P9-CFS-048

DISCOVER THE POWERS OF YOUR SUBCONSCIOUS MIND TO BRING HEALTH, WEALTH, AND HAPPINESS TO YOUR LIFE

WIN RICHES AND PROSPERITY

Free yourself of the negative attitudes that block your path to wealth. Master the three simple steps employed by successful businesspersons around the world.

REGAIN FORMER YOUTHFULNESS AND VIGOR

Find out why the mental and physical deterioration associated with aging is not natural, and how you can retain your youth.

WORK REAL MIRACLES IN THE LIVES OF OTHERS

Learn how to use Mental Transference to will health and vitality to a far-off loved one or friend in great need.

FIND NEW PEACE OF MIND

Discover how to use the Spiritual Law of Communion to bring yourself into radiant union with your own personal Higher Power.

The Power of Your Subconscious Mind

ONE OF THE MOST POWERFUL
SELF-HELP GUIDES EVER WRITTEN!

NOW REVISED & EXPANDED

Joseph Murphy, Ph.D., D.D.

Revised By Ian McMahan, Ph.D.

BANTAM BOOKS

NEW YORK   TORONTO   LONDON   SYDNEY   AUCKLAND

THE POWER OF YOUR SUBCONSCIOUS MIND

A Bantam Book / published by arrangement with Reward Books

PUBLISHING HISTORY

Prentice Hall original edition published June 1963
Bantam mass market edition published April 1982
Reward Books revised trade paperback edition published April 2000
Bantam revised mass market edition / January 2001

Published simultaneously in the United States and Canada

Bantam books are published by Bantam Books, a division of Random
House, Inc. Its trademark, consisting of the words "Bantam Books" and the
portrayal of a rooster, is Registered in U.S. Patent and Trademark Office and
in other countries. Marca Registrada. Bantam Books, 1540 Broadway, New
York, New York 10036.

PRINTED IN THE UNITED STATES OF AMERICA

OPM   10   9   8

Contents

5 MENTAL HEALINGS IN MODERN TIMES 63

6 PRACTICAL TECHNIQUES IN MENTAL HEALINGS 75

10 YOUR RIGHT TO BE RICH   122

15 YOUR SUBCONSCIOUS MIND AND YOUR HAPPINESS 186

16 YOUR SUBCONSCIOUS MIND AND HARMONIOUS HUMAN RELATIONS 196

17 How to Use Your Subconscious Mind for Forgiveness **212**

18 How Your Subconscious Removes Mental Blocks **227**

How This Book Can Work Miracles in Your Life

I have seen miracles happen to men and women in all walks of life all over the world. Miracles will happen to you, too—when you begin using the magic power of your subconscious mind. This book is designed to teach you that your habitual thinking and imagery mold, fashion, and create your destiny. For as a person thinketh in his subconscious mind, so is he.

DO YOU KNOW THE ANSWERS?

Why is one person sad and another person happy? Why is one person joyous and prosperous and another person poor and miserable? Why is one person fearful and anxious and another full of faith and confidence? Why does one person have a beautiful, luxurious home while another person lives out a meager existence in a slum?

Why is one person a great success and another an abject failure? Why is one speaker outstanding and immensely popular and another mediocre and unpopular? Why is one person a genius in her work or profession while another toils and moils all his life without doing or accomplishing anything worthwhile?

Why is one person healed of a so-called incurable disease and another isn't? Why is it so many good, kind, religious people suffer the tortures of the damned in their minds and bodies? Why is it many immoral and irreligious people succeed and prosper and enjoy radiant health? Why is one person happily married and another very unhappy and frustrated?

Is there an answer to these questions in the workings of your conscious and subconscious minds?

There most certainly is.

MY REASON FOR WRITING THIS BOOK

What motivated me to write this book was a deep desire to share with others the answers I have discovered to these and many similar questions. I have tried to explain the great fundamental truths of your mind in the simplest language possible. I believe that it is perfectly possible to explain the basic and fundamental laws of life and of your mind in ordinary everyday language. You will find that the language of this book is that used in your daily papers and current periodicals, in your business offices, in your home, and in the daily workshop.

I urge you to study this book and apply the techniques it outlines. As you do, I am absolutely convinced that you will lay hold of a miracle-working power that will lift you up from confusion, misery, melancholy, and failure. It will guide you to your true place, solve your difficulties, sever you from emotional and physical bondage, and place you on the royal road to freedom, happiness, and peace of mind.

This miracle-working power of your subconscious mind can heal you of your sickness, making you vital and strong again. In learning how to use your inner powers, you will open the prison door of fear and enter into a life described by Paul as the glorious liberty of the sons of God.

RELEASING THE MIRACLE-WORKING POWER

A personal healing will always be the most convincing evidence of our subconscious powers. Many years ago I managed to cure myself of a malignancy—in medical terminology it is called a sarcoma—by using the healing power of my subconscious mind, which created me and still maintains and governs all my vital functions.

The technique I applied then is explained in detail in this book. I feel sure that it will help others to trust the same Infinite healing presence lodged in the subconscious depths of all of us. Thanks to the kindly advice of an elderly doctor friend, I suddenly realized that it is natural to assume that the creative intelligence that made all my organs, fashioned my body, and started my heart can heal its own handiwork. The ancient proverb says, "The doctor dresses the wound and God heals it."

WONDERS HAPPEN WHEN YOU PRAY EFFECTIVELY

Scientific prayer is the harmonious interaction of the conscious and subconscious levels of mind scientifically directed toward a specific purpose. This book will teach you the scientific way to tap the realm of infinite power within you, enabling you to get what you really want in life. You desire a happier, fuller, and richer life. Begin to use this miracle-working power and smooth your way in daily affairs, solve business problems, and bring harmony in family relationships.

Be sure that you read this book several times. The many chapters will show you how this wonderful power works and how you can draw out the hidden inspiration and wisdom that is within you. Learn the simple techniques of impressing the subconscious mind. Follow the new scientific way in tapping the infinite storehouse. Read this book carefully, earnestly, and lovingly. Prove to yourself the amazing way it can help you. It may be—and I believe it will be—the turning point of your life.

EVERYBODY PRAYS

Do you know how to pray effectively? How long is it since you prayed as part of your everyday activities? In an emergency, in time of danger or trouble, in illness, and when death lurks, prayers pour forth.

Just follow the daily news. There are reports that people all over the country are praying for a child stricken with a so-called incurable ailment, for peace among nations, for a group of miners trapped in a flooded mine. Later we hear that when rescued, the miners say they prayed while waiting for rescue.

Certainly, prayer is an ever-present help in time of trouble. But why should you wait for trouble to make prayer an integral and constructive part of your life? The dramatic answers to prayer make headlines and are the subject of testimonies to the effectiveness of prayer. But what of the many humble prayers of children, the simple thanksgiving of grace at the table daily, the faithful devotions wherein the individual seeks only communion with God?

My work with people has led me to study the various approaches to prayer. I have experienced the power of prayer in my own life, and I have talked and worked with many others who have benefited greatly from the help of prayer. The problem usually is how to tell someone else how to pray. People who are in trouble have difficulty in thinking and acting reasonably. Their problems overwhelm them and block their ability to listen and understand. They need an easy formula to follow, an obviously workable pattern that is simple and specific.

UNIQUE FEATURE OF THIS BOOK

The unique feature of this book is its down-to-earth practicality. Here you will find simple, usable techniques and formulas that you can easily apply in your everyday life. I have taught these simple processes to men and women all over the world.

The special features of this book will appeal to you because they explain why you often get the opposite of what you prayed for. Thousands of times, people in all parts of the world have asked me, "Why is it I have prayed and prayed and got no answer?" In this book you will find the reasons for this common complaint. The explanation of the many ways of impressing the subconscious mind and getting the right answers make this an extraordinarily valuable book and an ever-present help in times of trouble.

WHAT DO YOU BELIEVE?

Contrary to what many people think, it is not the thing that is believed in that brings an answer to a person's prayer. Prayers are answered when the individual's subconscious mind responds to the mental picture or thought in his or her mind. This law of belief is the secret operating principle in all the religions of the world. It is the hidden reason for their psychological truth.

The Buddhist, the Christian, the Moslem, and the Jew may all get answers to their prayers, in spite of the enormous differences among their stated beliefs. How can this be? The answer is that it is not because of the particular creed, religion, affiliation, ritual, ceremony, formula, liturgy, incantation, sacrifices, or offerings, but solely because of belief or mental acceptance and receptivity about that for which they pray.

The law of life is the law of belief. Belief can be summed up briefly as a thought in your mind. As a person thinks, feels, and believes, so is the condition of his or her mind, body, and circumstances. A technique, a methodology based on an understanding of what you are doing and why you are doing it will help you to bring about a subconscious embodiment of all the good things of life. Essentially, answered prayer is the realization of your heart's desire.

DESIRE IS PRAYER

Everyone desires health, happiness, security, peace of mind, and true expression. But how many of us achieve all these goals? A university professor admitted to me recently, "I know that if I change my mental pattern and redirect my emotional life, my heart condition will improve. I *know* that. The problem is, I do not have any technique, process, or modus operandi. My mind wanders back and forth on my many problems, and I feel frustrated, unhappy, and defeated."

This professor had the *desire* for perfect health. What he needed was a knowledge of the way his mind worked. It was this that would enable him to fulfill his desire. By practicing the healing methods outlined in this book, he became whole and perfect.

THERE IS ONE MIND COMMON TO ALL INDIVIDUALS

The miracle-working powers of your subconscious mind existed before you and I were born, before any church or world existed. The great eternal truths and principles of life antedate all religions. It is with these thoughts in mind that I urge you in the following chapters to lay hold of this wonderful, magical, transforming power. It will bind up mental and physical wounds, proclaim liberty to the fear-ridden mind, and liberate you completely from the limitations of poverty, failure, misery, lack, and frustration.

All you have to do is unite mentally and emotionally with the good you wish to embody. The creative powers of your subconscious will respond accordingly. Begin now, today. Let wonders happen in your life! Keep on keeping on until the day breaks and the shadows flee away.

1
The Treasure House Within You

You have infinite riches within your reach. To gain them, all you have to do is open your mental eyes and behold the treasure house of infinity within you. There is a storehouse within you from which you can extract everything you need to live life gloriously, joyously, and abundantly.

Many people are closed off to their own potential because they do not know about this storehouse of infinite intelligence and boundless love within themselves. Whatever you want, you can draw it forth.

A magnetized piece of iron will lift about twelve times its own weight. But if you demagnetize this same piece of iron, it will not lift even a feather.

In the same way, there are two types of people. Those who are magnetized are full of confidence and faith. They know they are born to succeed and to win.

Others, so many others, are demagnetized. They are full of fears and doubts. When an opportunity comes, they say, "What if I fail? I might lose my money. People will laugh at me." People of this sort will not get very far in life. Their fear to go forward makes them simply stay where they are.

You can become a magnetized person when you discover and put to use the master secret of the ages.

THE MASTER SECRET OF THE AGES

Suppose someone asked you to name the master secret of the ages. What would you answer? Atomic energy? Interplanetary travel? Black holes? No, it is not any of these. Then what is this master secret? Where can one find it? How can it be understood and put into action?

The answer is extraordinarily simple. This secret is the marvelous, miracle-working power found in your own subconscious mind. This is the last place most people would look for it, which is the reason so few ever find it.

THE MARVELOUS POWER OF YOUR SUBCONSCIOUS

Once you learn to contact and release the hidden power of your subconscious mind, you can bring into your life more power, more wealth, more health, more happiness, and more joy.

You do not need to acquire this power. You already possess it. But you will have to learn how to use it. You must understand it so that you can apply it in all departments of your life.

If you follow the simple techniques and processes explained in this book, you can gain the necessary knowledge and understanding. You can be inspired by a new light, and you can generate a new force that enables you to realize your hopes and make all your dreams come true. Decide now to make your life grander, greater, richer, and nobler than ever before.

Within your subconscious depths lie infinite wisdom, infinite power, an infinite supply of all that is necessary. It is waiting there for you to give it development and expression. If you begin now to recognize these potentialities of your deeper mind, they will take form in the world without.

Provided you are open-minded and receptive, the infinite intelligence within your subconscious mind can reveal to you everything you need to know at every moment of time and point of space. You can receive new thoughts and ideas, bring forth new inventions, make new discoveries, create new works of art. The infinite intelligence in your subconscious can give you access to wonderful new kinds of knowledge. Let it reveal itself to you and it will open the way to perfect expression and true place in your life.

Through the wisdom of your subconscious mind, you can attract the ideal companion, as well as the right business associate or partner. It can show you how to get all the money you need and give you the financial freedom to be, to do, and to go as your heart desires.

It is your right to discover this inner world of thought, feeling, and power, of light, love, and beauty. Though invisible, its forces are mighty. Within your subconscious mind you will find the solution for every problem and the cause for every effect. Once you learn to draw out these hidden powers, you come into actual possession of the power and wisdom necessary to move forward in abundance, security, joy, and dominion.

I have seen the power of the subconscious lift people up out of crippled states, making them whole, vital, and strong once more. Their minds made them free to go out into the world to experience happiness, health, and joyous expression. There is a miraculous curative force in your subconscious that can heal the troubled mind and the broken heart. It can open the prison door of the mind and liberate you. It can free you from all kinds of material and physical bondage.

NECESSITY OF A WORKING BASIS

If you want to make progress in any field of endeavor, there is an essential first step. You must discover a working basis that is universal in its application. Before you can become skilled in the operation of your subconscious mind, you must understand its principles. Once that is achieved, you can practice its powers knowing the results you will certainly obtain. You can apply these powers for the definite specific purposes and goals you want to accomplish.

For many years I followed the profession of chemist. One of the first things I learned in my early training was that if you combine two atoms of hydrogen and one of oxygen, the product will be water—not occasionally or most of the time, *always*. If you take one atom of oxygen and one atom of carbon and combine them, you will produce carbon monoxide, a poisonous gas. But if you add another atom of oxygen, you will get carbon dioxide, a gas that is harmless to animals and vital to plants. These facts are universal and unchangeable. They are what we call *principles*.

The principles of chemistry, physics, and mathematics are no different in their workings from the principles of your subconscious mind. If you want to make use of chemical or physical forces, you must learn the principles of these fields. If you want to make use of the force of your subconscious mind, you must learn its principles.

Take the generally accepted principle, *Water seeks its own level*. This is a universal principle. It applies to water everywhere, at any time, and to all liquids that behave like water.

The ancient Egyptians knew this principle. They used it to make the foundations of the great pyramids perfectly level. Today, engineers use it when planning everything from an irrigation system to a hydroelectric power station.

Or take the principle, *Matter expands when heated.* This is true anywhere, at any time, and under all circumstances. If you heat a piece of steel, it will expand, whether the steel is found in China, England, India, or in an orbiting space station.

Matter expands when heated . . . This is a universal truth. It is also a universal truth that whatever you impress on your subconscious mind is expressed on the screen of space as condition, experience, and event.

Your prayer is answered because your subconscious mind is principle, and by principle I mean the way a thing works. For example, an important principle of electricity is that it works from a higher to a lower potential. You do not change the principle of electricity when you turn on a lamp or cook on an electric stove. No, you *use* the principle. By cooperating with nature, you can bring forth marvelous inventions and discoveries that bless humanity in countless ways.

Your subconscious mind is principle. It works according to the law of belief. You must know what belief is, why it works, and how it works. Your Bible says in a simple, clear, and beautiful way:

> Whosoever shall say unto this mountain, Be thou removed, and be thou cast into the sea; and shall not doubt in his heart, but shall believe that those things which he saith shall come to pass; he shall have whatsoever he saith.
>
> *MARK 11:23*

The law of your mind is the law of belief. This means to believe in the way your mind works, to believe in belief itself. The belief of your mind is the thought of your mind, just that and nothing else.

All your experiences, events, conditions, and acts are

produced by your subconscious mind in reaction to your thoughts. Remember, it is not the thing believed in, but the belief in your own mind that brings about the result. Stop accepting the false beliefs, opinions, superstitions, and fears that plague our humankind. Begin to believe in the eternal verities and truths of life that never change. At that point you will move onward, upward, and Godward.

All those who read this book and faithfully apply the principles of the subconscious mind that are set forth here will gain the ability to pray scientifically and effectively for themselves and for others. Your prayer is answered according to the universal law of *action and reaction*. Thought is incipient action. The reaction is the response from your subconscious mind that corresponds to the nature of your thought. Fill your mind with the concepts of harmony, health, peace, and goodwill, and wonders will happen in your life.

THE DUALITY OF MIND

You have only one mind, but that one mind possesses two distinct and characteristic functional parts. The frontier that separates the two is well known to students of the mind. The two functions of your mind are essentially different from each other. Each has its own separate and distinct attributes and powers.

Many names have been used to distinguish the two functions of the mind. These include the objective and the subjective mind, the conscious and the subconscious mind, the waking and the sleeping mind, the surface and the deep self, the voluntary and the involuntary mind, the male and the female mind, and many others. All of these, whatever their implications, are recognitions of this essential duality.

Throughout this book I use the terms *conscious* and

subconscious to represent the dual nature of your mind. If another set of terms comes more easily to you, by all means use it. The important starting point is to recognize and acknowledge the double nature of the mind.

THE CONSCIOUS AND THE SUBCONSCIOUS MINDS

A wonderful way to begin getting to know the two functions of your mind is to think of it as a garden. You are the gardener. You are planting seeds of thought in your subconscious mind all day long. Much of the time you are not even aware of doing so, because the seeds are based on your habitual thinking. As you sow in your subconscious mind, so shall you reap in your body and environment.

Imagine your subconscious mind as a bed of rich soil that will help all kinds of seeds to sprout and flourish, whether good or bad. If you sow thorns, will you gather grapes? If you sow thistles, will you harvest figs? Every thought is a cause, and every condition is an effect. This is the reason it is so essential that you take charge of your thoughts. In that way, you can bring forth only desirable conditions.

Begin now to sow thoughts of peace, happiness, right action, goodwill, and prosperity. Think quietly and with conviction on these qualities. Accept them fully in your conscious reasoning mind. Continue to plant these wonderful seeds of thought in the garden of your mind and you will reap a glorious harvest.

When your mind thinks correctly, when you understand the truth, when the thoughts deposited in your subconscious mind are constructive, harmonious, and peaceful, the magic working power of your subconscious will respond. It will bring about harmonious conditions, agreeable surroundings, and the best of everything. Once you begin to control your thought processes, you can apply the powers of your subconscious to any problem or difficulty. You will actually be consciously cooperating with the infinite power and omnipotent law that governs all things.

Look around you. Wherever you live, whatever circle of society you are part of, you will notice that the vast majority of people lives in the world without. Those who are more enlightened, however, are intensely involved with the world within. They realize—as you will, too—that the world within *creates* the world without. Your thoughts, feelings, and visualized imagery are the organizing principles of your experience. The world within is the only creative power. Everything you find in your world of expression has been created by you in the inner world of your mind, whether consciously or unconsciously.

Once you learn the truth about the interaction of your conscious and subconscious minds, you will be able to transform your whole life. If you want to change external conditions, you must change the cause. Most people try to change conditions and circumstances by working on those conditions and circumstances. This is a terrible waste of time and effort. They fail to see that their conditions flow from a cause. To remove discord, confusion, lack, and limitation from your life, you must remove the cause. That cause is the way you use your conscious mind, the thoughts and images you encourage in it. Change the cause, and you change the effect. It is just that simple.

We all live in an unfathomable sea of infinite riches. Your subconscious is very sensitive to your conscious thoughts. Those conscious thoughts form the matrix through which the infinite intelligence, wisdom, vital forces, and energies of your subconscious flow. Shape that matrix in a more positive direction and you redirect those infinite energies to your greater benefit.

Each chapter of this book gives concrete, specific illustrations of how to apply the laws of mind. Once you learn to use these techniques, you will experience abundance instead of poverty, wisdom instead of superstition and ignorance, peace instead of inner strife, success instead of failure, joy instead of sadness, light instead of darkness, harmony instead of discord, faith and confidence instead of fear. Could there be any more wonderful set of blessings than these?

Most of the great scientists, artists, poets, singers, writers, and inventors have had a deep understanding of the workings of the conscious and subconscious minds. It was this that gave them the power to accomplish their goals.

Once Enrico Caruso, the great operatic tenor, was struck with stage fright. Spasms caused by intense fear constricted the muscles of his throat. His vocal cords felt paralyzed, useless. He stood backstage, already in costume, while perspiration poured down his face. In just moments he was supposed to go out on the stage and sing, before an eager audience of thousands.

Trembling, he said, "I can't sing. They will all laugh at me. My career is finished."

He turned to go back to his dressing room, Then, suddenly, he stopped and shouted, "The Little Me is trying to strangle the Big Me within!"

He turned toward the stage again and stood taller. "Get out of here," he commanded, addressing the Little Me. "The Big Me wants to sing through me."

By the Big Me, Caruso meant the limitless power and wisdom of his subconscious mind. He began to shout, "Get out, get out, the Big Me is going to sing!"

His subconscious mind responded by releasing the vital

forces within him. When the call came, he walked out onstage and sang gloriously and majestically. The audience was enthralled.

From what you have already learned, you can see that Caruso understood the two levels of mind—the conscious or rational, and the subconscious or irrational level. Your subconscious mind is reactive. It responds to the nature of your thoughts. When your conscious mind (Caruso's Little Me) is full of fear, worry, and anxiety, the negative emotions these create in your subconscious mind (the Big Me) are released. They flood the conscious mind with a sense of panic, foreboding, and despair. When this happens to you, you can follow the example of the great Caruso. You can speak affirmatively and with a deep sense of authority to the irrational emotions generated in your deeper mind. You can say, "Be still. Be quiet. I am in control. You must obey me. You are subject to my command. You cannot intrude where you do not belong."

You will be fascinated to see what happens when you speak authoritatively and with conviction to the irrational movement of your deeper self. Your mind will be flooded with harmony and with peace. The subconscious is *subject* to the conscious mind. That is why it is called *sub*conscious or *subjective*.

Outstanding Differences and Modes of Operation

The conscious mind is like the navigator or captain at the bridge of a ship. He directs the ship. He sends orders to men and women in the engine room. They in turn control the boilers, instruments, gauges, and so on. The people in the engine room do not know where they are going; they follow orders. They would go on the rocks if the man on the bridge issued faulty or wrong instructions based on his findings with the compass, sextant, and other instruments. The people in the engine room obey him because he is in charge. Because he is supposed to know what he is doing, the members of the crew do not talk back to the captain; they simply carry out his orders.

The captain is the master of his ship, and his decrees are carried out. In the same way, your conscious mind is the captain and the master of your ship—your body, your environment, and all your affairs. Your subconscious mind takes the orders you give it, based upon what your conscious mind believes and accepts as true. It does not question the orders or the basis on which they are given.

If you repeatedly say to yourself, "I can't afford it," your subconscious mind takes you at your word. It sees to it that you will not be in a position to buy what you want. As long as you go on saying, "I can't afford that car, that vacation, that home," you can be sure your subconscious mind will follow your orders. You will go through life experiencing the lack of all these things, and you will believe that circumstances made it so. It will not occur to you that you have created those circumstances yourself, by your own negative, denying thoughts.

Last Christmas Eve, a young woman named Nina W., who is a student at the University of Southern California, strolled through an exclusive shopping area in Beverly Hills. Her mind was filled with anticipation. She was about to spend the holidays with her family in Buffalo, New York.

As Nina passed a shop window, a beautiful Spanish-leather shoulder bag caught her eye. She looked at it yearningly. Then she noticed the price tag and gasped.

She was about to say to herself, "I could never afford such an expensive bag."

Then she remembered something she had heard me say

at one of my lectures. "Never finish a negative statement. Reverse it immediately and wonders will happen in your life."

Staring through the glass, she said, "That bag is mine. It is for sale. I accept it mentally, and my subconscious sees to it that I receive it."

Later that day, Nina met her fiancé for a sendoff dinner. He arrived with an elegantly wrapped gift under his arm. Holding her breath, she unwrapped it. There was the identical leather shoulder bag she had looked at and identified as her own that same morning. She had filled her mind with the thought of expectancy. Then she had turned the matter over to her deeper mind, which has the power of accomplishment.

Later, Nina told me, "I didn't have the money to buy that bag, yet now it is mine. I have learned where to find money and all the things I need, and that is in the treasure house of eternity within me."

HOW HER SUBCONSCIOUS RESPONDED

A few months ago I received a letter from a woman named Ruth A. who had attended my lectures. She wrote:

> I am seventy-five years old, a widow with a grown family. I was living alone, on a small pension and Social Security. My life seemed barren, hopeless. Then I remembered your lecture about the powers of the subconscious mind. You said that ideas could be conveyed to the subconscious mind by repetition, faith, and expectancy. Could it be true? I decided to try. I had nothing to lose.
>
> I began to repeat frequently, with all the feeling I could muster, "I am wanted. I am loved. I am happily married to a kind, loving, and spiritual-minded man. I am secure and fulfilled."

I kept on doing this many times a day for about two weeks. One day at the corner drugstore, I was introduced to a retired pharmacist. I found him to be kind, understanding, and very religious. He was a perfect answer to my prayer. Within a week he proposed to me. Now we are on our honeymoon in Europe. I know that the intelligence within my subconscious mind brought both of us together in divine order.

Ruth discovered that the treasure house was within her. Her prayer was felt as true in her heart, and her affirmation sank down by osmosis into her subconscious mind, which is the creative medium. The moment she succeeded in bringing about a subjective embodiment, her subconscious mind brought about the answer through the law of attraction. Her deeper mind, full of wisdom and intelligence, brought her and her new husband together in divine order.

Be sure that you think on this:

Whatsoever things are true, whatsoever things are honest, whatsoever things are just, whatsoever things are pure, whatsoever things are lovely, whatsoever things are of good report; if there be any virtue, and if there be any praise, think on these things.

PHIL. 4:8

IDEAS WORTH REMEMBERING
1. The treasure house is within you. Look within for the answer to your heart's desire.
2. The great secret possessed by the great men of all ages was their ability to contact and release the powers of their subconscious mind. You can do the same.
3. Your subconscious has the answer to all problems. If you

suggest to your subconscious prior to sleep, "I want to get up at 6 A.M.," it will awaken you at that exact time.

4. Your subconscious mind is the builder of your body and can heal you. Lull yourself to sleep every night with the idea of perfect health, and your subconscious, being your faithful servant, will obey you.

5. Every thought is a cause, and every condition is an effect.

6. If you want to write a book, write a wonderful play, give a better talk to your audience, convey the idea lovingly and feelingly to your subconscious mind and it will respond accordingly.

7. You are like a captain navigating a ship. He or she must give the right orders, or the ship is wrecked. In the same way, you must give the right orders (thoughts and images) to your subconscious mind, which controls and governs all your experiences.

8. Never use such expressions as "I can't afford it" or "I can't do this." Your subconscious mind takes you at your word. It sees to it that you do not have the money or the ability to do what you want to do. Affirm, "I can do all things through the power of my subconscious mind."

9. The law of life is the law of belief. A belief is a thought in your mind. Do not believe in things that will harm or hurt you. Believe in the power of your subconscious to heal, inspire, strengthen, and prosper you. According to your belief is it done unto you.

10. Change your thoughts, and you change your destiny.

2
How Your Mind Works

Your mind is your most precious possession. It is always with you, but its most amazing powers will be yours only when you have learned how to use it. As we have seen, there are two levels to your mind—the conscious or rational level and the subconscious or irrational level. You think with your conscious mind, and whatever you habitually think sinks down into your subconscious mind, which then creates according to the nature of your thoughts. Your subconscious mind is the seat of your emotions. It is the creative mind. If you think good, good will follow; if you think evil, evil will follow. This is the way your mind works.

The most important point to remember is this: Once the subconscious mind accepts an idea, it begins to execute it. It is an astonishing and subtle truth that the law of the subconscious mind works for good and bad ideas alike. This law, when applied in a negative way, is the cause of failure, frustration, and unhappiness. When your habitual thinking is harmonious and constructive, however, you experience perfect health, success, and prosperity.

Peace of mind and a healthy body are inevitable once you begin to think and feel in the right way. Whatever you claim mentally and feel as true, your subconscious mind will accept and bring forth into your experience. All you have to do is get your subconscious mind to accept your idea. Once that happens, the law of your subconscious mind will bring forth the health, peace, and prosperity you desire. You give the command or decree, and your subconscious will faithfully reproduce the idea impressed upon it.

The law of your mind is this: The reaction or response you get from your subconscious mind will be determined by the nature of the thought or idea you hold in your conscious mind.

Psychologists and psychiatrists point out that when thoughts are conveyed to your subconscious mind, impressions are made in the brain cells. As soon as your subconscious accepts any idea, it proceeds to put it into effect immediately. Working by association of ideas, it uses every bit of knowledge that you have gathered in your lifetime to bring about its purpose. It draws on the infinite power, energy, and wisdom within you. It lines up all the laws of nature to get its way. Sometimes it seems to bring about an immediate solution to your difficulties, but at other times it may take days, weeks, or longer. *Its ways are past finding out.*

THE DIFFERENCES BETWEEN CONSCIOUS AND SUBCONSCIOUS

You must remember that the conscious and subconscious are not two minds. They are merely two spheres of activity within one mind. Your conscious mind is the reasoning mind. It is that phase of mind that chooses. For example, you choose your books, your home, and your partner in life. You make all your decisions with your conscious mind. On the other hand, without any conscious choice on your part, your heart is kept functioning automatically, and the vital functions of digestion, circulation, and breathing are carried on by your subconscious mind through processes independent of your conscious control.

Your subconscious mind accepts what is impressed upon it or what you consciously believe. It does not reason things out as your conscious mind does, and it does not argue with you controversially. Your subconscious mind is like a bed of soil that accepts any kind of seed, good or bad. Your thoughts are active; they are the seeds. Negative, destructive thoughts continue to work negatively in your subconscious mind. Sooner or later, they will emerge and take shape as an outer experience that corresponds to their content.

Remember, your subconscious mind does not engage in proving whether your thoughts are good or bad, true or false. It responds according to the nature of your thoughts or suggestions. For example, if you consciously assume that something is true, even though it may be false, your subconscious mind will accept it as true and proceed to bring about results that must necessarily follow *because* you consciously assumed it to be true.

Experiments by Psychologists

Psychologists and others have performed countless experiments on people who are in a hypnotic trance. This research shows clearly that the subconscious mind does not make the selections and comparisons that are necessary for a reasoning process. Your subconscious mind will accept any suggestions, however false. Having once accepted any suggestion, it responds according to the nature of the suggestion given.

To illustrate how suggestible your subconscious mind is, if a practiced hypnotist suggests to one of her subjects that she is Napoleon Bonaparte, or even a cat or a dog, the subject will act out the part with inimitable accuracy. Her personality becomes changed for the time being. She believes herself to be whatever the operator tells her she is.

A skilled hypnotist may suggest to one of his students in the hypnotic state that her back itches, to another that his nose is bleeding, to another that she is a marble statue, to another that she is freezing and the temperature is below zero. Each one will follow out the line of his particular suggestion, totally oblivious to all those surroundings that do not pertain to the hypnotic suggestion.

These simple illustrations portray the difference between your conscious, reasoning mind and your subconscious mind, which is impersonal, nonselective, and accepts as true whatever your conscious mind believes to be true. Hence the importance of selecting thoughts, ideas, and premises that bless, heal, inspire, and fill your soul with joy.

THE TERMS *OBJECTIVE* AND *SUBJECTIVE MIND* CLARIFIED

Your conscious mind is sometimes referred to as your *objective mind* because it deals with outward objects. The objective mind is aware of the objective world. Its media of observation are your five physical senses. Your objective mind is your guide and director in your contact with your environment. You gain knowledge through your five senses. Your objective mind learns through observation, experience, and education. As previously pointed out, the greatest function of the objective mind is that of reasoning.

Suppose you are one of the hundreds of thousands of tourists who visit the Grand Canyon every year. You would come to the conclusion that it is one of the world's most amazing natural wonders. This conclusion would be based on your observation of its incredible depth, the complex shaping of the rock formations, the beautiful play of colors among the different geological strata. This is the working of your objective mind.

Your subconscious mind is often referred to as your *subjective mind*. Your subjective mind is aware of its environment, but not by means of the physical senses. Your subjective mind perceives by intuition. It is the seat of your emotions and the storehouse of memory. Your subjective mind performs its highest functions when your objective senses are not functioning. In other words, it is that intelligence that makes itself known when the objective mind is suspended or in a sleepy, drowsy state.

Your subjective mind sees without the use of the natural organs of vision. It has the capacity of clairvoyance and clairaudience: It can see and hear events that are taking place elsewhere. Your subjective mind can leave your body, travel to distant lands, and bring back information that is often of the most exact and truthful character. Through your subjective mind you can read the thoughts of others, read the contents of sealed envelopes, or intuit the information on a computer disk without using a disk drive.

Once we understand the interaction of the objective and subjective minds, we are in a better position to learn the true art of prayer.

THE SUBCONSCIOUS CANNOT REASON LIKE YOUR CONSCIOUS MIND

Your subconscious mind does not have the ability to argue or dispute what it is told. If you give it wrong information, it will accept it as true. It will then work to make that information correct. It will bring your suggestions, *even those that were false*, to pass as conditions, experiences, and events.

Everything that has happened to you happened because

of thoughts impressed on your subconscious mind through belief. If you have communicated wrong or distorted concepts to your subconscious mind, it is of the most urgent importance to correct them. The sure way to do this is by repeatedly giving your subconscious mind constructive, harmonious thoughts. As these are frequently repeated, your subconscious mind accepts them. In this way, you can form new, healthier habits of thought and life, for your subconscious mind is the seat of habit.

The habitual thinking of your conscious mind establishes deep grooves in your subconscious mind. If your habitual thoughts are harmonious, peaceful, and constructive, your subconscious mind will respond by creating harmony, peace, and constructive conditions.

Have you fallen prey to fear, worry, and other destructive forms of thinking? The remedy is to recognize the power of your subconscious mind and decree freedom, happiness, and perfect health. Your subconscious mind, being creative and one with your divine source, will then start to create the freedom and happiness you have earnestly decreed.

THE TREMENDOUS POWER OF SUGGESTION

As you can see by what we have already discussed, your conscious mind serves as the "watchman at the gate." One of its most crucial functions is to protect your subconscious mind from false impressions. The reason this is so important goes back to one of the basic laws of mind: Your subconscious mind is very sensitive to suggestion.

As you know, your subconscious mind does not make comparisons or contrasts. It doesn't reason and think things out for itself. This latter function belongs to your conscious mind. No, your subconscious mind simply reacts to the impressions given to it by your conscious mind. It does not pick and choose among different courses of action. It merely takes what it is given.

Suggestion is a tremendously powerful force. Imagine that you are on board a ship that is rocking a bit from side to side. You approach a timid-looking fellow passenger and say, "Gee, you don't look so hot. Your face is practically green! I'm afraid you're about to be seasick. Can I help you to your cabin?"

The passenger turns pale. The suggestion you have just made about seasickness links up with her own fears and forebodings. She lets you escort her down belowdecks. Once she is there, your negative suggestion, which she accepted, comes true.

Different Reactions to the Same Suggestion

It is important to realize that different people will react in different ways to the same suggestion. This is because they have different subconscious conditioning or beliefs.

Suppose, instead of choosing a fellow passenger on the ship, you go up to a member of the crew. You say, "Hey, buddy, you don't look so great. Do you think you're about to be seasick?"

Depending on the sailor's temperament, he either laughs at your feeble joke or tells you to get lost. Your suggestion had no power over him, because the idea of seasickness was associated in his mind with his own immunity from it. Therefore, it called up not fear or worry, but self-confidence.

A dictionary will tell you that a suggestion is the act or instance of putting something into one's mind. It is the mental process by which the thought or idea that has been suggested is entertained, accepted, or put into effect. Remember, a suggestion cannot impose itself on the subconscious mind against the will of the conscious mind. Your conscious mind has the power to reject the suggestion.

The sailor had no fear of seasickness. He had convinced himself of his immunity, so the negative suggestion had no power to evoke fear. But your fellow passenger was already worried about becoming sick. Therefore your suggestion had power over her.

All of us have our own inner fears, beliefs, opinions. These inner assumptions rule and govern our lives. A suggestion has no power in and of itself. Its power arises from the fact that you accept it mentally. Only at that point do your subconscious powers begin to act according to the nature of the suggestion.

HOW HE LOST HIS ARM

For many years I gave a regular series of lectures at the London Truth Forum in Caxton Hall, which I founded a number of years ago. Dr. Evelyn Fleet, the director, told me about a man whose young daughter suffered from both crippling rheumatoid arthritis and the disfiguring and painful skin condition called psoriasis. They tried many treatments, but nothing the doctors did seemed to help. The man was near despair. Over and over he said, to himself and to his friends, "I would give my right arm to see my daughter cured."

According to Dr. Fleet, one day the family was out for a drive. Their car was involved in a head-on collision. The father's right arm was torn off at the shoulder. When he came home from the hospital, he discovered that his daughter's arthritis and skin condition had vanished.

You must be very careful to give your subconscious only those suggestions that heal, bless, elevate, and inspire you in all your ways. Remember, your subconscious mind doesn't understand a joke. It takes you at your word.

HOW AUTOSUGGESTION BANISHES FEAR

The term *autosuggestion* means suggesting something definite and specific to oneself. Like any tool, wrongly used it can cause harm, but used properly it can be extremely helpful.

Janet R. was a talented young singer. She was invited to try out for an important role in an opera production. She desperately wanted to audition, but she was also terribly apprehensive.

Three times before, when she had sung for directors, she had failed miserably. The reason was fear of failure. She had a wonderful voice, but she had been saying to herself, "When the time comes for me to sing, I'll sound awful. I'll never get the role. They won't like me. They'll wonder how I have the nerve even to try out. I'll go, but I know it'll be a failure."

Her subconscious mind accepted these negative autosuggestions as a request. It proceeded to manifest them and bring them into her experience. The cause was an involuntary autosuggestion. Her fears had become emotionalized and subjectified thoughts that in turn became her reality.

This young singer was able to overcome the force of her negative autosuggestions. She accomplished this by countering them with *positive* autosuggestion. What she did was this. Three times a day, she went alone into a quiet room. She sat down comfortably in an armchair, relaxed her body, and closed her eyes. She stilled her mind and body as best she could. Physical inertia favors mental passivity and renders the mind more receptive to suggestion.

To counteract the fear suggestion, she repeated to herself, "I sing beautifully. I am poised, serene, confident, and calm." At each sitting she repeated this statement slowly, quietly, and with feeling from five to ten times. She had three such sittings during the day and one immediately before going to sleep.

After one week, she was completely poised and confident. When the fateful day came, she gave a wonderful audition and was cast in the part.

How She Restored Her Memory

A woman of seventy-five had always been proud of her ability to remember. Like everyone, she forgot things now and then, but she paid no attention. However, as she got older, she began to notice these occasions and worry about them. Each time she forgot something, she said to herself, "I must be losing my memory because of my age."

As a result of this negative autosuggestion, more and more names and events slipped her mind. She was close to despair. Then, fortunately, she realized how she was damaging herself. She resolved to reverse the process.

Every time she felt the temptation to think, "I am losing my memory," she stopped herself. More than that, she deliberately reversed the procedure.

Several times a day, she practiced induced positive autosuggestion. She said to herself:

> From today onward, my memory is improving in every way. I will always remember whatever I need to know at every moment of time and point of space. The impressions I receive will be clear and definite. I will retain them automatically and easily. Whatever I want to recall will immediately present itself in the correct form in my mind. I am improving rapidly every day. Very soon my memory will be better than it has ever been before.

At the end of three weeks, her memory was back to normal.

HOW HE OVERCAME A NASTY TEMPER

I was consulted by a man whose marriage and career were both in serious trouble. Hugh D.'s problem was his constant irritability and bad temper. He was concerned about this himself, but if anyone tried to discuss it with him, he exploded in anger. He constantly told himself that everyone was picking on him and that he had to defend himself against them.

To counter this negative autosuggestion, I advised him to use positive autosuggestion. Several times a day—morning, noon, and at night prior to sleep—he was to repeat to himself:

> From now on, I shall grow more good-humored. Joy, happiness, and cheerfulness are now becoming my normal states of mind. Every day I am becoming more and more lovable and understanding. I will be a center of cheer and goodwill to all those around me, infecting them with my good spirits. This happy, joyous, and cheerful mood is now becoming my normal, natural state of mind. I am grateful.

After a month, his wife and his coworkers remarked on how much easier he was to get along with.

SOME COMMENTS ON HETEROSUGGESTION

The term *heterosuggestion* means suggestions from another person. In all ages and in every part of the world, the power of suggestion has played a dominant part in the life and thought of humankind. Political creeds, religious beliefs, and cultural customs all flourish and perpetuate themselves through the power of heterosuggestion.

Suggestion can be used as a tool to discipline and control ourselves. However, it can also be used to take control and command over others who have not been taught to understand the laws of mind. In its constructive form it is wonderful and magnificent. In its negative aspects it is one of the most destructive of all the response patterns of the mind. Its results can be enduring patterns of misery, failure, suffering, sickness, and disaster.

HAVE YOU ACCEPTED ANY OF THESE?

From the day we are born, we are bombarded with negative suggestions. Not knowing how to counter them, we unconsciously accept them and bring them into being as our experience.

Here are some examples of negative suggestions:

- You can't.
- You'll never amount to anything.
- You mustn't.
- You'll fail.
- You haven't got a chance.
- You're all wrong.
- It's no use.
- It's not what you know, but who you know.
- The world is going to the dogs.
- What's the use, nobody cares.
- There's no point to trying so hard.
- You're too old now.
- Things are getting worse and worse.
- Life is an endless grind.

- Love is for the birds.
- You just can't win.
- Watch out, you'll catch a terrible disease.
- You can't trust a soul.

By accepting heterosuggestions of this kind, you collaborate in bringing them to pass. As a child, you were helpless when faced with the suggestions of others who were important to you. You did not know any better. The mind, both conscious and unconscious, was a mystery you did not even wonder about.

As an adult, however, you are able to make choices. You can use constructive autosuggestion, which is a reconditioning therapy, to change the impressions made on you in the past. The first step is to make yourself aware of the heterosuggestions that are operating on you. Unexamined, they can create behavior patterns that cause failure in your personal and social life. Constructive autosuggestion can release you from the mass of negative verbal conditioning that might otherwise distort your life pattern, making the development of good habits difficult or even impossible.

You can counteract negative suggestions

Pick up the paper or turn on the television news. Every day, you hear dozens of stories that could sow the seeds of futility, fear, worry, anxiety, and impending doom. If you accept them and take them in, these thoughts of fear can cause you to lose the will for life. However, once you understand that you do not *have* to accept them, choices open up for you. You have within you the power to counteract all these destructive ideas by giving your subconscious mind constructive autosuggestions.

Check regularly on the negative suggestions that people make to you. You do not have to be at the mercy of destructive heterosuggestion. All of us have suffered from it in our childhood, in our teens, and in adulthood. If you look back, you can easily recall how parents, friends, relatives, teachers, and associates contributed in a campaign of negative suggestions. Study the things said to you, closely examine their underlying meaning, and you will discover that many of them were nothing more than a form of propaganda. Its concealed purpose was—and *is*—to control you by instilling fear in you.

This heterosuggestion process goes on in every home, office, factory, and club. You will find that many of the suggestions people make, whether they know it or not, are aimed at making you think, feel, and act as they want you to, in ways that are to their advantage, even if they are destructive to you.

How Suggestion Killed a Man

A distant relative of mine went to a celebrated crystal gazer in India and asked the woman to read his future. The seer told him that he had a bad heart. She predicted that he would die at the next new moon.

My relative was aghast. He called up everyone in his family and told them about the prediction. He met with his lawyer to make sure his will was up-to-date. When I tried to talk him out of his conviction, he told me that the crystal gazer was known to have amazing occult powers. She could do great good or harm to those she dealt with. He was convinced of the truth of this.

As the new moon approached, he became more and more withdrawn. A month before this man had been happy, healthy, vigorous, and robust. Now he was an invalid. On the predicted date, he suffered a fatal heart attack. He died not knowing he was the cause of his own death.

How many of us have heard similar stories and shivered a little at the thought that the world is full of mysterious uncontrollable forces? Yes, the world is full of forces, but they are neither mysterious nor uncontrollable. My relative killed himself, by allowing a powerful suggestion to enter into his subconscious mind. He believed in the crystal gazer's powers, so he accepted her prediction completely.

Let us take another look at what happened, knowing what we do about the way the subconscious mind works. Whatever the conscious, reasoning mind of a person believes, the subconscious mind will accept and act upon. My relative was in a suggestible state when he went to see the fortune teller. She gave him a negative suggestion, and *he accepted it.* He became terrified. He constantly ruminated on his conviction that he was going to die at the next new moon. He told everyone about it, and he prepared for his end. It was his own fear and expectation of the end, accepted as true by his subconscious mind, that brought about his death.

The woman who predicted his death had no more power than the stones and sticks in the field. Her suggestion in itself had no power to create or bring about the end she suggested. If he had known the laws of his mind, he would have completely rejected the negative suggestion and refused to give her words any attention. He could have gone about the business of living with the secure knowledge that he was governed and controlled by his own thoughts and feelings. The prophecy of the seer would have been like a rubber ball thrown at an armored tank. He could have easily neutralized and dissipated her suggestion with no harm to himself. Instead, through lack of awareness and knowledge, he allowed it to kill him.

In themselves, the suggestions of others have no power over you. Whatever power they have, they gain because you give it to them through your own thoughts. You have to give your mental consent. You have to entertain and accept the thought. At that point it becomes your own thought, and your subconscious works to bring it into experience.

Remember, you have the capacity to choose. Choose life! Choose love! Choose health!

THE POWER OF AN ASSUMED MAJOR PREMISE

Since the days of ancient Greece, philosophers and logicians have studied the form of reasoning called a *syllogism*. Your mind reasons in syllogisms. In practical terms, this means that whatever major premises your conscious mind assumes to be true, that determines the conclusion your subconscious mind will come to, no matter what the particular question or problem might be. If your premises are true, the conclusion *must* be true.

For example:

- Every virtue is praiseworthy;
- Kindness is a virtue;
- Therefore, kindness is praiseworthy.

Or this:

- All formed things change and pass away;
- The Pyramids of Egypt are formed things;
- Therefore, the Pyramids will change and pass away.

The first statement is referred to as the major premise, and the right conclusion must necessarily follow the right premise.

A college professor who attended some of my science-of-mind lectures in New York City's Town Hall came to speak with me afterward. He told me, "Everything in my life is topsy-turvy. I have lost health, wealth, and friends. Everything I touch turns out wrong."

I explained to him that his problems followed logically and directly from his self-destructive major premise. To change his life, he had to establish a new major premise in his thinking. He needed to accept as true the conviction that the infinite intelligence of his subconscious mind was guiding, directing, and prospering him spiritually, mentally, and materially. Once he did that, his subconscious mind would automatically direct him wisely in his decisions, heal his body, and restore his mind to peace and tranquillity.

This professor formulated an overall picture of the way he wanted his life to be. This was his major premise:

> Infinite intelligence leads and guides me in all my ways. Perfect health is mine, and the Law of Harmony operates in my mind and body. Beauty, love, peace, and abundance are mine. The principles of right action and divine order govern my entire life. I know my major premise is based on the eternal truths of life, and I know, feel, and believe that my subconscious mind responds according to the nature of my conscious mind's thinking.

Later he wrote me the following progress report: "I repeated the statements of my major premise slowly, quietly, and lovingly several times a day. I knew that they were sinking deep down into my subconscious mind. I was convinced by the laws of mind that results must follow. I am deeply grateful for the interview you gave me, and I would like to add that all departments of my life are changing for the better. It works!"

THE SUBCONSCIOUS DOES NOT ARGUE CONTROVERSIALLY

Your subconscious mind is all-wise. It knows the answers to all questions. However, it does not *know* that it knows. It does not argue with you or talk back to you. It does not say, "You must not impress me with suggestions of that sort."

When you say, "I can't do this," "I am too old now," "I can't meet this obligation," "I was born on the wrong side of the tracks," "I don't know the right politician," you are impregnating your subconscious with these negative thoughts. It responds accordingly. You are actually blocking your own good. You are bringing lack, limitation, and frustration into your life.

When you set up obstacles, impediments, and delays in your conscious mind, you are denying the wisdom and intelligence resident in your subconscious mind. You are actually saying in effect that your subconscious mind cannot solve your problem. This leads to mental and emotional congestion, followed by sickness and neurotic tendencies.

To realize your desires and overcome your frustration, affirm boldly several times a day:

> The infinite intelligence that gave me this desire leads, guides, and reveals to me the perfect plan for the unfolding of my desire. I know the deeper wisdom of my subconscious is now responding, and what I feel and claim within is expressed in the without. There is a balance, equilibrium, and equanimity.

On the other hand, if you say, "There is no way out; I

am lost; there is no way out of this dilemma; I am stymied and blocked," you will get no answer or response from your subconscious mind. If you want the subconscious to work for you, you have to give it the right request and get its cooperation. It is always working for you. It is controlling your heartbeat and breathing this minute. When you cut your finger, it sets in motion the complex process of healing. Its most fundamental tendency is lifeward. It is forever seeking to take care of you and preserve you.

Your subconscious has a mind of its own, but it accepts your patterns of thought and imagery. When you look for the answer to a problem, your subconscious will respond, but it expects you to come to a decision and to a true judgment in your conscious mind. You must acknowledge that the answer is in your subconscious mind. If you say, "I don't think there is any way out; I am all mixed up and confused; why don't I get an answer?" you are neutralizing your prayer. Like the soldier marking time, you use up vital energy but you do not move forward.

Still the wheels of your mind. Relax. Let go. Quietly affirm:

> My subconscious knows the answer. It is responding to me now. I give thanks because I know the infinite intelligence of my subconscious knows all things and is revealing the perfect answer to me now. My real conviction is now setting free the majesty and glory of my subconscious mind. I rejoice that it is so.

REVIEW OF HIGHLIGHTS

1. Think good, and good follows. Think evil, and evil follows. You are what you think all day long.
2. Your subconscious mind does not argue with you. It

accepts what your conscious mind decrees. If you say, "I can't afford it," your subconscious works to make it true. Select a better thought. Decree, "I'll buy it. I accept it in my mind."

3. You have the power to choose. Choose health and happiness. You can choose to be friendly, or you can choose to be unfriendly. Choose to be cooperative, joyous, friendly, lovable, and the whole world will respond. This is the best way to develop a wonderful personality.

4. Your conscious mind is the "watchman at the gate." Its chief function is to protect your subconscious mind from false impressions. Choose to believe that something good can happen and is happening now. Your greatest power is your capacity to choose. Choose happiness and abundance.

5. The suggestions and statements of others have no power to hurt you. The only power is the movement of your own thought. You can choose to reject the thoughts or statements of others and affirm the good. You have the power to choose how you will react.

6. Watch what you say. You have to account for every idle word. Never say, "I will fail; I will lose my job; I can't pay the rent." Your subconscious cannot take a joke. It brings all these things to pass.

7. Your mind is not evil. No force of nature is evil. It depends how you use the powers of nature. Use your mind to bless, heal, and inspire all people everywhere.

8. Never say, "I can't." Overcome that fear by substituting the following: "I can do all things through the power of my own subconscious mind."

9. Begin to think from the standpoint of the eternal truths and principles of life and not from the standpoint of fear, ignorance, and superstition. Do not let others do your

thinking for you. Choose your own thoughts and make your own decisions.

10. You are the captain of your soul (subconscious mind) and the master of your fate. Remember, you have the capacity to choose. Choose life! Choose love! Choose health! Choose happiness!

11. Whatever your conscious mind assumes and believes to be true, your subconscious mind will accept and bring to pass. Believe in good fortune, divine guidance, right action, and all the blessings of life.

3

The Miracle-Working Power of Your Subconscious

The power of your subconscious is beyond all measure. It inspires you and guides you. It calls up vivid scenes from the storehouse of memory. Your subconscious controls your heartbeat and the circulation of your blood. It regulates your digestion, assimilation, and elimination. When you eat a piece of bread, your subconscious mind transmutes it into tissue, muscle, bone, and blood. These processes are beyond the ken of the wisest person who walks the earth. Your subconscious mind controls all the vital processes and functions of your body. It knows the answer to all problems.

Your subconscious mind never sleeps, never rests. It is always on the job. You can discover the miracle-working power of your subconscious by plainly stating to your subconscious prior to sleep that you want a specific thing accomplished. You will be amazed and delighted to discover that forces within you will be released that lead to the result you wished for. Here is a source of power and wisdom that puts you directly in touch with omnipotence. This is the power that moves the world, guides the planets in their course, and causes the sun to shine.

Your subconscious mind is the source of your ideals, aspirations, and altruistic urges. It was through the subconscious mind that Shakespeare perceived and communicated great truths hidden from the average man of his day. It was through the subconscious mind that the Greek sculptor, Phidias, gained the art and skill to portray beauty, order, symmetry, and proportion in marble and bronze. The subconscious mind is the deep well from which great artists draw their awe-provoking power. It enabled the great Italian artist, Raphael, to paint his Madonnas, and the great German musician, Beethoven, to compose his symphonies.

Some years ago, I was invited to lecture at the Yoga Forest University, in Rishikesh, India. While I was there, I had a long conversation with a surgeon who was visiting from Bombay. From him, I learned the astonishing story of Dr. James Esdaille.

Esdaille was a Scottish surgeon who practiced in Bengal during the 1840s. This was before ether or other modern methods of chemical anesthesia began to be used. Nevertheless, between 1843 and 1846, Dr. Esdaille performed some four hundred major surgical operations of all kinds. These included amputations, removal of tumors and cancerous growths, and operations on the eye, ear, and throat. All these operations were performed under mental anesthesia only. Patients said they felt no pain, and none of them died during surgery.

Just as amazing, the mortality rate of Esdaille's patients following surgery was extremely low. This was well before Western scientists such as Louis Pasteur and Joseph Lister pointed out the bacterial origin of infection. No one realized that postoperative infections were due to unsterilized instruments and virulent organisms. Nevertheless, when Esdaille suggested to his patients, who were in a hypnotic state, that no infection or septic condition would develop, their subconscious minds responded to his suggestion. They set in motion the processes needed to fight off the life-threatening dangers of infection.

Think of it: Over a century and a half ago, this Scottish surgeon who had gone halfway around the world discovered how to use the miraculous wonder-working powers of the subconscious mind. It is enough to cause you to be seized with awe. The transcendental powers that inspired Dr. Esdaille and that protected his patients from mortal danger can be yours, too.

Your subconscious mind can give you independence of time and space. It can make you free of all pain and suffering. It can give you the answer to all problems, whatever they may be. There is a power and an intelligence within you that far transcends your intellect, causing you to marvel at the wonder of it all. All these experiences cause you to rejoice and believe in the miracle-working powers of your own subconscious mind.

YOUR SUBCONSCIOUS IS YOUR BOOK OF LIFE

Whatever thoughts, beliefs, opinions, theories, or dogmas you write, engrave, or impress on your subconscious mind, you will experience them as the objective manifestation of circumstances, conditions, and events. What you write on the inside, you will experience on the outside. You have two sides to your life, objective and subjective, visible and invisible, thought and its manifestation.

Your thought is received as a pattern of neural firings in your cerebral cortex, which is the organ of your conscious reasoning mind. Once your conscious or objective mind accepts the thought completely, it is transmitted to the older parts of the brain, where it becomes flesh and is made manifest in your experience.

As previously outlined, your subconscious cannot argue. It acts only from what you write on it. It accepts your verdict or the conclusions of your conscious mind as final. This is why you are always writing on the book of life, because your thoughts become your experiences. The American philosopher, Ralph Waldo Emerson, said, "Man is what he thinks all day long."

WHAT IS IMPRESSED IN THE SUBCONSCIOUS IS EXPRESSED

William James, the father of American psychology, said that the power to move the world is in your subconscious mind. Your subconscious mind is one with infinite intelligence and boundless wisdom. It is fed by hidden springs and is called the law of life. Whatever you impress upon your subconscious mind, the latter will move heaven and earth to bring it to pass. You must, therefore, impress it with right ideas and constructive thoughts.

The reason there is so much chaos and misery in the world is that so many people do not understand the interaction of their conscious and subconscious minds. When these two principles are in accord, in concord, in peace, and synchronously together, you will have health, happiness, peace, and joy. There is no sickness or discord when the conscious and subconscious work together harmoniously and peacefully.

In the ancient world, Hermes Trismegistus had the reputation of being the greatest, most powerful magus the world had ever known. When his tomb was opened, centuries after his passing, those who were in touch with the wisdom of the ancients waited with great expectancy and a sense of wonder. It was said that the greatest secret of the ages would be found within the tomb. And so it was. The secret was:

> As within, so without;
> As above, so below.

In other words, whatever you impress in your subconscious mind, that becomes expressed on the screen of space. This same truth was proclaimed by Moses, Isaiah, Jesus, Buddha, Zoroaster, Laotze, and all the illumined seers of the ages. Whatever you feel as true subjectively is expressed as conditions, experiences, and events. Motion and emotion must balance. As in heaven (your own mind), so on earth (in your body and environment). This is the great law of life.

You will find throughout all nature the law of action and reaction, of rest and motion. These two must balance, then there will be harmony and equilibrium. You are here to let the life principle flow through you rhythmically and harmoniously. The intake and the outgo must be equal. The impression and the expression must be equal. All your frustration is due to unfulfilled desire.

If you think negatively, destructively, and viciously, these thoughts generate destructive emotions that must be expressed and must find an outlet. These emotions, being of a negative nature, are frequently expressed as ulcers, heart trouble, tension, and anxieties.

What is your idea or feeling about yourself now? Every part of your being expresses that idea. Your vitality, body, financial condition, friends, and social status represent a perfect reflection of the idea you have of yourself. This is the real meaning of what is impressed in your subconscious mind and what is expressed in all phases of your life.

We injure ourselves by the negative ideas we entertain. How often have you wounded yourself by getting angry, fearful, jealous, or vengeful? These are the poisons that enter your subconscious mind. You were not born with these negative attitudes. Feed your subconscious mind life-giving thoughts and you will wipe out all the negative patterns lodged within it. As you continue to do this, all the past will be wiped out and remembered no more.

THE SUBCONSCIOUS HEALS A MALIGNANCY OF THE SKIN

The most convincing evidence anyone can have of the healing power of the subconscious mind is a personal healing. Over forty years ago I developed a malignancy of the skin. I went to the finest doctors, who tried the most advanced treatments medical science could offer. None of these helped. The malignancy got progressively worse.

Then, one day, a clergyman with a deep store of psychological knowledge told me the inner meaning of the 139th Psalm. He called my attention to the passage that reads:

> In thy book all my members were written, which in continuance were fashioned, when as yet there was none of them.

He explained that the term *book* meant my subconscious mind, which fashioned and molded all my organs from a tiny original cell. He pointed out that since my subconscious mind had made my body, it could also recreate it and heal it according to the perfect pattern within it.

This clergyman pointed to his watch. "This had a maker," he told me. "But before the watch could become an objective reality, the watchmaker had to have the idea of it clearly in mind. If for some reason the watch stopped working as it should, the watchmaker's idea of it would give him the knowledge he needed to fix it."

I understood what he was trying to tell me by this analogy. The subconscious intelligence that created my body was like the watchmaker. It knew exactly how to heal, restore, and direct all the vital functions and processes of my body. But for it to do this properly, I had to give it the perfect idea of health. This would act as cause, and the effect would be a healing.

I formulated a very simple and direct prayer.

My body and all its organs were created by the infinite intelligence in my subconscious mind. It knows how to heal me. Its wisdom fashioned all my organs, tissues, muscles, and bones. This infinite healing presence within me is now transforming every cell of my being, making me whole and perfect. I give thanks for the healing I know is taking place at this time. Wonderful are the works of the creative intelligence within me.

I repeated this simple prayer aloud, for about five minutes two or three times a day. After some three months, my skin was whole and perfect. The malignancy had vanished. My doctor was baffled, but I knew what had happened. I had given life-giving patterns of wholeness, beauty, and perfection to my subconscious mind. These forced out the negative images and patterns of thought lodged in my subconscious mind, which were the cause of all my trouble.

Nothing appears on your body except when the mental equivalent is first in your mind. As you change your mind by drenching it with incessant affirmatives, you change your body.

This is the basis of all healing.

Marvelous are thy works; and that my soul [subconscious mind] knoweth right well.

PSALM 139:14

How the Subconscious Controls All Functions of the Body

Whether you are awake or asleep, the ceaseless, tireless action of your subconscious mind controls all the vital functions of your body without any need for your conscious mind to intervene. While you are asleep, your heart continues to beat rhythmically. Your chest and diaphragm muscles pump air in and out of your lungs. There the carbon dioxide that is the byproduct of the activity of your body's cells is exchanged for the fresh oxygen you need to go on functioning. Your subconscious controls your digestive processes and glandular secretions, as well as all the other wondrously complex operations of your body. All this happens whether you are awake or asleep.

If you were forced to operate your body's functions with your conscious mind, you would certainly fail. You would probably die a very quick death. The processes are too complicated, too intertwined. The "heart-lung" machine that is used during open-heart surgery is one of the wonders of modern medical technology, but what it does is infinitely simpler than what your subconscious mind does twenty-four hours a day, year in, year out.

Suppose you were crossing the ocean in a supersonic jetliner and you wandered into the cockpit. You certainly would not know how to fly the plane, but you would not find it difficult to distract the pilot and cause a problem. In the same way, your conscious mind cannot operate your body, but it can get in the way of proper operation.

Worry, anxiety, fear, and depression interfere with the normal functioning of the heart, lungs, stomach, and intestines. The medical community is just beginning to appreciate how serious so-called "stress-related" diseases are. The reason is that these patterns of thought interfere with the harmonious functioning of your subconscious mind.

When you feel physically and mentally disturbed, the best thing you can do is to let go, relax, and still the wheels of your thought processes. Speak to your subconscious mind. Tell it to take over in peace, harmony, and divine order. You will find that all the functions of your body will become normal again. Be sure to speak to your subconscious mind with authority and conviction. It will respond by carrying out your command.

HOW TO GET THE SUBCONSCIOUS TO WORK FOR YOU

The first thing to realize is that your subconscious mind is always working. It is active night and day, whether you act upon it or not. Your subconscious is the builder of your body, but you cannot consciously perceive or hear that inner silent process. Your business is with your conscious mind and not your subconscious mind. Just keep your conscious mind busy with the expectation of the best, and make sure the thoughts you habitually think are based on things that are lovely, true, just, and harmonious. Begin now to take care of your conscious mind, knowing in your heart and soul that your subconscious mind is always expressing, reproducing, and manifesting according to your habitual thinking.

Remember, just as water takes the shape of the pipe it flows through, the life principle in you flows through you according to the nature of your thoughts. Claim that the healing presence in your subconscious is flowing through you as harmony, health, peace, joy, and abundance. Think of it as a living intelligence, a lovely companion on the way. Firmly believe it is continually flowing through you vivifying, inspiring, and prospering you. It will respond exactly this way. It is done unto you as you believe.

HEALING PRINCIPLE OF THE SUBCONSCIOUS RESTORES OPTIC NERVES

One of the most celebrated healing shrines in the world is at Lourdes, in southwestern France. The archives of the medical department of Lourdes are filled with dossiers that detail well-authenticated cases of what are termed miraculous healings. One example among many is the case of Madame Bire, who was blind, with optic nerves that were atrophied and useless. After she visited Lourdes, she regained her sight. Several doctors who examined her testified that her optic nerves were still useless, and yet, she saw! A month later, a reexamination found that her visual mechanism had been fully restored to normal.

I am thoroughly convinced that Madame Bire was *not* healed by the waters of the shrine. What healed her was her own subconscious mind, which responded to her belief. The healing principle within her subconscious mind responded to the nature of her thought. Belief is a thought in the subconscious mind. It means to accept something as true. The thought accepted executes itself automatically.

Undoubtedly, Madame Bire went to the shrine with expectancy and great faith. She knew in her heart she would receive a healing. Her subconscious mind responded accordingly, releasing the ever present healing forces. The subconscious mind that created the eye can certainly bring a dead nerve back to life. What the creative principle created, it can recreate. *According to your belief is it done unto you.*

HOW TO CONVEY THE IDEA OF PERFECT HEALTH TO YOUR SUBCONSCIOUS MIND

A Methodist minister I met in Johannesburg, South Africa, told me how he overcame an advanced case of lung cancer. The method he used was to convey the idea of perfect health to his subconscious mind. At my request, he sent me a detailed description of the process, which I now pass along to you.

Several times a day I would make certain that I was completely relaxed mentally and physically. I relaxed my body by speaking to it as follows:

"My feet are relaxed, my ankles are relaxed, my legs are relaxed, my abdominal muscles are relaxed, my heart and lungs are relaxed, my head is relaxed, my whole being is completely relaxed."

After about five minutes I would find myself drifting into a sleepy, drowsy state. Then I affirmed the following truth:

"The perfection of God is now being expressed through me. The idea of perfect health is now filling my subconscious mind. The image God has of me is a perfect image, and my subconscious mind recreates my body in perfect accordance with the perfect image held in the mind of God."

This minister had a remarkable healing. The technique he used is a simple, straightforward way of conveying the idea of perfect health to your subconscious mind.

Another wonderful way to convey the idea of health to your subconscious is through disciplined or scientific imagination. I told a man who was suffering from functional paralysis to make a vivid picture of himself walking around in his office, touching the desk, answering the telephone, and doing all the things he ordinarily would do if he were healed. I explained to him that this mental visualization of perfect health would be accepted by his subconscious mind.

He threw himself into the role. He actually felt himself back in the office. He knew that he was giving his subconscious mind something concrete and definite to work upon. His subconscious mind was the film upon which the visualization was impressed.

He continued this visualization discipline intensively for several weeks. Then, one day, the telephone rang at a time when everyone else was out. The telephone was twelve feet away from his bed. Nevertheless, he managed to answer it. His paralysis vanished from that hour on. The healing power of his subconscious mind had responded to his mental imagery, and a healing followed.

This man had suffered from a mental block that prevented nerve impulses generated in the brain from reaching his legs. Therefore, he could not walk. When he shifted his attention to the healing power within him, the power flowed through his focused attention, and he could walk again.

> Whatsoever ye shall ask in prayer, believing, ye shall receive.
> *MATT. 21:22*

IDEAS WORTH REMEMBERING

1. Your subconscious mind controls all the vital processes of your body and knows the answer to all problems.
2. Prior to sleep, turn over a specific request to your subconscious mind and prove its miracle-working power to yourself.
3. Whatever you impress on your subconscious mind is expressed on the screen of space as conditions, experi-

ences, and events. Therefore, you should carefully watch all ideas and thoughts entertained in your conscious mind.

4. The law of action and reaction is universal. Your thought is action, and the reaction is the automatic response of your subconscious mind to your thought. Watch your thoughts!

5. All frustration is due to unfulfilled desires. If you dwell on obstacles, delays, and difficulties, your subconscious mind responds accordingly, and you are blocking your own good.

6. The Life Principle will flow through you rhythmically and harmoniously if you consciously affirm: "I believe that the subconscious power that gave me this desire is now fulfilling it through me." This dissolves all conflicts.

7. You can interfere with the normal rhythm of your heart, lungs, and other organs by worry, anxiety, and fear. Feed your subconscious with thoughts of harmony, health, and peace, and all the functions of your body will become normal again.

8. Keep your conscious mind busy with the expectation of the best, and your subconscious will faithfully reproduce your habitual thinking.

9. Imagine the happy ending or solution to your problem, feel the thrill of accomplishment, and what you imagine and feel will be accepted by your subconscious mind, which will bring it to pass.

4
Mental Healings in Ancient Times

Through the ages, people in every continent, climate, and culture have instinctively known that somewhere there resided a healing power that could restore the abilities and functions of a person's body to its normal state of efficiency and good health. They believed that this strange power could be invoked under certain conditions and that if it were invoked properly, the alleviation of human suffering would follow. The history of all nations presents testimony in support of this belief.

In the early history of the world, the power of secretly influencing men for good or evil, including the healing of the sick, was said to be possessed by priests, priestesses, and holy people. They claimed to possess powers derived directly from God that included the healing of the sick. The procedures and processes of healing varied throughout the world, but they generally included supplications and offerings to the god; various ceremonies, such as the laying on of hands and incantations; and the use of amulets, talismans, rings, relics, and images.

For example, in the religions of antiquity priests in the ancient temples gave drugs to their patients and practiced hypnotic suggestions as they went to sleep. The patients were told that the gods would surely visit them in their sleep and heal them. Many healings followed.

The devotees of Hecate were told to mix lizards with resin, frankincense, and myrrh and pound all this together in the open air under the crescent moon. After performing these bizarre and mysterious rites, they prayed to the goddess, took the potion they had just compounded, and went to sleep. If their faith was strong enough, they saw the goddess in a dream. This rite, which sounds so strange, even fantastic, to our ears, was often followed by healings.

People in ancient times worked out many effective ways to tap the incredible power of the subconscious mind and use it for healing. While they knew that these procedures worked, however, they did not understand how or why they worked. Today, we can see that they were using potent suggestions to the subconscious mind. The rituals and potions and amulets appealed powerfully to the imagination of people and favored the acceptance by the subconscious mind of the insistent suggestions given by the healer. But the *work* of healing was done by the patient's own subconscious mind.

In all ages unofficial healers have obtained remarkable results in cases where authorized medical skill had failed and the patients had given up hope. This gives cause for thought. How do these healers in all parts of the world effect their cures? The answer is that these healings take place because the blind belief of the sick person released the healing power resident in his or her subconscious mind. The more fantastic and peculiar the remedies and methods used by the healers, the more likely the patients were to believe that anything so strange must be unusually powerful. Their aroused emotional state made it easier for them to accept the suggestion of health, in both their conscious and subconscious mind. This point will be discussed at greater length in the next chapter.

BIBLICAL ACCOUNTS ON THE USE OF THE SUBCONSCIOUS POWERS

> What things soever ye desire, when ye pray, believe that ye receive them, and ye shall have them.
>
> *MARK 11:24*

Reread this passage and pay close attention to the difference in tenses. The verbs *believe* and *receive* are in the present, but the verb *shall have* is in the future. The inspired writer is telling us something of the greatest importance by this seemingly minor difference in the grammar of the sentence. If we believe and accept as true the fact that our desire has *already* been accomplished and fulfilled, that it is *already* completed, then its realization will follow as a thing *in the future*.

The success of this technique relies on the confident conviction that the thought, the idea, the picture is already fact in mind. In order for anything to have substance in the realm of mind, it must be thought of as actually existing.

Here in a few cryptic words is a concise and specific direction for making use of the creative power of thought by impressing upon the subconscious the particular thing you desire. Your thought, idea, plan, or purpose is as real on its own plane as your hand or your heart. In following the biblical technique, you completely eliminate from your mind all consideration of conditions, circumstances, or anything that might imply a negative outcome. You are planting a seed (concept) in the mind that, if you leave it undisturbed, will infallibly germinate into external fruition.

The prime condition that Jesus insisted upon was faith.

Over and over again you read in the Bible, *According to your faith is it done unto you*. If you plant certain types of seeds in the ground, you have faith they will grow after their kind. This is the way of seeds, and trusting the laws of growth and agriculture, you know that the seeds will come forth after their kind.

The faith that is described in the Bible is a way of thinking, an attitude of mind, an inner certitude, knowing that the idea you fully accept in your conscious mind will be embodied in your subconscious mind and made manifest. Faith is, in a sense, accepting as true what your reason and senses deny. It is closing down, refusing to listen to the little, rational, analytical, conscious mind and embracing an attitude of complete reliance on the inner power of your subconscious mind.

Here is one of the best known examples of the biblical technique of healing:

> And when he was come into the house, the blind men came to him: and Jesus saith unto them, Believe ye that I am able to do this? They said unto him, Yea, Lord. Then touched he their eyes, saying, according to your faith be it unto you. And their eyes were opened; and Jesus straitly charged them, saying, see that no man know it.
>
> *MATT. 9:28–30*

By saying, *according to your faith be it unto you*, Jesus was openly appealing to the cooperation of the subconscious mind of the blind men. Their faith was their great expectancy, their inner feeling, their inner conviction that something miraculous would happen, that their prayer would be answered. And therefore it was. This is the time-honored technique of healing, utilized alike by all healing groups throughout the world, regardless of religious affiliation.

In saying, *see that no man know it,* Jesus was urging the healed patients not to discuss their healing with others. If they did so, they might be harassed by the skeptical and derogatory criticisms of the unbelieving. This in turn might have tended to undo the benefits they had received at the hand of Jesus by depositing thoughts of fear, doubt, and anxiety in the subconscious mind.

> . . . for with authority and power he commandeth the unclean spirits, and they came out.
>
> *LUKE 4:36*

When the sick came to Jesus to be healed, they were healed by their own faith, together with his faith and understanding of the healing power of the subconscious mind. Whatever he decreed, he felt inwardly to be true. He and the people needing help were in the one universal subjective mind, and his silent inner knowing and conviction of the healing power changed the negative destructive patterns in the patients' subconscious. The resultant healings were the automatic response to the internal mental change. His command was his appeal to the subconscious mind of the patients plus his awareness, feeling, and absolute trust in the response of the subconscious mind to the words that he spoke with authority.

MIRACLES AT VARIOUS SHRINES THROUGHOUT THE WORLD

On every continent, in every land, there are shrines at which cures take place. Some are world famous. Others are known only to those who live nearby. Whether celebrated or obscure, the healings that happen at these shrines happen for the same reasons and by way of the same powers of the subconscious mind.

I have visited several of the famous shrines in Japan. The central focus of the world-renowned shrine of Diabutsu is a gigantic bronze statue, forty-two feet tall. It depicts Buddha seated with folded hands, his head inclined in an attitude of profound contemplative ecstasy.

Here I saw young and old making offerings at its feet. Money, fruit, rice, and oranges were offered. Candles were lit, incense was burned, and prayers of petition were recited. I listened to the chant of a young girl as she intoned a prayer, bowed low, and placed two oranges as an offering. She was thanking Buddha for restoring her voice. She had lost her voice, but it was restored at the shrine. Her simple faith that Buddha would give her back her singing voice if she followed a certain ritual, fasted, and made certain offerings had helped to kindle faith and expectancy. The result was a conditioning of her mind to the point of belief. Her subconscious mind then responded to her belief.

The power of imagination and blind belief cannot be overstated. A wondrous example of this is the case of a relative of mine in Perth, in western Australia, who suffered from tuberculosis. His lungs were badly diseased. His son decided to help his father heal himself. He went to his father's home and told him he had recently met a wandering monk with strange powers.

This monk had just returned from a long stay at one of the most celebrated healing shrines in Europe. There he had acquired a small fragment of the True Cross, set in a ring that dated back to the Middle Ages. Over the centuries, countless sufferers had been healed after touching the ring or the fragment of the Cross.

When the son had heard this he had told the monk about his father's illness and begged to borrow the ring. The monk had agreed. The son then gave the monk a free-will offering of the equivalent of $500.

When the son showed his father the ring, the older man practically snatched it from him. He clasped the ring to his chest, prayed silently, and went to sleep. In the morning he was healed. All the clinic's tests proved negative.

Healings of this sort happen all the time. What is most significant about this one is that the son's amazing story was totally made up. In fact, he had picked up a splinter of ordinary wood from the sidewalk, taken it to a jeweler, and had it set in a gold ring of antique design. He then gave it to his father.

You know, of course, it was not the splinter of wood from the sidewalk that healed the father. No, it was his imagination aroused to an intense degree, plus the confident expectancy of a perfect healing. Imagination was joined to faith or subjective feeling, and the union of the two brought about a healing through the power of his subconscious mind.

The father never learned of the trick that had been played upon him. If he had, he might well have had a relapse. Instead, his tuberculosis never returned. He remained completely cured and passed away from other causes fifteen years later, at the age of eighty-nine.

ONE UNIVERSAL HEALING PRINCIPLE

It is a well-known fact that all the various schools of healing bring about documented cures of the most wonderful character. The most obvious conclusion that strikes your mind is that there must be some underlying organ and process that is common to them all. Indeed there is. The organ of healing is the subconscious mind, and the process of healing is faith.

Think deeply about these fundamental truths:

- You possess mental functions that have been distinguished by designating one the conscious mind and the other the subconscious mind.
- Your subconscious mind is constantly amenable to the power of suggestion.
- Your subconscious mind has complete control of the functions, conditions, and sensations of your body.

You surely know that symptoms of almost any disease can be induced in hypnotic subjects by suggestion. For example, a subject in the hypnotic state can develop a high temperature, flushed face, or chills according to the nature of the suggestion given. You can suggest to the person that he is paralyzed and cannot walk, and it will be so. You can hold a cup of cold water under the nose of the hypnotic subject and tell him, "This is full of pepper; smell it!" He will sneeze violently and repeatedly. What do you think caused him to sneeze? The water, or the suggestion?

If someone tells you he is allergic to Timothy grass, you can place a synthetic flower or an empty glass in front of his nose, when he is in a hypnotic state, and tell him it is Timothy grass. He will develop his usual allergic symptoms. This shows us that the cause of the symptoms is in the subconscious mind. Curing the symptoms also takes place in the subconscious mind.

Different schools of medicine, such as osteopathy, chiropractic, chi qong, acupuncture, and naturopathy, all produce remarkable healings. So do the rites and ceremonies of the various religious beliefs throughout the world. It is obvious that all of these healings are brought about through the subconscious mind—the only healer there is.

Notice how the subconscious mind heals a cut on your finger. It knows exactly how to do it. The doctor dresses the wound and says, "Nature heals it!" But "nature" is nothing more than another name for natural law, the law of the subconscious mind. The instinct of self-preservation is the first law of nature, and self-preservation is the foremost function of the subconscious mind. Your strongest instinct is the most potent of all autosuggestions.

WIDELY DIFFERENT THEORIES

Many different theories of healing have been advanced by different religious sects and prayer-therapy groups. There are a great number who claim that because their practice produces results, their theory therefore must be right. As we have seen in this chapter, this cannot be correct.

As you know, there are many varieties of healing. Franz Anton Mesmer (1734–1815), an Austrian physician who practiced in Paris, discovered that by applying magnets to a diseased body, he could cure that disease miraculously. He also performed cures with various other pieces of glass and metal. Later, he abandoned the use of these objects in favor of passing his hands over the patient's body. He claimed that the real source of his cures was what he called "animal magnetism." He theorized that some mysterious magnetic substance was transmitted from the healer's hands to the patient.

Mesmer lent his name to this method of treating disease, which came to be called mesmerism. Today we know it as hypnotism. Other physicians, jealous of Mesmer's success, claimed that all his healings were due to suggestion and nothing else. When pressed, however, they had to admit that they did not know how this power of suggestion created such amazing effects.

All of these groups—psychiatrists, psychologists,

osteopaths, chiropractors, physicians, and religious groups of every variety—are using the one universal power resident in the subconscious mind. Each may proclaim the healings are due to their theory, but the truth is far different. The process of all healing is a definite, positive, mental attitude, an inner attitude, or a way of thinking, called faith. Healing is due to a confident expectancy that acts as a powerful suggestion to the subconscious mind, releasing its healing potency.

One person does not heal by a different power than another. It is true that both may have their own theories or methods, but there is only one process of healing, and that is faith. There is only one healing power; namely, your subconscious mind. Select whatever theory, belief, and method that calls out to you. You can rest assured, if you have faith, you will get results.

VIEWS OF PARACELSUS

Philippus Paracelsus, a famous Swiss alchemist and physician, who lived from 1493 to 1541, was a great healer in his day. He stated what is now an obvious scientific fact when he said:

> Whether the object of your faith be real or false, you will nevertheless obtain the same effects. Thus, if I believed in Saint Peter's statue as I should have believed in Saint Peter himself, I shall obtain the same effects that I should have obtained from Saint Peter. But that is superstition. Faith, however, produces miracles; and whether it is true or false faith, it will always produce the same wonders.

The views of Paracelsus were echoed in the sixteenth century by Pietro Pomponazzi, an Italian philosopher, who wrote:

We can easily conceive the marvelous effects which confidence and imagination can produce, particularly when both qualities are reciprocated between the subjects and the person who influences them. The cures attributed to the influence of certain relics are the effect of their imagination and confidence. Quacks and philosophers know that if the bones of any skeleton were put in place of the saint's bones, the sick would nonetheless experience beneficial effects, if they believed that they were veritable relics.

Think what this implies. If you believe in the power of saints' bones, or in the healing properties of certain waters, or, like my Australian relative, in the miraculous effects of a fragment of wood, *you will get results* because of the powerful suggestion given to your subconscious mind. It is the latter that does the healing.

BERNHEIM'S EXPERIMENTS

Hippolyte Bernheim was professor of medicine at Nancy, France, early in the twentieth century. He was one of the first to explain how a physician's suggestion to the patient took effect because of the force of the subconscious mind.

Bernheim relates the story of a man whose tongue was paralyzed. Every form of treatment was tried, with no success at all. Then one day the man's doctor announced that he had learned of a new instrument that was certain to relieve his problem. The doctor then put a pocket thermometer in the patient's mouth. The patient imagined this was the instrument that was to save him. In a few moments he cried out joyfully that he could once more move his tongue freely.

Bernheim continues:

Among our cases, facts of the same sort will be found. A young girl came into my office, having suffered from complete loss of speech for nearly four weeks. After making sure of the diagnosis, I told my students that loss of speech sometimes yielded instantly to electricity, which might act simply by its suggestive influence. I sent for the induction apparatus. I applied my hand over the larynx and moved a little and said, "Now you can speak aloud." In an instant I made her say "a," then "b," then "Maria." She continued to speak distinctly; the loss of voice had disappeared.

Here Bernheim is showing the power of faith and expectancy on the part of the patient, which acts as a powerful suggestion to the subconscious mind.

PRODUCING A BLISTER BY SUGGESTION

Bernheim states that he produced a blister on the back of a patient's neck by applying a postage stamp and suggesting to the patient that it was a fly-plaster. This sort of demonstration has been confirmed by the experiments and experiences of many doctors in many parts of the world. These leave no doubt that structural changes in the body can be brought about as a result of oral suggestion to patients.

THE CAUSE OF BLOODY STIGMATA

Hemorrhages and bloody stigmata can be induced by means of suggestion.

As a demonstration of this, Dr. M. Bourru put a subject into a hypnotic trance, then gave him the following suggestion:

At four o'clock this afternoon, after the hypnosis, you will come into my office, sit down in this armchair and fold your arms across your chest. Your nose will then begin to bleed.

That afternoon, the young man did exactly as he had been told. After he crossed his arms, several drops of blood came from his left nostril.

On another occasion, the same investigator traced a patient's name on both his forearms with the dull point of an instrument while the patient was in a hypnotic trance. Bourru then said:

At four o'clock this afternoon you will go to sleep. Your arms will bleed along the lines I have traced, and your name will appear written on your arms in letters of blood.

The patient was carefully observed that afternoon. At four o'clock he fell asleep. On his left arm the letters stood out in bright relief, and in several places there were drops of blood. Although the letters gradually faded, they were still faintly visible three months afterward.

These facts demonstrate at once the correctness of the two fundamental propositions previously stated; namely, the constant amenability of the subconscious mind to the power of suggestion and the perfect control that the subconscious mind exercises over the functions, sensations, and conditions of the body.

All the foregoing phenomena dramatize vividly abnormal conditions induced by suggestion. They are conclusive proof that *as a man thinketh in his heart* [subconscious mind] *so is he.*

HEALING POINTS IN REVIEW

1. Remind yourself frequently that the healing power is in your subconscious mind.

2. Know that faith is like a seed planted in the ground; it grows after its kind. Plant the idea (seed) in your mind, water and fertilize it with expectancy, and it will become manifest.

3. The idea you have for a book, new invention, or play is real in your mind. This is why you can believe you have it now. Believe in the reality of your idea, plan, or invention, and as you do, it will become manifest.

4. In praying for another, know that your silent inner knowing of wholeness, beauty, and perfection can change the negative patterns of the other's subconscious mind and bring about wonderful results.

5. The miraculous healings you hear about at various shrines are due to imagination and blind faith that act on the subconscious mind, releasing the healing power.

6. All disease originates in the mind. Nothing appears on the body unless there is a mental pattern corresponding to it.

7. The symptoms of almost any disease can be induced in you by hypnotic suggestion. This shows you the power of your thought.

8. There is only one process of healing and that is faith. There is only one healing power; namely, your subconscious mind.

9. Whether the object of your faith is real or false, you will get results. Your subconscious mind responds to the thought in your mind. Look upon faith as a thought in your mind, and that will suffice.

5
Mental Healings in Modern Times

What is it that heals? Where is this healing power, and how can it be put to practical use? These are vital questions of deep concern to all of us. To all of them, the answer is the same: This healing power is in the subconscious mind of every person, and a changed mental attitude on the part of the sick person releases this healing power.

No mental- or religious-science practitioner, psychologist, psychiatrist, or medical doctor ever healed a patient. There is an old saying, "The doctor dresses the wound, but God heals it." The psychologist or psychiatrist makes effective change by removing the mental blocks in the patient so that the healing principle may be released, restoring the patient to health. In the same way, the surgeon removes the physical block, enabling the healing currents to function normally. No physician, surgeon, or mental-science practitioner can legitimately claim that he or she "healed the patient." The one healing power may be called by many different names—nature, life, God, creative intelligence—but in reality these are simply different ways to refer to subconscious power.

As we have already seen, there are many different ways

we can use to remove the mental, emotional, and physical blocks that inhibit the flow of the healing life principle animating all of us. The healing principle resident in your subconscious mind can and will, if properly directed by you or some other person, heal your mind and body of all disease. This healing principle operates in all people regardless of creed, color, or race. You do not have to belong to some particular church in order to use and participate in this healing process. Your subconscious will heal the burn or cut on your hand even if you profess to be an atheist or agnostic.

Modern mental healing is based on the truth that the infinite intelligence and power of your subconscious mind responds according to your faith. Mental-science practitioners or ministers follow the injunction of the Bible. That is, they go into their closet and shut the door, which means they still their minds, relax, let go, and think of the infinite healing presence within them. They close the door of their mind to all outside distractions as well as appearances, and then they quietly and knowingly turn over their request or desire to their subconscious mind, realizing that the intelligence of their mind will answer them according to their specific needs.

The most wonderful thing to know is this: Imagine the end desired and feel its reality; then the infinite life principle will respond to your conscious choice and your conscious request. This is the meaning of the text *believe you have received, and you shall receive*. This is what the modern mental scientist does when he or she practices prayer therapy.

ONE PROCESS OF HEALING

There is only one universal healing principle operating through everything—the cat, the dog, the tree, the grass, the wind, the earth—for everything is alive. This life principle operates through the animal, vegetable, and mineral kingdoms as instinct and the law of growth. Because humans are consciously aware of this life principle, we can consciously direct it to bless ourselves in countless ways.

There are many different approaches, techniques, and methods in using the universal power, but there is only one process of healing, which is faith, for *according to your faith is it done unto you.*

THE LAW OF BELIEF

All religions of the world represent forms of belief, and these beliefs are explained in many ways. The law of life is belief. What do you believe about yourself, life, and the universe? *It is done unto you as you believe.*

Belief is a thought in your mind that causes the power of your subconscious to be distributed into all phases of your life according to your thinking habits. You must realize that when the Bible speaks of belief, it is not talking about your belief in some ritual, ceremony, form, institution, or formula. It is talking about belief itself. The belief of your mind is simply the thought of your mind.

> If thou canst believe, all things are possible to him that believeth.
>
> *MARK 9:23*

It is foolish to believe in something that will hurt or harm you. Remember, it is not the thing believed in that hurts or harms you, but the belief or thought in your mind that creates the result. All your experiences, all your actions, and all the events and circumstances of your life are but the reflections and reactions to your own thought.

PRAYER THERAPY IS THE COMBINED FUNCTION OF THE CONSCIOUS AND SUBCONSCIOUS MIND SCIENTIFICALLY DIRECTED

Prayer therapy is the synchronized, harmonious, and intelligent function of the conscious and subconscious levels of mind specifically directed for a definite purpose. In scientific prayer or prayer therapy, you must know what you are doing and why you are doing it. You trust the law of healing. Prayer therapy is sometimes referred to as mental treatment. Another term is *scientific prayer*.

In prayer therapy you consciously choose a certain idea, mental picture, or plan that you desire to experience. You realize your capacity to convey this idea or mental image to your subconscious by feeling the reality of the state assumed. As you remain faithful in your mental attitude, your prayer will be answered. Prayer therapy is a definite mental action for a definite specific purpose.

Let us suppose that you decide to heal a certain difficulty by prayer therapy. You are aware that your problem or sickness, whatever it may be, must be caused by negative thoughts charged with fear and lodged in your subconscious mind. You realize that if you can succeed in cleansing your mind of these thoughts, you will get a healing.

You, therefore, turn to the healing power within your subconscious mind. You remind yourself of its infinite power and intelligence and its capacity to heal all conditions. As you dwell on these truths, your fear will begin to dissolve. The recollection of these truths battles and ultimately overcomes the erroneous beliefs.

You give thanks for the healing that you know will come. Then you keep your mind off the difficulty until you feel guided, after an interval, to pray again. While you are praying, you refuse to give any power to the negative conditions or to admit for a second that the healing will not come. This attitude of mind brings about the harmonious union of the conscious and subconscious mind, which releases the healing power.

FAITH HEALING, WHAT IT MEANS, AND HOW BLIND FAITH WORKS

What is popularly known as faith healing is *not* the faith spoken of in the Bible, which means a knowledge of the interaction of the conscious and subconscious mind. A faith healer is one who heals without any real scientific understanding of the powers and forces involved. He or she may claim a special gift of healing, and the sick person's blind belief in him or her or in his or her powers may bring results.

In many parts of the world, traditional healers treat their patients by dances, incantations, and invocations of spirits. A person may be healed by touching the relics of a saint, wearing special ritual garb, lighting a holy incense or candle, or drinking a mixture of brewed herbs. *Anything* that leads the patient to honestly believe in the method or process will make a healing more likely.

Any method that causes you to move from fear and worry to faith and expectancy will heal. Many people claim that because their individual theories produce results, they must therefore be correct and true. As we have already seen, this cannot be right.

To illustrate how blind faith works, think back to our discussion of the Swiss physician, Franz Anton Mesmer. In 1776 he claimed to have produced many cures by stroking the bodies of his patients with magnets. Later, he threw away his magnets and simply made passes with his hands at a short distance from the patient. This, too, worked. To explain the success of this new procedure, Mesmer evolved the theory of animal magnetism. This he held to be a fluid that pervades the universe but is most active in the human organism. He claimed that this magnetic fluid was being transmitted from his hands to the diseased bodies of his patients and that this transfer of animal magnetism was what healed them. People flocked to him, and many wonderful cures were reported.

Mesmer moved to Paris. There the government appointed a commission to investigate his cures. Its members included prominent physicians and members of the Academy of Science, of which Benjamin Franklin was a member. After a thorough inquiry, the commission admitted that Mesmer had produced confirmed cures. It held, however, that there was no evidence to prove the correctness of his magnetic-fluid theory. It suggested that the effects were due to the imagination of the patients.

Soon after this, Mesmer was driven into exile. He died in 1815. Shortly afterward, Dr. James Braid of Manchester, England, undertook to show that magnetic fluid had nothing to do with the production of the healings of Dr. Mesmer. Dr. Braid discovered that patients could be thrown into hypnotic sleep by suggestion. While they were in the hypnotic trance, he succeeded in producing many of the amazing phenomena that Mesmer had ascribed to animal magnetism.

You can readily see that all these cures were undoubtedly brought about by the active imagination of the patients together with a powerful suggestion of health to their subconscious minds. It is not unfair to call this blind faith, because neither the patients nor the practicioners understood how the cures were brought about.

SUBJECTIVE FAITH AND WHAT IT MEANS

The subjective or subconscious mind of an individual is as amenable to the control of his or her own conscious or objective mind as it is to the suggestions of another. It follows that whatever may be your objective belief, if you will assume to have faith actively or passively, your subconscious mind will be controlled by the suggestion, and your desire will be fulfilled.

The faith required in mental healings is a purely subjective faith. The way to attain it is to put an end to active opposition on the part of the objective or conscious mind.

For an effective healing of the body to take place, it is, of course, best if both the conscious and subconscious mind are in a state of fully accepting faith. However, it is not always essential. You can enter into a condition of passivity and receptivity by relaxing the mind and the body and getting into a sleepy state. In this drowsy state your passivity becomes receptive to subjective impression.

A man once asked me, "How is it that I got a healing through a certain minister? When he told me that there is no such thing as disease and that matter does not exist, I did not believe a word he said. I thought he was insulting my intelligence. And yet, I was healed. How could that be?"

As I told this man, the explanation is simple. He was quieted by soothing words and told to get into a perfectly passive condition, to say nothing and think of nothing for the time being. The minister also became passive. He affirmed quietly, peacefully, and constantly for about a half hour that this man would have perfect health, peace, harmony, and wholeness.

At the end of the half hour, the man felt immense relief and was restored to health.

It is easy to see that his subjective faith had been made manifest by his passivity under treatment, and the suggestions of perfect healthfulness by the minister were conveyed to his subconscious mind. The two subjective minds were then in rapport.

If the man had allowed his doubts about the healer's power and the correctness of his theory to surface, these would have acted as antagonistic autosuggestions. The minister's suggestions would have been seriously handicapped or even totally frustrated. In this sleepy, drowsy state, however, the resistance of the conscious mind was reduced to a minimum. The subconscious mind of the patient was receptive to the minister's suggestions. It performed its functions in harmony with those suggestions, and a healing followed.

THE MEANING OF ABSENT TREATMENT

Suppose while living in Los Angeles, you learned that your mother in New York City was seriously ill. Your first impulse might be to leave your home and job to go to her. But what if that were not possible? Would you have to give up any hope of lending the strength of your faith to the process of your mother's recovery?

No. While you might not be physically present, your prayers would go to her nonetheless. It is the Father within that doeth the work.

There is but one creative mind. The creative law of mind serves you. What you must do is induce an inner realization of health and harmony in your own mentality. Its response is automatic. This inner realization, acting through the subconscious mind, operates in turn on your mother's subconscious mind. Your thoughts of health, vitality, and perfection operate through the one universal subjective mind. They set in motion a law of the subjective side of life that manifests itself through her body as a healing.

In the mind principle, there is no time or space. The same mind operates through your mother—and through you—no matter where you may be. In reality there is no absent treatment as opposed to present treatment, for the universal mind is omnipresent. You do not try to send out thoughts or hold a thought. Your treatment is a conscious movement of thought. As you become conscious of the qualities of health, well-being, and relaxation, these qualities will be resurgent in the experience of your mother. Results will follow.

Here is an actual example of what is misleadingly called absent treatment. A woman in Los Angeles learned that her mother in New York had suffered a coronary thrombosis. She could not go to her mother's side, but she prayed as follows:

> The healing presence is right where my mother is. Her bodily condition is but a reflection of her thought-life, like shadows cast on the screen. I know that in order to change the images on the screen I must change what they reflect. I now project in my own mind the image of wholeness, harmony, and perfect health for my mother.
>
> The infinite healing presence that created my mother's body and all her organs is now saturating every atom of her being, and a river of peace flows through every cell of her body. The doctors are divinely guided and directed, and whoever touches my mother is guided to do the right thing.
>
> I know that disease has no ultimate reality; if it had, no one could be healed. I now align myself with the infinite principle of love and life, and I know and decree that

> harmony, health, and peace are now being expressed in my mother's body.

She prayed in this manner several times a day. After a few days, her mother had a remarkable recovery. Her cardiologist was amazed and complimented her on her great faith in the power of God.

The conclusion arrived at in the daughter's mind and accepted by her with perfect faith set in motion the creative energy within the universal subconscious mind. This manifested itself through her mother's body as perfect health and harmony. What the daughter felt as true about her mother was simultaneously expressed in the experience of her mother.

RELEASING THE KINETIC ACTION OF THE SUBCONSCIOUS MIND

A psychologist friend of mine told me that a biopsy had shown the presence of cancerous cells in a vital organ. Her oncologist recommended a painful and dangerous treatment. Before agreeing, my friend tried another approach. Every night before going to sleep she quietly affirmed, "Every cell, nerve, tissue, and organ is now being made whole, pure, and perfect. My whole body is being restored to health and harmony."

A complete healing followed in about a month's time. Subsequent tests showed that the cancerous cells were no longer present.

I was very impressed by this, but also curious. I asked her why she repeated her affirmation prior to sleep. She told me, "Once it is set in motion in a certain direction, the kinetic action of the subconscious mind continues throughout your sleep. That is why it is so critical to give the subconscious mind something beneficial to work on as you drop off into slumber."

This was a very wise answer. Notice also that in thinking of harmony and perfect health, she never referred to her condition by name.

I strongly suggest that you stop talking about your ailments or giving them a name, especially in the hours leading up to sleep. The only sap from which they draw life is your attention and fear of them. Like the above-mentioned psychologist, become a mental surgeon. Then your troubles will be cut off the way dead branches are pruned from a tree.

On the other hand, if you are constantly naming your aches and symptoms and discussing them, you give them power over you. You inhibit the kinetic action that releases the healing power and energy of your subconscious mind. Furthermore, by the law of your own mind, these imaginings tend to take shape, *As the thing I greatly feared.* Fill your mind with the great truths of life and walk forward in the light of love.

SUMMARY OF YOUR AIDS TO HEALTH

1. Find out what it is that heals you. Realize that correct directions given to your subconscious mind will heal your mind and body.
2. Develop a definite plan for turning over your requests or desires to your subconscious mind.
3. Imagine the end desired and feel its reality. Follow it through, and you will get definite results.
4. Decide what belief is. Know that belief is a thought in your mind and that what you think you create.
5. It is foolish to believe in sickness or in anything that will hurt or harm you. Believe in perfect health, prosperity, peace, wealth, and divine guidance.
6. Great and noble thoughts upon which you habitually dwell become great acts.

7. Apply the power of prayer therapy in your life. Choose a certain plan, idea, or mental picture. Unite mentally and emotionally with that idea. As you remain faithful to your mental attitude, your prayer will be answered.

8. Always remember, if you really want the power to heal, you can have it through faith, which means a knowledge of the working of your conscious and subconscious mind. Faith comes with understanding.

9. Blind faith means that a person may get results in healing without any scientific understanding of the powers and forces involved.

10. Learn to pray for your loved ones who may be ill. Quiet your mind. Your thoughts of health, vitality, and perfection operating through the one universal subjective mind will be felt and made manifest in the mind of your loved one.

6
Practical Techniques in Mental Healings

When an engineer sets out to build a bridge or design a spacecraft, he or she approaches the problem with a known, familiar technique and a set of practiced skills and methods. These techniques, skills, and methods must be learned. In the same way, there are recognized techniques, skills, and methods for governing, controlling, and directing your life. These methods and techniques are primary.

In building the Golden Gate Bridge, the engineers first had to understand mathematical principles, stresses, and strains. Second, they developed in their minds a visualization of the ideal bridge across the bay. The third step was the application of tried and proven methods by which the principles were implemented. When these three steps were completed, the bridge took form and generations of motorists began to drive across it.

If you want your prayers to be answered, you must start with the proper techniques and methods. The way in which your prayer is answered is a scientific way. Nothing happens by chance. This is a world of order and laws. In this chapter you will find practical techniques for the unfolding and nurturing of your spiritual life. Your prayers must not remain up in the air like a balloon. They must go somewhere and accomplish something in your life.

When we analyze prayer, we discover there are many different approaches and methods. We will not consider in this book the formal, ritual prayers used in religious services. These have an important place in group worship, but that is not our focus here. We are immediately concerned with effective methods of *personal* prayer that can be applied in your daily life and used to help yourself and others.

Prayer is the formulation of an idea concerning something we wish to accomplish. Prayer is the soul's sincere desire. Your desire *is* your prayer. It comes out of your deepest needs, and it reveals the things you want in life. *Blessed are they that hunger and thirst after righteousness: for they shall be filled.* That is the real nature of prayer, the effective expression of life's hunger and thirst for peace, harmony, health, joy, and all the other blessings of life.

THE PASSING-OVER TECHNIQUE FOR IMPREGNATING THE SUBCONSCIOUS

As we have seen, the secret of effective prayer is to imbue the subconscious mind with the desired outcome. One of the simplest ways to do this is what is called the *passing-over technique*. This consists essentially of inducing the subconscious mind to take over your request as handed it by the conscious mind. This passing-over is best accomplished in a dreamlike state.

Know that in your deeper mind is infinite intelligence and infinite power. Just calmly think over what you want; visualize its coming into fuller fruition from this moment forward. Be like the little girl who had a very bad cough and a sore throat. She declared firmly and repeatedly, "It is passing away now. It is passing away now." It passed away in about an hour. Use this technique with complete simplicity and naivete.

YOUR SUBCONSCIOUS WILL ACCEPT YOUR BLUEPRINT

If you were building a new home for yourself and your family, you would take an intense interest in the blueprint for your home. You would want to make sure that the builders followed your blueprint to the last detail. You would keep watch over the materials they used. Knowing that the future life of your home depends on the quality of the materials used to construct it, you would select only the best cement, insulation, electrical wiring, roofing, and so on.

Does it not make sense to take the same care with your mental home and your mental blueprint for happiness and abundance?

All your experiences and everything that enters into your life depend upon the nature of the mental building blocks that you use in the construction of your mental home. If your blueprint is full of mental patterns of fear, worry, anxiety, or lack, and if you are despondent, doubtful, and cynical, then the quality of the mental materials you are installing in your mind will come forth as more toil, care, tension, anxiety, and limitation of all kinds.

The most fundamental and the most far-reaching activity in life is that which you build into your mentality every waking hour. Your word is silent and invisible; nevertheless, it is real.

You are building your mental home all the time, and your thoughts and mental imagery represent your blueprint. Hour by hour, moment by moment, you can build radiant health, success, and happiness by the thoughts you think, the ideas you harbor, the beliefs you accept, and the scenes you rehearse in the hidden studio of your mind. This stately mansion, upon the construction of which you are perpetually engaged, is your personality, your identity in this plane, your whole life story on this earth.

Get a new blueprint; build silently by realizing peace, harmony, joy, and goodwill in the present moment. By dwelling upon these things and claiming them, your subconscious will accept your blueprint and bring all these things to pass: *By their fruits ye shall know them.*

THE SCIENCE AND ART OF TRUE PRAYER

The term *science* means a body of knowledge that is coordinated, arranged, and systematized. Let us think more closely about the science and art of true prayer. This body of knowledge deals with the fundamental principles of life. It describes techniques and processes that can be demonstrated in your life and in the life of any human being who applies them faithfully. The art is your technique or process, and the science behind it is the definite response of creative mind to your mental picture or thought.

> Ask, and it shall be given you; seek, and ye shall find; knock, and it shall be opened unto you.
>
> *MATT. 7:7*

What does this celebrated verse tell us? It clearly means that you shall receive that for which you ask. It shall be opened to you when you knock, and you shall find that for which you are searching. This teaching implies the definiteness of mental and spiritual laws. There is always a direct response from the infinite intelligence of your subconscious mind to your conscious thinking. If you ask for bread, you will not receive a stone.

You must ask *believing*, if you are to receive. Your mind moves from the thought to the thing. Unless there is first an image in the mind, it cannot move, for there would be nothing for it to move toward. Your prayer, which is your mental act, must be accepted as an image in your mind before the power from your subconscious will play upon it and make it productive. You must reach a point of acceptance in your mind, an unqualified and undisputed state of agreement.

This contemplation should be accompanied by a feeling of joy and restfulness in foreseeing the certain accomplishment of your desire. The sound basis for the art and science of true prayer is your knowledge and complete confidence that the movement of your conscious mind will gain a definite response from your subconscious mind, which has boundless wisdom and infinite power. By following this procedure, your prayers will be answered.

THE VISUALIZATION TECHNIQUE

The easiest and most obvious way to formulate an idea is to visualize it, to see it in your mind's eye as vividly as if it were alive. You can see with the naked eye only what already exists in the external world. In a similar way, that which you can visualize in your mind's eye already exists in the invisible realms of your mind. Any picture you have in your mind is the substance of things hoped for and the evidence of things not seen. What you form in your imagination is as real as any part of your body. The idea and the thought are real and will one day appear in your objective world if you are faithful to your mental image.

This process of thinking forms impressions in your mind. These impressions in turn become manifested as facts and experiences in your life. Architects visualize the type of building they want. They see it as they desire it to be when completed. Their imagery and thought-processes become a plastic mold from which the building will emerge. It may be beautiful or ugly, a skyscraper or a one-story shack, but it begins as a visualization. The architect's mental imagery is projected as it is drawn on paper. Eventually, the contractor and construction workers gather the essential materials, and the building progresses until it stands finished, conforming perfectly to the mental patterns of the architect.

I always use the visualization technique before I speak to an audience. I quiet the wheels of my mind so that I may present to the subconscious mind my images of thought. Then I picture the entire auditorium. Its seats are filled with men and women who are all illumined and inspired by the infinite healing presence within each one. I see them as radiant, happy, and free.

Having first built up the idea in my imagination, I quietly sustain it there as a mental picture while I imagine I hear people saying, "I am healed," "I feel wonderful," "I am transformed." I keep this up for ten minutes or more. I let myself know and feel that each person's mind and body are saturated with love, wholeness, beauty, and perfection. My awareness grows to the point where in my mind I can hear the voices of the multitude proclaiming their health and happiness. Then I release the whole picture and go on the platform.

Almost every time I speak, having used this technique, some people stop by afterward to tell me their prayers were answered.

MENTAL-MOVIE METHOD

As the old saying proclaims, "A picture is worth a thousand words." The fact must be stressed that the subconscious mind will bring to pass any picture held in the mind and backed by faith: *Act as though I am, and I will be.*

A number of years ago I was in the Midwest on a lecture tour that took me to several states. I wanted to have a permanent base in the area so that I could serve those who needed my help. My travels carried me far away, but I did not forget the idea of a permanent base. One evening in Spokane, Washington, I relaxed on a couch in my hotel room. I immobilized my attention. In a quiet, passive manner I imagined that I was talking to a large audience. I said to those listening, "I am glad to be here; I have prayed for this ideal opportunity."

I saw that imaginary audience in my mind's eye, and I felt the reality of it all. I played the role of the actor and dramatized this mental movie. I felt satisfied that this picture was being conveyed to my subconscious mind, which would bring it to pass in its own way. The next morning, on awakening, I felt a great sense of peace and satisfaction. A few days later I received a call from an organization in the Midwest, asking me to take over as director. I did so, and I enjoyed several years of deeply fulfilling work there.

The method I have just described is often referred to as "the mental-movie method." I have received a great many letters from people who have read my books or heard me speak, telling me of the wonderful results they have obtained by using this technique.

One area in which the mental movie method seems especially useful is in selling property. If you have a home or property for sale, I suggest that you first satisfy yourself in your own mind that your price is right and fair to both you and the eventual buyer. After having done this, quiet your mind, relax, let go, and get into a drowsy, sleepy state that reduces all mental effort to a minimum. Now picture the check in your hands, rejoice in the check, give thanks for the check, and go off to sleep feeling the naturalness of the whole mental movie created in your mind.

You must act as if this is already an objective reality. When you do, the subconscious mind will take it as an impression. Then, the infinite intelligence will draw to you the buyer who really wants to have the property and who will love it and prosper in it. Through the deeper currents of the mind, the buyer and the seller are brought together. A mental picture held in the mind, backed by faith, will come to pass.

THE BAUDOIN TECHNIQUE

Charles Baudoin was a professor at the Rousseau Institute in France. He was a brilliant psychotherapist and a research director of the New Nancy School of Healing. He discovered that the best way to impress the subconscious mind is to enter into a drowsy, sleepy state, or a state akin to sleep, in which all effort was reduced to a minimum. Then the idea can be conveyed to the subconscious in a quiet, passive, receptive way, by reflection.

As Baudoin explained:

A very simple way of securing this [impregnation of the subconscious mind] is to condense the idea which is to be the object of suggestion, to sum it up in a brief phrase which can be readily graven on the memory, and to repeat it over and over again as a lullaby.

A few years ago, a young widow in Los Angeles found herself caught up in a prolonged and bitter family dispute. Her late husband had left his entire estate to her, but his sons and daughters from a previous marriage had filed suit to break the will. Her offers of a settlement were spurned.

When she asked me for my help, I explained the Baudoin technique to her. I urged her to condense the idea of her need into a phrase of a few words that could be easily impressed on her memory. The phrase she found was "It is finished in divine order." To her, these words meant that infinite intelligence, operating through the laws of her subconscious mind, would bring about a harmonious conclusion through the principle of harmony.

Every night for ten nights she sat in an armchair, systematically relaxed her body, and entered into the sleepy state. Once in a sleepy state, she affirmed slowly, quietly, and feelingly the statement, "It is finished in divine order," over and over again. She found herself achieving a sense of inner peace and an all-pervading tranquillity; then she went off into her deep, normal sleep.

On the morning of the eleventh day, she woke up with a sense of well-being and a conviction that it was indeed finished. Her attorney called her that same day. The opposing attorney and his clients were willing to settle. A harmonious agreement was reached, and the lawsuit was dropped.

THE SLEEPING TECHNIQUE

When you enter into a sleepy, drowsy state, effort is reduced to a minimum. The conscious mind is submerged to a great extent when in a sleepy state. The reason for this is that the highest degree of outcropping of the subconscious occurs just prior to sleep and just after we awaken. In this state the negative thoughts, which tend to neutralize your desire and so prevent acceptance by your subconscious mind, are no longer present.

Suppose you want to get rid of a destructive habit. Assume a comfortable posture, relax your body, and be still. Get into a sleepy state, and in that sleepy state, say quietly, over and over as a lullaby, "I am completely free from this habit; harmony and peace of mind reign supreme." Repeat these words slowly, quietly, and lovingly for five or ten minutes night and morning. Each time you repeat the words the emotional value becomes greater. When the urge comes to repeat the negative habit, repeat this formula out loud to yourself. By this means you induce the subconscious to accept the idea, and a healing follows.

THE "THANK-YOU" TECHNIQUE

In the Bible, Paul recommends that we make known our requests with praise and thanksgiving. Some extraordinary results follow this simple method of prayer. The thankful heart is always close to the creative forces of the universe, causing countless blessings to flow toward it by the law of reciprocal relationship, based on a cosmic law of action and reaction.

Recently a young mother told me of her experience with this technique. She said, "I was out of work and broke, with three small children to feed and clothe. I didn't know where to turn. Then I heard you explain that we should be thankful even before our prayers are answered. It was as if a light had gone on in my mind. I knew I had to try it."

Every night and morning for about three weeks, this woman repeated the words, "Thank you, Father, for my wealth." She did this in a relaxed, peaceful manner and continued until the feeling or mood of thankfulness dominated her mind. She imagined she was addressing the infinite power and intelligence within, though she knew, of course, that she could not literally see the creative intelligence or infinite mind. She was seeing with the inner eye of spiritual perception, realizing that her thought-image of wealth was the first cause, relative to the money, position, and food she needed. Her thought-feeling was the substance of wealth, untrammeled by antecedent conditions of any kind.

By repeating, "Thank you, Father," over and over, the woman's mind and heart were lifted up to the point of acceptance. When thoughts of lack, poverty, and distress came into her mind, she would say again, "Thank you, Father," as often as necessary. She knew that as she kept up the thankful attitude, she would recondition her mind to the idea of wealth. This is exactly what happened.

This mother's prayer had an interesting sequel. Shortly after she began to pray in the way just described, she met a former employer on the street whom she had not seen in five years. The former employer offered her a responsible, well-paid position. He even advanced her a temporary loan to tide her over until her first paycheck. As she said to me, "I'll never forget the amazing power of 'Thank you, Father.' It has worked wonders for me."

THE AFFIRMATIVE METHOD

The effectiveness of an affirmation is determined largely by your understanding of the truth and meaning that underlie the words *In praying use not vain repetition.* The power of your affirmation lies in the intelligent application of definite and specific positives. Suppose a schoolchild adds three and three and puts down seven on the blackboard. The teacher affirms with mathematical certainty that three and three are six; therefore, the child changes the figures accordingly. The teacher's statement did not *make* three and three equal six. This was already a mathematical truth that in turn caused the child to rearrange the figures on the blackboard.

It is abnormal to be sick; it is normal to be healthy. Health is the truth of your being. When you affirm health, harmony, and peace for yourself or another, and when you realize these are universal principles of your own being, you rearrange the negative patterns of your subconscious mind based on your faith and understanding of that which you affirm.

The result of the affirmative process of prayer depends on conforming to the principles of life, regardless of appearances. Consider for a moment: There is a principle of mathematics but none of error. There is a principle of truth but none of dishonesty. There is a principle of intelligence but none of ignorance. There is a principle of harmony but none of discord. There is a principle of health but none of disease, and there is a principle of abundance but none of poverty.

I chose to use the affirmative method when my sister was about to be operated on for the removal of gallstones in a hospital in England. Her diagnosis was based on the usual hospital tests and X-ray procedures. She asked me to pray for her recovery. I was over six thousand miles away, but this did not disturb me. There is no time or space in the mind principle. Infinite mind or intelligence is present in its entirety at every point simultaneously.

Several times a day I withdrew all thought from the contemplation of my sister's symptoms and from the corporeal personality altogether. Calmly, confidently, I affirmed as follows:

> This prayer is for my sister Catherine. She is relaxed and at peace, poised, balanced, serene, and calm. The healing intelligence of her subconscious mind that created her body is now transforming every cell, nerve, tissue, muscle, and bone of her being according to the perfect pattern of all organs lodged in her subconscious mind. Silently, quietly, all distorted thought patterns in her subconscious mind are removed and dissolved, and the vitality, wholeness,

and beauty of the life principle are made manifest in every atom of her being. She is now open and receptive to the healing currents that are flowing through her like a river, restoring her to perfect health, harmony, and peace. All distortions and ugly images are now washed away by the infinite ocean of love and peace flowing through her, and it is so.

At the end of two weeks, my sister had another examination. Her X-rays were negative. Her doctor admitted that she showed a remarkable healing and called off the scheduled surgery.

To affirm is to state that it is so. As you maintain this attitude of mind as true, regardless of all evidence to the contrary, you will receive an answer to your prayer. Your thought can only affirm, for even if you deny something, you are actually affirming the presence of what you deny. Repeating an affirmation, knowing what you are saying and why you are saying it, leads the mind to that state of consciousness where it accepts that which you state as true. Keep on affirming the truths of life until you get the subconscious reaction that satisfies.

THE ARGUMENTATIVE METHOD

This method is just what its name implies. It stems from the amazing work of Dr. Phineas Parkhurst Quimby, a pioneer in mental and spiritual healing who lived and practiced in Belfast, Maine, over a century ago. He was really the father of psychosomatic medicine and the first psychoanalyst. He also had a remarkable capacity to diagnose clairvoyantly the cause of the patient's trouble, pains, and aches.

In brief, the argumentative method as employed so successfully by Quimby consists of spiritual reasoning. You convince the patient and yourself that the sickness is due to false beliefs, groundless fears, and negative patterns lodged in the subconscious mind. You reason it out clearly in your mind and convince your patient that the disease or ailment is due only to a distorted, twisted pattern of thought that has taken form in the body. This wrong belief in some external power and external causes has now externalized itself as sickness and can be changed by changing the thought patterns.

You explain to the sick person that the basis of all healing is a change of belief. You also point out that the subconscious mind created the body and all its organs; therefore, it knows how to heal it, can heal it, and is doing so now as you speak. You argue in the courtroom of your mind that the disease is a shadow of the mind based on disease-soaked, morbid thought-imagery. You continue to build up all the evidence you can muster on behalf of the healing power within, which created all the organs in the first place, and which has a perfect pattern of every cell, nerve, and tissue within it.

Then, you render a verdict in the courthouse of your mind in favor of yourself and your patient. You liberate the sick one by faith and spiritual understanding. Your mental and spiritual evidence is overwhelming. Since there is but one mind, what you feel as true is made manifest in the experience of the patient, and a healing follows.

THE ABSOLUTE METHOD IS LIKE MODERN ULTRASOUND THERAPY

Many people throughout the world practice this form of prayer treatment with wonderful results. The person using the absolute method mentions the name of the patient. Then she silently thinks of God and His qualities and attributes, such as, God is all bliss, boundless love, infinite intelligence, all-powerful, boundless wisdom, absolute harmony, indescribable beauty, and perfection. As she quietly thinks along these lines her consciousness is lifted into a new spiritual dimension. She feels the infinite ocean of God's love dissolving everything unlike itself in the mind and body of the patient for whom she is praying. She feels all the power and love of God are now focused on the patient. Whatever is bothersome or vexing is now completely neutralized in the presence of the infinite ocean of life and love.

The absolute method of prayer might be compared to the latest developments in ultrasound therapy. These were explained to me recently by a distinguished physician in Los Angeles. The device she uses in her work generates powerful sound waves at extremely high frequencies. When these are focused on areas of the body where there are abnormal tissues, the affected cells resonate to the ultrasound and respond to it.

To the degree that we rise in consciousness by contemplating the qualities and attributes of God, we generate spiritual waves of harmony, health, and peace. Those on whom these waves are focused then resonate to them and respond. Many remarkable healings have been achieved by this technique of prayer.

A CRIPPLED PERSON WALKS

Dr. Quimby often used the absolute method in the later years of his healing career.

One of his manuscripts describes how he healed a crippled woman. He was called on to visit this woman, who was lame, aged, and bedridden. He states that her ailment was due to the fact that she was imprisoned by a creed so small and contracted that she could not stand upright and move about. She was living in the tomb of fear and ignorance. Because she took the Bible literally, it frightened her.

"In this tomb," Quimby said, "was the presence and power of God trying to burst the bands, break through the bonds, and rise from the dead."

When the woman would ask others for an explanation of some passage of the Bible, the answer would be a stone; then she would hunger for the bread of life. Dr. Quimby diagnosed her case as a mind cloudy and stagnated due to excitation and fear, caused by the inability to see clearly the meaning of the passage of the Bible that she had been reading. This showed itself in her body by the heavy and sluggish feeling that would terminate as paralysis.

At this point Quimby asked her what was meant in the Bible verses:

> Yet a little while am I with you, and then I go unto Him that sent me. Ye shall seek me, and shall not find me: and where I am, thither ye cannot come.
>
> *JOHN 7:33–34*

She replied that it meant Jesus went to heaven. Quimby explained what it really meant by telling her that *being with her a little while* meant his explanation of her symptoms, feelings, and their causes. He had compassion and sympathy for her momentarily, but he could not remain in that mental state. The next step was *to go to Him that sent us.* This, Quimby pointed out, was the creative power of God in all of us.

Quimby immediately traveled in his mind and contemplated the divine ideal; that is, the vitality, intelligence, harmony, and power of God functioning in the sick person. This is why he said to the woman, "Therefore, where I go you cannot come, for you are in your narrow, restricted belief, and I am in health."

This prayer and explanation produced an instantaneous sensation, and a change came over her mind. She walked without her crutches! Quimby said it was one of the most singular of all his healings. She was, as it were, dead to error, and to bring her to life or truth was to raise her from the dead. Quimby quoted the resurrection of Christ and applied it to her own Christ or health; this produced a powerful effect on her. He also explained to her that the truth that she accepted was the angel or idea that rolled away the stone of fear, ignorance, and superstition. This then released the healing power of God, which made her whole.

THE DECREE METHOD

Power goes into our word according to the feeling and faith behind it. When we realize the power that moves the world is moving on our behalf and is backing up our word, our confidence and assurance grow. You do not try to add power to power. There must be no mental striving, coercion, force, or mental wrestling.

A young woman used the decree method on a young man who was constantly phoning her, pressing her for dates. She found it very difficult to get rid of him. When he began to show up at her workplace, she realized that she had to do something drastic at once.

Several times a day, she put herself into a quiet state and repeatedly decreed as follows:

> I release J___ R_____ unto God.   He is in his true place at all times. I am free, and he is free. I now decree that my words go forth into infinite mind and it brings it to pass. It is so.

According to her, the young man immediately disappeared from her life. She has never seen him since. She says, "It was as if the ground swallowed him up."

Thou shalt decree a thing, and it shall be established unto thee: and the light shall shine upon thy ways.

JOB 22:28

SERVE YOURSELF WITH SCIENTIFIC TRUTH

1. Be a mental engineer and use tried and proven techniques in building a grander and greater life.

2. Your desire is your prayer. Picture the fulfillment of your desire now and feel its reality, and you will experience the joy of the answered prayer.

3. Desire to accomplish things the easy way—with the sure aid of mental science.

4. You can build radiant health, success, and happiness by the thoughts you think in the hidden studio of your mind.

5. Experiment scientifically until you personally prove that there is always a direct response from the infinite intelligence of your subconscious mind to your conscious thinking.

6. Feel the joy and restfulness in foreseeing the certain accomplishment of your desire. Any mental picture you have in your mind is the substance of things hoped for and the evidence of things not seen.

7. A mental picture is worth a thousand words. Your subconscious will bring to pass any picture held in the mind backed by faith.

8. Avoid all effort or mental coercion in prayer. Get into a sleepy, drowsy state and lull yourself to sleep feeling and knowing that your prayer is answered.

9. Remember that the thankful heart is always close to the riches of the universe.

10. To affirm is to state that it is so, and as you maintain this

attitude of mind as true, regardless of all evidence to the contrary, you will receive an answer to your prayer.

11. Generate waves of harmony, health, and peace by thinking of the love and the glory of God.

12. What you decree and feel as true will come to pass. Decree harmony, health, peace, and abundance.

7

The Tendency of the Subconscious Is Lifeward

Over ninety percent of your mental life is subconscious. If you fail to make use of this marvelous power, you condemn yourself to live within very narrow limits.

Your subconscious processes are always lifeward and constructive. Your subconscious is the builder of your body and maintains all its vital functions. It is on the job twenty-four hours a day and never sleeps. It is always trying to help and preserve you from harm.

Your subconscious mind is in touch with infinite life and boundless wisdom, and its impulses and ideas are always lifeward. The great aspirations, inspirations, and visions for a grander and nobler life spring from the subconscious. Your profoundest convictions are those you cannot argue about rationally because they do not come from your conscious mind; they come from your subconscious mind.

Your subconscious speaks to you in intuitions, impulses, hunches, intimations, urges, and ideas. It is always telling you to rise, transcend, grow, advance, adventure, and move forward to greater heights. The urge to love, to save the lives of others, comes from the depths of your subconscious. For example, during the great San Francisco earthquake and fire of April 18, 1906, invalids and handicapped people who had been confined to bed for long periods of time rose up and performed amazing feats of bravery and endurance. The intense desire welled up within them to save others at all costs, and their subconscious responded accordingly.

Great artists, musicians, poets, speakers, and writers tune in with their subconscious powers and become animated and inspired. Robert Louis Stevenson, before he went to sleep, used to charge his subconscious with the task of evolving stories for him while he slept. He was accustomed to ask his subconscious to give him a good, marketable thriller whenever his bank account was low. Stevenson said the intelligence of his deeper mind gave him the story piece by piece, like a serial. This shows how your subconscious will speak lofty and wise sayings through you that your conscious mind knows nothing about.

Mark Twain confided to the world on many occasions that he never worked in his life. All his humor and all his great writings were the result of his ability to tap the inexhaustible reservoir of his subconscious mind.

HOW THE BODY PORTRAYS THE WORKINGS OF THE MIND

The interaction of your conscious and subconscious mind requires a similar interaction between the corresponding systems of nerves. The cerebrospinal or voluntary system is the organ of the conscious mind. The autonomic system is the organ of the subconscious mind. The voluntary nervous system is the channel through which you receive conscious perception by means of your physical senses and exercise voluntary control over the movement of your body. This system has its control center in the cerebral cortex of the brain.

The autonomic nervous system, sometimes referred to as the involuntary nervous system, has its centers of activity in other parts of the brain, including the cerebellum, the brain stem, and the amygdala. These organs have their own connections to the major systems of the body and support their vital functions even when conscious awareness is absent.

The two systems may work separately or synchronously. For example, when a perception of danger arrives at the switching center in the cerebellum, messages are sent both to the conscious cortex and to the subconscious amygdala. The person's defensive abilities may start to respond to the danger even before the danger is consciously noticed and evaluated.

A simple way of looking at the mental and physical interaction is to realize that your conscious mind grasps an idea that is parallel to a corresponding series of electrical impulses in your voluntary system of nerves. This in turn causes a similar current to be generated in your involuntary system of nerves, thus handing the idea over to your subconscious mind, which is the creative medium. This is how your thoughts become things.

Every thought entertained by your conscious mind and accepted as true is sent by your cortex to the other organs of the brain that support your subconscious mind, to be made into your flesh and to be brought forth into your world as a reality.

THERE IS AN INTELLIGENCE THAT TAKES CARE OF THE BODY

When you study the cellular system and the structure of the organs, such as eyes, ears, heart, liver, bladder, and so on, you discover that they consist of groups of cells that form a group intelligence that allows them to function together. They are able to take orders and carry them out in deductive function at the suggestion of the master mind (conscious mind).

A careful study of the single-celled organism shows you what goes on in your complex body. Though the monocellular organism has no organs, it still gives evidence of mind action and reaction performing the basic functions of movement, alimentation, assimilation, and elimination.

Many say there is an intelligence that will take care of your body if you let it alone. This is true in a sense. The difficulty is that the conscious mind always interferes with its sensory evidence based on outer appearances. These lead to the sway of false beliefs, fears, and mere opinion. When fears, false beliefs, and negative patterns are made to register in your subconscious mind through psychological, emotional conditioning, there is no other course open to the subconscious mind except to act on the blueprint specifications offered it.

THE SUBCONSCIOUS MIND WORKS CONTINUALLY FOR THE COMMON GOOD

The subjective self within you works continuously for the general good, reflecting an innate principle of harmony behind all things. Your subconscious mind has its own will, and it is very real in itself. It functions night and day, whether you will it or not. It is the builder of your body, but you cannot see, hear, or feel it building. All this is a silent process. Your subconscious has a life of its own that is always moving toward harmony, health, and peace. This is the divine norm within it, seeking expression through you at all times.

How humans interfere with the innate principle of harmony

To think correctly, scientifically, we must know the "Truth." As the ancient saying puts it, "Ye shall know the truth, and the truth shall set you free." To know the truth is to be in harmony with the infinite intelligence and power of your subconscious mind, which is always moving lifeward.

Every thought or action that is not harmonious, whether through ignorance or design, will result in discord and limitation of all kinds.

Scientists inform us that you build a new body every eleven months; so from a physical standpoint you are really only eleven months old. If you build defects back into your body by thoughts of fear, anger, jealousy, and ill will, you have no one to blame but yourself.

You are the sum total of your own thoughts. You can keep from entertaining negative thought and imagery. The way to get rid of darkness is with light; the way to overcome cold is with heat; the way to overcome the negative thought is to substitute the good thought. Affirm the good, and the bad will vanish.

Why it's normal to be healthy, vital, and strong, abnormal to be sick

The average child born into the world is perfectly healthy, with all its organs functioning perfectly. This is the normal state, and we should remain healthy, vital, and strong. The instinct of self-preservation is the strongest instinct of your nature, and it constitutes a most potent, ever present, and constantly operative truth, inherent in your nature. All your thoughts, ideas, and beliefs must operate with greater potentiality when they are in harmony with the innate life-principle in you, which is forever seeking to preserve and protect you along all lines. It follows from this that normal conditions can be restored with greater ease and certainty than abnormal conditions can be induced.

It is abnormal to be sick. The condition of sickness simply means you are going against the stream of life and thinking negatively. The law of life is the law of growth; all nature testifies to the operation of this law by silently, constantly expressing itself in growth. Where there is growth and expression, there must be life; where there is life there must be harmony; and where there is harmony, there is perfect health.

If your thought is in harmony with the creative principle of your subconscious mind, you are in tune with the innate principle of harmony. If you entertain thoughts that are not in accordance with the principle of harmony, these thoughts cling to you, harass you, worry you, and finally bring about disease, and if persisted in, possibly death.

In the healing of disease, you must increase the inflow and distribution of the vital forces of your subconscious mind throughout your system. This can be done by eliminating thoughts of fear, worry, anxiety, jealousy, hatred, and every other destructive thought. These tend to tear down and destroy your nerves and glands—body tissue that controls the elimination of all waste material and keeps the organism in a state of purity.

Pott's disease cured

Pott's disease, or tuberculosis of the spine, used to be a terrible scourge of children. One child who contracted it was named Frederick Elias Andrews, of Indianapolis, Indiana. The disease made him a twisted cripple who could not walk and had to go about on his hands and knees. His physician pronounced him incurable.

Andrews refused to accept that verdict. He began to

pray. He created his own affirmation, repeating it over and over many times a day and mentally absorbing the qualities he needed:

> I am whole, perfect, strong, powerful, loving, harmonious, and happy.

He made this prayer the last utterance on his lips at night and the first in the morning. He prayed for others as well, sending out thoughts of love and health.

This attitude of mind and way of prayer returned to him multiplied many times. His faith and perseverance paid off with big dividends. When thoughts of fear, anger, jealousy, or envy drew his attention, he would immediately start his counteracting force of affirmation going in his mind. His subconscious mind responded according to the nature of his habitual thinking. He became a strong, straight, well-formed man.

This is the meaning of the statement in the Bible:

> Go thy way, thy faith hath made thee whole.
>
> *MARK 10:52*

How Faith in Your Subconscious Powers Makes You Whole

A young man who came to my lectures on the healing power of the subconscious mind had severe eye trouble. His ophthalmologist told him he would have to have a delicate, risky operation. After learning about the scientific basis of prayer, the young man said to himself, "My subconscious made my eyes, and it can heal me."

Each night, as he went to sleep, he entered into a drowsy, meditative state, the condition akin to sleep. His attention was immobilized and focused on the eye doctor. He imagined the doctor was in front of him, and he plainly heard, or imagined he heard, the doctor saying to him, "A miracle has happened!" He heard this over and over again every night for five minutes or so before going to sleep.

Three weeks later he had another appointment with the ophthalmologist who had examined his eyes. The physician examined him again, then exclaimed, "This is a miracle!"

What had happened? This man impressed his subconscious mind, using the eye doctor as an instrument or means of convincing it and conveying the idea. Through repetition, faith, and expectancy he impregnated his subconscious mind. His subconscious mind had made his eye. It held within it the perfect pattern or blueprint of the eye's normal, healthy structure. Once impregnated with the idea of restoring the eye to its healthy state, it immediately proceeded to heal the eye. This is another example of how faith in the healing power of your subconscious can make you whole.

POINTERS TO REVIEW

1. Your subconscious is the builder of your body and is on the job twenty-four hours a day. You interfere with its life-giving pattern by negative thinking.
2. Charge your subconscious with the task of evolving an answer to any problem, prior to sleep, and it will answer you.
3. Watch your thoughts. Every thought accepted as true is sent by your conscious cortex to your subconscious brain structures and is brought into your world as a reality.
4. Know that you can remake yourself by giving a new blueprint to your subconscious mind.
5. The tendency of your subconscious is always lifeward. Your job is with your conscious mind. Feed your subconscious mind with premises that are true. Your sub-

conscious is always reproducing according to your habitual mental patterns.

6. You build a new body every eleven months. Change your body by changing your thoughts and keeping them changed.

7. It is normal to be healthy. It is abnormal to be ill. There is within the innate principle of harmony.

8. Thoughts of jealousy, fear, worry, and anxiety tear down and destroy your nerves and glands, bringing about mental and physical diseases of all kinds.

9. What you affirm consciously and feel as true will be made manifest in your mind, body, and affairs. Affirm the good and enter into the joy of living.

8

How to Get the Results You Want

Not all prayers are answered. Everyone knows that. Skeptics see this as evidence that prayer does not work. What they overlook is that for prayer to work, it must be used effectively, with a clear understanding of its scientific basis. Only then can we know why a particular prayer was not effective and arrive at a practical method to make it more effective.

What if you find your prayers are not answered as you would like? What then? You must understand the principal reasons for such a failure. These are: lack of confidence and too much effort. Many people block answers to their prayers by failing to fully comprehend the workings of their subconscious mind. When you know how your mind functions, you gain a measure of confidence.

You must remember that whenever your subconscious mind accepts an idea, it immediately begins to execute it. It uses all its mighty resources to that end. It mobilizes all the mental and spiritual laws of your deeper mind. This law is true for good ideas, but it holds true for bad ideas as well. Consequently, if you use your subconscious mind negatively, it brings trouble, failure, and confusion. When you use it constructively, it brings guidance, freedom, and peace of mind.

The right answer is inevitable when your thoughts are positive, constructive, and loving. From this it is obvious that the only thing you have to do in order to overcome failure is to get your subconscious to accept your idea or request. Feel its reality now and the law of your mind will do the rest. Turn over your request with faith and confidence, and your subconscious will take over and answer for you.

Any time you try to force your subconscious mind to do something for you, you will fail. The results you want will become more distant instead of closer. Your subconscious mind does not respond to mental coercion. It responds to your faith or conscious mind acceptance.

Your failure to get results may also be a consequence of mentally making such statements as

- Things are getting worse.
- I will never get an answer.
- I see no way out.
- It is hopeless.
- I don't know what to do.
- I'm all mixed up.

When you use such statements, you get no response or cooperation from your subconscious mind. Like a soldier marking time, you go neither forward nor backward. In other words, you don't get anywhere.

Imagine that you got into a taxi and gave the driver a half dozen different directions. He would become hopelessly confused. He might refuse to take you anywhere. Even if he tried to follow your instructions, chances are he would not be able to. Where you would end up is anybody's guess.

It is the same when working with the enormous powers

of your subconscious mind. You must have a clear-cut idea in your mind. You must arrive at the definite decision that there is a way out, a solution to the vexing problem in sickness. Only the infinite intelligence within your subconscious knows the answer. When you come to that clear-cut conclusion in your conscious mind, your mind is then made up, and *according to your belief is it done unto you.*

EASY DOES IT

A homeowner whose furnace broke down during a bitter cold snap called a repairman. The repairman came at once. Within half an hour, the furnace was working again. The repairman then gave the homeowner a bill for $200.

"What!" the outraged homeowner exclaimed. "It took you no time at all. All you did was replace one small part. How can you have the nerve to charge me $200 for a little gizmo that can't be worth more than five dollars?"

The repairman shrugged. "I charged you only two dollars for the broken part," he said. "That's what I had to pay for it."

The homeowner waved the bill in his face. "Two dollars!" he yelled. "This says $200!"

"That's right," the repairman said. "The other $198 is for knowing what was wrong and how to fix it."

Your subconscious mind is the master mechanic, the all-wise one. It knows the ways and means of healing any organ of your body. Decree health, and your subconscious will establish it, but relaxation is the key. "Easy does it."

Do not let yourself get bogged down in thinking about details and means. Know what the end result will be. Get the feel of the happy solution to your problem, whether it is health, finances, or personal relationships. Remember how you felt after you recovered from a serious illness. Bear in mind that your feeling is the touchstone of all subconscious demonstration. Your new idea must be felt subjectively in a finished state, felt not as something that may come to pass in the future, but as something that is actually coming to pass at this moment.

USE IMAGINATION, NOT WILLPOWER

Enlisting the powers of your subconscious mind is not like pushing against an obstacle. Working harder does not lead to better results. Use no willpower. Instead, visualize the end and the state of freedom it produces. You will find your intellect trying to get in the way, trying to find ways to solve the problem and impose those ways on your subconscious.

Resist this. Put away your intellectual problem-solving skills. Persist in maintaining a simple, childlike, miracle-making faith. Picture yourself without the ailment or problem. Imagine the emotional gratification of the freedom state you seek. Cut out all red tape from the process. The simple way is the best.

HOW DISCIPLINED IMAGINATION WORKS WONDERS

A wonderful way to get a response from your subconscious mind is through disciplined or scientific imagination. As we have seen, the subconscious mind is the architect and builder of the body. It controls all your vital functions.

The Bible says, *Whatsoever ye shall ask in prayer, believing, ye shall receive.* To believe is to accept something as true, to live in the state of being it. As you sustain this mood, you shall experience the joy of the answered prayer.

THE THREE STEPS TO SUCCESS IN PRAYER

Successful prayer requires three basic steps:

1. Acknowledge or admit the problem.
2. Turn the problem over to the subconscious mind, which alone knows the most effective solution or way out.
3. Rest with a sense of deep conviction that it is done.

Doubts and hesitations only weaken your prayer. Do not say to yourself, "I wish I could be healed" or "I hope this works." Your feeling about the work to be done sets the tone. Harmony is yours. Know that health is yours.

You become effective by becoming a vehicle for the infinite healing power of the subconscious mind. Pass on the idea of health to your subconscious mind with complete conviction; then relax. Give yourself over to its power. Say to the condition and circumstance, "This, too, shall pass." Through relaxation and conviction, you impregnate your subconscious mind. This enables the kinetic energy behind the idea to take over and bring it into concrete realization.

WHY YOU MAY GET THE OPPOSITE OF WHAT YOU PRAY FOR

Emile Coué was a celebrated French psychologist whose lectures gained him many admirers and followers in the United States. One of his important insights was this:

When your desires and imagination are in conflict, your imagination invariably gains the day.

He referred to this as the law of reverse effort.

Suppose you were asked to walk along a narrow plank that

was resting on the floor. You would do it easily, without question. But now suppose the same plank were twenty feet up, stretching between two walls. Would you walk it? *Could* you?

Probably not. Your desire to walk the length of the plank would come into conflict with your imagination. You would imagine yourself toppling off the plank and falling a long way to the ground. You might very much *want* to walk across the plank, but your fear of falling would keep you from being able to do it. The more effort you put into conquering your imagination or suppressing it, the greater strength is given to the dominant idea of falling.

The thought "I will use my willpower to overcome my *failure*," reinforces the thought of failure. Mental effort often leads to self-defeat, creating the opposite of what is desired. To focus on the need to exert willpower is to emphasize the condition of powerlessness. It is like deciding that you will do all you can not to think of a green hippopotamus. The decision makes the idea of a green hippo dominate the mind, and the subconscious always responds more to the dominant idea. Your subconscious will accept the stronger of two contradictory propositions.

Maybe you find yourself thinking

- I want a healing; why can't I get it?
- I try so hard, why don't I get results?
- I must force myself to pray harder.
- I must use all the willpower I have.

You must realize where your error lies. You are trying too hard! Never try to compel the subconscious mind to accept your idea by exercising willpower. Such attempts are doomed to failure. All too often, you end up getting the opposite of what you prayed for. The effortless way is better.

Have you ever had something like this happen to you? You have to take an examination of some kind. You have put in a lot of time studying and reviewing the material. You feel as if you know it well. But when you face a blank exam page, you find that your mind is even more blank. All your knowledge of the subject has suddenly deserted you. You can't recall a single relevant thought. You grit your teeth and summon all the powers of your will, but the harder you try, the farther the knowledge seem to flee.

Frustrated, you leave the examination room. The mental pressure eases. Suddenly the answers you were hunting for so desperately a few minutes ago flow tantalizingly back into your mind. You told yourself you knew the material, and sure enough, you did . . . but not when you needed to. The mistake you made was to try to force yourself to remember. By the law of reversed effort, this led not to success, but to failure. What you got was the opposite of what you asked or prayed for.

THE CONFLICT OF DESIRE AND IMAGINATION MUST BE RESOLVED

To use mental force or willpower is to presuppose that there is opposition. But the act of imagining opposition *creates* opposition. If your attention is focused on the obstacles to obtaining what you desire, it is no longer concentrating on the *means* to obtain your desire.

In the Bible, it is said:

> If two of you shall agree on earth as touching any thing that they shall ask, it shall be done for them of my Father which is in heaven.
>
> *MATT. 18:19*

Who are these two who are spoken of? They stand for the harmonious union or agreement between your conscious and subconscious on any idea, desire, or mental image. When there is no longer any quarrel between the different parts of your mind, your prayer will be answered. The two agreeing may also be represented as you and your desire, your thought and feeling, your idea and emotion, your desire and imagination.

You avoid all conflict between your desires and imagination by entering into a drowsy, sleepy state that brings all effort to a minimum. The conscious mind is submerged to a great extent when in a sleepy state. The best time to impregnate your subconscious is just prior to sleep. The reason for this is that the highest degree of outcropping of the subconscious occurs just before going to sleep and just after we awaken. In this state the negative thoughts and imagery that tend to neutralize your desire and so prevent acceptance by your subconscious mind no longer present themselves. When you imagine the reality of the fulfilled desire and feel the thrill of accomplishment, your subconscious brings about the realization of your desire.

A great many people solve all their dilemmas and problems by the play of their controlled, directed, and disciplined imagination. They know that whatever they imagine and feel as true *will* and *must* come to pass.

A young woman named Shara G. came to me close to despair. She was involved in a lengthy, complicated lawsuit that had been through one postponement after another, with no end in sight. Her deepest desire was for a harmonious solution to the suit. Her mental imagery, however, was full of failure, loss, bankruptcy, and poverty. The result was just as Coué would have predicted. Her imagination prevailed over her desire, and the suit dragged on and on.

At my suggestion, Shara put herself into a sleepy, drowsy

state each night at bedtime, then began to imagine the best possible ending to her problem. She put herself into a state of feeling it to the best of her ability. She knew that the image in her mind had to agree with her heart's desire.

As she became drowsy, she began to imagine as vividly as possible a meeting with her lawyer after the lawsuit was settled. She heard herself asking him questions about the outcome and listening to his explanations. She heard him telling her over and over again, "The case has been settled out of court. This is a perfectly harmonious solution."

During the day, when fear thoughts came into her mind, Shara would run her mental videotape of the meeting with her lawyer, complete with words and gestures. She imagined his smile, his mannerisms, the sound of his voice, the specific words he used. She did this so often, so faithfully, that her fears were counteracted before she even knew they had tried to come into her mind.

At the end of a few weeks, her attorney called her. He confirmed what she had been imagining and feeling as true. The lawsuit was settled, and she knew that the settlement was one she could accept as harmonious.

This is really what the Psalmist meant when he wrote:

Let the words of my mouth [your thoughts and mental images] and the meditations of my heart [your feeling, nature, emotion] be acceptable in thy sight, O Lord [the law of your subconscious mind], my strength, and my redeemer [the power and wisdom of your subconscious mind that can redeem you from sickness, bondage, and misery].

PSALM 19:14

IDEAS WORTH RECALLING

1. Mental coercion or too much effort shows anxiety and fear that block your answer. Easy does it.
2. When your mind is relaxed and you accept an idea, your subconscious goes to work to execute the idea.
3. Think and plan independently of traditional methods. Know that there is always an answer and a solution to every problem.
4. Do not be overly concerned with the beating of your heart, with the breathing of your lungs, or the functions of any organ of your body. Lean heavily upon your subconscious and proclaim frequently that Divine right action is taking place.
5. The feeling of health produces health, the feeling of wealth produces wealth. How do you feel?
6. Imagination is your most powerful faculty. Imagine what is lovely and of good report. You are what you imagine yourself to be.
7. You avoid conflict between your conscious and subconscious in the sleepy state. Imagine the fulfillment of your desire over and over again prior to sleep. Sleep in peace and wake in joy.

9

How to Use the Power of Your Subconscious for Wealth

If you are having financial difficulties, if you are trying to make ends meet, it means you have not convinced your subconscious mind that you will always have plenty and some to spare. You know men and women who work a few hours a week and make fabulous sums of money. They do not strive or slave hard. Do not believe the story that the only way you can become wealthy is by the sweat of your brow and hard labor. It is not so; the effortless way of life is the best. Do the thing you love to do, and do it for the joy and thrill of it.

I know an executive in Los Angeles who receives a six-figure salary. Last year he went on a nine-month cruise seeing the world and its beauty spots. He said to me that he had succeeded in convincing his subconscious mind that he is worth that much money. He told me that there are people in his organization earning about one-tenth as much as he does who know more about the business than he does and could probably manage it better. However, they have no ambition and no creative ideas. They are not interested in the wonders of their subconscious mind.

WEALTH IS OF THE MIND

Wealth is ultimately nothing more than a subconscious conviction on the part of the individual. You will not become a millionaire by saying, "I am a millionaire, I am a millionaire." You will grow into a wealth consciousness by building into your mentality the idea of wealth and abundance.

YOUR INVISIBLE MEANS OF SUPPORT

The trouble with most people is that they have no invisible means of support. When business falls away, the stock market drops, or they take a loss on their investments, they seem helpless. The reason for such insecurity is that they do not know how to tap the subconscious mind. They are unacquainted with the inexhaustible storehouse within.

Someone with a poverty-type mind finds himself in poverty-stricken conditions. Someone else, with a mind filled with ideas of wealth, is surrounded by everything he needs. It was never intended that we should lead a life of indigence. You can have wealth, everything you need, and plenty to spare. Your words have power to cleanse your mind of wrong ideas and to instill right ideas in their place.

THE IDEAL METHOD FOR BUILDING A WEALTH CONSCIOUSNESS

Perhaps you are saying as you read this chapter, "I need wealth and success." This is what you do: Repeat for about five minutes to yourself three or four times a day, "Wealth. Success." These words have tremendous power. They represent the inner power of the subconscious mind. Anchor your mind on this substantial power within you; then conditions and circumstances corresponding to their nature and quality will be manifested in your life. You are not saying, "I am wealthy," you are dwelling on real powers within you. There is no conflict in the mind when you say, "Wealth." Furthermore, the feeling of wealth will well up within you as you dwell on the idea of wealth.

The feeling of wealth produces wealth; keep this in mind at all times. Your subconscious mind is like a bank, a sort of universal financial institution. It magnifies whatever you deposit or impress upon it whether it is the idea of wealth or of poverty. Choose wealth.

WHY YOUR AFFIRMATIONS FOR WEALTH FAIL

I have talked to many people over the years whose usual complaint is "I have said for weeks and months, 'I am wealthy, I am prosperous,' and nothing has happened." I discovered that when they said, "I am prosperous, I am wealthy," they felt within that they were lying to themselves.

One man told me, "I have affirmed that I am prosperous until I am tired. Things are now worse. I knew when I made the statement that it was obviously not true." His statements were rejected by the conscious mind, and the opposite of what he outwardly affirmed and claimed was made manifest.

Your affirmation succeeds best when it is specific and when it does not produce a mental conflict or argument. The statements made by this man made matters worse because they suggested his lack. Your subconscious accepts what you really feel to be true, not just idle words or statements. The dominant idea or belief is always accepted by the subconscious mind.

HOW TO AVOID MENTAL CONFLICT

The following is the ideal way to overcome this conflict for those who have this difficulty. Make this practical statement frequently, particularly prior to sleep: "By day and by night I am being prospered in all of my interests." This affirmation will not arouse any argument because it does not contradict your subconscious mind's impression of financial lack.

I suggested to one businessman whose sales and finances were extremely low and who was greatly worried that he sit down in his office, become quiet, and repeat this statement over and over: "My sales are improving every day." This statement engaged the cooperation of the conscious and subconscious mind, and results followed.

DON'T SIGN BLANK CHECKS

You sign blank checks when you make such statements as "There is not enough to go around," "There is a shortage," "I will lose the house because I can't meet the mortgage," and so forth. If you are full of fear about the future, you are also writing a blank check and attracting negative conditions to you. Your subconscious mind accepts your fear and negative statement as your request and proceeds in its own way to bring obstacles, delays, lack, and limitation into your life.

YOUR SUBCONSCIOUS GIVES YOU COMPOUND INTEREST

To him that hath the feeling of wealth, more wealth shall be added; to him that hath the feeling of lack, more lack shall be added. Your subconscious multiplies and magnifies whatever you deposit in it. Every morning as you awaken, deposit thoughts of prosperity, success, wealth, and peace. Dwell upon these concepts. Busy your mind with them as often as possible. These constructive thoughts will find their way as deposits in your subconscious mind, and bring forth abundance and prosperity.

WHY NOTHING HAPPENED

I can hear you saying, "Oh, I did that, and nothing happened." You did not get results because you indulged in fear thoughts perhaps ten minutes later and neutralized the good you had affirmed. When you place a seed in the ground, you do not dig it up again later in the day. You let it take root and grow.

Suppose, for example, you are about to say, "I will not be able to make that payment." Before you get further than "I will—" stop the sentence. Change it into a constructive statement, such as, "I will be prospered in all my ways."

TRUE SOURCE OF WEALTH

Your subconscious mind is never short of ideas. There are within it an infinite number of ideas ready to flow into your conscious mind and appear as cash in your pocket in countless ways. This process will continue to go on in your mind regardless of whether the stock market goes up or down, or whether the pound sterling or dollar drops in value. Your wealth is never truly dependent on bonds, stocks, or money in the bank; these are only symbols—necessary and useful, of course, but only symbols.

The point I want to emphasize is that if you convince your subconscious mind that wealth is yours and that it is always circulating in your life, you will always and inevitably have it, regardless of the form it takes.

TRYING TO MAKE ENDS MEET AND THE REAL CAUSE

There are many people who claim that they are always trying to make ends meet. They seem to have a great struggle to meet their obligations. Have you listened to their conversation? In many instances their conversation runs along this vein. They are constantly condemning those who have succeeded in life and who have raised their heads above the crowd. Perhaps they are saying, "Oh, that fellow has a racket; he is ruthless: he is a crook."

This is why they lack. They are constantly condemning the thing they claim to desire and want. The reason they speak critically of their more prosperous associates is because they are envious and covetous of the other's prosperity. The quickest way to cause wealth to take wings and fly away is to criticize and condemn others who have more wealth than you.

A COMMON STUMBLING BLOCK TO WEALTH

There is one emotion that is the cause of the lack of wealth in the lives of many. Most people learn this the hard way. It is envy. For example, if you see a competitor depositing large sums of money in the bank and you have only a meager amount to deposit, does it make you envious? The way to overcome this emotion is to say to yourself, "Isn't it wonderful! I rejoice in that man's prosperity. I wish for him greater and greater wealth."

To entertain envious thoughts is devastating, because it places you in a negative position. Therefore, wealth flows away from you instead of to you. If you are ever annoyed or irritated by the prosperity or great wealth of another, claim immediately that you truly wish for him or her greater wealth in every possible way. This will neutralize the negative thoughts in your mind and cause an ever greater measure of wealth to flow to you by the law of your own subconscious mind.

RUBBING OUT A GREAT MENTAL BLOCK TO WEALTH

If you are worried and critical about someone who you claim is making money dishonestly, stop worrying about him. If your suspicions are correct, you know that such a person is using the law of mind negatively. In time, the law of mind will take care of him. Be careful not to criticize him for the reasons previously indicated. Remember: The block or obstacle to wealth is in your own mind. You can now destroy that mental block. This you may do by getting on mental good terms with everyone.

SLEEP AND GROW RICH

As you go to sleep at night, practice the following technique. Repeat the word "Wealth" quietly, easily, and feelingly. Do this over and over again, just like a lullaby. Lull yourself to sleep with the one word, "Wealth." You should be amazed at the result. Wealth should flow to you in avalanches of abundance. This is another example of the magic power of your subconscious mind.

SERVE YOURSELF WITH THE POWERS OF YOUR MIND

1. Decide to be wealthy the easy way, with the infallible aid of your subconscious mind.
2. Trying to accumulate wealth by the sweat of your brow and hard labor is one way to become the richest man in the graveyard. You do not have to strive or slave hard.

3. Wealth is a subconscious conviction. Build into your mentality the idea of wealth.

4. The trouble with most people is that they have no invisible means of support.

5. Repeat the word "Wealth" to yourself slowly and quietly for about five minutes prior to sleep and your subconscious will bring wealth to pass in your experience.

6. The feeling of wealth produces wealth. Keep this in mind at all times.

7. Your conscious and subconscious mind must agree. Your subconscious accepts what you feel to be true. The dominant idea is always accepted by your subconscious mind. The dominant idea should be wealth, not poverty.

8. You can overcome any mental conflict regarding wealth by affirming frequently, "By day and by night I am being prospered in all of my interests."

9. Increase your sales by repeating this statement over and over, "My sales are improving every day; I am advancing, progressing, and getting wealthier every day."

10. Stop writing blank checks, such as, "There is not enough to go around" or "There is a shortage," and so forth. Such statements magnify and multiply your loss.

11. Deposit thoughts of prosperity, wealth, and success in your subconscious mind and the latter will give you compound interest.

12. What you consciously affirm, you must not mentally deny a few moments later. This will neutralize the good you have affirmed.

13. Your true source of wealth consists of the ideas in your mind. You can have an idea worth millions of dollars. Your subconscious will give you the idea you seek.

14. Envy and jealousy are stumbling blocks to the flow of wealth. Rejoice in the prosperity of others.
15. The block to wealth is in your own mind. Destroy that block now by getting on good mental terms with everyone.

10

Your Right to Be Rich

You have a fundamental right to be rich. You are here to lead the abundant life and be happy, radiant, and free. You should, therefore, have all the money you need to lead a full, happy, and prosperous life.

You are here to grow, expand, and unfold spiritually, mentally, and materially. You have the inalienable right to fully develop and express yourself in all your potentials. An important aspect of that is the ability, should you so choose, to surround yourself with beauty and luxury.

Why be satisfied with just enough to go around when you can enjoy the riches of your subconscious mind? In this chapter, you will learn to make friends with money. Once you do, you will always have all you need and more. Don't let anyone make you feel doubtful or ashamed of your desire to be rich. At its deepest level, it is a desire for a fuller, happier, more wonderful life. It is a cosmic urge. It is not only good, but very good.

MONEY IS A SYMBOL

Money is a symbol of exchange. To you it is a symbol not only of freedom from want, but of beauty, refinement, abundance, and luxury. It is also a symbol of the economic health of the nation. When your blood is circulating freely in your body, you are healthy. When money is circulating freely in your life, you are economically healthy. When people begin to hoard money, to put it away in tin boxes and become charged with fear, they become economically ill.

As a symbol, money has taken many forms throughout the centuries. Almost anything you can think of has served as money at some time and place in history—gold and silver, of course, but also salt, beads, and trinkets of various kinds. In early times people's wealth was often determined by the number of sheep and oxen they owned. Now we use currency and other negotiable instruments. One reason is obvious. It is much more convenient to write a check than to carry a few sheep around with you to pay bills.

HOW TO WALK THE ROYAL ROAD TO RICHES

Once you understand the powers of your subconscious mind, you have within your grasp a road map to the royal road to riches of all kinds—spiritual, mental, or financial. Anyone who has taken the trouble to learn the laws of mind believes and knows definitively that she will never want. Regardless of economic crises, stock-market fluctuations, recessions, strikes, galloping inflation, or even war, she will always be amply supplied.

The reason for this is that she has conveyed the idea of wealth to her subconscious mind. As a result, it keeps her supplied wherever she may be. She has convinced herself in her mind that money is forever flowing freely in her life and that there is always a wonderful surplus available to her. As she decrees it, so it is. Should there be a financial collapse tomorrow and everything she possesses becomes worthless, she will still attract wealth. She will come through the crisis comfortably and likely even gain advantage from it.

WHY YOU DO NOT HAVE MORE MONEY

As you read this chapter, you may be thinking, "I deserve a bigger income than I have." In my opinion, that is true of most people. They really do deserve to have more—but they are not likely to get it. One of the most important reasons these people do not have more money is that they silently or openly condemn it. They refer to money as "filthy lucre." They tell their children and friends that "the love of money is the root of all evil." Coupled with this as a reason they do not prosper is that they have a sneaky subconscious feeling there is some special virtue in poverty. This subconscious pattern may be due to early-childhood training, or it may be based on a false interpretation of scriptures.

MONEY AND A BALANCED LIFE

One time a man came up to me and said, "I am broke. But that's all right. I do not like money. It is the root of all evil." These statements represent the thinking of a confused, neurotic mind. Love of money to the exclusion of everything else will cause you to become lopsided and unbalanced. You are here to use your power or authority wisely. Some people crave power, others crave money.

If you set your heart on money exclusively and say, "Money is all I want; I am going to give all my attention to amassing money; nothing else matters," you can get money and gain a fortune, but at what cost! You have forgotten that you are here to lead a balanced life. You must also satisfy the hunger for peace of mind, harmony, love, joy, and perfect health.

By making money your sole aim, you made a wrong choice. You thought that was all you wanted, but you found after all your efforts that it was not only the money you needed. No one on his deathbed wishes he had spent more time making money! You also desire true expression of your hidden talents, true place in life, beauty, and the joy of contributing to the welfare and success of others. By learning the laws of your subconscious mind, you could have a million dollars or many millions, if you wanted them, and still have peace of mind, harmony, perfect health, and perfect expression.

POVERTY IS A MENTAL ILLNESS

There is no virtue in poverty. It is an illness like any other mental illness. If you were physically ill, you would realize there was something wrong with you. You would seek help and try to cure the condition at once. In the same way, if you do not have enough money constantly circulating in your life, there is something radically wrong with you.

The urge of the life principle in you is toward growth, expansion, and the life more abundant. You are not here to live in a hovel, dress in rags, and go hungry. You should be happy, prosperous, and successful.

WHY YOU MUST NEVER CRITICIZE MONEY

Cleanse your mind of all weird and superstitious beliefs about money. Do not ever regard money as evil or filthy. If you do, you cause it to take wings and fly away from you.

Remember that you lose what you condemn. You cannot attract what you criticize.

GETTING THE RIGHT ATTITUDE TOWARD MONEY

Here is a simple technique you may use to multiply money in your experience. Use the following statements several times a day:

> I like money. I love it. I use it wisely, constructively, and judiciously. Money is constantly circulating in my life. I release it with joy, and it returns to me multiplied in a wonderful way. It is good and very good. Money flows to me in avalanches of abundance. I use it for good only, and I am grateful for my good and for the riches of my mind.

HOW THE SCIENTIFIC THINKER LOOKS AT MONEY

Suppose you discovered a rich vein of gold, silver, lead, copper, or iron in the ground. Would you announce that these things are evil? Of course not! All evil comes from humankind's darkened understanding, from ignorance, from false interpretation of life, and from misuse of the subconscious mind.

Since money is simply a symbol, we could just as easily use lead or tin or some other metal as a medium of exchange. In the earlier part of the twentieth century, U.S. dimes and quarters were made of silver. At times, they contained ten cents or twenty-five cents worth of silver. Then the government started making them of cheaper metals. But the worth of a quarter is still twenty-five cents, even if the metal that makes it up is worth far less than that.

A physicist will tell you that the only difference between one metal and another is the kind and number of elementary particles in its atoms. If you direct a stream of particles at a block of one metal, you can change it into another. The alchemist's ancient dream of producing gold from baser metals is now within our grasp. But so what? Gold is no more virtuous, or evil, than lead. They are different substances with different properties, that's all. It is only because of the long history in which gold was considered especially precious that people love it—or hate it—more than they do lead.

How to Attract the Money You Need

Many years ago I met a young man in Australia who told me that his fondest dream was to become a physician. He was taking science classes and doing brilliantly, but he had no way to pay for medical school. His parents were both dead. To support himself, he cleaned doctors' offices in the local hospital's professional building. I explained to him that a seed planted in the soil attracts to itself everything it needs for its proper unfolding. All he had to do was to take a lesson from the seed and plant the required idea in his subconscious mind.

Every night, as this young man went to sleep, he visualized a medical diploma with his name in big, bold letters. He found it easy to create a sharp, detailed image of the diploma. Part of his job was to dust and polish the framed diplomas hanging on the walls of the doctors' offices, and he studied them as he cleaned them.

He persisted with this visualization technique every night for about four months. Then one of the doctors whose office he cleaned asked if he would like to become a physician's assistant. The doctor paid for him to attend a training program where he learned a wide variety of medical skills, then gave him a job as his assistant. He was so impressed with the young man's brilliance and determination that he later helped him through medical school. Today, this young man is a prominent doctor in Montreal, Canada.

This young man's success came because he had learned the law of attraction. He discovered how to use his subconscious mind the right way. This involved making use of an age-old law that says, "Having clearly seen the end, you have willed the means to the realization of the end." The end in this case was to become a physician. He was able to imagine, see, and feel the reality of being a doctor. He lived with the idea. He sustained it, nourished it, and loved it. At last, through his visualization, the idea penetrated the layers of his subconscious mind. It became a conviction. That conviction then attracted to him everything that was needed for the fulfillment of his dream.

WHY SOME PEOPLE DO NOT GET A RAISE IN PAY

Let us say you work for a large corporation. You believe that you are underpaid. You resent the fact that you are not appreciated by your employers. You constantly mull over your conviction that you deserve more money and greater recognition.

By setting yourself in mental opposition to your employer, you are subconsciously severing your ties with that organization. You are setting a process in motion. Then, one day, your superior tells you, "We have to let you go." In a real sense, you dismissed yourself. Your superior was simply acting as the instrument through which your own negative mental state was confirmed. This is an example of the law of action and reaction. The action is your thought, and the reaction is the response of your subconscious mind.

OBSTACLES AND IMPEDIMENTS ON THE PATHWAY TO RICHES

From time to time, you have probably heard someone say, "Anybody who makes a lot of money has to be some kind of crook."

The person who talks—and thinks—this way is usually suffering from a financial illness. Maybe he is bitter and envious of former friends who have been more successful and now have greater resources. If so, this person is creating his own difficulties. Entertaining negative thoughts about those friends and condemning their wealth causes prosperity and wealth to flee. Would you stay with someone who condemns you? Of course not; and neither will wealth. This person is chasing away the thing he is praying for.

He is praying in two ways. On the one hand he is saying, "I wish wealth to flow to me now." But in the next breath, he is saying, "That fellow's wealth is a dirty, evil thing." This contradiction is a signpost on the road to poverty and misery. Always make it a special point to rejoice in the wealth of another person.

PROTECT YOUR INVESTMENTS

If you are seeking guidance regarding investments, or if you are worried about your stocks or bonds, quietly claim, "Infinite intelligence governs and watches over all my financial transactions. Whatsoever I do shall prosper." If you do this frequently, with perfect faith and confidence, you will find that you will be guided to make wise investments. Moreover, you will be protected from loss, because you will be prompted to sell any risky securities or holdings before any loss accrues to you.

YOU CANNOT GET SOMETHING FOR NOTHING

In large stores the management hires guards and store detectives to keep people from stealing. Every day they catch a number of people trying to get something for nothing. Anyone who does such a thing is steeped in a mental atmosphere of lack and limitation. In trying to steal from others, they are robbing themselves of peace, harmony, faith, honesty, integrity, goodwill, and confidence.

Furthermore, their messages to their subconscious minds draw to them all manner of loss: loss of character, prestige, social status, and peace of mind. These people do not understand how their minds work. They lack faith in the source of supply. If only they would mentally call on the powers of their subconscious mind and claim that they are guided to their true expression, they would find work and abundance. Then, by honesty, integrity, and perseverance, they would become a credit to themselves and to society at large.

YOUR CONSTANT SUPPLY OF MONEY

The path to freedom, comfort, and a constant supply of needed wealth lies in recognizing the powers of your subconscious mind and the creative power of your thought or mental image. Accept the abundant life in your own mind. Your mental acceptance and expectancy of wealth has its own mathematics and mechanics of expression. As you enter into the mood of opulence, all things necessary for the abundant life will come to pass.

Let this be your daily affirmation; write it in your heart: I am one with the infinite riches of my subconscious mind. It is my right to be rich, happy, and successful. Money flows to me freely, copiously, and endlessly. I am forever conscious of my true worth. I give of my talents freely, and I am wonderfully blessed financially. It is wonderful!

STEP UP THIS WAY TO RICHES

1. Be bold enough to claim that it is your right to be rich. Your deeper mind will honor your claim.

2. You don't want just enough to go around. You want all the money you need to do all the things you want to do, when you want to do them. Get acquainted with the riches of your subconscious mind.

3. When money is circulating freely in your life, you are economically healthy. Look at money like the tide and you will always have plenty of it. The ebb and flow of the tide is constant. When the tide is out, you are absolutely sure that it will return.

4. Knowing the laws of your subconscious mind, you will always be supplied regardless of what form money takes.

5. One reason many people simply make ends meet and never have enough money is that they condemn money. What you condemn takes wings and flies away.

6. Do not make a god of money. It is only a symbol. Remember that the real riches are in your mind. You are here to lead a balanced life—this includes acquiring all the money you need.

7. Don't make money your sole aim. Claim wealth, happiness, peace, true expression, and love, and personally radiate love and goodwill to all. Then your subconscious mind will give you compound interest in all these fields of expression.

8. There is no virtue in poverty. It is a disease of the mind. You should heal yourself of this mental conflict or malady at once.

9. You are not here to live in a hovel, to dress in rags, or to go hungry. You are here to lead the life more abundant.

10. Never use the term "filthy lucre" or say "I despise money." You lose what you criticize. Money in itself is neither good nor bad, but thinking of it in either light makes it so.

11. Repeat frequently, "I like money. I use it wisely, constructively, and judiciously. I release it with joy, and it returns a thousandfold."

12. Money is not evil any more than copper, lead, tin, or iron that you may find in the ground are. All evil is due to ignorance and misuse of the mind's powers.

13. To picture the end result in your mind causes your subconscious to respond and fulfill your mental picture.

14. Stop trying to get something for nothing. There is no such thing as a free lunch. You must give to receive. If you give mental attention to your goals, ideals, and enterprises, your deeper mind will back you up. The key to wealth is to apply the laws of the subconscious mind by impregnating it with the idea of wealth.

11
Your Subconscious Mind as a Partner in Success

The true inner meaning of success is to be successful at the enterprise of living. A long period of peace, joy, and happiness on this plane may be termed success. The eternal experience of these qualities is the everlasting life spoken of by Jesus. The real things of life, such as peace, harmony, integrity, security, and happiness, are intangible. They come from the deep self of human beings. Meditating on these qualities builds these treasures of heaven in our subconscious. That is the true place where

> . . . moth and rust do not consume, and where thieves do not break through and steal.
>
> *MATT. 6:20*

THE THREE STEPS TO SUCCESS

The vital first step to success is to find out the thing you love to do, then do it. Unless you love your work, you cannot possibly consider yourself successful at it, even if all the rest of the world hails you as a great success. Loving your work, you have a deep desire to carry it out. If someone is drawn to become a psychiatrist, it is not enough for her to get a diploma and hang it on the wall. She will want to keep up with the field, attend conventions, and continue studying the mind and its workings. She will visit other clinics and pore over the latest scientific journals. In other words, she will work to keep herself informed in the most advanced methods of alleviating human suffering, because she puts the interests of her patients first.

But what if, as you read these words, you find yourself thinking, "I can't take the first step, because I don't know what it is I want to do. How on earth do I find a field of effort that I will love?"

If that is your situation, pray for guidance in this way:

The infinite intelligence of my subconscious mind reveals to me my true place in life.

Repeat this prayer quietly, positively, and lovingly to your deeper mind. As you persist with faith and confidence, the answer will come to you as a feeling, a hunch, or a tendency in a certain direction. It will come to you clearly and in peace, and as an inner silent awareness.

The second step to success is to specialize in some particular branch of work and strive to excel in it. Suppose a student chooses chemistry as a profession. He should concentrate on one of the many branches in this field and give all his time and attention to his chosen specialty. His enthusiasm should make him want to know all there is available about his field; if possible, he should know more than anyone else. The young man should become ardently interested in his work and should desire to use it to serve the world.

He that is greatest among you, let him become your servant. There is an enormous contrast between this attitude of mind and that of someone who wants only to make a living or just "get by." "Getting by" is not true success. People's motives must be greater, nobler, and more altruistic. They must serve others, thereby casting their bread upon the waters.

The third step is the most important one. You must be sure that the thing you want to do does not contribute only to your own success. Your desire must not be selfish. It must benefit humanity. The path of a complete circuit must be formed. In other words, your idea must go forth with the purpose of blessing or serving the world. It will then come back to you magnified and full of blessings. If you work only for your own benefit, you do not complete this essential circuit. You may appear to be successful, but the short-circuit you have generated in your life may lead over time to limitation or sickness.

THE MEASURE OF TRUE SUCCESS

At this point you may be thinking, "What about that guy I saw a show about? The one who made hundreds of millions of dollars from shady stock deals? He's as big a success as you'll ever see, and I don't think he cares a bit about benefiting humanity."

Such cases are all too common, but we must be careful to understand them for what they are. Someone may seem to succeed for a while, but money obtained by fraud often takes wings and flies away. Even if it does not, when we rob from another, we rob from ourselves. The mood of lack and limitation that led to our behavior manifests itself in other ways as well, in our body, our home life, our relationships with others.

What we think and feel, we create. We create what we believe. Even though someone may have accumulated a fortune fraudulently, he is not successful. There is no success without peace of mind. What good is a person's accumulated wealth if he cannot sleep nights, is sick, or has a guilt complex?

I once met a professional criminal in London who told me something of his exploits. He had amassed a large fortune that allowed him to live in luxury in his house outside London and his summer home in France. In luxury, yes, but *not* in comfort. He was in constant dread of being arrested by Scotland Yard. He had many inner disorders that were undoubtedly caused by his constant fear and deep-seated guilt complex. He knew he had done wrong. This deep sense of guilt attracted all kinds of trouble to him.

Later, I heard that he had voluntarily turned himself in to the police and had served a prison sentence. After his release from prison, he sought psychological and spiritual counsel and became transformed. He went to work and became an honest, law-abiding citizen. He found what he loved to do and was happy.

A successful person loves her work and expresses herself fully. Success is contingent upon a higher ideal than the mere accumulation of riches. The person of success is the person who possesses great psychological and spiritual understanding. Many of the great business leaders of today depend upon the correct use of their subconscious minds for their success. They cultivate the ability to see an upcoming project as if it were already complete. Having seen and felt the fulfillment of their prayers, their subconscious minds bring about their realization. If you imagine an objective clearly, you will be provided with the necessities, in ways you know not of, through the wonder-working power of your subconscious mind.

In considering the three steps to success you must never forget the underlying power of the creative forces of your subconscious mind. This is the energy behind all the steps in any plan of success. Your thought is creative. Thought fused with feeling becomes a subjective faith or belief,

> . . . and according to your belief is it done unto you.
>
> *MATT. 9:29*

Once you understand that you possess a mighty force within you that is capable of bringing to pass all your desires, you gain both confidence and a sense of peace. Whatever your field of action may be, you should learn the laws of your subconscious mind. When you know how to apply the powers of your mind and when you are expressing yourself fully and giving of your talents to others, you are on the sure path to true success. If you are about God's business, or any part of it, God, by his nature, is for you, so who can be against you? With this understanding there is no power in heaven or on earth that can withhold success from you.

HOW HE MADE HIS DREAM COME TRUE

In Hollywood, I met an actor whose name is probably familiar to every moviegoer or television fan. He confided to me that he had grown up on a small farm in the Midwest. His family was just scraping by. His only entertainment was an old black-and-white TV that barely pulled in two channels. Even so, he began to dream of being an actor. The dream occupied him more and more.

"All the time I was out working in the fields," he said, "or driving the cows back to the barn, I imagined that I could see my name in big letters on the marquee of a great theater. I saw every detail—the crowds of fans, the interviewers clamoring to speak to me. I kept this up for years.

"Finally, I left home. I came to Los Angeles and got work as an extra in films and TV shows. Before long, I got my first starring role. The night of the premiere, I drove to the theater and almost fainted. There was my name in lights, there were the crowds and the news reporters, all just as I had imagined them as a child."

He added, "I, more than anyone, understand how the power of sustained imagination can bring success."

HER DREAM PHARMACY BECAME A REALITY

Some years ago I got to know a young pharmacist named Mary S. She worked in the prescription department of a big chain drugstore. One day while she was filling a prescription for me, we started talking. I asked her how she liked her work.

"Oh, it's fine," she said. "Between my salary and commissions, I do okay, and the company has a good profit-sharing program. With any luck, I'll be able to retire while I'm still young enough to enjoy life."

I was silent for a moment. Then I asked, "Was that the way you thought it would be as a child, when you decided you wanted to be a pharmacist?"

Her face grew troubled. "Well, no," she replied. "I guess not. I always saw myself with my own store. I wanted to walk down the street and have people say hello to me and call me by name. And I'd know all their names, because I was their druggist. You're going to think this is strange, but I even dreamed about having parents call me in the middle of the night because their kid was sick. I'd pull my clothes on over my pajamas and go down to the store to get them the medicine they needed. Not much like a nine-to-five job behind a counter at the back end of a big store, is it?"

"It certainly isn't," I said. "But why shouldn't you follow your dream? Wouldn't you be happier and more productive? Raise your sights. Get out of this place. Start your own store."

"How can I?" she said, shaking her head. "That takes big money, and we're just getting by from month to month."

My response was to share with her a wonderful fact: Whatever she could conceive as true, she could bring into being. I went on to tell her something about the powers of her subconscious mind. She soon understood that if she could succeed in impregnating her subconscious mind with a clear and specific idea, those powers would somehow bring it to pass.

She began to imagine that she was in her own store. She mentally arranged the bottles, dispensed prescriptions, and imagined waiting on customers who were also her neighbors and friends. She also visualized a big bank balance. Mentally she worked in that imaginary store. Like a good actor, she lived the role. *Act as though I am, and I will be.* She put herself wholeheartedly into the act, living, moving, and acting on the assumption that she owned the store.

Several years later, Mary wrote me to say what had happened to her life since our conversation. The chain store she worked for went under because of competition from a larger store at a new mall. She found a job as a traveling representative for a major drug company, handling a territory that covered several states.

One day her work took her to a small town on the western edge of her territory. There was only one drugstore in town. She had never been there before, but the moment she walked in, she recognized it. It was exactly the store she had visualized so clearly in her imagination.

Flabbergasted, she told the elderly owner of the drugstore about this amazing coincidence. In turn, the owner confided that he was about ready to retire but did not want to sell a store that had been in his family for three generations to some big corporation.

After several discussions, the owner offered to lend her the money to buy the store. She would be able to make the payments on the loan out of the profits of the business. The young woman moved her family to the town and soon was able to make a down payment on a big old house within walking distance of the store. Now, when she walks to work in the morning, everyone she passes says hello and calls her by name. They know her, because she is their druggist.

USING THE SUBCONSCIOUS MIND IN BUSINESS

Some years ago I gave a lecture to a group of business executives on the powers of imagination and the subconscious mind. In the course of the lecture, I described how the great German poet Goethe used his imagination wisely when confronted with difficulties and predicaments.

According to Goethe's biographers, he was accustomed to filling many hours quietly holding imaginary conversations. He would imagine one of his friends sitting across from him, answering him in the right way. In other words, if he were concerned over any problems, he imagined his friend giving him the right or appropriate answer, accompanied with his usual gestures and tonal qualities of the voice. He made the entire imaginary scene as real and as vivid as possible.

One of the people present at this lecture was a young stockbroker. She proceeded to adopt the technique of

Goethe. She began to have imaginary conversations with a multimillionaire investor who knew her and had once congratulated her on her wise and sound judgment in recommending stocks. She dramatized this imaginary conversation until she had psychologically fixed it as a form of belief in her mind.

This broker's inner talking and controlled imagination certainly agreed with her aim, which was to make sound investments for her clients. Her main purpose in life was to make money for her clients and to see them prosper financially by her wise counsel. She is still using her subconscious mind in her business, and she is a brilliant success in her field. She was recently interviewed in an article in a major financial magazine.

A BOY OF SIXTEEN TURNS FAILURE INTO SUCCESS

Sixteen-year-old Todd M. told me, "I'm failing everything. I don't know why. I guess I'm just stupid. Maybe I'd better drop out of school before they flunk me out."

As we talked further, I discovered that the only thing wrong with Todd was his attitude. He felt indifferent toward his studies and resentful toward some of his teachers and fellow students.

I taught him how to use his subconscious mind to succeed in his studies. He began to affirm certain truths several times a day, particularly at night just prior to sleep and first thing after awakening in the morning. As we have seen, these are the best times to impregnate the subconscious mind.

He affirmed as follows:

I realize that my subconscious mind is a storehouse of memory. It retains everything I read and hear from my teachers. I have a perfect memory at my disposal, if I

> choose to use it. The infinite intelligence of my subconscious mind constantly reveals to me everything I need to know on all my examinations, whether written or oral. I radiate love and goodwill to all my teachers and fellow students. I sincerely wish for them success and all good things.

Todd is now enjoying a greater freedom than he has ever known. He is now receiving all A's. He constantly imagines the teachers and his parents congratulating him on his success in his studies.

HOW TO BECOME SUCCESSFUL IN BUYING AND SELLING

In buying or selling, remember that your conscious mind is the starter and your subconscious mind is the motor. You must start the motor to enable it to perform its work. Your conscious mind awakens the power of your subconscious mind.

The first step in conveying your clarified desire, idea, or image to the deeper mind is to relax, immobilize the attention, get still, and be quiet. This quiet, relaxed, and peaceful attitude of mind prevents extraneous matter and false ideas from interfering with your mental absorption of your ideal. Furthermore, in the quiet, passive, and receptive attitude of mind, effort is reduced to a minimum.

The second step is to begin to imagine the reality of the end you desire. For example, you may wish to buy a home. In your relaxed state of mind, you affirm as follows:

> The infinite intelligence of my subconscious mind is all-wise. It reveals to me now the ideal home that meets all my requirements and that I can afford. I am now turning this request over to my subconscious mind. I know it responds

according to the nature of my request. I release this request with absolute faith and confidence in the same way that a farmer deposits a seed in the ground, trusting implicitly in the laws of growth.

The answer to your prayer may come from an advertisement in the paper or from a friend. Or you may be guided directly to a particular home that is exactly what you are seeking. There are many ways in which your prayer may be answered. The principal knowledge, in which you may place your confidence, is that the answer always comes, provided you trust the working of your deeper mind.

Suppose, instead of wanting to buy, you want to sell a home, land, or any kind of property. The same approach of trusting the infinite intelligence of your subconscious mind will give you the guidance you seek. When I sold my own home in Los Angeles, I used a technique that many real-estate brokers I have spoken to are now using with remarkable and speedy results.

I placed a sign on the lawn in front of my home that read, "For sale by owner." That night, as I was going to sleep, I asked myself, "Suppose you find a buyer for the house, what will you do next?" The answer was "I'll take down the 'For Sale' sign and throw it in the garbage."

Against the inner screen of my mind, I projected a detailed scenario. I took hold of the sign, pulled it up from the ground, placed it on my shoulder, and carried it to the trash cans at the back of the house. As I threw it in the garbage, I said, "Thanks for your help, but I don't need you anymore!"

I went to sleep feeling the deep inner satisfaction of knowing that it was finished.

The next day a man gave me a deposit on the house and said, "You can throw that sign away. You don't need it anymore."

I followed his advice. I pulled the sign up and took it to the garbage. The outer action conformed to the inner. There is nothing new about this. *As within, so without.* In other words, according to the image impressed on your subconscious mind, so it is on the objective screen of your life. The outside mirrors the inside. External action follows internal action.

Here is another effective method used in selling homes, land, or any kind of property. Affirm slowly, quietly, and feelingly as follows:

> Infinite intelligence attracts to me the buyer for this home who wants it and who prospers in it. This buyer is being sent to me by the creative intelligence of my subconscious mind, which makes no mistakes. This buyer may look at many other homes, but mine is the only one he wants and will buy, because he is guided by the infinite intelligence within him. I know the buyer is right, the time is right, and the price is right. Everything about it is right. The deeper currents of my subconscious mind are now in operation bringing both of us together in divine order. I know that it is so.

Remember always that what you are seeking is also seeking you. Whenever you want to sell a home or property of any kind, there is always someone who wants what you have to offer. By using the powers of your subconscious mind correctly, you free your mind of all sense of competition and anxiety in buying and selling.

HOW SHE SUCCEEDED IN GETTING WHAT SHE WANTED

There is a young woman, Margaret T., who regularly attended my lectures and classes. Because of where she lived, she had to change buses three times to get to the hall. It took her one and a half hours each way to attend a lecture. In one of my lectures, she heard me explain how a young man who needed a car in his work received one.

She went home and experimented with the technique I had outlined in my lecture. She later wrote me a letter telling me how she had applied my methods and what followed. I publish it here with her permission.

Dear Dr. Murphy:

I knew that I had to have a car for my personal growth. There was no other way I could go on attending your lectures regularly. I decided that, as long as I was trying to obtain a car, I should try to obtain the car I had always dreamed about, which is a Cadillac.

In my imagination I went through all the steps I would go through if I were actually buying and driving a car. I saw myself going into the showroom and test driving the model I was interested in. I claimed that Cadillac as my own over and over again.

I kept the mental picture of getting into the car, driving it, feeling the upholstery, and so on, consistently for over two weeks. Last week I drove to your lecture in a Cadillac. My uncle in Inglewood had passed away and left me his Cadillac and his entire estate.

A SUCCESS TECHNIQUE EMPLOYED BY MANY OUTSTANDING EXECUTIVES

Many prominent business executives quietly use the abstract term "success" over and over many times a day until they reach a conviction that success is theirs. They know that the idea of success contains all the essential elements of success. Likewise, you can begin now to repeat the word "success" to yourself with faith and conviction. Your subconscious mind will accept it as true of you, and you will be under a subconscious compulsion to succeed.

You are compelled to express your subjective beliefs, impressions, and convictions. What does *success* imply to you? You want, undoubtedly, to be successful in your home life and in your relationships with others. You wish to be outstanding in your chosen work or profession. You wish to possess a beautiful home, and all the money you need to live comfortably and happily. You want to be successful in your prayer life and in your contact with the powers of your subconscious mind.

You are a business executive also because you are in the business of living. Become a successful executive by imagining yourself doing what you long to do and possessing the things you long to possess. Become imaginative; mentally participate in the reality of the successful state. Make a habit of it. Go to sleep feeling successful every night and perfectly satisfied, and you will eventually succeed in implanting the idea of success in your subconscious mind. Believe you were born to succeed, and wonders will happen as you pray.

PROFITABLE POINTERS

1. Success means successful living. When you are peaceful, happy, joyous, and doing what you love to do, you are successful.

2. Find out what you love to do, then do it. If you don't know your true expression, ask for guidance, and the lead will come.
3. Specialize in your particular field and try to know more about it than anyone else.
4. Those who are successful are not selfish. Their main desire in life is to serve humanity.
5. There is no true success without peace of mind.
6. A successful person possesses great psychological and spiritual understanding.
7. If you imagine an objective clearly, you will be provided with the necessities through the wonder-working power of your subconscious mind.
8. Your thought fused with feeling becomes a subjective belief, and according to your belief is it done unto you.
9. The power of sustained imagination draws forth the miracle-working powers of your subconscious mind.
10. If you are seeking promotion in your work, imagine your employer, supervisor, or loved one congratulating you on your promotion. Make the picture vivid and real. Hear the voice, see the gestures, and feel the reality of it all. Continue to do this frequently, and through frequent occupancy of your mind, you will experience the joy of the answered prayer.
11. Your subconscious mind is a storehouse of memory. For a perfect memory, affirm frequently: "The infinite intelligence of my subconscious mind reveals to me everything I need to know at all times, everywhere."
12. If you wish to sell a home or property of any kind, affirm slowly, quietly, and feelingly as follows: "Infinite intelligence attracts to me the buyer for this house or property, who wants it, and who prospers in it." Sustain this

awareness, and the deeper currents of your subconscious mind will bring it to pass.

13. The idea of success contains all the elements of success. Repeat the word "success" to yourself frequently with faith and conviction and you will be under a subconscious compulsion to succeed.

12

How Scientists Use the Subconscious Mind

Many of the most creative scientists in history have realized the true importance of the subconscious mind. Edison, Marconi, Einstein, and many others have used the subconscious mind to give them the insight and the "know-how" to bring about their great achievements. The ability to bring into action the power of the subconscious mind is one of the most important factors in determining the success of great scientific and research workers.

One of the most amazing examples of this can be found in the life of the celebrated chemist, Friedrich von Stradonitz. He had been struggling for a long time to understand the chemical structure of the hydrocarbon called benzine. This is a compound that contains six atoms of carbon and six of hydrogen. Stradonitz was constantly perplexed by the problem. All his efforts seemed to lead nowhere.

Unable to solve the riddle, tired and exhausted, Stradonitz turned the matter over completely to his subconscious mind. Shortly afterward, as he was about to board a London bus, his subconscious presented his conscious mind with a sudden flash. In his mind, Stradonitz saw the image of a snake biting its own tail and turning around like a pinwheel. This message from his subconscious mind inspired him to orient his search in a different direction. Soon he arrived at the long-sought answer, the circular arrangement of atoms that is known as the benzine ring.

HOW A DISTINGUISHED SCIENTIST BROUGHT FORTH HIS INVENTIONS

Nikola Tesla was a brilliant pioneer in the field of electricity. The Tesla coil, an exhibit in science museums that is always a favorite with children, was only one of his inventions. This is a charged metal sphere. When someone touches it, the static electricity makes his or her hair stand straight up. Tesla also experimented with the concept of broadcasting energy. His ideas on this topic are still considered revolutionary.

Tesla was a convinced user of the power of the subconscious mind. Whenever he had an idea for a new invention or a new research direction, he would build it up in his imagination, then turn it over to his subconscious mind. He knew that his subconscious mind would reconstruct and reveal to his conscious mind all the parts needed for its manufacture in concrete form. Through quietly contemplating every possible improvement, he wasted no time on correcting defects. He was able to give the technicians working with him the perfect end product of his mind.

In an interview, he said, "Invariably, my device works as I imagined it should. In twenty years there has not been a single exception."

HOW A FAMOUS NATURALIST SOLVED HIS PROBLEM

Professor Louis Agassiz of Harvard University was one of the most distinguished American naturalists of the nineteenth century. He discovered the great powers of his subconscious mind while he slept. The following example comes from a biography of Agassiz, written by his widow.

He had been for two weeks striving to decipher the some-
what obscure impression of a fossil fish on the stone slab
in which it was preserved. Weary and perplexed, he put
his work aside at last, and tried to dismiss it from his mind.
Shortly after, he waked one night persuaded that while
asleep he had seen his fish with all the missing features
perfectly restored. But when he tried to hold and make fast
the image it escaped him. Nevertheless, he went early to
the Jardin des Plantes, thinking that on looking anew at the
impression he should see something which would put him
on the track of his vision. In vain—the blurred record was
as black as ever. The next night he saw the fish again, but
with no more satisfactory result. When he awoke it disappeared from his memory as before. Hoping that the same
experience might be repeated, on the third night he placed
a pencil and paper beside his bed before going to sleep.

Accordingly, toward morning the fish reappeared in
his dream, confusedly at first, but at last with such distinct-
ness that he had no longer any doubt as to its zoological
characters. Still half dreaming, in perfect darkness, he
traced these characters on the sheet of paper at the bedside. In the morning he was surprised to see in his noctur-
nal sketch features which he thought it impossible the fossil
itself should reveal. He hastened to the Jardin des Plantes,
and, with his drawing as a guide, succeeded in chiseling
away the surface of the stone under which portions of the
fish proved to be hidden. When wholly exposed it corre-
sponded with his dream and his drawing, and he succeeded in classifying it with ease.

HOW AN OUTSTANDING PHYSICIAN SOLVED THE PROBLEM OF DIABETES

In the 1920s, Dr. Frederick Banting, a brilliant Canadian physician and researcher, focused his attention on the ravages of diabetes. At that time medical science offered no effective method of arresting the disease. Dr. Banting spent considerable time experimenting and studying the international literature on the subject, but every path he explored seemed to be a dead end.

One night, exhausted by still another long day of what seemed to be wasted efforts, he fell asleep. While he lay sleeping, his subconscious mind instructed him to extract the residue from the degenerated pancreatic duct of dogs. This inspiration led him to the discovery of insulin, which has helped countless millions of people since.

You will note that Dr. Banting had been consciously dwelling on the problem for some time, seeking a solution, a way out. His subconscious responded accordingly.

It does not follow that you will always get an answer overnight. The answer may not come for some time. Do not be discouraged. Keep on turning the problem over every night to the subconscious mind prior to sleep, as if you had never done it before.

If you continue to experience a delay in arriving at a solution, maybe you are thinking of the question you are presenting to your subconscious mind as a major one that will take a long time to solve. This would not be surprising. We are usually tempted to believe our problems are difficult. If they weren't, they wouldn't be problems. However, this is a mistake. Your subconscious mind is timeless and spaceless. Go to sleep believing you have the answer *now*. Do not postulate that the answer will have to wait to come in the future. Have an abiding faith in the outcome. Become convinced now as you read this book that there is an answer and a perfect solution for you.

HOW A SCIENTIST ESCAPED FROM A SOVIET CONCENTRATION CAMP

Dr. Lothar von Blenk-Schmidt, an outstanding electronics engineer, was locked up in a Soviet prison camp during World War II. He credits his survival and eventual escape to freedom to the powers of his subconscious mind.

> I was a prisoner of war in a coal mine in Russia, and I saw men dying all around me in that prison compound. We were watched over by brutal guards, arrogant officers, and sharp, fast-thinking commissars. After a short medical checkup, a quota of coal was assigned to each person. My quota was three hundred pounds per day. In case any man did not fill his quota, his small food ration was cut down, and in a short time he was resting in the cemetery.
>
> I started concentrating on my escape. I knew that my subconscious mind would somehow find a way. My home in Germany was destroyed, my family wiped out; all my friends and former associates were either killed in the war or were in concentration camps.
>
> I said to my subconscious mind, "I want to go to Los Angeles, and you will find the way." I had seen pictures of Los Angeles and I remembered some of the boulevards very well as well as some of the buildings.
>
> Every day and night I would imagine I was walking down Wilshire Boulevard with an American girl whom I met in Berlin prior to the war (she is now my wife). In my imagination we would visit the stores, ride buses, and eat in the restaurants. Every night I made it a special point to drive my imaginary American automobile up and down the boulevards of Los Angeles. I made all this vivid and

real. These pictures in my mind were as real and as natural to me as one of the trees outside the prison camp.

Every morning the chief guard would count the prisoners as they were lined up. He would call out "one, two, three," etc., and when seventeen was called out, which was my number in sequence, I stepped aside. In the meantime, the guard was called away for a minute or so, and on his return he started by mistake on the next man as number seventeen. When the crew returned in the evening, the number of men was the same, and I was not missed, and the discovery would take a long time.

I walked out of the camp undetected and kept walking for twenty-four hours, resting in a deserted town the next day. I was able to live by fishing and killing some wildlife. I found coal trains going to Poland and traveled on them by night, until finally I reached Poland. With the help of friends, I made my way to Lucerne, Switzerland.

One evening at the Palace Hotel, Lucerne, I had a talk with a man and his wife from the United States of America. This man asked me if I would care to be a guest at his home in Santa Monica, California. I accepted, and when I arrived in Los Angeles, I found that their chauffeur drove me along Wilshire Boulevard and many other boulevards which I had imagined so vividly in the long months in the Russian coal mines. I recognized the buildings which I had seen in my mind so often. It actually seemed as if I had been in Los Angeles before. I had reached my goal.

I will never cease to marvel at the wonders of the subconscious mind. Truly, it has ways we know not of.

HOW ARCHAEOLOGISTS AND PALEONTOLOGISTS RECONSTRUCT ANCIENT SCENES

Your subconscious mind has a memory of everything that has ever happened in the history of our species. Archeologists studying ancient ruins and the countless artifacts left by the people of former cultures can put imaginative perception to marvelous use in their work. Their subconscious mind can aid them in reconstructing ancient scenes. The dead past becomes alive once more. Looking at the fragments of these ancient buildings and studying the pottery, statuary, tools, and household utensils of earlier civilizations, the scientist is able, through the common data banks of the universal mind, to know how, when, and why these objects were created.

The keen concentration and disciplined imagination of the scientist awakens the latent powers of the subconscious mind. This gives him the ability to clothe the ancient structures with roofs and surround them with gardens, pools, and fountains. The fossil remains are clothed with eyes, sinews, and muscles, and they again walk and talk. The past becomes the living present, and we find that in mind there is no time or space. Through disciplined, controlled, and directed imagination, you can be a companion of the most scientific and inspired thinkers of all time.

HOW TO RECEIVE GUIDANCE FROM YOUR SUBCONSCIOUS

When you have to make what you think will be a difficult decision, or when you fail to see the solution to your problem, begin at once to think constructively about it. If you are fearful and worried, you are not really thinking. True thinking is free from fear.

Here are the steps of a simple technique you can use to receive guidance on any subject.

- Quiet the mind and still the body. Tell the body to relax; it has to obey you. It has no volition, initiative, or self-conscious intelligence. Your body is an emotional disk that records your beliefs and impressions.
- Mobilize your attention; focus your thought on the solution to your problem.
- Try to solve it with your conscious mind.
- Think how happy you would be about the perfect solution. Sense the feeling you would have if the perfect answer were yours now.
- Let your mind play with this mood of happiness and contentment in a relaxed way; then drop off to sleep.
- When you awaken, if you do not have the answer, get busy with something else. While you are preoccupied with something else, it is possible that the answer will pop into your mind.

In receiving guidance from the subconscious mind, the simple way is the best. Here is an illustration. I once lost a valuable ring that was a family heirloom. I looked everywhere for it, but it was nowhere to be found. I was worried and distressed by the loss.

That night I talked to my subconscious mind, in the same way that I would talk to anyone. Before dropping off to sleep, I said to it, "You know all things. You know where that ring is, and you now reveal to me where it is."

In the morning, I woke up suddenly with these words ringing in my ear: "Ask Robert!"

This seemed very strange to me. The only Robert I could think of offhand was the nine-year-old son of my next-door neighbors. Why should he know anything about the location of my ring? However, I followed the inner voice of intuition.

I found Robert in his yard and described the ring to him. "You haven't seen it, have you?" I asked.

"Oh, sure," he replied. "I found it in the bushes yesterday when I was playing hide and seek. I didn't know whose it was, so I took it inside and put it on my desk. I was going to put up a sign about it, but I forgot."

The subconscious mind will always answer you if you trust it.

HIS SUBCONSCIOUS REVEALED THE LOCATION OF HIS FATHER'S WILL

Hugo R. was a young man who attended my lectures in Los Angeles. He told me of his experience with the power of the subconscious mind. His father had died suddenly, apparently leaving no will. However, his sister told him that their father had once mentioned making his will and told her that he had done his best to make it fair to everyone.

Hugo realized that if his late father were ruled to have died intestate (without a will), the property would be divided up according to rules made by the state. It was not likely that this would fit their father's desires. Moreover, legal fees would consume much of the estate. He and his sister looked everywhere, but they could not locate the will. They began to wonder whether the will existed at all.

Then Hugo remembered what he had learned about using the subconscious mind. Before going to sleep, he talked to his deeper mind, saying, "I now turn this request over to the subconscious mind. It knows where my father's will is and reveals it to me." Then he condensed his request down to one word, "Answer." He repeated it over and over again, like a lullaby. He went to sleep with the word "Answer" echoing in his mind.

The next morning, he woke up with a tremendous urge

to visit a certain bank in downtown Los Angeles. He wondered about this. Had he heard his father mention it once? Had he noticed a letter from the bank in his father's mail? He didn't know, but he did know that he had to check out this hunch. He went to the bank that morning. Eventually, a bank officer confirmed that there was a safe-deposit box in the vault registered in the name of his late father. When the box was opened, the missing will was discovered inside.

Your thought, as you go to sleep, arouses the powerful latency that is within you. Suppose you are wondering if you should sell your home, buy a certain stock, sever a partnership, move to New York or stay in Los Angeles, dissolve the present contract or take a new one. Do this: Sit quietly in your armchair or at the desk in your office. Remember that there is a universal law of action and reaction. The action is your thought. The reaction is the response from your subconscious mind. The subconscious mind is reactive and reflexive; that is its nature. It rebounds, rewards, and repays. It follows the law of correspondence. It responds by corresponding. As you contemplate right action, you will automatically experience a reaction or response in yourself that represents the guidance or answer of your subconscious mind.

In seeking guidance, you simply think quietly about right action. This means that you are using the infinite intelligence resident in the subconscious mind to the point where it begins to use you. From there on, your course of action is directed and controlled by the subjective wisdom within you, which is all-wise and omnipotent. Your decision will be right. There will be only right action because you are under a subjective compulsion to do the right thing. I use the word *compulsion* because the law of the subconscious is compulsion.

THE SECRET OF GUIDANCE

The secret of guidance or right action is to mentally devote yourself to the right answer until you find its response in you. The response is a feeling, an inner awareness, an overpowering hunch whereby you know that you know. You have used the power to the point where it begins to use you. You cannot possibly fail or make one false step while operating under the subjective wisdom within you. You will find that all your ways are pleasantness and all your paths are peace.

HIGHLIGHTS TO RECALL

1. Remember that the subconscious mind has determined the success and wonderful achievements of all great scientific workers.

2. By giving your conscious attention and devotion to the solution of a perplexing problem, your subconscious mind gathers all the necessary information and presents it full-blown to the conscious mind.

3. If you are wondering about the answer to a problem, try to solve it objectively. Get all the information you can from research and also from others. If no answer comes, turn it over to your subconscious mind prior to sleep, and the answer always comes. It never fails.

4. You do not always get the answer overnight. Keep on turning your request over to your subconscious until the day breaks and the shadows flee away.

5. You delay the answer by thinking it will take a long time or that it is a major problem. Your subconscious has no problem, it knows only the answer.

6. Believe that you have the answer now. Feel the joy of the answer and the way you would feel if you had the perfect answer. Your subconscious will respond to your feeling.

7. Any mental picture, backed by faith and perseverance, will come to pass through the miracle-working power of your subconscious. Trust it, believe in its power, and wonders will happen as you pray.

8. Your subconscious is the storehouse of memory, and within your subconscious are recorded all your experiences since childhood.

9. Scientists meditating on ancient scrolls, temples, fossils, and other evidence are able to reconstruct scenes of the past and make them alive today. Their subconscious mind comes to their aid.

10. Turn over your request for a solution to your subconscious prior to sleep. Trust it and believe in it, and the answer will come. It knows all and sees all, but you must not doubt or question its powers.

11. The action is your thought, and the reaction is the response of your subconscious mind. If your thoughts are wise, your actions and decisions will be wise.

12. Guidance comes as a feeling, an inner awareness, an overpowering hunch whereby you know that you know. It is an inner sense of touch. Follow it with the simplicity of faith.

13
Your Subconscious and the Wonders of Sleep

You spend about eight out of every twenty-four hours, or one third of your entire life, in sleep. This is an inexorable law of life. Sleep is a divine law, and many answers to our problems come to us when we are sound asleep.

Many people have advocated the theory that you get tired during the day, that you go to sleep to rest the body, and that a reparative process takes place while you sleep. This is a gross misunderstanding. *Nothing* rests in sleep. Your heart, lungs, and all your vital organs function while you are asleep. If you eat prior to sleep, the food is digested and assimilated. Your skin secretes perspiration. Your nails and hair continue to grow.

In the same way, your subconscious mind never rests or sleeps. It is always active, controlling all your vital forces. The healing process takes place more rapidly while you are asleep, because there is no interference from your conscious mind. Remarkable answers are given to you while you are asleep.

WHY WE SLEEP

One of the earliest scientific researchers to carry out serious investigations into sleep was Dr. John Bigelow. He was able to show that at night, while asleep, you receive constant impressions through the sensory nerves connected to the eyes, ears, nose, and subcutaneous nerves. The neural network of the brain is also quite active.

Dr. Bigelow's research led him to a conclusion that is closely aligned with the information presented in this book. He said that the main reason we sleep is in order that "the nobler part of the soul is united by abstraction to our higher nature and becomes a participant in the wisdom and foreknowledge of the gods."

PRAYER, A FORM OF SLEEP

Throughout the day, your conscious mind gets involved with vexations, strife, and contentions. It needs to be able to withdraw periodically from sense evidence and the objective world and commune silently with the inner wisdom of your subconscious mind. By claiming guidance, strength, and greater intelligence in all phases of your life, you will be enabled to overcome all difficulties and solve your daily problems.

This regular withdrawal from sense evidence and the noise and confusion of everyday living is also a form of sleep. That is, you become asleep to the world of the senses and alive to the wisdom and power of your subconscious mind.

STARTLING EFFECTS OF SLEEP DEPRIVATION

Lack of sleep can cause you to become irritable, moody, and depressed. All human beings need a minimum of six hours' sleep to be healthy. Most people need more. Those who think they can get along on less are fooling themselves.

Medical researchers who have investigated sleep processes and deprivation of sleep point out that severe insomnia has preceded psychotic breakdown in some instances.

Remember, you are spiritually recharged during sleep. Adequate sleep is essential to produce joy and vitality in life.

YOU NEED MORE SLEEP

One way to find out why we need sleep is to look at what happens when we do not get it. In 1964, a seventeen-year-old boy named Randy Gardner set out to win a place in the *Guinness Book of World Records*. He kept himself awake for 264 hours—eleven straight days! Later tests showed that he had suffered no permanent damage. However, during the time he was keeping himself awake, his thinking processes deteriorated. His speech became slurred. He suffered from memory lapses. In the later hours, he started to experience hallucinations.

Most people who are chronically short on sleep do not go to such extremes. However, they too may suffer from serious effects. According to the National Highway Traffic Safety Administration, as many as 200,000 traffic accidents a year are related to sleep problems. One driver in five has at least occasionally dozed off at the wheel. As a result, drivers are five to ten times more likely to have an accident late at night than during the daytime.

Experiments with volunteers have shown that a tired brain craves sleep so hungrily that it will sacrifice anything to get it. After only a few hours of sleep loss, subjects start experiencing fleeting naps called "lapses" or microsleep. These happen three or four times an hour. During them, just as in "real" sleep, the person's eyelids close and his or her brain waves become slower.

At first, each of these lapses lasts just a fraction of a second, but as hours of sleep loss mount, the lapses take place more often and last longer, for as much as two or three seconds. Even if the subjects had been piloting an airliner in a thunderstorm, they still couldn't have resisted microsleeps for those few priceless seconds.

SLEEP BRINGS COUNSEL

Sandra F. is a young woman in Los Angeles who has often listened to my radio talks. She told me that she had been offered a position in New York City at twice her present salary. She could not decide whether or not to accept the new job. Before going to sleep, she prayed in these words:

> The creative intelligence of my subconscious mind knows what is best for me. Its tendency is always lifeward, and it reveals to me the right decision, which blesses me and all concerned. I give thanks for the answer that I know will come to me.

She repeated this simple prayer over and over as a lullaby as she drifted to sleep. In the morning, she had a persistent feeling that she should not accept the offer. She rejected it. Later events verified her inward sense of knowing. A few months after the job offer, the company went bankrupt.

The conscious mind may be correct on the objectively known facts. However, it was the intuitive faculty of the subconscious mind that realized the problems with the company and prompted her accordingly.

SAVED FROM CERTAIN DISASTER

The wisdom of your subconscious mind can instruct you and protect you, if you pray for right action as you go to sleep.

Many years ago, I was offered a lucrative assignment in the Far East. I prayed for guidance and the right decision as follows:

> Infinite intelligence within me knows all things. The right decision is revealed to me in divine order. I will recognize the answer when it comes.

I repeated this simple prayer over and over as a lullaby prior to sleep. That night, I had a dream in which an old friend came to me. He held out a newspaper and said, "Read these headlines! Do not go!" The headlines of the newspaper trumpeted stories of violence, unrest, and war—all of which occurred not long afterward in the area where I had been asked to go.

Your subconscious mind is all-wise. It knows all things. Often it will speak to you, but in a voice that your conscious mind will immediately accept. In the dream I just related, which doubtless saved me from putting myself in a situation of grave danger, my subconscious mind projected its warning in the guise of a person whom I trusted and respected.

To some, a warning may come in the form of a mother who appears in a dream. She tells the person not to go here or there, and the reason for the warning. Sometimes your subconscious will warn you in your waking hours. You think you hear a voice that sounds like that of your mother or some loved one. You stop and turn, looking for its source. Later you find that if you had gone on the way you were going, you might have been struck on the head by an object falling from a window.

YOUR FUTURE IS IN YOUR SUBCONSCIOUS MIND

Remember that because your future is the result of your habitual thinking, it is already in your mind unless you change it through prayer. In the same way, the future of a country is in the collective subconscious of the people of that nation. There is nothing strange in the dream I had wherein I saw the headlines of the newspapers long before the events they spoke of. Those events had already taken place in the minds of those who would bring them about. All their plans were already engraved on that great recording instrument, the collective subconscious of the universal mind. Tomorrow's events are in your subconscious mind. So are next week's and next month's. They may be perceived by a highly psychic or clairvoyant person.

No disaster or tragedy can happen to you if you decide to pray. Nothing is predetermined or foreordained. Your mental attitude—the way you think, feel, and believe—determines your destiny. You can, through scientific prayer, mold, fashion, and create your own future. *Whatsoever a man soweth, that shall he also reap.*

A CAT NAP NETS HIM $15,000

Years ago, one of my students mailed me a newspaper clipping about a man named Ray Hammerstrom who worked as a roller in a Pittsburgh steel mill. The mill had recently installed a new machine that controlled the delivery of newly forged steel bars to what were called cooling beds. Despite the best efforts of the installers, the machine could not be made to work properly. Engineers worked on it for several days, but to no avail.

Hammerstrom thought a lot about the problem. He tried to figure out a new design that might work. Nothing came to him. One afternoon he lay down for a nap. As he fell asleep, he thought about the switch problem. During his nap, he had a dream in which he saw a perfect design for the faulty switch. When he awoke, he sketched his new design according to the outline of his dream.

This visionary cat nap won Hammerstrom a check for

$15,000, the largest award the firm had ever given an employee for a new idea.

HOW A PROFESSOR SOLVED HIS PROBLEM IN SLEEP

Dr. H. V. Helprecht was an eminent professor of Assyrian at the University of Pennsylvania. In his memoirs, he recounted an amazing experience.

> One Saturday evening I had been wearying myself, in the vain attempt to decipher two small fragments of agate which were supposed to belong to the finger rings of some Babylonians.
>
> About midnight, weary and exhausted, I went to bed and dreamed the following remarkable dream: A tall, thin priest of Nippur, about forty years of age, led me to the treasure chamber of the temple . . . a small, low-ceilinged room without windows, while scraps of agate and lapis-lazuli lay scattered on the floor. Here he addressed me as follows: "The two fragments which you have published separately on pages 22 and 26 belong together, are not finger rings. The first two rings served as earrings for the statue of the god; the two fragments [you have] are the portions of them. If you will put them together you will have confirmation of my words." . . . I awoke at once . . . I examined the fragments . . . and to my astonishment found the dream verified. The problem was then at last solved.

This demonstrates clearly the creative manifestation of his subconscious mind, which knew the answer to all his problems.

HOW THE SUBCONSCIOUS WORKED FOR A FAMOUS WRITER WHILE HE SLEPT

In one of his books, *Across the Plains*, Robert Louis Stevenson devotes a whole chapter to the topic of dreams. He was a vivid dreamer. It was his persistent habit to give specific instructions to his subconscious every night prior to sleep. He would request his subconscious to evolve stories for him while he slept. For example, if his bank account was low, his command to his subconscious would be something like this: "Give me a good thrilling novel that will be marketable and profitable." His subconscious responded magnificently.

Stevenson recounts,

> These little brownies [the intelligences and powers of his subconscious] can tell me a story piece by piece, like a serial, and keep me, its supposed creator, all the while in total ignorance of where they aim.
>
> That part of my work which is done when I am up and about [while he is consciously aware and awake] is by no means necessarily mine, since all goes to show that the brownies have a hand in it even then.

SLEEP IN PEACE AND WAKE IN JOY

If you suffer from insomnia, you will find the following prayer very effective. Repeat it slowly, quietly, and lovingly prior to sleep.

> My toes are relaxed, my ankles are relaxed, my abdominal muscles are relaxed, my heart and lungs are relaxed, my hands and arms are relaxed, my neck is relaxed, my brain is relaxed, my face is relaxed, my eyes are relaxed, my whole mind and body are relaxed.

I fully and freely forgive everyone, and I sincerely wish for them harmony, health, peace, and all the blessings of life. I am at peace, I am poised, serene, and calm. I rest in security and in peace. A great stillness steals over me, and a great calm quiets my whole being as I realize the Divine Presence within me. I know that the realization of life and love heals me.

I wrap myself in the mantle of love and fall asleep filled with goodwill for all. Throughout the night peace remains with me, and in the morning I shall be filled with life and love. A circle of love is drawn around me. *I will fear no evil, for Thou art with me.* I sleep in peace, I wake in joy, and in *Him I live, move, and have my being.*

Summary of Your Aids to the Wonders of Sleep

1. If you are worried that you will not wake up on time, suggest to your subconscious mind prior to sleep the exact time you wish to arise and it will awaken you. It needs no clock. Do the same thing with all problems. There is nothing too hard for your subconscious.

2. Your subconscious never sleeps. It is always on the job. It controls all your vital functions. Forgive yourself and everyone else before you go to sleep and healing will take place much more rapidly.

3. Guidance is given you while you are asleep, sometimes in a dream. The healing currents are also released, and in the morning you feel refreshed and rejuvenated.

4. When troubled by the vexations and strife of the day, still the wheels of your mind and think about the wisdom and intelligence lodged in your subconscious

mind, which is ready to respond to you. This will give you peace, strength, and confidence.

5. Sleep is essential for peace of mind and health of body. Lack of sleep can cause irritation, depression, and mental disorders. You need eight hours' sleep.

6. Medical research scholars point out that insomnia sometimes precedes psychotic breakdowns.

7. You are spiritually recharged during sleep. Adequate sleep is essential for joy and vitality in life.

8. Your tired brain craves sleep so hungrily that it will sacrifice anything to get it. Many who have fallen asleep at the wheel of an automobile can testify to this.

9. Many sleep-deprived people have poor memories and lack proper coordination. They become befuddled, confused, and disorientated.

10. Sleep brings counsel. Prior to sleep, claim that the infinite intelligence of your subconscious mind is guiding and directing you. Then, watch for the lead that comes, perhaps on awakening.

11. Trust your subconscious completely. Know that its tendency is always lifeward. Occasionally, your subconscious answers you in a very vivid dream and a vision in the night. You can be forewarned in a dream in the same way as the author of this book was warned.

12. Your future is in your mind now, based on your habitual thinking and beliefs. Claim infinite intelligence leads and guides you and that all good is yours, and your future will be wonderful. Believe it and accept it. Expect the best, and invariably the best will come to you.

13. If you are writing a novel, play, or book, or are working on an invention, speak to your subconscious mind at

night and claim boldly that its wisdom, intelligence, and power are guiding, directing, and revealing to you the ideal play, novel, book or are revealing the perfect solution, whatever it may be. Wonders will happen as you pray this way.

14
Your Subconscious Mind and Marital Problems

All marital trouble is caused by a failure to properly understand the functions and powers of the mind. Friction between husband and wife will disappear when each partner uses the law of mind correctly. By praying together they stay together. The contemplation of divine ideals, the study of the laws of life, the mutual agreement on a common purpose and plan, and the enjoyment of personal freedom bring about that harmonious marriage, that wedded bliss, that sense of oneness where the two become one.

The best time to prevent divorce is before marriage. There is nothing wrong with deciding to get out of a very bad situation. But why get into the bad situation in the first place? Would it not be better to give attention to the real cause of marital problems, to really get at the root of the matter in the first place?

The problems of marital unhappiness, discord, separation, and divorce are no different from all other problems of men and women. They can be traced directly to a lack of knowledge of the working and interrelationship of the conscious and subconscious mind.

THE MEANING OF MARRIAGE

To be genuine, a marriage must begin on a sound spiritual basis. It must be of the heart, and the heart is the chalice of love. Honesty, sincerity, kindness, and integrity are all aspects of love. Each partner should be perfectly honest and sincere with the other. It is not a true marriage when a man marries a woman to lift his ego or because he wants to share her money or social position. This indicates a lack of sincerity, honesty, and true love. Such a marriage is a farce, a sham, and a masquerade.

If a woman says, "I am tired of working. I want to get married because I want security," her major premise is false. She is not using the laws of mind correctly. Her security depends upon her knowledge of the interaction of the conscious and subconscious mind and its application.

A woman (or a man) will never lack for wealth or health if she applies the techniques outlined in the chapters of this book. Her wealth can come to her independent of her husband, parents, or anyone else. A woman is not dependent on her husband for health, peace, joy, inspiration, guidance, love, wealth, security, happiness, or anything in the world. Her security and peace of mind come from her knowledge of the powers within her and from the constant use of the laws of her own mind in a constructive fashion.

HOW TO ATTRACT THE IDEAL HUSBAND

If you have studied the chapters that precede this one, you are now acquainted with the way your subconscious mind works. You know that whatever you impress upon it will be experienced in your world. Begin now to impress your subconscious mind with the qualities and characteristics you desire in a man.

The following is an excellent technique: Sit down at night in your armchair, close your eyes, let go, relax the body, become very quiet, passive, and receptive. Talk to your subconscious mind and say to it,

> I am now attracting a man into my experience who is honest, sincere, loyal, faithful, peaceful, happy, and prosperous. These qualities that I admire are sinking down into my subconscious mind now. As I dwell upon these characteristics, they become a part of me and are embodied subconsciously.
>
> I know there is an irresistible law of attraction and that I attract to me a man according to my subconscious belief. I attract that which I feel to be true in my subconscious mind.
>
> I know I can contribute to his peace and happiness. He loves my ideals, and I love his ideals. He does not want to make me over; neither do I want to make him over. There is mutual love, freedom, and respect.

Practice this process of impregnating your subconscious mind. Then, you will have the joy of attracting to you a man possessing the qualities and characteristics you mentally dwelt upon. Your subconscious intelligence will open up a pathway, whereby both of you will meet, according to the irresistible and changeless flow of your own subconscious mind. Have a keen desire to give the best that is in you of love, devotion, and cooperation. Be receptive to this gift of love which you have given to your subconscious mind.

HOW TO ATTRACT THE IDEAL WIFE

To draw to yourself the life partner that you seek, affirm as follows:

I now attract the right woman who is in complete accord with me. This is a spiritual union because it is divine love functioning through the personality of someone with whom I blend perfectly. I know I can give to this woman love, light, peace, and joy. I feel and believe I can make this woman's life full, complete, and wonderful.

I now decree that she possesses the following qualities and attributes: She is spiritual, loyal, faithful, and true. She is harmonious, peaceful, and happy. We are irresistibly attracted to each other. Only that which belongs to love, truth, and beauty can enter my experience. I accept my ideal companion now.

As you think quietly and with deep interest on the qualities and attributes that you admire in the companion you seek, you will build the mental equivalent into your mentality. Then, the deeper currents of your subconscious mind will bring both of you together in divine order.

NO NEED FOR THIRD MISTAKE

Recently Sheila B., a woman with many years of experience as an administrator, said to me, "I have had three husbands and all three have been passive and submissive. They all depended on me to make all decisions and govern everything. Why do I attract such men?"

I asked her if she had known before getting married the second time that her prospective husband had a similar character to her first husband.

"Of course not," she said emphatically. "If I had known he was such a milquetoast, I wouldn't have had anything to do with him. And the same goes for my third."

Sheila's trouble did not lie with the men she married. It was a result of her own personality make-up. She was a very assertive person with a strong need to stay in control of every situation she found herself in. On one level she wanted a partner who would be submissive and passive so that she could play the dominant role.

At the same time, her deeper need was for a partner who would be her equal. Her subconscious picture attracted to her the sort of man that she subjectively wanted, but once she found one, she discovered that he did not meet her real needs. She had to learn to break this pattern by adopting the right prayer process.

HOW SHE BROKE THE NEGATIVE PATTERN

Sheila B. finally learned a simple truth. When you believe you can have the type of partner you idealize, it is done unto you as you believe.

To break the old subconscious pattern and attract to herself the ideal mate, Sheila used the following prayer:

> I am building into my mentality the type of man I deeply desire. The man I attract for a husband is strong, powerful, loving, successful, honest, loyal, and faithful. He finds love and happiness with me. I love to follow where he leads.
>
> I know he wants me, and I want him. I am honest, sincere, loving, and kind. I have wonderful gifts to offer him. They are goodwill, a joyous heart, and a healthy body. He offers me the same. It is mutual. I give and I receive.
>
> Divine intelligence knows where this man is, and the

deeper wisdom of my subconscious mind is now bringing both of us together in its own way, and we recognize each other immediately. I release this request to my subconscious mind which knows how to bring my request to pass. I give thanks for the perfect answer.

She prayed in this way every day, first thing in the morning and last thing before going to sleep. She affirmed these truths in the confident knowledge that through frequent occupation of the mind she would reach the mental equivalent of what she sought.

THE ANSWER TO HER PRAYER

Several months went by. Sheila had a number of dates and social engagements, but none of the men she met was what she was looking for. She began to wonder if her quest was hopeless. She found herself starting to question, waiver, doubt, and vacillate. At that point, she reminded herself that the infinite intelligence was bringing it to pass in its own way. There was nothing to be concerned about. When she received the final decree in her divorce proceedings, it brought her a great sense of release and mental freedom.

Soon afterward, she took a new position as head administrator in a medical group practice. The first day she was on the job, one of the senior physicians came by her office to introduce himself. He had been out of town at a medical conference the day she had interviewed for the position.

The minute he walked in, she knew he was the man she was praying for. Apparently he knew it, too. He proposed to her before a month had passed. Their subsequent marriage was ideally happy. This physician was not the passive or submissive type. He was strong, confident, and decisive. Well respected in his field, a former college athlete, he was also a deeply spiritual man.

Sheila got what she prayed for because she claimed it mentally until she reached the point of saturation. In other words, she mentally and emotionally united with her idea, and it became a part of her.

SHOULD I GET A DIVORCE?

Divorce is very much an individual question. There cannot be a general answer that is valid for everyone. In some cases, of course, there should never have been a marriage in the first place. In other cases, divorce is not a solution. Divorce may be right for one person and wrong for another. A person who is divorced may be far more sincere and noble than many married people who are perhaps living a lie.

For example, I was once consulted by a woman whose husband beat her and stole from her to support a drug habit. She had been brought up to believe that marriage is sacred and forever and that consequently divorce is immoral. I explained to her that true marriage is of the heart. If two hearts blend harmoniously, lovingly, and sincerely, that is the ideal marriage. The pure action of the heart is love.

Following this explanation she knew what to do. She knew in her heart that there is no divine law that compelled her to be browbeaten, intimidated, and beaten, simply because someone once said, "I pronounce you man and wife."

If you are in doubt as to what to do, ask for guidance. Know that there is always an answer and that you will receive it. Follow the lead that comes to you in the silence of your soul. It speaks to you in peace.

DRIFTING INTO DIVORCE

I once spoke with a young couple who had been married for only a few months but were already seeking a divorce. I discovered that the young man had a constant fear that his wife would leave him. He expected rejection and believed that she would be unfaithful to him. These thoughts haunted his mind and became an obsession with him.

His mental attitude was one of separation and suspicion. She felt unresponsive to him, but this was a result of his own feeling. The atmosphere of separation operating through his subconscious mind brought about a condition or action in accordance with the mental pattern behind it. There is a law of action and reaction, or cause and effect. The thought is the action, and the response of the subconscious mind is the reaction.

His wife left home and asked for a divorce—exactly what he had feared and believed she would do.

DIVORCE BEGINS IN THE MIND

Divorce takes place first in the mind; the legal proceedings follow after. These two young people were full of resentment, fear, suspicion, and anger. These attitudes weaken, exhaust, and debilitate the whole being. They learned that hate divides and that love unites. They began to realize what they had been doing with their minds. Neither of them knew the law of mental action. They were misusing their minds and bringing chaos and misery on themselves.

At my suggestion, this couple got back together and experimented with prayer therapy. They began to radiate love, peace, and goodwill to each other. Each one practiced radiating harmony, health, peace, and love to the other, and they alternated in the reading of the Psalms every night. As a result of this sincere effort on their part, and the impregnation of their subconscious minds with beneficial impulses, their marriage is growing more beautiful every day.

THE NAGGING WIFE

Many times the reason a wife nags is because she gets no attention. Her legitimate craving for love and affection expresses itself in a way that pushes her partner farther away. Give your wife attention, and show your appreciation. Praise and exalt all her many good points.

Another type of nagging reflects a desire to make the partner conform to a particular pattern. There are few quicker ways to drive a partner away. Wives and husbands must be on their guard not to be scavengers, always looking for petty faults or errors in each other. Let each give attention and praise for the constructive and wonderful qualities in the other.

THE BROODING HUSBAND

If a man begins to brood or grows morbid against his wife because of things she said or did, he is, psychologically speaking, committing adultery. One of the meanings of adultery is idolatry, which means giving attention to or uniting mentally with that which is negative and destructive. When a man is silently resenting his wife and is full of hostility toward her, he is unfaithful. He is not faithful to his marriage vows, which are to love, cherish, and honor her all the days of his life.

The man who is brooding, bitter, and resentful can swallow his sharp remarks, abate his anger, and go to great lengths to be considerate, kind, and courteous. He can deftly skirt the differences. Through praise and mental effort, he can get out of the habit of antagonism. As he soaks his subconscious mind with thoughts of peace, harmony, and love, he will find that he gets along better not only with his wife, but with everyone in his life. Assume the harmonious state, and eventually you will find peace and harmony.

THE GREAT MISTAKE

It is a great mistake to discuss your marital problems or difficulties with neighbors and relatives. Suppose, for example, a wife tells a neighbor, "John treats my mother abominably, drinks to excess, and is constantly abusive and insulting."

This wife is degrading and belittling her husband in the eyes of everyone she speaks to. Moreover, as she discusses and dwells upon the shortcomings of her husband, she is actually creating these states within herself. Who is thinking and feeling it? She is! And as you think and feel, so are you.

Relatives will usually give you the wrong advice. It is usually biased and prejudiced because it is not given in an impersonal way. Any advice you receive which violates the golden rule, which is a cosmic law, is not good or sound.

It is well to remember that no two human beings ever lived beneath the same roof without clashes of temperament, periods of hurt, and strain. Never display the unhappy side of your marriage to your friends. Keep your quarrels to yourself. Refrain from criticism and condemnation of your parmer.

DON'T TRY TO REMAKE YOUR PARTNER

Husbands and wives must not try to make their partners over into a second edition of themselves. The tactless attempt to change them is an affront, a statement that they are not worthy in themselves. These attempts are always foolish and many times lead to the destruction of the marriage. Attempting to alter someone destroys pride and self-esteem and arouses a spirit of contrariness and resentment that can prove fatal to the marriage bond.

Adjustments are needed, of course. None of us is perfect, and that holds for marriage partners as well. But if you have a good look inside your own mind and study your character and behavior, you will find enough shortcomings to keep you busy the rest of your life. If you think, "I will make him or her over into what I want," you are looking for trouble and the divorce court. You are asking for misery. You will have to learn the hard way that there is no one to change but yourself.

PRAY TOGETHER AND STAY TOGETHER THROUGH STEPS IN PRAYER

The first step: Never carry over from one day to another accumulated irritations arising from little disappointments. Be sure to forgive each other for any sharpness before you retire at night. The moment you awaken in the morning, claim infinite intelligence is guiding you in all your ways. Send out loving thoughts of peace, harmony, and love to your marriage partner, to all members of the family, and to the whole world.

The second step: Say grace at breakfast. Give thanks for the wonderful food, for your abundance, and for all your blessings. Make sure that no problems, worries, or arguments shall enter into the table conversation; the same applies at dinnertime. Say to your wife or husband, "I appreciate all you are doing, and I radiate love and goodwill to you all day long."

The third step: The husband and wife should alternate in praying each night. Do not take your marriage partner for granted. Show your appreciation and love. Think appreciation and goodwill, rather than condemnation, criticism, and nagging. The way to build a peaceful home and a happy marriage is to use a foundation of love, beauty, harmony, mutual respect, faith in God, and all things good. Read the 23rd,

27th, and 91st Psalms, the 11th chapter of Hebrews, the 13th chapter of I Corinthians, and other great texts of the Bible before going to sleep. As you practice these truths, your marriage will grow more and more blessed through the years.

REVIEW YOUR ACTIONS

1. Ignorance of mental and spiritual laws is the cause of all marital unhappiness. By praying scientifically together, you stay together.

2. The best time to prevent divorce is before marriage. If you learn how to pray in the right way, you will attract the right mate for you.

3. Marriage is the union of a man and woman who are bound together by love. Their hearts beat as one, and they move onward, upward, and Godward.

4. Marriage does not guarantee happiness. People find happiness by dwelling on the eternal truths of God and the spiritual values of life. Then, the man and woman can contribute to each other's happiness and joy.

5. You attract the right mate by dwelling on the qualities and characteristics you admire in a woman or a man. Then your subconscious mind will bring you together in divine order.

6. You must build into your mentality the mental equivalent of what you want in a marriage partner. If you want to attract an honest, sincere, and loving partner in life, you must be honest, sincere, and loving yourself.

7. You do not have to repeat mistakes in marriage. When you really believe you can have the type of man or woman you idealize, it is done unto you as you believe. To believe is to accept something as true. Accept your ideal companion now mentally.

8. Do not wonder how, why, or where you will meet the mate you are praying for. Trust implicitly the wisdom of your subconscious mind. It has the power to carry out its mission. You don't have to assist it.

9. You are mentally divorced when you indulge in peeves, grudges, ill will, and hostility toward your marriage.partner. You are mentally dwelling with error in your mind. Adhere to your marriage vows, "I promise to cherish, love, and honor him (or her) all the days of my life."

10. Cease projecting fear patterns to your marriage partner. Project love, peace, harmony, and goodwill, and your marriage will grow more beautiful and more wonderful through the years.

11. Radiate love, peace, and goodwill to each other. These vibrations are picked up by the subconscious mind resulting in mutual trust, affection, and respect.

12. A nagging partner is usually seeking attention and appreciation. He or she is craving love and affection. Praise and exalt their many good points. Show them that you love and appreciate them.

13. Partners who love each other do not do anything unloving or unkind in word, manner, or action. Love is what love does.

14. In marital problems, always seek expert advice. You would not go to a carpenter to pull a tooth; neither should you discuss your marriage problems with relatives or friends. If you need counsel, go to a trained person.

15. Never try to make over your wife or husband. These attempts are always foolish and tend to destroy the pride and self-esteem of the other. Moreover, they arouse a spirit of resentment that can prove fatal to the marriage bond. Cease trying to make the other a second edition of yourself.

16. Pray together and you will stay together. Scientific prayer solves all problems. Mentally picture your wife as she ought to be, joyous, happy, healthy, and beautiful. See your husband as he ought to be, strong, powerful, loving, harmonious, and kind. Maintain this mental picture, and you will experience the marriage made in heaven, which is harmony and peace.

15

Your Subconscious Mind and Your Happiness

William James, father of American psychology, said that the greatest discovery of the nineteenth century was not in the realm of physical science. The greatest discovery was the power of the subconscious touched by faith. In every human being is that limitless reservoir of power that can overcome any problem in the world.

True and lasting happiness will come into your life the day you get the clear realization that you can overcome any weakness—the day you realize that your subconscious can solve your problems, heal your body, and prosper you beyond your fondest dream.

You may have been very happy when you became engaged to the partner of your dreams. You may have felt happy when you graduated from college, when you got married, when your child was born, or when you won a great victory or a prize. You could go on and list other experiences that have made you happy. However, no matter how marvelous these experiences are, they do not give real lasting happiness. They are transitory.

The Book of Proverbs gives the answer: *Whosoever trusteth in the Lord, happy is he.* When you trust in the Lord (the power and wisdom of your subconscious mind) to lead, guide, govern, and direct all your ways, you will become poised, serene, and relaxed. As you radiate love, peace, and goodwill to all, you are really building a superstructure of happiness for all the days of your life.

YOU MUST CHOOSE HAPPINESS

Happiness is a state of mind. There is a phrase in the Bible that says, *Choose ye this day whom ye will serve.* You have the freedom to choose happiness. This may seem extraordinarily simple, and it is. Perhaps this is why people stumble on the way to happiness; they do not see the simplicity of the key to happiness. The great things of life are simple, dynamic, and creative. They produce well-being and happiness.

St. Paul reveals to you how you can think your way into a life of dynamic power and happiness in these words:

> Finally, brethren, whatsoever things are true, whatsoever things are honest, whatsoever things are just, whatsoever things are pure, whatsoever things are lovely, whatsoever things are of good report; if there be any virtue, and if there be any praise, think on these things.
>
> *PHIL. 4:8*

HOW TO CHOOSE HAPPINESS

Begin now to choose happiness. This is how you do it: When you open your eyes in the morning, say to yourself,

> Divine order takes charge of my life today and every day. All things work together for good for me today. This is a new and wonderful day for me. There will never be another day like this one. I am divinely guided all day long, and whatever I do will prosper. Divine love

surrounds me, enfolds me, and enwraps me, and I go forth in peace.

Whenever my attention wanders away from that which is good and constructive, I will immediately bring it back to the contemplation of that which is lovely and of good report. I am a spiritual and mental magnet attracting to myself all things that bless and prosper me. I am going to be a wonderful success in all my undertakings today. I am definitely going to be happy all day long.

Start each day in this manner; then you will be choosing happiness, and you will be a radiant, joyous person.

HE MADE IT A HABIT TO BE HAPPY

A number of years ago, I stayed for about a week in a farmer's house in Connemarra on the west coast of Ireland. My host seemed always to be singing and whistling and was full of good humor. I asked him the secret of his happiness.

"Sure, it's a habit with me," he replied. "Every morning when I awaken and every night before I go to sleep, I bless my family, the crops, the cattle, and I thank God for the wonderful harvest."

This farmer had made a practice of this for over forty years. As you know, thoughts repeated regularly and systematically sink into the subconscious mind and become habitual. He discovered that happiness is a habit.

YOU MUST DESIRE TO BE HAPPY

There is one important point to remember about being happy. You must sincerely desire to be happy. There are people who have been depressed, dejected, and unhappy so long that were they suddenly made happy by some wonderful, good, joyous news, they would react like the woman who once said to me, "It is wrong to be so happy!" They have become so accustomed to the old mental patterns that they do not feel at home being happy. They long to return to their familiar depressed, unhappy state.

I knew an elderly woman in England who had arthritis for many years. She would pat herself on the knee and say, "My arthritis is bad today. I can't possibly go out. My arthritis keeps me miserable." As a result of her condition, this woman got a lot of attention from her son, daughter, and neighbors. She really wanted her arthritis. She enjoyed her "misery," as she called it. On the level of her subconscious mind, she did not really want to be happy.

I suggested a curative procedure to her. I wrote down some biblical verses and told her that if she gave attention to these truths, her mental attitude would undoubtedly change. Her faith and confidence would be restored to health. She was not interested. Like many people, she suffered from a peculiar mental, morbid streak. She enjoyed being miserable and sad, or at least she enjoyed the benefits her misery brought her.

WHY CHOOSE UNHAPPINESS?

Many people choose unhappiness without realizing that they are doing so. They do so by entertaining such ideas as these:

- Today is a black day; everything is going to go wrong.
- I am not going to succeed.
- Everyone is against me.
- Business is bad, and it is going to get worse.
- I'm always late.
- I never get the breaks.
- He can, but I can't.

If you have this attitude of mind the first thing in the morning, you will attract all these experiences to you, and you will be very unhappy.

Begin to realize that the world you live in is determined largely by what goes on in your mind. Marcus Aurelius, the great Roman philosopher and sage, said, "A man's life is what his thoughts make of it." The leading American philosopher of the nineteenth century, Ralph Waldo Emerson, said, "A man is what he thinks all day long." The thoughts you habitually entertain in your mind have the tendency to actualize themselves in physical conditions.

Make certain you do not indulge in negative thoughts, defeatist thoughts, or unkind, depressing thoughts. Recall frequently to your mind that you can experience nothing outside your own mentality.

IF I HAD A MILLION DOLLARS, THEN I'D BE HAPPY

Wealth in and of itself will not make you happy. On the other hand, it is not a deterrent to happiness. Today, many people try to buy happiness by buying things—a high-definition television, the latest car, expensive designer clothes, a house in the country. But happiness cannot be purchased or procured in that way.

The kingdom of happiness is in your thought and feeling. Too many people have the idea that it takes something artificial to produce happiness. Some say, "If I were elected mayor, made CEO of the corporation, featured on the society page of the paper, I would be happy."

The truth is that happiness is a mental and spiritual state. A promotion or external honor will not yield happiness. Your strength, joy, and happiness consist in finding out the law of divine order and right action lodged in your subconscious mind and applying these principles in all phases of your life.

HE FOUND HAPPINESS TO BE THE HARVEST OF A QUIET MIND

When I was lecturing in San Francisco some years ago, I was approached by a man who was very unhappy and dejected over the way his business was going. He was the general manager of a corporation. His heart was filled with resentment toward the vice president and the president of the company. He felt that their opposition to his ideas was leading the company in a terrible direction. Profits were declining, as was market share. The company's share price was also going down, which concerned him greatly because much of his compensation was in the form of stock options.

This is how he solved his business problem: The first thing each morning he affirmed quietly as follows:

> All those working in our corporation are honest, sincere, cooperative, faithful, and full of goodwill to all. They are mental and spiritual links in the chain of this corporation's growth, welfare, and prosperity. I radiate love, peace, and goodwill in my thoughts, words, and deeds to my two associates and to all those in the company.
>
> The president and the vice president of our company are divinely guided in all their undertakings. The infinite intelligence of my subconscious mind makes all decisions through me. There is only right action in all our business transactions and in our relationship with each other.
>
> I send the messengers of peace, love, and goodwill before me to the office. Peace and harmony reign supreme in the minds and hearts of all those in the company, including myself. I now go forth into a new day, full of faith, confidence, and trust.

This business executive repeated the preceding meditation slowly three times in the morning, feeling the truth of what he affirmed. When fearful or angry thoughts came into his mind during the day, he would say to himself, "Peace, harmony, and poise govern my mind at all times."

As he continued disciplining his mind in this manner, all the harmful thoughts ceased to come, and peace came into his mind. He reaped the harvest.

Subsequently, he wrote me to the effect that at the end of about two weeks of reordering his mind, the president and the vice president called him into the office, praised his operations and his new constructive ideas, and remarked how fortunate they were in having him as general manager. He was very happy in discovering that man finds happiness within himself.

THE BLOCK OR STUMP IS NOT REALLY THERE

Years ago a friend told me the story of a horse that had been frightened by a snake next to a stump on the road. From then on, every time the horse came to that same stump, he shied. The farmer dug the stump out, burned it, and leveled the road. It didn't help. For years afterward, every time the horse passed the place where the stump had been, he shied. The horse was shying at the *memory* of a stump.

There is no block to your happiness save in your own thought life and mental imagery. Are fear or worry holding you back? Fear is a thought in your mind. You can dig it up this moment by supplanting it with faith in success, achievement, and victory over all problems.

I knew a man whose business went bankrupt. He said to me, "I made mistakes, but I've learned a lot from them. I am going back into business, and I will be a tremendous success." He faced up to that stump in his mind. He did not whine or complain. Instead, he dug up the stump of failure. Through believing in his inner powers to back him up, he banished all fear thoughts and old depressions. Believe in yourself, and you will succeed and be happy.

THE HAPPIEST PEOPLE

The happiest person is the one who constantly brings forth and practices what is best in himself or herself. Happiness and virtue complement each other. Not only are the best the happiest, but the happiest are usually the best in the art of living life successfully. God is the highest and best in you. Express more of God's love, light, truth, and beauty, and you will become one of the happiest persons in the world today.

Epictetus, the Greek stoic philosopher, said,

> There is but one way to tranquility of mind and happiness; let this, therefore, be always ready at hand with thee, both when thou wakest early in the morning, and all the day long, and when thou goest late to sleep, to account no external things thine own, but commit all these to God.

SUMMARY OF STEPS TO HAPPINESS

1. William James said that the greatest discovery of the nineteenth century was the power of the subconscious mind touched by faith.

2. There is tremendous power within you. Happiness will come to you when you acquire a sublime confidence in this power. Then you will make your dreams come true.

3. You can rise victorious over any defeat and realize the cherished desires of your heart through the marvelous power of your subconscious mind. This is the meaning of *Whosoever trusteth in the Lord* [spiritual laws of the subconscious mind], *happy is he.*

4. You must choose happiness. Happiness is a habit. It is a good habit on which to ponder often.

Whatsoever things are true, whatsoever things are honest, whatsoever things are just, whatsoever things are pure, whatsoever things are lovely, whatsoever things are of good report; if there be any virtue, and if there be any praise, think on these things.

PHIL. 4:8

5. When you open your eyes in the morning, say to yourself, "I choose happiness today. I choose success today. I choose right action today. I choose love and goodwill for all today. I choose peace today." Pour life, love, and interest into this affirmation, and you have chosen happiness.

6. Give thanks for all your blessings several times a day. Furthermore, pray for the peace, happiness, and prosperity of the members of your family, your associates, and all people everywhere.

7. You must sincerely desire to be happy. Nothing is accomplished without desire. Desire is a wish with wings of imagination and faith. Imagine the fulfillment of your desire, feel its reality, and it will come to pass. Happiness comes in answered prayer.

8. By constantly dwelling on thoughts of fear, worry, anger, hate, and failure, you will become depressed and unhappy. Remember, your life is what your thoughts make of it.

9. You cannot buy happiness with all the money in the world. Some millionaires are happy, some are unhappy. Many people with little worldly wealth are happy, and some are unhappy. Some married people are happy, and some unhappy. Some single people are happy, and some are unhappy. The kingdom of happiness is in your thought and feeling.

10. Happiness is the harvest of a quiet mind. Anchor your thoughts on peace, poise, security, and divine guidance, and your mind will be productive of happiness.

11. There is no block to your happiness. External things are not causative. They are effects, not causes. Take your cue from the only creative principle within you. Your thought is cause, and a new cause produces a new effect. Choose happiness.

12. The happiest person is the one who brings forth the highest and the best in himself or herself. God is the highest and the best in him or her, for the kingdom of God is within.

16
Your Subconscious Mind and Harmonious Human Relations

A vital concept you have learned from studying this book is that your subconscious mind is like a recording machine that faithfully reproduces whatever you impress upon it. This is one of the reasons the Golden Rule is so central to creating and maintaining a harmonious balance in your relationships with others.

> All things whatsoever ye would that men should do unto you, do ye even so to them.
>
> *MATT. 7:12*

This lesson has both outer and inner meanings. The inner meaning concerns the connection between your conscious and subconscious mind. To paraphrase the Scripture:

- As you would want people to think about you, think you about them in like manner.
- As you would want people to feel about you, feel you also about them in like manner.
- As you would want people to act toward you, act you toward them in like manner.

For example, you may be polite and courteous to someone in your office, but when her back is turned, you are very critical and resentful toward her in your mind. Such negative thoughts are highly destructive to you. It is like taking poison. The negative energy you are generating robs you of vitality, enthusiasm, strength, guidance, and goodwill. As these negative thoughts and emotions sink into your subconscious, they cause all kinds of difficulties and maladies in your life.

THE MASTER KEY TO HAPPY RELATIONSHIPS WITH OTHERS

> Judge not, that ye be not judged. For with what judgment ye judge, ye shall be judged: and with what measure ye mete, it shall be measured to you again.
>
> *MATT 7:1–2*

The key to harmonious relations with others lies in the close study of these verses and the application of the inner truths they represent. To judge is to think, to arrive at a mental verdict or conclusion in your mind. The thought you have about the other person is *your* thought, because *you* are thinking it. Your thoughts are creative. Therefore, you actually create in your own experience what you think and feel about the other person. The suggestion you give to another, you give to yourself as well, because your mind is the creative medium.

This is why it is said, *For with what judgment ye judge, ye shall be judged.* This means that in applying standards and criteria to others, you create those standards and criteria in your subconscious, which then applies them to you. Once you know this law and understand the way your subconscious mind works, you will always be careful to think, feel, and act right toward others, for in doing so you are creating a situation of right action, feeling, and thought toward yourself.

And with what measure ye mete, it shall be measured to you again. The good you do for others comes back to you in like measure; and the evil you do returns to you by the law of your own mind. If someone cheats and deceives another, he is actually cheating and deceiving himself. His sense of guilt and mood of loss inevitably will attract loss to him in some way, at some time. His subconscious records his mental act and reacts according to the mental intention or motivation.

Your subconscious mind is impersonal and unchanging, neither considering persons nor respecting religious affiliations or institutions of any kind. It is neither compassionate nor vindictive. The way you think, feel, and act toward others returns at last upon yourself.

THE DAILY HEADLINES MADE HIM SICK

Begin now to observe yourself. Observe your reactions to people, conditions, and circumstances. Record them in a notebook for later study. How do you respond to the events and news of the day? It makes no difference if all the other people were wrong and you alone were right. If the news disturbs you, it is your evil because your negative emotions robbed you of peace and harmony.

A woman wrote me to ask for help with her husband. She explained that he went into a rage every time he read what certain columnists wrote in the newspaper. She added that this constant reaction of anger and suppressed rage on his part was very bad for his high blood pressure. His doctor had told him that he had to find some way to reduce his stress through emotional reconditioning.

I invited this man to come see me. I explained to him the way his mind functions. He understood that it was emotionally immature to get angry over an article in the newspaper, but he had not known the damage his anger was causing to his own mind and body.

He began to realize that he should give the columnist the freedom to express himself even if he disagreed with him politically, religiously, or in any other way. In the same manner, the columnist ought to give him the freedom to write a letter to the newspaper disagreeing with his published statements. He learned that he could disagree without being disagreeable. He awakened to the simple truth that it is never what some other person says or does that affects him. Rather, it is his own reaction to what is said or done that matters.

This explanation helped this man achieve a cure. He realized that with a little practice he could master his morning tantrums. His wife later told me that he eventually learned to laugh at what the columnists he so disliked had to say. He also learned to laugh at himself for reacting so strongly. The newspaper articles no longer have power to disturb, annoy, and irritate him. His hypertension is more under control as a result of his increased emotional poise and serenity.

I HATE WOMEN, BUT I LIKE MEN

Cynthia R. was an executive secretary with a large corporation. She came to me because she felt very bitter toward some of the women in her office. She believed they were gossiping and, as she said, spreading vicious lies about her. When I asked, she admitted that she had many problems in her relationships with other women. She said, "I hate women, but I like men."

As I continued to talk with her, I discovered that Cynthia spoke to the people she supervised in a very haughty, imperious, and irritable tone of voice. There was a certain pomposity in her way of speaking, and I could see where her tone of voice would affect some people unpleasantly. She did not realize this. For her, the important point was that her coworkers took delight in making things difficult for her.

If all the people in your office or factory annoy you, isn't it possible that this annoyance and turmoil may be due to some subconscious pattern or mental projection that is coming from you? We all know that a dog will react ferociously if you hate or fear dogs. Animals pick up your subconscious vibrations and react accordingly. Is it so outrageous to say that human beings are just as sensitive as dogs, cats, and other animals in this regard?

To this woman who hated women, I suggested a process of prayer. I explained to her that when she began to identify herself with spiritual values and commenced to affirm the truths of life, her hatred of women would completely disappear, along with the vocal patterns and mannerisms that communicated that hatred to others. She was surprised to learn that our emotions show up in our speech, actions, writings, and in all phases of our life.

As a result of our conversation, Cynthia stopped behaving in her typical resentful and angry way. She established a pattern of prayer that she practiced regularly, systematically, and conscientiously in the office.

This was the prayer she used with such success:

I think, speak, and act lovingly, quietly, and peacefully. I now radiate love, peace, tolerance, and kindliness to all those who criticized me and gossiped about me. I anchor my thoughts on peace, harmony, and goodwill to all.

Whenever I am about to react negatively, I say firmly to myself, "I think, speak, and act from the standpoint of the principle of harmony, health, and peace within myself."

Creative intelligence leads, rules, and guides me in all my ways.

The practice of this prayer transformed her life. She found that the atmosphere of criticism and annoyance in her workplace gradually disappeared. Her coworkers became friends and companions in life's journey. She discovered the truth, that we have no one to blame and no one to change but ourselves.

HIS INNER SPEECH HELD BACK HIS PROMOTION

One day Jim S., a sales representative, came to see me. He was deeply upset by the difficulties he had working with the sales manager of his organization. Jim had been with the company ten years without receiving any promotion or recognition of any kind. He showed me his sales figures. I could easily see that they were higher proportionately than those of the other sales representatives in the territory. His explanation was that the sales manager did not like him. He claimed that he was unjustly treated. At conferences the manager ridiculed his suggestions and at times was actively rude to him.

After discussing his situation in greater detail, I suggested to Jim that the cause was to a great degree within himself. His concept and belief about his superior bore witness to the reaction of this man. The measure we mete shall be measured to us again. Jim's mental measure or concept of the sales manager was that he was mean, prejudiced, and cantankerous. Jim was filled with bitterness and hostility toward the executive. On his way to work he conducted a vigorous conversation with himself filled with criticism, mental arguments, recriminations, and denunciations of his sales manager.

What Jim gave out mentally, he was inevitably bound to get back. By the end of our conversation, Jim realized that his inner speech was highly destructive. The intensity and force of his silent thoughts and emotions, the mental condemnation and vilification of the sales manager that he rehearsed entered into his own subconscious mind. This brought about the negative response from his boss, as well as creating other personal, physical, and emotional disorders.

At my urging, Jim began to pray frequently as follows:

> I am the only thinker in my universe. I am responsible for what I think about my boss. My sales manager is not responsible for the way I think about him. I refuse to give power to any person, place, or thing to annoy me or disturb me. I wish health, success, peace of mind, and happiness for my boss. I sincerely wish him well, and I know he is divinely guided in all his ways.

He repeated this prayer out loud slowly, quietly, and feelingly, knowing that his mind is like a garden and that whatever he plants in the garden will come forth like seeds after their kind.

I also taught him to practice visualization or mental imagery prior to sleep. He created a scenario in which his superior congratulated him on his fine work, praised his zeal and enthusiasm, and remarked on the wonderful response he obtained from customers. He felt the reality of all this. He felt his boss's handshake, heard the tone of his voice, and saw him smile. He made a real mental movie, dramatizing it to the best of his ability. Night after night he replayed this mental movie, knowing that his subconscious mind was the receptive medium on which his conscious imagery would be impressed.

Gradually, by a process of what we can think of as mental and spiritual osmosis, the impression was made on his subconscious mind. The expression automatically came forth. Jim's sales manager subsequently called him up to San Francisco, congratulated him, and gave him a promotion to division sales manager, with greatly increased responsibilities and a subtantial raise in salary. Once Jim changed his concept and estimate of his boss, his subconscious mind saw to it that his boss responded accordingly.

BECOMING EMOTIONALLY MATURE

What someone else says cannot really annoy or irritate you unless you *permit* it to disturb you. The only path by which another person can upset you is through your own thought. If you get angry, you have to go through four stages in your mind. You begin to think about what was said. You decide to get angry and generate an emotion of rage. Then you decide to act. Perhaps you talk back and react in kind. As you see, the thought, emotion, reaction, and action all take place in your own mind.

What does it mean to be emotionally mature? It means that you move beyond the natural, but childish, tendency to respond negatively to the criticism and resentment of others. No one likes to be criticized or belittled. However, we have the ability to choose how to react when it happens. The mature choice is to refrain from responding in a similarly negative way. Responding in kind means to descend to the level of belittling criticism and to become one with the negative atmosphere of the other. Identify yourself with your own aim in life. Do not permit any person, place, or thing to deflect you from your inner sense of peace, tranquillity, and radiant health.

THE MEANING OF LOVE IN HARMONIOUS HUMAN RELATIONS

Sigmund Freud, the founder of psychoanalysis and one of the most important figures in the history of psychology, said that unless the personality has love, it sickens and dies. Love includes understanding, goodwill, and respect for the divinity in the other person. The more love and goodwill you emanate and exude, the more comes back to you.

If you puncture someone else's ego and wound her estimate of herself, you cannot gain her goodwill. Recognize that everyone wants to be loved and appreciated. Everyone needs to feel important in the world. Realize that the other person is conscious of her true worth. Like yourself, she feels the dignity of being an expression of the one life-principle animating all people. As you do this consciously and knowingly, you build up the other person, and she returns your love and goodwill.

SHE HATED HER AUDIENCES

Marie C. had always dreamed of being an actress. She studied theater in college, then had the good fortune to be hired by an important regional theater company in a part of the country she did not know at all. The first time she performed with the company, the audience booed her. Dismayed and angry, she decided that the people of that region were stupid, ignorant, and backward. She hated them all. After a miserable time, she was dropped from the company. She moved back to the area where she had grown up, and left the stage to work as a waitress.

One day a friend invited her to go to a lecture in Town Hall in New York City. The topic was "How to Get Along with Ourselves." This lecture changed her life. She began to see that she had overreacted to her early experience with the regional company. She admitted to herself that the play she had been in that first time was not good and that, as a new member of the company, she had probably not been at her best. The fault did not lie with the people in the audience, but with the way she accepted their reaction, then turned it back on them in the form of negative energy.

Marie decided to return to the stage and to her lifelong dream of being an actress. She began to pray sincerely for the audience and for herself. She poured out love and goodwill every night before stepping onto the stage. She made it a habit to claim that the peace of God filled the hearts of all present and that all present were lifted up and inspired. During each performance she sent out love vibrations to the audience. Today, she has an important career in theater. She transmits her goodwill and esteem to others, and they return it in kind.

HANDLING DIFFICULT PEOPLE

It should not come as a surprise that some people in the world are difficult. They are twisted and distorted mentally. They are malconditioned. Many are mental delinquents who have become argumentative, uncooperative, cantankerous, cynical, and sour on life. They are sick psychologically. Their minds have become deformed and distorted, perhaps because of experiences they have had in the past.

What do you do when you have to deal with someone like this? The temptation is to turn their negative energy back on them in the form of dislike. But to do that, you first have to take their negativity into yourself, with all the bad effects that will have on your own being. Strive instead to "return good for evil." This creates an armor that keeps their difficult and unpleasant attitudes from affecting you, and your transmission of compassion and understanding will set in motion the process of changing them.

MISERY LOVES COMPANY

The hateful, frustrated, distorted, and twisted personality is out of tune with the infinite. The person resents those who are peaceful, happy, and joyous. Usually he criticizes, condemns, and vilifies those who have been very good and kind to him. His attitude is this: Why should they be so happy when I am so miserable? He wants to drag them down to his own level. The old saying is still true, that "misery loves company." Once you understand this, you remain unmoved, calm, and dispassionate.

A man named Bruce T. who attended my lectures in London told me of his experience with this process. He had become active in a volunteer organization that was concerned with beautifying the community where he lived. Most of the volunteers were genuinely interested in working on planting gardens, sprucing up rundown areas, and repairing dilapidated buildings. One member, however, opposed every measure that anyone suggested. More than that, he constantly attacked the motives of the others. He made the meetings of the group so unpleasant that attendance began to decline.

Some of the other members came to Bruce. They suggested that they band together and expel the grouch from the organization. He was about to go along with this plan when he realized that to do so would be to perpetuate the man's twisted attitudes within himself. Instead, he began to visualize the man changing into a pleasant, cooperative member of the group. Before each meeting, Bruce went into a quiet corner and repeated,

I think, speak, and act in true accord with the principle of harmony and peace within myself. All who bind themselves to the goals of our organization do so with kindness and purpose in divine order. There is no discord, no unpleasantness. Creative intelligence leads, rules, and guides us in all we do.

After several weeks, the man who had caused so much trouble proposed a new initiative. He presented it in such an agreeable and cooperative manner that he won the approval of everyone else in the organization, including those who had wanted to kick him out.

THE PRACTICE OF EMPATHY IN HUMAN RELATIONS

A young woman named Alice O. visited me recently. She told me that she had long hated another young woman in the office where she worked. Her reason was that the other woman was prettier, happier, and more prosperous than she. The crowning blow came when the other woman became engaged to marry the CEO of the company, whom Alice had long admired.

One day after the marriage took place, the woman she so disliked came into work with her daughter from a previous marriage. Alice had not known her coworker had a child or even that she had been married before. Because of a congenital problem, the woman's daughter wore a steel leg brace. Alice overheard her say to her mother, "Mommy, is this where my new daddy works too? I love this place, because it is so full of people I love."

"My heart suddenly went out to that little girl," Alice told me. "I knew how happy she must feel. I got a vision of how happy this woman was, against odds I had not even known about. All of a sudden I felt love for her. I went into her office and wished her all the happiness in the world. And I meant it."

In that moment, Alice experienced what psychologists call *empathy*. This is not the same thing as sympathy, in which we understand the feelings of others. It is more. It means imaginatively projecting yourself into the mental attitudes and states of the other person. When Alice projected her mental mood or the feeling of her heart into that of the other woman, it was as if she began to think through the other woman's experience. She was thinking and feeling as the other woman, and also as the child, because she had also projected herself into the mind of the child.

Any time you feel tempted to injure or think ill of another, project yourself mentally into the mind of Moses and think from the standpoint of the Ten Commandments. If you are prone to be envious, jealous, or angry, project yourself into the mind of Jesus and think from that standpoint, and you will feel the truth of the words *Love ye one another*.

APPEASEMENT NEVER WINS

Do not permit people to take advantage of you and gain their point by temper tantrums, crying jags, or other forms of emotional blackmail. These people are dictators who try to enslave you and make you do their bidding. Be firm but kind, and refuse to yield. Appeasement never wins. Refuse to contribute to their delinquency, selfishness, and possessiveness. Remember, do that which is right. You are here to fulfill your ideal and remain true to the eternal verities and spiritual values of life, which are eternal.

Give no one in all the world the power to deflect you from your goal, your aim in life, which is to express your hidden talents to the world, to serve humanity, and to reveal more and more of God's wisdom, truth, and beauty to all people in the world. Remain true to your ideal. Know definitely and absolutely that whatever contributes to your peace, happiness, and fulfillment must of necessity bless all people who walk the earth. The harmony of the part is the harmony of the whole; for the whole is in the part, and the part is in the whole. All you owe the other, as Paul says, is love, and love is the fulfilling of the law of health, happiness, and peace of mind.

PROFITABLE POINTERS IN HUMAN RELATIONS

1. Your subconscious mind is a recording machine that reproduces your habitual thinking. Think good of the other, and you are actually thinking good about yourself.
2. A hateful or resentful thought is a mental poison. Do not think ill of another for to do so is to think ill of yourself. You are the only thinker in your universe, and your thoughts are creative.
3. Your mind is a creative medium; therefore, what you think and feel about the other, you are bringing to pass in your own experience. This is the psychological meaning of the Golden Rule. As you would that others should think about you, think you about them in the same manner.
4. To cheat, rob, or defraud another brings lack, loss, and limitation to yourself. Your subconscious mind records your inner motivations, thoughts, and feelings. When these are negative, loss, limitation, and trouble come to you in countless ways. What you do to the other, you are doing to yourself.

5. The good you do, the kindness proffered, the love and good you send forth will all come back to you multiplied in many ways.

6. You are responsible for the way you think about the other. Remember, the other person is not responsible for the way you think about him or her. Your thoughts are reproduced. What are you thinking now about the other person?

7. Become emotionally mature and permit other people to differ with you. They have a perfect right to disagree with you, and you have the same freedom to disagree with them. You can disagree without being disagreeable.

8. Just as animals are able to pick up fear vibrations, many people are just as sensitive. The thoughts you believe are hidden are actually broadcast by your voice, your facial expressions, and your body language. This is true both for positive and negative thoughts.

9. Your inner speech, representing your silent thoughts and feelings, is experienced in the reactions of others toward you.

10. Wish for the other what you wish for yourself. This is the key to harmonious human relations.

11. Change your concept and estimate of your employer. Feel and know he or she is practicing the Golden Rule and the law of love, and he or she will respond accordingly.

12. Another person cannot annoy you or irritate you except if you permit him or her to. Your thought is creative; you can bless the other person. If someone calls you an insulting name, you have the freedom to reply, "God's peace fills your soul."

13. Love is the answer to getting along with others. Love is

understanding, goodwill, and a respect for the divinity of the other.

14. Have compassion and understanding for those whose negative conditioning has made them difficult and unpleasant. The divine spark is within them, just as it is within everyone. To understand all is to forgive all.

15. Rejoice in the success, promotion, and good fortune of others. In doing so, you attract good fortune to yourself.

16. Never yield to another's emotional scenes and tantrums. Appeasement never wins. Do not be a doormat. Adhere to that which is right. Stick to your ideal, knowing that the mental outlook that gives you peace, happiness, and joy is right, good, and true. What blesses you, blesses all.

17. All you owe any person in the world is love, and love is wishing for everyone what you wish for yourself—health, happiness, and all the blessings of life.

17

How to Use Your Subconscious Mind for Forgiveness

Life plays no favorites. God is life, and this life-principle is flowing through you at this moment, as you read and think upon these words. God loves to express himself through you as harmony, peace, beauty, joy, and abundance. This is called the will of God or the tendency of life.

If you set up resistance in your mind to the flow of life through you, this emotional congestion will snarl up your subconscious mind and cause all kinds of negative conditions. God has nothing to do with the unhappy or chaotic conditions in the world. All these conditions are brought about by the negative and destructive thinking of our species. Therefore, it is a serious mistake to blame God for your trouble or sickness.

Many persons habitually set up mental resistance to the flow of life by accusing and reproaching God for the sin, sickness, and suffering of mankind, Others cast the blame on God for their pains, aches, loss of loved ones, personal tragedies, and accidents. They are angry at God, and they believe he is responsible for their misery.

As long as people entertain such negative concepts about God, they will experience automatic negative reactions from their subconscious minds. What they fail to understand is that they are punishing themselves. They must see the truth, find release, and give up all condemnation, resentment, and anger against anyone or any power outside themselves. Otherwise, they cannot go forward into a healthy, happy, or creative activity. At the instant these people entertain a God of love in their minds and hearts, at the instant they believe that God is a loving Father who watches over them, cares for them, guides them, sustains and strengthens them, this concept and belief about God or the life-principle will be accepted by their subconscious mind, and they will find themselves blessed in countless ways.

LIFE ALWAYS FORGIVES YOU

The life-principle holds a bottomless fund of forgiveness for you. It forgives you when you cut your finger. The subconscious intelligence within you sets about immediately to repair it. New cells build bridges over the cut. If you contract an infection from a harmful organism, life forgives you and sets about surrounding and annihilating the invader. If you burn your hand, the life-principle reduces the edema and congestion and gives you new skin, tissue, and cells.

Life holds no grudges against you. It is always forgiving you. Life brings you back to health, vitality, harmony, and peace, *if* you cooperate by thinking in harmony with nature. Negative, hurtful memories, bitterness, and ill will clutter up and impede the free flow of the life-principle within you.

HOW SHE BANISHED THAT FEELING OF GUILT

Harriet G. worked late at the office every day. She often did not go home until after midnight. She expected that her superiors and coworkers would pat her on the back because she worked so hard. They didn't. Since she was usually the only one who stayed so late, the others didn't even know about her unusual devotion. Meanwhile, her family life was in serious trouble. Her husband and two sons hardly knew what she looked like. When her younger son's Little League team made the local playoffs, Harriet not only missed the game, she even forgot to ask who won. To top it off, Harriet's doctor warned her that she was developing dangerously high blood pressure.

Harriet came to talk to me after her husband told her he wanted a separation. I asked her why she shut her husband out of her life and showed so little interest in her boys. At first she tried to say that she had to work so hard just to keep up with her job. I asked if her coworkers put in as much time as she did. No, she admitted, the others in her company kept pretty normal hours, and they were not any better at the job than she was.

I suggested to her why she was working so arduously.

"There is something eating you inside," I told her. "If there weren't, you would not act this way. You are punishing yourself for something."

For a while, she resisted this suggestion. She kept trying to say that her working habits were normal, that other people were lazy. Finally, however, she admitted that she had a deep sense of guilt. Fifteen years earlier, after her father died, she had served as executor of the estate. She had deliberately kept from turning over a large sum of money to her younger brother.

"Why did you do that?" I asked. "Was it a question of greed?"

"Of course not!" she replied. "My brother . . . well, he had a terrible drug problem. I knew what would happen to the money if I turned it over to him. I told myself I was saving it for him, for when he got himself straightened out."

"And . . . ?" I probed.

Harriet took a deep breath. "It never happened. He killed himself. Maybe he didn't do it on purpose, but it came to the same thing. He was only twenty-six. I keep thinking . . . what if I hadn't kept the money? Maybe he would have used it to go into some kind of rehab program. He might still be with us. It's my fault he's dead."

I asked her, "If you had it to do over again, what would you do?"

"I don't know," she said, shaking her head. "But I know I'd try harder to help my brother, instead of being down on him because he had a problem."

"But at the time, did you feel you were justified?" I asked. "Did you feel you were doing the right thing?"

"Sure," she told me. "But now I'm sure it was wrong. That money wasn't mine."

"So you would not do it now?"

"No, I wouldn't," she replied. Her face grew stern. "But that doesn't matter. I can never be forgiven for what I did. I stole from my only brother, and he died. It's only right that God should punish me. I deserve it."

I explained to her that God was not punishing her. She was punishing herself. If you misuse the laws of life, you will suffer accordingly. If you put your hand on a naked charged wire, you will get a shock. The forces of nature are not evil; it is your use of them that determines whether they have a good or evil effect. Electricity is not evil; it depends on whether you use it to light up your home or give someone a fatal shock. The only sin is ignorance of the law, and the only punishment is the automatic reaction of people's misuse of the law.

If you misuse the principles of chemistry, you may blow up your workplace. If you strike your hand against a board, you may cause your hand to bleed. The board is not at fault. The fault lies with your misuse of it.

Eventually I helped Harriet realize that God does not condemn or punish anyone. All her suffering was due to the reaction of her subconscious mind to her own negative and destructive thinking. What she needed was forgiveness, but the true meaning of forgiveness is to forgive yourself. Forgiveness is getting your thoughts in line with the divine law of harmony. Self-condemnation is called *hell* (bondage and restriction); forgiveness is called *heaven* (harmony and peace).

The burden of guilt and self-condemnation was lifted from her mind, and she had a complete healing. The next time she had a checkup, her blood pressure had become normal. The explanation was the cure.

A MURDERER LEARNED TO FORGIVE HIMSELF

Arthur O. murdered a man in Europe many years ago. When he came to me, he was suffering from great mental anguish and torture. He believed that God must punish him for his terrible deed. I asked him what had happened. He explained that he had found out that the other man was having an affair with his wife. He had come upon them unexpectedly, as he returned from hunting, and shot the man in a moment of mad rage. The legal system did not take a very harsh view of his deed; he had to serve only a few months in prison.

When he was released from jail, Arthur divorced his wife and emigrated to the United States. After several years, he met and married an American woman. He and his wife have been blessed with three lovely children. He has made a successful career in a field where he is in a position to help many people. His colleagues like and respect him. None of this seems to help. All this time later, he still blames himself for what he did.

After hearing Arthur's story, I explained to him that scientists tell us every cell of our bodies is replaced every eleven months. Both physically and psychologically, he was no longer the same man who had committed murder, and he had not been for many years. Moreover, he had clearly transformed himself both mentally and spiritually. He was now full of love and goodwill for humanity. The person who committed the crime years before was long since mentally and spiritually dead. In refusing to forgive himself, Arthur was condemning an innocent man.

This explanation had a profound effect upon him. He said it was as if a great weight had been lifted from his mind. He realized for the first time the inner significance of the following truth in the Bible:

> Come now, let us reason together, saith the Lord: though your sins be as scarlet, they shall be as white as snow; though they be red like crimson, they shall be as wool.
>
> *ISAIAH 1:18*

CRITICISM CANNOT HURT YOU WITHOUT YOUR CONSENT

A schoolteacher named Ramona K. came to me after a lecture. She told me that recently she had had to give a speech. Afterward, one of her fellow teachers sent her a note full of criticism. She said that Ramona spoke too fast, swallowed some of her words, and couldn't be heard. Her diction was poor and her text rambled.

Ramona was hurt and angry. She felt deep resentment toward her critic and tried to avoid any contact with her at school.

When I questioned her, Ramona eventually admitted that she deserved many of the criticisms. She was not experienced at speaking to an adult audience. She had been nervous beforehand, and afterward she was simply glad that she had gotten through it. That was the reason she had been so wounded by her coworker's criticisms. It was as if somebody had blasted a toddler for not running fast enough, when simply managing to walk was an amazing feat.

As we talked, Ramona began to see that her first reaction had been childish. She came to agree that the letter was really a blessing and a much-needed corrective. She decided to perfect her lecturing skills by signing up for a course in public speaking at a nearby college. In the meantime, she called up the writer of the note to thank her for her interest and input.

How to be compassionate

What if the letter Ramona received was totally incorrect? What if she had good reason to think that the criticisms it made of her speech were simply wrong? In that case, Ramona would have had to realize that something about her speech, whether its manner or its content, had upset the prejudices, superstitions, or narrow sectarian beliefs of the note's writer. The problem would lie not with her but with the writer.

To understand this is to take an essential first step toward compassion. The next logical step would be to pray for the other person's peace, harmony, and understanding. You cannot be hurt when you know that you are master of your thoughts, reactions, and emotions. Emotions follow thoughts, and you have the power to reject all thoughts that may disturb or upset you.

Left at the altar

Some years ago I was asked to perform a marriage ceremony at a nearby church. The young man did not appear. At the end of two hours, the would-be bride shed a few tears. She then said to me, "I prayed for divine guidance. This may be the answer to my prayer, for He never faileth."

Her reaction was to restate her faith in God and all things good. She had no bitterness in her heart, because, as she said, "Much as I longed for it, I think this marriage must not have been right action, because my prayer was for right action, not just for me, but for both of us." This young woman sailed serenely through an experience that might have sent another person into an emotional tailspin.

Tune in with the infinite intelligence within your subconscious depths. Trust the answer as unquestioningly as you trusted your mother and father when they held you in their arms. This is the high road to poise and mental and emotional health.

IT IS WRONG TO MARRY; SEX IS EVIL AND I AM EVIL

A young woman who heard me speak came up to me afterward. She told me her name was Carol. I was struck by her appearance. She wore a very plain black dress and black stockings. Her face was pale and bland, without a single touch of lipstick or other makeup. Her manner, too, was subdued yet somehow watchful, as if she imagined that those around her might suddenly start acting in an outrageous way.

Soon Carol was telling me about her upbringing. She was raised by her mother, who taught her to believe that it was a sin to dance, to play cards, to swim, or to go out with men. According to her mother, all men were evil. Sex was nothing but debauchery, inspired by the devil. If she disobeyed these commandments, if she failed to follow them exactly and to the letter, she would burn eternally in hell.

When Carol went out with young men in the office where she worked, she felt a deep sense of guilt. She was convinced that God would punish her. A young man she felt close to asked her to marry him, but she refused. As she said to me, "It is wrong to marry; sex is evil and I am evil." This was her early conditioning speaking.

Of course this young woman felt full of guilt. How could she not? It was impossible for her to live up to her mother's beliefs. It was impossible to avoid the thought that there was something *wrong* with those beliefs. The life-principle that flows through all of us was struggling for recognition and expression.

I suggested to Carol that she try to learn how to forgive herself. To forgive means to give for. She had to give up all these false beliefs for the truths of life and a new estimate of herself.

Carol came to me once weekly for about ten weeks. I taught her what I have learned about the workings of the conscious and subconscious mind, just as I have set it forth in this book. As she gradually came to see that she had been brainwashed, mesmerized, and conditioned by an ignorant, superstitious, bigoted, and frustrated mother, she started to live a wonderful life.

At my suggestion, Carol began to wear more attractive clothes. She visited the cosmetics department of a downtown store for a free comprehensive "makeover." She took dancing lessons and learned to drive. She also learned to swim, to play cards, and to talk with young men. She broke away completely from her family and began to love and value life.

As Carol discovered her inner nature, she began to pray for a companion by claiming that infinite spirit would attract to her a man who harmonized with her thoroughly. One evening as she left my office, a man was waiting to see me. I casually introduced them. Six months later, they were married. They are still married and happy with one another.

FORGIVENESS IS NECESSARY FOR HEALING

And when ye stand praying, forgive, if ye have ought
against any . . .

MARK 11:25

Forgiveness of others is essential to mental peace and radiant
health. You must forgive everyone who has ever hurt you if
you want perfect health and happiness. Forgive yourself by
getting your thoughts in harmony with divine law and order.
You cannot forgive yourself completely until you have forgiven others first. To refuse to forgive yourself is nothing
more or less than spiritual pride or ignorance.

In the psychosomatic field of medicine today, it is being
constantly emphasized that resentment, condemnation of
others, remorse, and hostility are behind a host of maladies
ranging from arthritis to cardiac disease. The stress caused by
these negative emotions can directly affect the immune system of the body, leaving you open to infection and disease.

Specialists in stress-related disorders point out that people who were hurt, mistreated, deceived, or injured often
react by filling themselves with resentment and hatred for
those who hurt them. This reaction causes inflamed and fes-
tering wounds in their subconscious minds. There is only one
remedy. They have to cut out and discard their hurts, and the
one and only sure way to do this is by forgiveness.

FORGIVENESS IS LOVE IN ACTION

The essential ingredient in the art of forgiveness is the willingness to forgive. If you sincerely desire to forgive the other,
you are more than halfway over the hurdle. Of course you
understand that to forgive another does not necessarily mean

that you like him or want to associate with him or her. You cannot be compelled to like someone. That would be as if the government tried to legislate goodwill, love, peace, or tolerance. You are not going to like a person simply because someone orders you to do so. However—and this is a crucial point—we can love people without liking them.

The Bible says, *Love ye one another.* Impossible as this may sound at first, anyone can do it who really wants to do it. Love means that you wish for the other health, happiness, peace, joy, and all the blessings of life. There is only one prerequisite, and that is sincerity. You are not being magnanimous when you forgive, you are really being selfish, because what you wish for the other, you are actually wishing for yourself. The reason is that you are thinking it and you are feeling it. As you think and feel, so are you. Could anything be simpler than that?

TECHNIQUE OF FORGIVENESS

Here is a simple but effective method to bring about forgiveness in yourself. It will work wonders in your life as you practice it. Quiet your mind, relax, and let go. Think of God and his love for you, and then affirm:

> I fully and freely forgive [think of the name of the offender]. I release him (her) mentally and spiritually. I completely forgive everything connected with the matter in question. I am free, and he (she) is free. It is a marvelous feeling.
>
> This is my day of general amnesty. I release anybody and everybody who has ever hurt me, and I wish for each and everyone health, happiness, peace, and all the blessings of life. I do this freely, joyously, and lovingly. Whenever I think of the person or persons who

hurt me, I say, "I have released you, and all the blessings of life are yours." I am free and they are free. It is wonderful!

The great secret of true forgiveness is that once you have forgiven the person, it is unnecessary to repeat the prayer. Whenever the person comes to your mind, or the particular hurt happens to enter your mind, wish the delinquent well, and say, "Peace be unto you." Do this as often as the thought enters your mind. You will find that after a few days the thought of the person or experience will return less and less often, until it fades into nothingness.

THE ACID TEST FOR FORGIVENESS

Prospectors and jewelers use what is called an acid test to tell if a metal is real gold or an imitation. There is an acid test for forgiveness, too. Imagine that I tell you something wonderful about someone who has wronged you, cheated you, or defrauded you. If you sizzle at hearing the good news about this person, the roots of hatred are still in your subconscious mind, playing havoc with you.

Suppose you had a very painful dental procedure last year and you tell me about it now. If I ask whether you are in pain from it now, you would give me an astonished look and say, "Of course not! I remember the pain, but I don't feel it any longer."

That is the whole story. If you have truly forgiven someone, you will remember the incident, but you will no longer feel the sting or hurt of it. This is the acid test of forgiveness. You must meet it psychologically and spiritually. Otherwise, you are simply deceiving yourself. You are not practicing the true art of forgiveness.

TO UNDERSTAND ALL IS TO FORGIVE ALL

Once you understand the creative law of your own mind, you stop blaming other people and conditions for making or marring your life. You realize that your own thoughts and feelings create your destiny. Furthermore, you are aware that externals are not the causes and conditioners of your life and your experiences. To think that others can mar your happiness, that you are the football of a cruel fate, that you must oppose and fight others for a living—all these ideas reveal their destructive nature once you understand that thoughts are things. This principle is clearly set forth in the Bible:

> For as a man thinketh in his heart, so is he.
>
> *PROVERBS 23:7*

SUMMARY OF YOUR AIDS TO FORGIVENESS

1. God, or life, is no respecter of persons. Life plays no favorites. Life, or God, seems to favor you once you begin to align yourself with the principles of harmony, health, joy, and peace.

2. God, or life, never sends disease, sickness, accident, or suffering. We bring these things on ourselves by our own negative destructive thinking, based upon the law *As we sow, so shall we reap*.

3. Your concept of God is the most important thing in your life. If you really believe in a God of Love, your subconscious mind will respond by bringing countless blessings to you. Believe in a God of Love.

4. Life, or God, holds no grudge against you. Life never condemns you. Life heals a cut on your hand. Life forgives you if you burn your finger. It reduces the edema and restores the part to wholeness and perfection.

5. Your guilt complex is a false concept of God and life. God, or life, does not punish or judge you. You do this to yourself by the subconscious effects of your false beliefs, negative thinking, and self-condemnation.

6. God, or life, does not condemn or punish you. The forces of nature are not evil. The effect of their use depends on how you use the power within you. You can use electricity to kill someone or to light the house. You can use water to drown a child or quench his thirst. Good and evil come right back to the thought and purpose in a person's own mind.

7. God, or life, never punishes. People punish themselves by their false concepts of God, life, and the universe. Their thoughts are creative, and they create their own misery.

8. If another criticizes you, and these faults are within you, rejoice, give thanks, and appreciate the comments. This gives you the opportunity to correct the particular fault.

9. You cannot be hurt by criticism when you know that you are master of your thoughts, reactions, and emotions. This gives you the opportunity to pray for and bless the other, thereby blessing yourself.

10. When you pray for guidance and right action, take what comes. Realize it is good and very good. Then there is no cause for self-pity, criticism, or hatred.

11. There is nothing good or bad, but thinking makes it so. There is no evil in the desire for food, sex, wealth, or true expression. It depends on how you use these urges, desires, or aspirations. Your desire for food can be met without killing someone for a loaf of bread.

12. Resentment, hatred, ill will, and hostility are behind a host of maladies. Forgive yourself and everybody else by pouring out love, life, joy, and goodwill to all who have

hurt you. Continue until such time as you can meet them in your mind and know that you are at peace with them.

13. To forgive is to give something for. Give love, peace, joy, wisdom, and all the blessings of life to the other, until there is no sting left in your mind. This is the acid test of forgiveness.

14. If someone has hurt you, lied about and vilified you, and has said all manner of evil about you, is your thought of that person negative? If so, you have not yet forgiven. The roots of hatred are still in your subconscious mind, playing havoc with you and your good. The only way to wither those roots is with love. Wish for the person all the blessings of life. This is the meaning of *Forgive until seventy times seven.*

18

How Your Subconscious Removes Mental Blocks

What can you do if you are faced with a difficult situation and you cannot see your way clear? The solution lies within the problem. Every question implies its own answer. The infinite intelligence within your subconscious mind knows all and sees all. It has the answer and is revealing it to you now . . . but you must *listen*. You must follow the urgings of your subconscious mind with perfect confidence. Once you achieve this new mental attitude, that the creative intelligence within you is bringing about a happy solution, you will find the answer you seek. Rest assured that such an attitude of mind will bring order, peace, and meaning to all your undertakings.

HOW TO BREAK OR BUILD A HABIT

We are all creatures of habit. Habit is a function of our subconscious minds. We learned to swim, ride a bicycle, dance, and drive a car by consciously doing these things over and over again until they established tracks in our subconscious minds. Then, the automatic habit action of the subconscious mind took over. This is sometimes referred to as "second nature," that is, the reaction of the subconscious mind to the thinking and acting that makes up our "first" nature.

If we create our own habits, it follows that we are free to *choose* good habits or bad habits. If you repeat a negative thought or act over a period of time, you will place yourself under the compulsion of a habit. The law of your subconscious is compulsion.

HOW HE BROKE A BAD HABIT

When Bob J. came to me, he was close to despair. "I've lost my job, my wife, and my family to drink," he told me. "My wife won't even speak to me on the phone. She won't let me see our daughter. I don't know where to turn."

"Have you tried to stop drinking?" I asked.

"Of course I have," he said. "Lots of times. And I have stopped, too, for a little while. Then I get an uncontrollable urge, and the next thing I know, I'm coming off a two-week bender. It's terrible!"

Time and again these experiences had occurred to this unfortunate man. He realized that binge drinking had become a habit, and he saw that he had to change the habit and establish a new one. However, his continued efforts to suppress his cravings made matters only worse. His repeated failures convinced him that he was hopeless and powerless to control his urge or obsession. This idea of being powerless operated as a tremendous suggestion to his subconscious mind and aggravated his weakness, making his life a succession of failures.

I taught him to harmonize the functions of the conscious and subconscious mind. When these two cooperate, the idea or desire implanted in the subconscious mind is realized. His reasoning mind agreed that if the old habit path or track had carried him into trouble, he could consciously form a new path to freedom, sobriety, and peace of mind.

He knew that while his destructive habit had become automatic, he had acquired it through his conscious choice. He realized that if he had been conditioned negatively, he also could be conditioned positively. As a result, he stopped thinking that he was powerless to overcome the habit. He achieved a clear understanding that there was no obstacle to his healing other than his own thought. Therefore, there was no occasion for great mental effort or mental coercion.

THE POWER OF HIS MENTAL PICTURE

Bob began to make a practice of relaxing his body and getting into a drowsy, meditative state. Then he filled his mind with the picture of the desired end, knowing his subconscious mind could bring it about the easiest way. He imagined his daughter giving him a welcoming hug and saying, "Oh, Daddy, it's so wonderful to have you home again!"

Regularly, systematically, he sat down and meditated in this way. When his attention wandered, he made it a habit to immediately recall the mental picture of his daughter with her smile and the scene of his home enlivened by her cheerful voice. All this brought about a reconditioning of his mind. It was a gradual process. He kept it up. He persevered, knowing that sooner or later he would establish a new habit pattern in his subconscious mind.

I told him that he could liken his conscious mind to a camera, that his subconscious mind was the sensitive plate on which he registered and impressed the picture. This made a profound impression on him. His whole aim became to firmly impress the picture on his mind and develop it there. Films are developed in the dark; likewise, mental pictures are developed in the darkroom of the subconscious mind.

FOCUSED ATTENTION

Bob understood that his conscious mind was like a camera, so he used no effort. There was no mental struggle. He quietly adjusted his thoughts and focused his attention on the scene before him until he gradually identified with the picture. He became absorbed in the mental atmosphere, repeating the mental movie frequently.

There was no room for doubt that a healing would follow. When there was any temptation to drink, he would switch his imagination from any thoughts of drinking bouts to the feeling of being at home with his family. He was successful because he confidently expected to experience the picture he was developing in his mind. Today he is sober, reunited with his family, successful in his career, and radiantly happy.

SHE SAID A JINX WAS FOLLOWING HER

"For the last three months, I've been running into one roadblock after another. I really think I've got a jinx following me!"

Ruth B. was the founder of a firm that handles billing and record-keeping for professionals. Her company was very successful at first, but then something changed.

"I don't get it," she told me. "Suddenly it's as if all the doors that were opening to me are jammed shut. Time after time, I bring potential clients right to the point of signing on the dotted line. Then, at the eleventh hour, they back out. What's going on?"

"How long have you had this problem?" I asked.

"Like I said, about three months," she replied. "Since the middle of April."

Curious, I asked, "What makes you so sure about the date? Did anything in particular happen then?"

She scowled. "You better believe it! I was making a pitch to a certain orthodontist. I'm not going to say his name, but if your kid has braces, you probably know him. I laid it all out. I showed him how much time and effort and money he'd save if my outfit handled all his clerical scutwork. He saw the sense of it and made a verbal commitment. But when I mailed him the contract, first he stalled, then he backed out. I was fit to be tied!"

"And after that . . . ?" I probed.

"It started happening over and over," Ruth said. For a moment she covered her eyes. "I'm jinxed! There's no other explanation."

"Yes, there is," I told her. I explained that her irritation and resentment toward the orthodontist had given her a subconscious belief that other prospective clients would also back out on her. This belief set up a pattern of frustration, hostility, and obstacles. She gradually built up in her mind an expectation of last-minute cancellations. Once this was impressed upon her subconscious mind, it began to bring about the conditions she dreaded. And each successive failure strengthened the conviction that she was doomed to fail. She had established a vicious circle.

As we continued to talk, Ruth began to see that the trouble was in her own mind. She realized that the cure was to change her mental attitude. She began to meditate in this manner:

I realize I am one with the infinite intelligence of my subconscious mind, which knows no obstacle, difficulty, or delay. I live in the joyous expectancy of the best. My deeper mind responds to my thoughts. I know that the work of the infinite power of my subconscious cannot be hindered. Infinite intelligence always finishes successfully whatever it begins.

Creative wisdom works through me bringing all my plans and purposes to completion. Whatever I start, I bring to a successful conclusion. My aim in life is to give wonderful service, and all those whom I contact are blessed by what I have to offer. All my work comes to full fruition in divine order.

She repeated this prayer every morning before going to call on her customers. She also prayed each night before going to sleep. In a short time she had established a new habit pattern in her subconscious mind. Soon she was once again successful in convincing prospective clients to sign up with her company. All thought of being the victim of a jinx was forgotten.

How Much Do You Want What You Want?

The story is told that a young man asked Socrates how he could get wisdom.

"Come with me," Socrates replied. He took the lad to a river and shoved his head underwater. He held it there until the boy struggled for air. Then he let him go.

Once the boy regained his composure, Socrates asked him, "What did you desire most when your head was underwater?"

"I wanted air," the boy told him.

Socrates nodded slowly. "When you want wisdom as much as you wanted air when you were immersed in the water," he said, "you will receive it."

In the same way, when

- you have an intense, sincere desire to overcome a certain block in your life;
- you come to a clear-cut decision that there is a way out;
- you confidently decide that that is the course you wish to follow,

then victory and triumph are assured.

If you really want peace of mind and inner calm, you will get it. It doesn't matter how unjustly you have been treated, or how unfair the boss has been, or what a mean scoundrel someone has proved to be. All this makes no difference to you when you awaken to your mental and spiritual powers. You know what you want, and you will definitely refuse to let the thieves (thoughts) of hatred, anger, hostility, and ill will rob you of peace, harmony, health, and happiness.

Once you learn the habit of identifying your thoughts immediately with your aim in life, you cease to become upset by people, conditions, news, and events. Your aim is peace, health, inspiration, harmony, and abundance. Feel a river of peace flowing through you now. Your thought is the immaterial and invisible power, and you choose to let it bless, inspire, and give you peace.

WHY HE COULD NOT BE HEALED

Allan S. was a field representative for a major textbook distributor. He was married, with four children, but he was also involved in a secret relationship with another woman during his business trips. When he came to see me, he was nervous and irritable. He could not get to sleep without pills. He had high blood pressure and an assortment of internal pains that his doctor could not diagnose or relieve. To make matters worse, he was drinking heavily.

As we quickly discovered, the cause of all this was a deep unconscious sense of guilt. The religious creed he had been brought up in was deeply lodged in his subconscious mind. It placed great stress on the sanctity of the marriage vows, yet he was violating them flagrantly and constantly. He drank to excess in a vain attempt to heal the wound of guilt. Just as an invalid might take morphine and codeine for severe pains, he was taking alcohol for the pain or wound in his mind. It was the old story of adding fuel to the fire.

THE EXPLANATION AND THE CURE

He listened to my explanation of how his mind worked. He faced his problem, considered it carefully, and made a decision to give up his illicit relationship. He also realized that his drinking was an unconscious attempt to escape. The hidden cause lodged in his subconscious mind had to be eradicated. Only then would healing follow.

He began to impress his subconscious mind three times a day, using this prayer:

> My mind is full of peace, poise, balance, and equilibrium. The infinite lies stretched in smiling repose within me. I am not afraid of anything in the past, the present, or the future. The infinite intelligence of my subconscious mind leads, guides, and directs me in all ways.
>
> I now meet every situation with faith, poise, calmness, and confidence. I am now completely free from the habit. My mind is full of inner peace, freedom, and joy. I forgive myself; then I am forgiven. Peace, sobriety, and confidence reign supreme in my mind.

As he repeated this prayer, he was fully aware of what he was doing and why he was doing it. Knowing what he was doing gave him necessary faith and confidence. I explained to him that as he spoke these statements out loud, slowly, lovingly, and meaningfully, they would gradually sink into his subconscious mind. Like seeds, they would grow after their kind. His ears heard the sound, and the healing vibrations of the words reached his subconscious mind and obliterated all the negative mental patterns that had caused his problems. Light dispels darkness. The constructive thought destroys the negative thought. He became a transformed man within a month.

REFUSING TO ADMIT IT

If you are an alcoholic or drug addict, admit it. Do not dodge the issue. Many people remain alcoholics because they refuse to admit it.

Your disease is an instability, an inner fear. You are refusing to face life, and so you try to escape your responsibilities through the bottle. As an alcoholic you have no free will. You may think you have. You may even boast about your willpower.

If you are a habitual drunkard and you assert boldly, "I will not touch it anymore," you do not have the power to make this assertion come true. The reason is that you do not know where to *locate* the power.

You are living in a psychological prison of your own making. You are bound by your beliefs, opinions, training, and environmental influences. Like most people, you are a creature of habit. You are conditioned to react the way you do.

BUILDING IN THE IDEA OF FREEDOM

You can build the idea of freedom and peace of mind into your mentality so that it reaches your subconscious depths. The latter, being all-powerful, will free you from all desire for alcohol. At that point, you will achieve a new understanding of how your mind works. You will discover within yourself the infinite resources to back up your statement and prove the truth to yourself.

FIFTY-ONE PERCENT HEALED

If you have a keen desire to free yourself from any destructive habit, you are already fifty-one percent healed. When your desire to give up the bad habit is greater than your need to continue it, you will be amazed to discover that complete freedom is but a step away.

Whatever thought you anchor the mind upon, the mind magnifies. Engage the mind on the concept of freedom (that is, freedom from the destructive habit) and peace of mind. Keep it focused on this new direction of attention. In doing so, you generate feelings that gradually pervade the concept of freedom and peace. Whatever idea you emotionalize in this way is accepted by your subconscious and brought to pass.

THE LAW OF SUBSTITUTION

Realize that something good can come out of your suffering. You have not suffered in vain. However, it is foolish to continue to suffer.

If you continue as an alcoholic, it will bring about mental and physical deterioration and decay. Realize that the power in your subconscious is backing you up. Even though you may be seized with melancholia, you can begin to imagine the joy of freedom that is in store for you.

This is the law of substitution. Your imagination took you to the bottle. Let it now take you to freedom and peace of mind. You will suffer a little, but it is for a constructive purpose. You will bear it like a mother in the pangs of childbirth, and you will bring forth a child of the mind. Your subconscious will give birth to sobriety.

CAUSE OF ALCOHOLISM

The real cause of alcoholism is negative and destructive thinking; *for as humans thinketh, so are they.* The alcoholic has a deep sense of inferiority, inadequacy, frustration, and defeat. Often these are accompanied by a deep inner hostility. He or she has countless alibis to explain his or her drinking, but in reality the sole reason is in the person's *thought life.*

THREE MAGIC STEPS

The first step: Get still; quiet the wheels of the mind. Enter into a sleepy, drowsy state. In this relaxed, peaceful, receptive state, you are preparing for the second step.

The second step: Take a brief phrase that can be graven readily on the memory and repeat it over and over as a lullaby. Use the phrase "Sobriety and peace of mind are mine now, and I give thanks." To prevent the mind from wandering, repeat it aloud or sketch its pronunciation with the lips and tongue as you say it mentally. This helps its entry into the subconscious mind. Do this for five minutes or more. You will find a deep emotional response.

The third step: Just before going to sleep, practice what Johann von Goethe, the great German poet, used to do. Imagine a friend or loved one with you. Your eyes are closed, you are relaxed and at peace. The loved one or friend is subjectively present, and is saying to you, "Congratulations!"

You see the smile; you hear the voice. You mentally

touch the hand; all is real and vivid. The word *congratulations* implies complete freedom. Hear it over and over until you get the subconscious reaction that satisfies.

KEEP ON KEEPING ON

When fear knocks at the door of your mind, or when worry, anxiety, and doubt cross your mind, behold your vision, your goal. Think of the infinite power within your subconscious mind, which can generate your thinking and imagining. This will give you confidence, power, and courage. Keep on, persevere, *until the day breaks, and the shadows flee away.*

REVIEW YOUR THOUGHT POWER

1. The solution lies within the problem. The answer is in every question. Infinite intelligence responds to you as you call upon it with faith and confidence.
2. Habit is the function of your subconscious mind. There is no greater evidence of the marvelous power of your subconscious than the force and sway habit holds in your life. You are a creature of habit.
3. You form habit patterns in your subconscious mind by repeating a thought or act over and over until it establishes tracks in the subconscious mind and becomes automatic.
4. You have freedom to choose. You can choose a good habit or a bad habit. Prayer is a good habit.
5. Whatever mental picture, backed by faith, you behold in your conscious mind, your subconscious mind will bring to pass.
6. The only obstacle to your success and achievement is your own thought or mental image.

7. When your attention wanders, bring it back to the contemplation of your good or goal. Make a habit of this. This is called disciplining the mind.

8. Your conscious mind is the camera, and your subconscious mind is the sensitive plate on which you register or impress the picture.

9. The only jinx that follows anyone is a fear thought repeated over and over in the mind. Break the jinx by knowing that whatever you start you will bring to a conclusion in divine order. Picture the happy ending and sustain it with confidence.

10. To form a new habit, you must be convinced that it is desirable. When your desire to give up the bad habit is greater than your desire to continue, you are already fifty-one percent healed.

11. The statements of others cannot hurt you except through your own thoughts and mental participation. Identify yourself with your aim, which is peace, harmony, and joy. You are the only thinker in your universe.

12. Excessive drinking is an unconscious desire to escape. The cause of alcoholism is negative and destructive thinking. The cure is to think of freedom, sobriety, and perfection and to feel the thrill of accomplishment.

13. Many people remain alcoholics because they refuse to admit their problem.

14. The law of your subconscious mind, which held you in bondage and inhibited your freedom of action, will give you freedom and happiness. It depends on how you use it.

15. Your imagination took you to the bottle; let it take you to freedom by imagining you are free.

16. The real cause of alcoholism is negative and destructive thinking. *As a man thinketh in his heart* [subconscious mind], *so is he.*
17. When fear knocks at the door of your mind, let faith in God and all things good open the door.

19

How to Use Your Subconscious Mind to Remove Fear

One of my students was invited to speak at the annual banquet of his professional association. He told me he was panic-stricken at the thought of speaking before a thousand people, many of whom were influential in his field. He overcame his fear this way: For several nights he sat calmly in an armchair for about five minutes. He said to himself slowly, quietly, and positively:

> I am going to master this fear. I am overcoming it now. I speak with poise and confidence. I am relaxed and at ease.

In this way, he set into operation a definite law of mind. When the time came, he overcame his fear and gave a very successful speech.

The subconscious mind is amenable to suggestion. It is *controlled* by suggestion. When you still your mind and relax, the thoughts of your conscious mind sink into the subconscious. The process is similar to osmosis, in which fluids separated by a porous membrane intermingle. As these positive seeds, or thoughts, sink into the subconscious area, they grow after their kind, and you become poised, serene, and calm.

PEOPLE'S GREATEST ENEMY

It has been said that people's greatest enemy is fear. Fear is behind failure, sickness, and poor human relations. Millions of people are afraid of the past, the future, old age, insanity, and death. But fear is a thought in your mind. This means that you are afraid of your own thoughts.

A small child can be paralyzed with fear when a playmate says there is a monster under the bed who will grab him in the night. But when the parent turns on the light and shows there is no monster, he is freed from fear. The fear in the mind of the child was every bit as real as if there were really a monster there. He was healed of a false thought in his mind. The thing he feared did not exist. In the same way, most of your fears have no reality. They are merely a conglomeration of sinister shadows, and shadows have no reality.

DO THE THING YOU FEAR

Ralph Waldo Emerson, the great nineteenth-century philosopher and poet, said, "Do the thing you are afraid to do, and the death of fear is certain."

There was a time when I was filled with unutterable fear at the thought of standing before an audience and speaking. If I had given way to this fear, terrible as it was, I am sure you would not now be reading this book. I would never have been able to share with others what I have learned about the workings of the subconscious mind.

The way I overcame this fear was to follow Emerson's advice. Quaking inside, I went before audiences and spoke. Gradually I became less fearful, until at last I was comfortable enough to enjoy what I was doing. I even grew to look forward to speaking engagements. I did the thing I was afraid to do, and the death of fear was certain.

When you affirm positively that you are going to master your fears, and you come to a definite decision in your conscious mind, you release the power of the subconscious, which flows in response to the nature of your thought.

BANISHING STAGE FRIGHT

In an earlier chapter, I described the case of Janet R., a young opera singer whose career had been sidetracked by a terrible case of stage fright. When she was invited to audition for a major role in an opera production, she realized that this might well be her last chance at success. Yet her stage fright was as powerful as ever. Unless she managed to deal with it, she knew she would fail once again.

The way she overcame her fear was to isolate herself in a room and do her best to relax both her body and mind. To counteract the fear suggestion that dominated her subconscious mind, she repeated slowly, quietly, and with feeling the words "I sing beautifully. I am poised, serene, confident, and calm."

She repeated these words from five to ten times at each sitting. By the end of one week she felt poised and confident. When the time came, she gave an outstanding audition.

If you adapt this procedure to your situation and carry it out sincerely and confidently, the death of fear is certain.

FEAR OF FAILURE

I often get visits from students at a nearby university. One complaint many of them share is what we can call suggestive amnesia during examinations. They all tell me the same thing: "I know the material cold before the exam, and I remember all the answers after the exam. But when I'm in the classroom staring down at a blank exam booklet, my mind goes totally blank!"

A great many of us have had similar experiences. The explanation lies in one of the major laws of the subconscious mind. The idea that realizes itself is the one to which we give the most concentrated attention. In talking with these students, I find that they are most attentive to the idea of failure. As a result, it is failure that the subconscious mind brings into reality. The fear of failure itself creates the experience of failure, by way of a temporary amnesia.

A medical student named Sheila A. was one of the most brilliant students in her class. Yet when she faced a written or oral examination, she found herself going blank at even simple questions. I explained the reason to her. She had been worrying and brooding over the chances of failure for several days before the exam. These negative thoughts became charged with fear.

Thoughts enveloped in the powerful emotion of fear are realized in the subconscious mind. In other words, this young student was requesting her subconscious mind to see to it that she failed, and that is exactly what it did. On the day of the examination she found herself stricken with suggestive amnesia.

HOW SHE OVERCAME HER FEAR

As Sheila studied the working of her subconscious mind, she learned that it is the storehouse of memory. It had a perfect record of everything she had heard and read during her medical training. Moreover, she learned that the subconscious mind is responsive and reciprocal. The way to be in deep rapport with it is to be relaxed, peaceful, and confident.

Every night and morning, she began to imagine her parents congratulating her on her wonderful record. She would hold an imaginary letter from them in her hand. As she began to contemplate this happy result, she called forth a corresponding or reciprocal response or reaction in herself.

Under this consistent stimulation, the all-wise and omnipotent power of the subconscious took over. It dictated and directed her conscious mind accordingly. She imagined the end, thereby willing the means to the realization of the end. After following this procedure, she had no trouble passing her subsequent exams. The subjective wisdom of her subconscious mind took over and *compelled* her to give an excellent account of herself.

FEAR OF WATER

When I was about ten years old, I accidentally fell into a swimming pool. I had never learned to swim. I flailed my arms, but it did no good. I felt myself sinking. I can still remember the terror as the dark water surrounded me. I tried to gasp for air, but my mouth filled with water. At the last moment, another boy noticed my plight. He jumped in and pulled me out. This experience sank into my subconscious mind. The result was that for years I feared the water.

Then one day I mentioned this irrational fear of mine to a wise elderly psychologist.

"Go down to the swimming pool," he told me. "Look at the water. It is simply a chemical compound, made up of two atoms of hydrogen and one of oxygen. It has no will, no awareness. But you have *both*."

I nodded, wondering where this was leading.

"Once you understand that the water is essentially passive," he continued, "say out loud in a strong voice, 'I am going to master you. By the powers of mind, I will dominate you.' Then go into the water. Take swimming lessons. Use your inner powers to overcome the water."

I did as I was told. Once I assumed a new attitude of mind, the omnipotent power of the subconscious responded, giving me strength, faith, and confidence. It enabled me to overcome my fear, and I mastered the water. Today I swim every morning for both health and pleasure. Do not permit water to master you. Remember, you are the master of the water.

MASTER TECHNIQUE FOR OVERCOMING ANY PARTICULAR FEAR

Here is a technique for overcoming fear that I have taught from the lecture platform to thousands of people. It works like a charm. Try it!

Suppose you are afraid of swimming. Begin now to sit still for five or ten minutes three or four times a day. Put yourself into a state of deep relaxation. Now imagine you are swimming. Subjectively, you *are* swimming. Mentally you have projected yourself into the water. You feel the brisk coolness of the water and the movement of your arms and legs. It is all real, vivid, and a joyous activity of the mind.

This is not idle daydreaming. You understand that what you are experiencing in your imagination will be developed in your subconscious mind. Then you will be compelled to express the image and likeness of the picture you impressed on your deeper mind. When you next attempt to swim, it is the joy that will surface. This is the law of the subconscious.

You can apply the same technique to other fears. If you are afraid of high places, imagine you are taking a stroll in the mountains. Feel the reality of it all. Enjoy the pure air, the alpine flowers, the thrilling scenery. Know that as you continue to do this mentally, you will come to do it physically with ease and comfort.

HE BLESSED THE ELEVATOR

Jonathan M. is an executive with a large corporation. For many years he was terrified to ride in an elevator. He would walk up seven flights of stairs to his office every morning to avoid the elevator ride. When he had to meet with people from other companies whose offices were on high floors, he always found some excuse to meet them at his own office or at a restaurant. Business trips out of town were torture for him. He had to call ahead, to make sure his hotel room was on a low floor and that he would be able to use the stairs.

This fear was the product of his subconscious mind, perhaps in response to some experience that he had long since forgotten on a conscious level. Once he learned this, he set about to change it. He began to bless the elevator every night and several times a day. In a calm, confident mood, he repeated to himself:

> The elevator in our building is a wonderful idea. It came out of the universal mind. It is a boon and a blessing to all our employees. It gives wonderful service. It operates in divine order. I ride in it in peace and joy. I remain silent now while the currents of life, love, and understanding flow through the patterns of my thought.
>
> In my imagination I am now in the elevator, and I step out into my office. The elevator is full of our employees. I talk to them, and they are friendly, joyous, and free. It is a wonderful experience of freedom, faith, and confidence. I give thanks.

He continued this prayer for ten days. On the eleventh day, he walked into the elevator with other members of his company and felt completely free.

NORMAL AND ABNORMAL FEAR

A newborn baby has only two basic fears, the fear of falling and the fear of sudden loud noises. These are perfectly normal. They serve as a sort of alarm system given you by nature as a means of self-preservation.

Normal fear is good. You hear an automobile coming down the road toward you and you step aside to survive. The momentary fear of being run over is overcome by your action.

All other fears are abnormal. They were caused by particular experiences or were passed along to you by parents, relatives, teachers, and others who influenced your early years.

ABNORMAL FEAR

Abnormal fear takes hold when people let their imagination run riot. I knew a woman who was invited to go on a trip around the world by plane. She began to cut out of the newspapers all reports of airplane catastrophes. She even ordered a videotape of *The World's Worst Airplane Crashes*. She imagined herself going down in the ocean and drowning. This is abnormal fear. Had she persisted in this, there is a strong chance that she would have attracted to herself what she feared most.

Another example of someone who suffered from abnormal fear is a businessman in New York who was very successful and prosperous. He created his own private mental motion picture in which his company was forced into bankruptcy and he lost everything. The more he ran this mental movie of failure, the more he sank into a deep depression. He refused to stop this morbid imagery. He kept telling his wife, "This can't last," "The boom will end any day now," "It's all hopeless, we're going to go broke."

His wife later told me that in the end he did go bankrupt. All the things he imagined and feared came to pass. The things he feared did not exist, but he brought them to pass by constantly fearing, believing, and expecting financial disaster. As Job said, *The thing I feared has come upon me.*

The world is full of people who are afraid that something terrible will happen to their children or that some dread catastrophe will befall them. When they read about an epidemic of some rare disease, they live in fear that they will catch it. Some imagine they have the disease already. All this is abnormal fear.

THE ANSWER TO ABNORMAL FEAR

If you find yourself beset with an abnormal fear, you must strive to move mentally to the opposite. If you remain at the extreme of fear, you will suffer stagnation plus mental and physical deterioration. When fear arises, one of the basic laws of the subconscious mind immediately brings with it a desire for something opposite to the thing feared.

Place your attention on the thing immediately desired. Get absorbed and engrossed in your desire. Know that the subjective always overturns the objective. This attitude will give you confidence and lift your spirits. The infinite power of your subconscious mind is moving on your behalf. It cannot fail. Therefore, peace and assurance are yours.

EXAMINE YOUR FEARS

The head of sales for a major multinational corporation confided that when he first began working as a salesperson, he had to walk around the block five or six times before he could get up the nerve to call on a customer.

His supervisor was both very experienced and very perceptive. One day she said to him, "Don't be afraid of the monster hiding behind the door. There is no monster. You are the victim of a false belief."

The supervisor went on to tell him that whenever she felt the first stirrings of a fear, she stood up to it. She stared it in the face, looking it straight in the eye. When she did that, she always found that her fear faded and shrank into insignificance.

HE LANDED IN THE JUNGLE

A former U.S. Army chaplain named John N. told me that during World War II, the plane he was in was hit and damaged by antiaircraft fire. He had to bail out over the jungle-clad mountains of New Guinea. Of course he was frightened, but he knew that fear came in two varieties, normal and abnormal. The abnormal kind, which was trying to take control of him, was a close relative of panic.

He decided to do something about his fear immediately. He began to talk to himself, saying, "John, you can't surrender to your fear. Your fear is a desire for safety and security, and a way out."

He stood in the center of a small clearing and calmed his breathing. He pushed away the first symptoms of panic. As soon as he felt more relaxed, he began to claim, "Infinite intelligence, which guides the planets in their courses, is now leading and guiding me out of this jungle to safety." He kept saying this out loud to himself for ten minutes or more.

"Suddenly," John told me, "I felt something start to stir inside me. It was a mood of confidence and faith. I was drawn to one side of the clearing. There I found the faint trace of a path, and I began to walk. Two days later, I miraculously came upon a small village where the people were friendly. They fed me, then took me to the edge of the jungle, where a rescue plane picked me up."

John's changed mental attitude saved him. His confidence and trust in the subjective wisdom and power within him gave him the solution to his problem.

He added, "If I had started to bemoan my fate and indulge my fears, the monster fear would have conquered me. I probably would have died of fear and starvation."

HE DISMISSED HIMSELF

Rafael S. was an executive in a major foundation. He admitted to me that for three years he had been terrified he would lose his position. He was always imagining failure. He kept expecting his subordinates to be promoted over his head. The thing he feared did not exist, save as a morbid anxious thought in his own mind. His vivid imagination dramatized the loss of his job until he became increasingly nervous and inefficient. Finally he was asked to resign.

In reality, Rafael dismissed himself. His constant negative imagery, the flood of fear suggestions he sent to his subconscious mind, caused the subconscious mind to respond and react accordingly. It led him to make mistakes and foolish decisions. These in turn created his failure. He might never have been fired if he had immediately moved to the opposite in his mind.

THEY PLOTTED AGAINST HIM

During a world lecture tour, I had a two-hour conversation with a prominent government official in one of the countries I visited. I found that this man had a deep sense of inner peace and serenity. He said that although he is constantly showered with abuse by newspapers that support the opposition party, he never allows it to disturb him. His practice is to sit still for fifteen minutes in the morning and realize that in the center of himself is a deep, still ocean of peace. Meditating in this way, he generates tremendous power, which overcomes all manner of difficulties and fears.

A few months earlier, he had received a midnight call from a panicky colleague. According to his coworker, a group of people were plotting against him. They intended to overthrow his administration by force, with help from dissident elements of the country's armed forces.

In reply, the official told his colleague, "I am going to sleep now in perfect peace. We can discuss this tomorrow at 10:00 A.M."

As he explained to me, "I know that no negative thought can ever manifest itself unless I emotionalize the thought and accept it mentally. I refuse to entertain their suggestion of fear. Therefore, no harm can come to me unless I allow it."

Notice how calm he was, how cool, how serene! He did not get overwrought and start tearing his hair or wringing his hands. At his center he found the still water, an inner peace, and there was a great calm.

DELIVER YOURSELF FROM ALL YOUR FEARS

In the Bible there is a perfect formula for casting out fear:

> I sought the Lord, and He heard me, and delivered me from all my fears.
>
> *PSALM 34:4*

Lord is an ancient word meaning *law*—the power of your subconscious mind.

Learn the wonders of your subconscious. Understand how it works and functions. Master the techniques given to you in this chapter. Put them into practice now, today! Your subconscious will respond, and you will be free of all fears. *I sought the Lord, and He heard me, and delivered me from all my fears.*

STEP THIS WAY TO FREEDOM FROM FEAR

1. Do the thing you are afraid to do, and the death of fear is certain. If you say to yourself with perfect confidence and faith, "I am going to master this fear," you will.
2. Fear is a negative thought in your mind. Supplant it with a constructive thought. Fear has killed millions. Confidence is greater than fear. Nothing is more powerful than faith in God and the good.
3. Fear is person's greatest enemy. It is behind failure, sickness, and bad human relations. Love casts out fear. Love is an emotional attachment to the good things of life. Fall in love with honesty, integrity, justice, goodwill, and success. Live in the joyous expectancy of the best, and invariably the best will come to you.
4. Counteract fear suggestions with the opposite, such as,

"I sing beautifully; I am poised, serene, and calm." It will pay fabulous dividends.

5. Fear is behind the suggestive amnesia that strikes during examinations. You can overcome this by affirming frequently, "I have a perfect memory for everything I need to know." Imagine a friend congratulating you on your brilliant success on the exam. Persevere and you will win.

6. If you are afraid to cross water, swim. In your imagination swim freely, joyously. Project yourself into the water mentally. Feel the chill and thrill of swimming across the pool. Make it vivid. As you do this subjectively, you will be compelled to go into the water and conquer it. This is the law of your mind.

7. If you are afraid of closed places, such as elevators, mentally ride in an elevator while sincerely blessing all its parts and functions. You will be amazed how quickly the fear will be dissipated.

8. You were born with only two fears, the fear of falling and the fear of noise. All your other fears were acquired. Get rid of them.

9. Normal fear is good. Abnormal fear is very bad and destructive. To constantly indulge in fear thoughts results in abnormal fear, obsessions, and complexes. To fear something persistently causes a sense of panic and terror.

10. You can overcome abnormal fear when you know the power of your subconscious mind can change conditions and bring to pass the cherished desires of your heart. Give your immediate attention and devotion to your desire, which is the opposite of your fear. This is the love that casts out fear.

11. If you are afraid of failure, give attention to success. If you are afraid of sickness, dwell on perfect health. If you

are afraid of an accident, dwell on the guidance and protection of God. If you are afraid of death, dwell on eternal life. God is life, and that is your life now.

12. The great law of substitution is the answer to fear. Whatever you fear has its solution in the form of your desire. If you are sick, you desire health. If you are in the prison of fear, you desire freedom. Expect the good. Mentally concentrate on the good, and know that your subconscious mind answers you always. It never fails.

13. The things you fear do not really exist except as thoughts in your mind. Thoughts are creative. This is why Job said, *The thing I feared has come upon me.* Think good and good follows.

14. Look at your fears; hold them up to the light of reason. Learn to laugh at your fears. That is the best medicine. Nothing can disturb you but your own thought. The suggestions, statements, or threats of other persons have no power. The power is within you, and when your thoughts are focused on that which is good, then God's power is with your thoughts of good.

15. There is only one creative power, and it moves as harmony. There are no divisions of quarrels in it. Its source is love. This is why God's power is with your thoughts of good.

20

How to Stay Young in Spirit Forever

Your subconscious mind never grows old. It is timeless, ageless, and endless. It is a part of the universal mind of God, which was never born and will never die.

Fatigue or old age does not have an impact on any spiritual quality or power. Patience, kindness, veracity, humility, goodwill, peace, harmony, and brotherly love are attributes and qualities that never grow old. If you continue to generate these qualities here on this plane of life, you will always remain young in spirit.

Years alone are not responsible for bringing about degenerative disorders. It is not time itself, but the *fear* of time that has a harmful aging effect on our minds and bodies. Indeed, the neurotic fear of the effects of time may well be the cause of premature aging.

During the many years of my public life, I have had occasion to study the biographies of famous men and women who have continued their productive activities into the years well beyond the normal span of life. Some of them even achieve their greatness for the first time in old age. It has also been my privilege to meet and get to know countless individuals of no special prominence who, in their lesser sphere, belong among those hardy mortals who have proved that old age itself does not destroy the creative powers of the mind and body.

HE HAD GROWN OLD IN HIS THOUGHT LIFE

A few years ago I called on an old friend in London, England. He had recently turned eighty. For many people, this is a cause for rejoicing, but unfortunately not for him. I was deeply shocked when I saw him. He looked and felt weak, even ill, although he admitted that his doctor had not found any particular medical problem.

"Doctors are idiots," he proclaimed. "I know very well what my disease is. It is life itself!"

I asked him what he meant.

"No one wants or needs me," he cried. "And why should they? I'm of no use to anyone. We are born, we grow up. We get old and we die, and that's the end of the story."

I saw that, in a way, he was right in his understanding of his illness. He was sick, not because of life, but because of the way he *viewed* life. His mental attitude of futility and worthlessness had brought about his sickness. He was looking forward only to senescence, and after that—nothing. Indeed, he had grown old in his thought life, and his subconscious mind made manifest everything he was expecting and dreading.

AGE IS THE DAWN OF WISDOM

Unfortunately, many people have the same attitude as this unhappy man. They are afraid of what they term "old age," the end, and extinction. What this really means is that they are afraid of life. Yet life is endless. Age is not the flight of years, but the dawn of wisdom.

Wisdom is the awareness of the tremendous spiritual powers in your subconscious mind and the knowledge of how to apply these powers to lead a full and happy life. Get it out of your head once and for all that sixty-five, seventy-five, or eighty-five years of age is synonymous with the end for you or anybody else. It can be the beginning of a glorious, fruitful, active, and most productive life pattern, better than you have ever experienced. Believe this, expect it, and your subconscious will bring it to pass.

WELCOME THE CHANGE

Old age is not a tragic occurrence. What we call the aging process is really change. It is to be welcomed joyfully and gladly. Each phase of human life is a step forward on a path that has no end. We have enormous powers that transcend the limits of our bodily powers. We have marvelous senses that transcend the limits of our five physical senses.

Life is spiritual and eternal. We need never grow old, for life, or God, cannot grow old. The Bible says that God is life. Life is self-renewing, eternal, indestructible, and is the reality of all people.

LIFE IS

A woman once asked Thomas Edison, the electrical wizard, "Mr. Edison, what is electricity?"

He replied, "Madame, electricity is. Use it."

Electricity is the name we give an invisible power that we do not fully comprehend. Yet we learn all we can about the principles of electricity and its uses. We use it in countless ways.

Scientists cannot see an electron with their eyes, yet they accept it as a scientific fact, because it is the only valid conclusion that coincides with other experimental evidence. We cannot see life. However, we know we are alive. Life is, and we are here to express it in all its beauty and glory.

MIND AND SPIRIT DO NOT GROW OLD

The Bible says,

> And this is life eternal, that they might know thee the only
> true God.

JOHN 17:3

Anyone who thinks or believes that the earthly cycle of birth, adolescence, youth, maturity, and old age is all there is to life is indeed to be pitied. Such a person has no anchor, no hope, no vision. To that person life has no meaning.

This type of belief brings frustration, stagnation, cynicism, and a sense of hopelessness that leads to neurosis and mental aberrations of all kinds. What if you can no longer play a fast game of tennis or swim as fast as your children? What if your body has slowed down, or you walk with a slow step? Remember, life is always clothing itself anew. What people call death is but a journey to a new city in another dimension of life.

I say to those who come to my lectures that they should accept what we call old age gracefully. Age has its own glory, beauty, and wisdom that belong to it. Peace, love, joy, beauty, happiness, wisdom, goodwill, and understanding are qualities that never grow old or die.

Ralph Waldo Emerson, poet and philosopher, said, "We do not count a man's years until he has nothing else to count."

Your character, the quality of your mind, your faith, and your convictions are not subject to decay.

YOU ARE AS YOUNG AS YOU THINK YOU ARE

I give public lectures in Caxton Hall in London, England, every few years. Following one of these lectures, a surgeon came up to speak to me.

"I am eighty-four years of age," he told me. "I operate every morning, visit patients in the afternoons, and I write for medical and other scientific journals in the evening."

His attitude was that he was as useful as he believed himself to be and as young as his thoughts. He said to me, "It's true what you said just now. A person is as strong as he thinks he is, and as valuable as he thinks he is."

This surgeon has not surrendered to advancing years. He knows that he is immortal. His final comment to me was "If I should pass on tomorrow, I will find myself helping and curing people in the next dimension, not with a surgeon's scalpel, but with mental and spiritual surgery."

YOUR GRAY HAIRS ARE AN ASSET

Don't ever walk away from an opportunity while thinking, "I'm too old to take this on." That way lies stagnation and mental death. If you become convinced you are finished, your subconscious mind will accept that belief and bring it into reality. Some people are old at thirty, while others are young at eighty. The mind is the master weaver, the architect, the designer, and the sculptor. The playwright George Bernard Shaw was still active at ninety, and the artistic quality of his mind had not relaxed from active duty.

I meet men and women who tell me that some employers almost slam the door in their faces when they say they are over forty. This attitude on the part of employers is cold, callous, and completely void of compassion and understanding.

Who decreed that you must be under thirty-five years of age to receive consideration? The reasoning behind this is shallow and specious. If the employer would stop to think, he or she would realize that the person was not selling his or her age or gray hair. Rather, the person would be willing to give of his or her talents, experience, and wisdom gathered through years of experience in the marketplace of life.

AGE IS AN ASSET

Your age should be a distinct asset to any organization, because of your practice and application through the years of the principles of the Golden Rule and the law of love and goodwill. Your gray hair, if you have any, should stand for greater wisdom, skill, and understanding. Your emotional and spiritual maturity should be a tremendous blessing to any organization.

People should not be shunted to the sidelines at sixty-five, or at any particular chronological age. That is a time of life when they could be most useful in handling personnel problems, making plans for the future, making decisions, and guiding others in the realm of creative ideas based on their experience and insight into the nature of the business.

BE YOUR AGE

"I've had it with this business!" a Hollywood scriptwriter told me. "I've done first-rate work for years. I know my craft as well as anyone in town. I've won awards at festivals around the world."

Puzzled, I asked, "Then what's wrong?"

He threw up his hands. "The last story conference I went to, this thirty-year-old studio executive told me I couldn't relate to today's audiences. When I tried to argue, he informed me that he didn't want any scripts that weren't geared to the minds and tastes of boys twelve to eighteen! I walked out."

This is a tragic state of affairs. How are the great masses of people expected to become emotionally and spiritually mature if they are fed such a diet? They are being blinded to the potential they have within them for personal growth. They are told that they must glorify youth, even though in reality *youth* stands for inexperience, lack of discernment, and hasty judgment.

I CAN KEEP UP WITH THE BEST OF THEM

I know dozens of people in their sixties and older who spend their time in a frantic campaign to stay young. They take fad drugs, follow fad diets, waste their money on flimsy exercise machines whose virtues are touted on late night television. Those with greater resources go in for spa treatments, liposuction, and cosmetic surgery. Their constant, futile cry is, "Look, I can keep up with the best of them!"

These people should remember a great truth:

> As a man thinketh in his heart, so is he.
>
> *PROV. 23:7*

Diets, multivitamins, and supports of all kinds will not keep these people young. They must realize that they grow old or remain young in accordance with their processes of thinking. Your subconscious mind is conditioned by your thoughts. If your thoughts are constantly on the beautiful, the noble, and the good, you will remain spiritually young regardless of your chronological years.

FEAR OF OLD AGE

Job said, *The thing which I greatly feared is come upon me.*
Many people fear old age. They are uncertain about the
future, because they anticipate mental and physical deterioration as the years advance. What they think and feel comes
to pass.

You grow old when you lose interest in life, when you
cease to dream, to hunger after new truths, and to search for
new worlds to conquer. When your mind is open to new
ideas and new interests and when you raise the curtain and
let in the sunshine and inspiration of new truths of life and
the universe, you will be young and vital.

YOU HAVE MUCH TO GIVE

Whether you are sixty-five or ninety-five years of age, you
must realize you have much to give. You can help stabilize,
advise, and direct the younger generation. You can give the
benefit of your knowledge, your experience, and your wisdom. You can always look ahead, for at all times you are gazing into infinite life. You will find that you can never cease to
unveil the glories and wonders of life. Try to learn something
new every moment of the day and you will find your mind
will always be young.

ONE HUNDRED AND TEN YEARS OLD

Some years ago while lecturing in Bombay, India, I was
introduced to a man whose friends told me was one hundred
ten years old. He had the most beautiful face I have ever seen.
He seemed transfigured by the radiance of an inner light.
There was a rare beauty in his eyes. I could see he had grown
old in years with gladness and with no indication that his
mind had dimmed its lights.

RETIREMENT—A NEW VENTURE

Be sure that your mind never retires. Your mind must be like a parachute—it's of no use at all unless it opens up. Be open and receptive to new ideas. I have seen people of sixty-five and seventy retire. They seemed to rot away, and in a few months passed on. They obviously felt that their life had come to an end, and because they thought so, it *was* so.

Retirement can be a new venture, a new challenge, a new path, the beginning of the fulfillment of a long dream. It is inexpressibly depressing to hear someone say, "What will I do now that I am retired?" He or she is saying, in effect, "I am mentally and physically dead. My mind is bankrupt of ideas."

All this is a false picture. The real truth is that you can accomplish more at ninety than you did at sixty, because each day you are growing in wisdom and understanding of life and the universe through your new studies and interest.

HE GRADUATED TO A BETTER JOB

Frank W. is an executive who lives near me. He was forced out of his job a few months ago. The company told him it was because of a new restructuring plan, but he believed his age of sixty-five lay behind the decision.

"Do you feel bitter about being the victim of discrimination?" I asked him. "Are you going to sue?"

He laughed ruefully. "I could, I suppose. And I guess I might very well win in court. But why should I spend my time and energy that way? I haven't lost my job, the company has lost my services."

He paused, then added, "The way I look at it, I just got my promotion from kindergarten to the first grade."

"How do you mean?"

"Well, for instance," he replied, "when I graduated from

high school, I climbed to the next rung of the ladder by going to college. I took a step forward in my education and understanding of life in general. My career was another step, or maybe a few steps. Now I've been liberated to do things I've always wanted to do. In other words, being let go is still another step upward on the ladder of life."

Frank came to the wise conclusion that he was no longer going to concentrate on making a living. Now he was going to give all his attention to living life. He had been a passionate amateur photographer for years. He made a commitment to take courses in photographic technique at a nearby art institute. Later he went on a voyage around the world. At each place he visited, he took dozens of rolls of film. He now lectures before various groups, lodges, and clubs and is in constant demand.

There are countless ways of taking an interest in something worthwhile outside yourself. Become enthusiastic over new creative ideas, make spiritual progress, and continue to learn and to grow. In this manner you remain young in heart, because you are hungering and thirsting after new truths, and your body will reflect your thinking at all times.

YOU MUST BE A PRODUCER AND NOT A PRISONER OF SOCIETY

Laws that prohibit employers from discriminating against men and women because of age are a step in the right direction, but laws alone cannot alter the way people think. Someone of sixty-five years may be younger mentally, physically, and physiologically than many people of thirty. We are here to enjoy the fruits of our labor, to be a producer and not a prisoner of society that sentences us to idleness because of our age.

A person's body slows down gradually as he or she advances through the years, but his conscious mind can be made much more active, alert, alive, and quickened by the inspiration from his or her subconscious mind. The mind, in reality, never grows old. Job said,

> Oh that I were as in months past, as in the days when God preserved me; When his candle shined upon my head, and when by his light I walked through darkness; As I was in the days of my youth, when the secret of God was upon my tabernacle.
>
> *JOB 29:2–4*

SECRET OF YOUTH

To recapture the days of your youth, feel the miraculous, healing, self-renewing power of your subconscious mind moving through your whole being. Know and feel that you are inspired, lifted up, rejuvenated, revitalized, and recharged spiritually. You can bubble over with enthusiasm and joy, as in the days of your youth, for the simple reason that you can always mentally and emotionally recapture that joyous state.

The candle that shines upon your head is divine intelligence. It reveals to you everything you need to know. It enables you to affirm the presence of your good, regardless of appearances. You walk by the guidance of your subconscious mind, because you know that the dawn appears and the shadows flee.

GET A VISION

Instead of saying, "I am old," say, "I am wise in the way of the divine life." Don't let the corporation, newspapers, or statistics hold a picture before you of old age, declining years, decrepitude, senility, and uselessness. Reject it, for it is a lie. Refuse to be hypnotized by such propaganda. Affirm life—not death. Get a vision of yourself as happy, radiant, successful, serene, and powerful.

YOUR MIND DOES NOT GROW OLD

The pioneering heart surgeon Michael DeBakey developed the first roller pump for blood in 1932. His pump is still used for heart bypass surgery. At the age of ninety, Dr. DeBakey got permission to start clinical trials on a new invention, a tiny pump that can be implanted in the chests of those with severe heart disease. Not content with research, DeBakey pursued an active surgical schedule as well. A colleague said, "It would take other people five or six lifetimes to do what he's done."

DeBakey summed up his philosophy at ninety this way: "As long as you have challenges and are physically and mentally able, life is stimulating and invigorating."

HIS MIND ACTIVE AT NINETY-NINE

My father learned the French language at sixty-five years of age and became an authority on it at seventy. He began the study of Gaelic when he was over sixty and became an acknowledged and famous teacher of the subject. He assisted my sister at an institute of higher education until he passed away at ninety-nine. His mind was as clear at ninety-nine as it had been when he was twenty. In fact, his reasoning powers became even sharper with age. Truly, you are as old as you think and feel.

We need our senior citizens

Marcus Porcius Cato, the Roman patriot, learned Greek at eighty. Madame Ernestine Schumann-Heink, the great German-American contralto, reached the pinnacle of her musical success after she became a grandmother.

The Greek philosopher Socrates learned to play musical instruments when he was eighty years old. Michelangelo was painting his greatest canvases at eighty. At eighty, Cios Simonides won the prize for poetry, Johann von Goethe finished *Faust*, and Leopold von Ranke commenced his *History of the World*, which he finished at ninety-two.

Alfred, Lord Tennyson wrote a magnificent poem, "Crossing the Bar," at eighty-three. Isaac Newton was hard at work close to eighty-five. At eighty-eight John Wesley was directing, preaching, and guiding Methodism.

Jeanne Louise Calment of Arles, France, was not famous as these people were famous. In her youth, she once met a famous man, the painter Vincent van Gogh, but that did not bring her any particular notice. It was not until after her one-hundredth birthday that those around her began to pay attention. For her, it was the occasion to give up riding her bicycle every day!

On Calment's one-hundred-tenth birthday, she received greetings and good wishes from around the world. Her one-hundred-eighteenth birthday made her the oldest documented human in history. When asked how she had done it, she said, "I took pleasure when I could. I acted clearly and morally and without regret. I'm very lucky." At one hundred twenty-two, her smile was as radiant and contagious as ever.

Let us place our senior citizens in high places and give them every opportunity to bring forth the flowers of Paradise.

If you are retired, get interested in the laws of life and the wonders of your subconscious mind. Do something you have always wanted to do. Study new subjects and investigate new ideas.

Pray as follows:

> As the hart panteth after the water brooks, so panteth my soul after thee, O God.
>
> *PSALM 42:1*

THE FRUITS OF OLD AGE

> His flesh shall be fresher than a child's: he shall return to the days of his youth.
>
> *JOB 33:25*

Old age really means the contemplation of the truths of God from the highest standpoint. Realize that you are on an endless journey, a series of important steps in the ceaseless, tireless, endless ocean of life. Then, with the Psalmist you will say,

> They shall still bring forth fruit in old age; they shall be fat and flourishing.
>
> *PSALM 92:14*

> But the fruit of the Spirit is love, joy, peace, patience, gentleness, goodness, faith, meekness, temperance: against such there is no law.
>
> *GALATIANS 5:22–23*

You are a child of infinite life, which knows no end, and you are an heir to eternity.

PROFITABLE POINTERS

1. Patience, kindness, love, goodwill, joy, happiness, wisdom, and understanding are qualities that never grow old. Cultivate them and express them and remain young in mind and body.

2. The neurotic fear of the effects of time may well be the cause of premature aging.

3. Age is not the flight of years; it is the dawn of wisdom in the mind of humans.

4. The most productive years of your life can be from sixty-five to ninety-five.

5. Welcome the advancing years. It means you are moving higher on the path of life, which has no end.

6. God is life, and that is your life now. Life is self-renewing, eternal, and indestructible and is the reality of all humans. You live forever, because your life is God's life.

7. You cannot see your mind, but you know you have a mind. You cannot see spirit, but you know that the spirit of the game, the spirit of the artist, the spirit of the musician, and the spirit of the speaker is real. Likewise, the spirit of goodness, truth, and beauty moving in your mind and heart are real. You cannot see life, but you know you are alive.

8. Old age may be called the contemplation of the truths of God from the highest standpoint. The joys of old age are greater than those of youth. Your mind is engaged in spiritual and mental athletics. Nature slows your body so that you may have the opportunity to meditate on things divine.

9. We do not count a man's years until he has nothing else

to count. Your faith and convictions are not subject to decay.

10. You are as young as you think you are. You are as strong as you think you are. You are as useful as you think you are. You are as young as your thoughts.

11. Your gray hairs are an asset. You are not selling your gray hairs. You are selling your talent, abilities, and wisdom that you have garnered through the years.

12. Fad diets and expensive pills won't keep you young. *As a man thinketh, so is he.*

13. Fear of old age can bring about physical and mental deterioration. *The thing I greatly feared has come upon me.*

14. You grow old when you cease to dream and when you lose interest in life. You grow old if you are irritable, crotchety, petulant, and cantankerous. Fill your mind with the truths of God and radiate the sunshine of his love—this is youth.

15. Look ahead, for at all times you are gazing into infinite life.

16. Your retirement is a new venture. Take up new studies and interests. You can do the things you always wanted to do when you were so busy making a living. Give your attention to living life.

17. Become a producer and not a prisoner of society. Don't hide your light under a bushel.

18. The secret of youth is love, joy, inner peace, and laughter. In God there is fullness of joy. In God there is no darkness at all.

19. You are needed. Some of the great philosophers, artists, scientists, writers, and others accomplished their greatest work after they were eighty years old.

20. The fruits of old age are love, joy, peace, patience, gentleness, goodness, faith, meekness, and temperance.
21. You are a child of the infinite life that knows no end. You are an heir to eternity. You are wonderful!

Index

Nobody could have written this book better than Bill Hybels. Full of practical advice, hard-won wisdom, and spiritual insights, *Simplify* contains everything you need to create a God-first schedule that will radically simplify your life. And when you do, you'll find a freedom you'd almost forgotten was possible.

ANDY STANLEY
Senior pastor of North Point Ministries

I learned a long time ago that if I didn't take control of my schedule and my money, they would always take control of me. Learning when and how to say no has given me more freedom than you can imagine. It's a word I always teach young leaders, and it's a message I'm glad Bill Hybels is bringing in *Simplify*.

DAVE RAMSEY
New York Times bestselling author and nationally syndicated radio show host

It has been said, "Beware when a naked man offers you a shirt." But Bill Hybels writing a book on simplicity is exactly the opposite, because he speaks from a well of experience. I treasure his perspective because he has led through complexity for several decades and echoes what great leaders always say: Simplicity is the key to making a complex life successful. Thank you, Bill.

DR. HENRY CLOUD
Leadership expert, psychologist, and bestselling author

My dad has always inspired me to live with more intention and clarity, and always helped me navigate the steps from here to there. I'm thrilled that his wisdom is now in a format that I can hand out to friends, and I will, because I don't know who doesn't need this kind of rich thinking about what it means to live with focus and sanity and peace. I love these ideas, and I can't wait to share this book.

SHAUNA NIEQUIST
Proud daughter, author of *Bread and Wine*, www.shaunaniequist.com

As a wife, mum, founder of an anti-trafficking organization, and church leader, it's quite easy to feel overwhelmed or frenetic at times. But I desire to be anchored in the truth of God's Word and lead a busy life well. In *Simplify*, Bill Hybels helps to guide us into a soul detox from being exhausted to energized, frenetic to faithful. Ultimately, it's taught me to be more by doing less, building a life on health and wholeness, not cluttered chaos.

CHRISTINE CAINE
Founder of The A21 Campaign and bestselling author of *Undaunted*

No one can truly impact a complex, broken outer world if they do not have a simple, healthy inner world. Bill has navigated exceedingly complex demands for many years; in *Simplify* he shares concrete steps into the "easy yoke" of Jesus, learned in the pressure cooker of real life.

JOHN ORTBERG
Senior pastor of Menlo Park Presbyterian Church and author of *Who Is This Man?*

If you have ever ached inside because life is so complicated, this is the book for you. In *Simplify*, Bill Hybels walks you on a journey to redefine your perspective, realign your priorities, and reignite your faith in Christ. This book will not only give you hope, but also practical truths to live the life you always hoped was possible.

CRAIG GROESCHEL
Pastor of LifeChurch.tv and author of *Fight: Winning the Battles That Matter Most*

Bill Hybels's masterful and courageous work, *Simplify: Ten Practices to Unclutter Your Soul*, has again brought clear answers to questions we're all asking. Read and digest these principles. They have become my personal assignment for this next season.

WAYNE CORDEIRO
Pastor of New Hope Christian Fellowship

BILL HYBELS

simplify.

ten practices to unclutter your soul

**TYNDALE™
MOMENTUM**

*An Imprint of
Tyndale House Publishers, Inc.*

Visit Tyndale online at www.tyndale.com.

Visit Tyndale Momentum online at www.tyndalemomentum.com.

TYNDALE is a registered trademark of Tyndale House Publishers, Inc. *Tyndale Momentum* and the Tyndale Momentum logo are trademarks of Tyndale House Publishers, Inc. Tyndale Momentum is an imprint of Tyndale House Publishers, Inc.

Simplify: Ten Practices to Unclutter Your Soul

Designed by Jacqueline L. Nuñez

Library of Congress Cataloging-in-Publication Data

Hybels, Bill.
    Simplify : ten practices to unclutter your soul / Bill Hybels.
      pages cm
    Includes bibliographical references.
    ISBN 978-1-4143-9122-9 (hc)
  1. Simplicity—Religious aspects—Christianity. 2. Spiritual life—Christianity. 3. Christian life.
I. Title.
    BV4647.S48H93 2014
    248.4—dc23   2014009469

ISBN 978-1-4143-9712-2 (International Trade Paper Edition)

Printed in the United States of America

20	19	18	17	16	15	14
7	6	5	4	3	2	1

To Henry and Mac, the two little grandboys who turned
a tough Dutch guy into a shameless idiot.

Contents

from exhausted to energized

Replenishing Your Energy Reserves

A GOOD PORTION of my work these days involves coaching and mentoring leaders, both here in the United States and around the world. Increasingly, whether I'm speaking with leaders at home or abroad, at Willow Creek or in other circles of my life, I hear the same words repeated over and over: *exhausted, overwhelmed, overscheduled, anxious, isolated, dissatisfied.* It's a bipartisan issue—young and old, rich and poor, professionals and parents, women and men, Republicans and Democrats. And it's a global issue—I've heard these words in English and in countless foreign languages.

It was startling to hear these words so often. I began to realize that, as leaders and Christ followers, we needed to address this situation. So whenever I had a chance, I began openly discussing burnout, stress, and dissatisfaction. My gut told me the topics might strike a chord with people, because they certainly struck a chord with me.

I grossly underestimated the impact.

As I explored the concerns that leave people feeling isolated, overwhelmed, and exhausted, and as I sought to formulate a framework for how to tackle the diverse complexities of these issues, I began using the term *simplify*. How do we *simplify* our lives? The term stuck. The very word seemed to energize people.

Perhaps they hoped I would unveil a closely held secret, a key to the universe that would help them uncomplicate their frazzled lives. Perhaps they assumed I was well beyond these issues in my own experience and hoped I might whisk some crumbs of wisdom off the mahogany table of my life into their waiting and eagerly cupped hands.

Not so! Those who know me well can tell you I've spent the majority of my adult life wrestling with the same dark swarm of words I've lately been hearing from leaders across the globe. I am nowhere near immune. I know far too much about being overwhelmed and overscheduled and exhausted. I know all too well what it feels like to be anxious, dissatisfied, wounded, and spent. As I've talked about these issues, I have been both a student and a teacher, to be sure. You'll see in the pages you're about to read that I'm a serious fellow learner on the topic of simplifying our lives.

> Simplified living is about more than doing less. It's being who God called us to be.

I am not naturally inclined to lead a simple life. I feel a strong sense of responsibility to the calling God has entrusted to me—not just at work, but also with my family, the relationships I invest in, the recreation I need for my mental health, and the travel my work requires. I don't foresee my life slowing to a lounge-by-the-pool pace anytime soon, if ever. Can you relate?

Simplified living is about more than doing less. It's being who God called us to be, with a wholehearted, single-minded focus. It's walking away from innumerable lesser opportunities in favor of the few to which we've been called and for which we've been created. It's a lifestyle that allows us, when our heads hit the pillow at night, to reflect with gratitude that our day was well invested and the varied responsibilities of our lives are in order.

If we don't change how we live, our overcomplicated world will begin to feel frighteningly normal. We will become accustomed to life at a frantic pace, no longer able to discriminate between the important and the unessential. And that's the danger: When we fritter away our one and only life doing things that don't *really* matter, we sacrifice the things that do matter. Through more misses than hits, I have experienced the high cost of allowing my life to get out of control. My desire is to spare you some of the pain of learning these lessons as I did—the hard way.

What if your life could be different? What if you could be certain you were living the life God called you to live and building a legacy for those you love? If you crave a simpler life anchored by the priorities that matter most, roll up your sleeves: Simplified living requires more than just organizing your closets or cleaning out your desk drawer. It requires *uncluttering your soul.* By examining core issues that lure you into frenetic living, and by eradicating the barriers that leave you exhausted and overwhelmed, you can stop doing the stuff that doesn't matter and build your life on the stuff that does.

> Simplified living requires more than just organizing your closets or cleaning out your desk drawer. It requires *uncluttering your soul.*

In my experience, a handful of key practices are vital to keeping my soul clutter-free. These practices help me overcome the barriers that keep me from living the life "to the full" that Jesus promises in John 10:10. In each chapter of this book, I invite you to examine one of these practices, assess what Scripture has to say about it, hold up a mirror to your own life, and then take action.

There are no shortcuts to simplified living. Untangling yourself from the overscheduled, overwhelming web of your current life is not for the faint of heart. It's honest, rigorous work. As I tell leaders whenever I speak on the subject, action *is* required. That's why each chapter of this book concludes with Action Steps—questions about what keeps you in bondage to such frenetic, cluttered patterns, as well as hands-on practices for eradicating clutter from your soul and moving toward a simplified life. I challenge you to go beyond reading each chapter merely for theory. Don't let an intellectual nod to the concept of simplified living inoculate you against making actual changes in your actual life. Rather, *apply* what you read with *courage* and *grit*.

I can tell you from my own experience that simplifying your life will produce immediate rewards. Each day will have a clear purpose, and each relationship will receive the investment it's due. And without the needless clutter clanging around in your soul, you'll be able to hear—and respond to—each whisper from God.

This is what I know: *Change is possible*. Whether you're teetering on the edge of a cluttered collapse or you're just starting to realize that some minor life adjustments are in order, you *can* simplify. You may well *have to* simplify to live the life God is inviting you to live. As you begin to implement these key practices, they will become habits that create simplified days, then months, then years, and eventually a lifetime that brings satisfaction and fulfillment. Making these course corrections will produce a life you'll be glad to have lived when you look in the rearview mirror.

You've been warned: This process is not for the faint of heart. Action on your part *is* required. Still game? Let's dive in.

"TELL HER TO HELP ME!"

Of all the people Jesus interacted with during His three-year teaching ministry, Scripture records only one person whom He redirected in the area of simplicity: a good friend of His, a woman named Martha.

Jesus had hundreds of followers during His ministry—not just the twelve disciples—but He chose only a handful to be in His inner friendship circle. Three were His disciples: Peter, James, and John. And there were three others: Mary, Martha, and Lazarus, siblings who were faithful supporters of His ministry. They lived in a little suburb of Jerusalem called Bethany, which still exists today. Jesus stayed with them from time to time and deeply valued their hospitality.

The incident I'm about to describe took place as the demands on Jesus were growing. The more He taught, the more people wanted from Him—more healings, more miracles, more of everything He could offer. His days were increasingly packed. So occasionally, Jesus called a time-out and retreated to the serenity of the guest quarters in Bethany, where He could wind down for a day or two and refuel in the company of His closest friends. Here's how Luke describes one such visit:

> As Jesus and his disciples were on their way, he came to a village where a woman named Martha opened her home to him. She had a sister called Mary, who sat at the Lord's feet listening to what he said. But Martha was distracted by all the preparations that had to be made. She came to him and asked, "Lord, don't you care that my sister has left me to do the work by myself? Tell her to help me!"
>
> "Martha, Martha," the Lord answered, "you are worried and upset about many things, but few things are needed—or indeed only one. Mary has chosen what is better, and it will not be taken away from her."[1]

You can see the dynamics of this situation shaping up from a mile away. Mary and Martha have had no time to prepare for this drop-in visit by Jesus and twelve dusty disciples. But Jesus feels comfortable enough in His friendship with them that He stops by for some replenishing time.

Mary decides to go with the flow and pulls up a chair. Perhaps she says something to Jesus like, "I'm so glad You stopped by. How's it been going on the road? How big a pain have the Pharisees been lately? You can tell us; we're friends. What You share in Bethany stays in Bethany."

Meanwhile, Martha has busied herself in the kitchen getting a meal going. She is frantically trying to play the role of accommodating hostess, tending to the physical needs of Jesus and His disciples—appetizers, entrées, and drinks. It begins to grate on her that Mary is simply lounging in the other room with Jesus, catching up on the latest events.

After a while, Martha snaps. She loses it. She's clearly ticked. Perhaps she had already attempted some subtle cues to get her sister to give her a hand with the food. First she may have peeked around the corner and given Mary the stink-eye—the look that says, *Get in here and help me!* Then maybe she started dropping pans to get Mary's attention. My wife, Lynne, used to do that with me. When she thought I wasn't helping enough, she'd "accidentally" let a few pans crash to the kitchen floor. After about the fifth pan—I was a little slow on the draw—I would catch a clue: "That's the signal!" And I'd head for the kitchen to pitch in.

We don't know whether Mary has missed, or has chosen to ignore, her sister's hints that she needs help, but at a certain point, Martha bursts into the room and interrupts the conversation Mary is having with Jesus. She doesn't address Mary; she addresses Jesus directly with an opening salvo: "Lord, don't You care?"

The irony here is thick. "Don't You care?" she asks the Lord of the universe, the one who left heaven's splendor to put on human flesh and descend into first-century Palestine; who has been out on the road, teaching and healing and serving others until He's absolutely exhausted; and who will soon bleed and die for the redemption of everyone in the world, including Martha.

"Don't You care?"

I picture Martha in this scene with a wooden spoon in her hand. She gets right up in Jesus' face: "You tell her to help me! Order that lazy sister of mine into the kitchen before I do something with this spoon!"

If I were Jesus, I would have had several ideas running through my mind about what Martha could do with that spoon. But Jesus doesn't escalate the conflict. He doesn't power up on Martha. He doesn't say, "How dare you speak to the Son of God this way . . ." According to the text, He simply says her name twice: "Martha, Martha." In other words, "Easy does it, Martha. Take a chill pill."

> Jesus doesn't escalate the conflict. He doesn't say, "How dare you speak to the Son of God this way . . ."

Then, with genuine kindness, He makes an observation: "You are worried and upset about many things."

He can tell she's overwhelmed, overscheduled, and exhausted— the very words that define our culture. And He invites her to put down her spoon and take a couple of deep breaths.

"So many things are occupying your mind right now," He says. "They're churning you up inside. You're making My visit much more complicated than I want it to be."

I picture Jesus clarifying the lines, taking advantage of a teachable moment for everyone in the room: "Martha, can I simplify something for you? Whenever I stop by, it's not for the food. If I wanted a five-star dinner, I could arrange for one—I just fed five thousand people a couple of weeks ago, you know. And I made some awesome chardonnay at a wedding reception once. I can arrange for food and drink anywhere, anytime. When I stop by to visit, it's for friendship, for connection, to be with you. I come here for the life-giving, life-exchanging engagement, for fellowship. That's all, really."

In Luke's text, Jesus tells Martha something that I, too, often need to be reminded of: *Few things are needed—indeed only one.*

Martha was missing what mattered most; but not Mary. She got it.

"Mary has chosen the good part," Jesus says, "and I'm not going to take it away from her. I will not send her into the kitchen to do a dozen things that don't really matter in the big picture."

By affirming Mary's choice, Jesus invites Martha to set down her spoon and follow her sister's example.

Your heart and mine yearn for an antidote to all the drivenness and busyness in our lives. The antidote isn't getting it all done in the kitchen—or the office, or the mall. The antidote is leaving that stuff—sometimes undone—to sit down for an unrushed conversation with Jesus.

> Your heart and mine yearn for an antidote to all the drivenness and busyness in our lives.

What a terrific story. In a few short words, Jesus teaches us about His values and priorities.

I also find it fascinating that the Gospel of Luke juxtaposes the Mary and Martha story with the parable of the Good Samaritan.[2] On the heels of teaching His followers to be active and help those in need, Jesus strikes a different note in His response to Martha's activism. "In all your activity," He says, "don't lose sight of relationship."

Unrushed. Unhurried. Let's sit down and get caught up with each other.

Relationship.

WAKE-UP CALL

Some years back, I had a "moment" that was far uglier than Martha's ugly moment. At the time, I had felt depleted not just for days, not just for weeks, but for *months*. Things had gotten so bad that, one by one, my wife and kids had subtly suggested that maybe I should spend some time at our family cottage in Michigan. *Alone.* Their unanimous, unspoken message was loud and clear: *You're over the edge. You're no fun around here. Go inflict yourself* on *yourself for a few days. In another state!*

It didn't take a genius to crack the code. So I packed my duffel bag.

As I walked down the long hallway to our garage, our little dog saw me coming—and he dove out of the way into the laundry room. Even the dog knew I was on edge. It seemed I was the last to notice.

On my drive over to the cottage that day, I had my wooden spoon out, just like Martha, and I was giving God an earful. I complained about the elders of our church: "They have unrealistic expectations!" I complained about the staff: "They always want stuff from me, and they rarely thank me." Then the spoon grew to the size of a canoe paddle, and I complained about our congregation: "They think I'm just a sermon machine, and they don't really care about me as a person."

For the entire three-hour drive, I was shaking the spoon. When I arrived at the cottage, I deposited my duffel bag in the bedroom and headed to the kitchen to make something to eat. When I opened the fridge and discovered there was no food, my complaints continued: "Whoever stayed here last hasn't given any thought to the one who would be coming over next—*the one who pays the bills!* They don't give a rip about me either!"

So I drove to the little grocery store in town to pick up a bag of groceries. And I was none too happy about it, believe me.

After I paid the cashier, I walked toward the screen-door exit. Out of the corner of my eye, I spotted a guy I'd seen around town before—a wounded Vietnam vet in his wheelchair. I noticed he was also moving toward the door. I calculated his speed and compared it to mine. I calculated his angle and compared it to mine. And I remember thinking, *Are you kidding me? He and I are going to reach the door at exactly the same time. He's going to be moving slowly because he's in the wheelchair, and I suppose I should be courteous and help him. . . .*

And here was my next thought: *What else could go wrong for me today, God? What else could go wrong?*

In that same split second, God took the scales off my eyes, and I looked into the cesspool of resentment, exhaustion, and darkness that filled my heart. And I'm not kidding you—when I saw it in all its ugliness, I felt my knees grow weak. I thought I might vomit right there in the store.

> God took the scales off my eyes, and I looked into the cesspool of resentment, exhaustion, and darkness that filled my heart.

I pulled it together enough to help the guy navigate the doorway, but the moment I exited that tiny grocery store, I had to admit to God and to myself that I was more concerned about the *fifteen seconds* longer it had taken me to get through the door than I was about the fifteen *years* that soldier had spent in a wheelchair after injuries sustained while serving our country.

Reeling from that realization, I walked to my truck, climbed in, put my head on the steering wheel, and lost it: *What has happened to me? Who have I become?*

I had to admit: *I hate who I've become.* And then I begged, "God, help me. God, help me. God, help me."

That was my rock-bottom moment, when I finally realized the price of depletion. Coming to my senses in the parking lot of that little grocery store was like when an alcoholic wakes up in his neighbor's wheelbarrow at three o'clock in the morning and finally admits, "I drink too much. How did this happen?" I just sat there, asking God, "How did this happen? How did I become this overwhelmed, overscheduled, exhausted person who is devoid of compassion and angry at everybody? How did this happen?"

Before I left the parking lot that day, I made a vow: *Never again will I allow myself to get this depleted. The cost is too high. Never again.* And to this day, I have a maniacal aversion to depletion. I know what I'm like when I get to the edge. I know what I'm capable of. And I'm not going there again.

I know I disappoint a lot of people when they ask me to do things for them and I feel I must say no:

"Please do my wedding."

"Would you please mentor my son?"

"Can you please get behind my cause?"

"Will you please . . . ?"

As a pastor and as a friend, it's hard for me to say no to the many wonderful people I'd like to help and the many wonderful things I'd like to do around our church and around the world. But I have learned the hard way how important it is to not let myself get completely spent. I've already bottomed out once, and that was more than enough. Depletion harms the people around me, and it damages my soul.

When you decide that you never want to live on empty again, you start paying more attention to the replenishment side of the equation. If you choose to live with more energy reserves in your life, you will without a doubt disappoint some people. Trust me, you have to *fight* to keep your life replenished. No one else can keep your tank full. It's up to you to protect your energy reserves and priorities.

> When you decide that you never want to live on empty again, you start paying more attention to the replenishment side of the equation.

I don't know if you've ever hit rock bottom like I did, but I know I'm not alone in the exhaustion game. A depleted dad from Willow Creek told me recently that he almost took a swing at his fifteen-year-old son. The dad had been running on fumes for about six months, and when he and his son got into an argument a few weeks back, he very nearly did the unthinkable. Thankfully, he caught himself about mid-swing and was so horrified by his anger that he called me to talk about it; he also called a Christian counselor. That dad was in shock: "I was this close to punching *my son*. What has happened to me?" Depletion can be costly.

Another guy told me, "I'm suing a business friend out of sheer anger. I don't care if I win the case; I just want to mess with his life." I told him, "Uh, I think you're a little over the edge. I think you're on empty, friend. If you're doing lawsuits for sport, you've been at the bottom of your energy reserves for far too long."

And then a Willow Creek couple I know filed for bankruptcy. Both husband and wife overspend when they're depleted—and they've been depleted for a long time, so they've just been going to the mall and racking up charges. Now their credit cards are maxed out and they're behind on their mortgage, and if something doesn't change soon, they will lose everything.

Suing for sport or overspending to the point of bankruptcy? That's depleted living.

HOW FULL IS YOUR BUCKET?

I warned you: The path to simplicity is not for the faint of heart. It's a process that requires total honesty. So let me pose the question: How depleted are you? How long has it been since you have felt fully replenished?

Jesus told Martha that her only hope was to pull up a chair, unplug from all the busyness, and begin a conversation with the only one who could restore her frenetic heart, settle her spirit, and get her heading back to true north. Is the same true for you?

Allow me to ask a follow-up question: Would an honest conversation with Jesus, in an unrushed setting, help you, too?

Of all the leaders I've had the opportunity to meet—from CEOs to nonprofit execs to politicians to church leaders—guess which type is most likely to have a problem with being overwhelmed, overscheduled, and exhausted?

Senior pastors! Card-carrying, seminary-graduated women and men of the cloth. Exhaustion runs rampant among pastors. This subject comes up in every city, every country, every culture, and every language group in which I've had the privilege of doing some mentoring and training. It's a universal theme.

Here's what I often do with my exhausted pastor friends: First, I draw a simple picture of a bucket, on a whiteboard or a napkin, depending on the setting. I ask, "What does your life feel like when your energy bucket is filled to the brim? What does it feel like when you're filled up with God, when you're connected to Jesus Christ, when things in your family are running on all cylinders, when your schedule is sane, when you're eating right and exercising and sleeping properly? How does it feel to be filled up and replenished?"

Here's how they describe full-bucket living:

- "I'm at my best when I'm filled up."
- "I pray my best prayers."
- "I feel the presence of God more consistently."
- "I'm more attentive to the whispers of the Holy Spirit."
- "I hear the voice of God more often than when I'm depleted."
- "I love my spouse and my family well."
- "I love perfect strangers. Heck, I even love Packer fans!"[3] (When I hear this in Chicago, it's impressive!)
- "When I'm filled up, I make better decisions about my schedule. I'm careful not to overcommit."
- "I make better food choices and rest choices."
- "I feel more creative, more soulful."
- "I feel eager to do God's bidding."

Sometimes, a pastor will get real quiet for a minute and then say, "When I'm all filled up, I live the life that Jesus desires for me: life in all its fullness, a life characterized by that peace that passes human understanding." With a nostalgic nod, these pastors reflect fondly on times when they were all filled up, living a life-to-the-full kind of life.

How about you? Can you recall a time when you were living that way? When you were replenished and filled up? When you were living soulfully, restfully, creatively, lovingly, playfully, prayerfully? My guess is you can recall a handful of such times in your life. (If not, keep reading—there's hope!) I can recall such times too—and increasingly they are becoming the norm rather than the exception, as I seek to master the art of simplified living. It can be done.

Hold on to that image for a second, and let's switch gears. Let's talk about times when you're depleted—toxically depleted. Your bucket is empty. You have nothing left to give. What does that feel like?

When I ask people this question, no matter where I am in the world, the first word that comes out of their mouths is *resentment*. They resent someone or something—just like Martha coming out of the kitchen shaking a wooden spoon at Mary and Jesus. She was resentful. "Jesus, don't You care? My sister's a deadbeat. We can't order takeout. Your disciples are mooches. And they never help with the dishes."

Resentment. Ever feel it? I do.

Another word I hear frequently is *irritated*. Some of us are easily irritated when we get depleted. Something minor goes wrong, and it sets us off, all out of proportion. We snap at our spouse, we lose our temper at work, we kick the dog.

Some of us withdraw and become passive.

Some of us isolate and become loners.

Some of us overeat, overdrink, or overmedicate.

Some of us overwork.

I feel horrible admitting it, but overwork is *my* approach. My colleagues know it's true. When I'm depleted, I put my shoulder to the wheel and work like a mad banshee, pushing myself and everyone around me mercilessly.

And let me confess something that makes me extra lovable: When I'm in one of my overworking spells, I get mad at anyone who *isn't* overworking. I get irritated if someone is whistling in the hallways at Willow. I think, *What are you whistling about? You should be working harder instead of whistling! You're clearly under-challenged. Step into my office and I'll straighten that out!*

> When we get depleted, we get scattered. We lose our ability to focus, and we jump from one distraction to the next with little to show for it.

Sometimes when we get depleted, we get scattered. We lose our ability to focus, and we jump from one distraction to the next with little to show for it. We confuse *motion* with *progress.*

Some of us over-rev. We get all the plates spinning at some ridiculous RPM. When people look at us, they just shake their heads. *Whoa! This is going to end badly.*

Some of us, when we get depleted, escape into movies, cheesy novels, or television. We waste hour upon hour trolling Facebook, Pinterest, or Instagram, admiring others' lives instead of living our own.

Some of us overspend. When we get totally depleted, we go to the mall with credit cards, looking for the type of quick high that fits in a shopping bag.

Some of us turn to pornography. Those who don't have the energy or emotional health to pursue intimacy in a healthy way often go after it in the shadows. If you look at what's underneath the skyrocketing use of pornography these days, a lot of it is connected to depletion, isolation, and exhaustion. In the same way, some people have affairs. (Sometimes several.)

I think it's safe to say that none of us are at our best when we're depleted.

If you find yourself shaking that wooden spoon—or that canoe paddle—and you're telling God what to do, and you're mad at the world, maybe it's time for you to hear God say to you, "Let's sit down together. We've got some things to work out, you and Me. You've lost a connection with Me somewhere. You've lost your bearings on true north, and now you're just spinning. But I have a better plan."

REPLENISHING YOUR ENERGY RESERVES

Here's where things get fun. Not simple—in fact, a little bit complicated—but fun.

What sorts of things fill your bucket? What refuels you? What activities or engagements restore your energy levels? What do you need to do to start pouring new streams of replenishment into your badly depleted life? What relationships inspire you? What do you read that elevates your perspective? What in your life is actually a bucket-filler for you?

Quite often, people will say to me, "I have no idea. I haven't been replenished in so long that I don't even know what those things would be." Can you relate? Perhaps you've been empty for so long, you've forgotten what fills your bucket. You've forgotten what replenishes your soul. If that's you . . . no worries. We will explore what some of those things might be. And by the time you finish the Action Steps in this chapter, I'm confident you will have a game plan for keeping your bucket filled.

> There's no point in filling the bucket without first patching the holes.

PATCHING HOLES

Before you can formulate a plan for keeping your bucket filled, it's important to understand *why* you're so depleted in the first place. There's no point in filling the bucket without first patching the holes.

Sometimes, people are afraid to say no to their bosses or their spouses or their kids, so they say yes to another last-minute project or commitment that they know will deplete them beyond what is wise. Sometimes, people derive a disproportionate amount of their self-worth from being overachievers. They keep doing and doing, thinking that what matters most is the end product, not the process. Sometimes, people feel an undercurrent of guilt for taking time to do things that fill their buckets, as if someone will judge them for having fun or for spending time doing something for *themselves* rather than for others. This is especially true of those who work in compassion-related fields.

But this is backward thinking. When your tank is empty, you have nothing to offer anyone else. You can't give what you don't have. Engaging in replenishment activities is not a form of selfish entertainment; it's vital to the end goal of living your one and only life at its best. Be unapologetic about it. Prioritize and protect these replenishment streams in your life.

When you get depleted, it's tempting to start looking around for someone to pull you out. But let me state with crystal clarity: It's *your* responsibility to fill your bucket—not your boss's, not your board's, not your church's, not your staff's, not your spouse's. It's your own responsibility to keep your own bucket filled, to identify streams of replenishing energy that will take you from a depleted state to where your tank is filled to the brim and overflowing.

Let's examine five bucket-filling streams.

FIVE KEYS TO REPLENISHMENT
Connecting with God

No doubt you've seen a picture of Michelangelo's most famous painting on the ceiling of the Sistine Chapel, "The Creation of Adam," in which he portrays God and Adam with their hands outstretched toward one another. God is leaning and straining toward Adam, and His fingertip almost touches Adam's hand, which is more relaxed, not nearly as intent on its mission.

The very hand of heaven reaching for the hand of man.

Now, imagine Adam's hand reaching out another six inches, grabbing firmly ahold of God's hand, and hanging on to it tightly. That image captures the single biggest bucket-filler in my life: *being firmly hand-in-hand with God.*

When I feel God's love, when the Holy Spirit is bubbling within my spirit, when I'm in conversations with Him throughout my day, hearing His whispers, trying to be present and responsive to Him— when I'm really in a dialed-in relationship with God—it's the single most replenishing dynamic in my life.

Sometimes just a sentence or two from Him spoken into the depths of my heart can change my entire day. *You're doing good, Bill. I'm proud of you.* That means so much to me! Sometimes an encouraging phrase from God in the middle of a tough day can take my bucket from 25 percent full to 75 percent full.

> When I feel God's love . . . it's the single most replenishing dynamic in my life.

When I'm really connected with God, I'm far less concerned about other people's opinions of me or their plans and expectations for my life. I'm quicker to stay on God's agenda. I'm able to remind myself, *Hey, I don't need to fulfill someone else's agenda, because I have my hand in the hand of the one whose plans and purposes my life is all about.*

Being right with God and tuned in to Him and walking close with Him simplifies my life. It filters out all the noise of everyone else who wants my attention.

Perhaps you've never really connected with God to begin with. If you've always sensed somewhere deep in the core of your being that there is more to life, I challenge you to reach out your hand to Him. He loves you, and He will grasp any humbled hand that comes His way. Maybe you have long withheld your hand from His, and today is the day you need to apologize for your waywardness and stick out your hand and say, "God, I need You in my life." He will become that replenishing force for you. The powerful touch of God on a human life is a game changer. It has been for me. It can be for you.

If you're not in the daily habit of reaching for God's hand and listening for His agenda, let me offer you a challenge: Find a spot in your home—for me, it's a wooden rocking chair by the fireplace—and sit there for fifteen minutes a day, connecting with God. Read His Word, open up your life to Him, and listen for His whispers. When you're in that chair and you're in a right relationship with God, it secures your identity. It simplifies your agenda. You won't be so tempted to run out and do all the other stuff that doesn't matter a hill of beans to God.

So, chair time. Start there.

There are many other avenues that can help you connect with God. Gary Thomas's book *Sacred Pathways: Discover Your Soul's Path to God* describes ten "spiritual pathways" that help Christ followers express their love for God.[4] Most of us utilize more than one pathway to augment our hand-in-hand connection to Him. Do you connect with God best through solitude? Through nature? Through tradition, loving others, music? By discovering the spiritual pathway that fits best with your unique temperament, you can more readily keep your hand-in-hand relationship with God tight. If you're not sure how to connect with God, use part of your fifteen minutes in the chair, as I described above, to explore your relationship with Him in ways that resonate with how He wired you.

Spending time with God each day is the antidote to one energy-killer in particular: *image management.* Many of us drain an exorbitant amount of energy from our buckets by constantly maintaining our personal image: *I've got to look good for so-and-so. I've got to speak well in front of this person. I've got to produce such and such for that person.* When we're connected with God and we're secure in our identity as His daughters and sons, we can spend all that energy on stuff that meets God's agenda for our lives, rather than on image management. Life is simpler when we have only one agenda to meet: God's. For me, the number one priority in my daily, weekly, monthly, and annual rhythm is to stay as closely connected with God as I possibly can. It is by far the biggest replenisher in my life.

Family

A second replenisher—and this is a huge one for me as well—is family. Family looks different for each one of us. For me, family is my wife, son, daughter, son-in-law, and grandsons. And whether you're married or single, there is the "family" of friends you have gathered around you, people God has brought into your life who are family to you. These relationships are important replenishers.

> As I stay deeply connected with my family, these relationships pour refreshment into my bucket.

My family is not a burden to me. Far from it! My wife and kids fill me up, and now I have two grandsons who tip my bucket to overflowing. As I stay deeply connected with my family, these relationships pour refreshment into my bucket. On any given day, I'll exchange e-mails with Todd, our son who lives out of state, and texts with our daughter, Shauna, and her husband, Aaron, as well as texts and phone calls with Lynne. Even when Lynne or I travel out of the country, we stay closely connected. I love my family, and they refurbish my soul. Even when we have an occasional conflict—as every family does—these people don't drain me. We work things through and get back on track.

Family is one of the greatest blessings in my life. I build into the members of my family, and they build into me. We have a new little guy running around our family these days: our younger grandson, Mac, who is two. That kid has brought so much joy into my life. Before I was a grandfather, I couldn't see it coming—how much it would change me. But my grandkids have proven to be major replenishers in my life.

I'm glad it helps out Shauna and Aaron when Lynne and I babysit, but frankly, I do it for myself. My grandchildren fill me up! I'm with them as often as I can be. Psalm 127:3 says, "Children are a gift from God."[5] If I'm too busy for my own kids and grandkids, then I'm too busy. They ought to be a big part of my life, and I want to be a big part of theirs.

Not every family relationship is replenishing. Family systems are complex, and they require intentionality. Maybe it's time to make amends with some family members to get your relationship back on track so they're on the replenishing side instead of the energy-draining side. Relationships are tricky, and if yours are not life giving, you may have some work to do when we dive deeper into this topic in chapters 5 and 7. But for now, think about how you can make your family a life-giving source of replenishment.

Satisfying Work

Another key replenisher for me is satisfying work. I love my job. It gives me energy every time I set foot on our campus at Willow Creek. I am surrounded by gifted, passionate leaders who are terrific at what they do. I have a fantastic team of staff members who report directly to me. We have a broader leadership team of about twenty, who lead the rest of the staff and the various ministries we have. And we have a world-class board of elders. I also work with the Willow Creek Association's board and leadership team. And I have an executive assistant, Jean, whose joy is outright contagious and whose skills match or surpass any executive assistant on the planet.

King Solomon says it just right, in my view: "It is good and proper for people to find satisfaction—replenishment—in their labor."[6]

Friend, life is short. If your job sucks the life out of you week after week, year after year, you will never be able to keep your energy bucket filled. Get on your knees every single day and pray, "God, either help me change my attitude about this job or help my job to change. Help me change departments, change employers, or change careers."

If your job drains you again and again, perhaps you're not in the right vocation.

Believe me, I know this is a very complicated subject. In today's economy, you don't just run out and quit your job. I understand that. And perhaps the job that would satisfy your soul and fill your bucket doesn't bring the money you need to stay afloat in this season. But prayerfully evaluate what truly matters. What are your needs, versus your wants? Begin praying that God will lead you to a vocation that brings the provision you need and also fills your bucket.

> Life is short. If your job sucks the life out of you, you will never be able to keep your energy bucket filled.

I could tell countless stories of friends who walked away from lucrative marketplace jobs to take less pay and fewer perks, putting their hands to the plow of jobs that bring them deep satisfaction. We have many such people on staff at Willow. I am currently walking alongside a friend who just sold his mansion-sized home and moved his family into a nearby rental. He is stepping out of a high-income business to attend seminary, and his family is helping him follow God's whisper to pursue a career that will fill his bucket in a way that his wealth-producing marketplace job did not.

When I see people who are consistently filled up, I often discover they're quite satisfied with what they do vocationally. God, in His love for you, would love for your job to be a bucket-filler and not a bucket-drainer. I believe you can trust Him for that, in His wisdom and His timing.

Recreation

The fourth replenisher was a problem area for me during the first fifteen years of my ministry at Willow Creek. My days of church building and parenting small children were extraordinarily intense, and I had no form of recreation in my life whatsoever. How could I take time to go have fun when people were still far from God? When there were still people with needs that had to be met, and ministries that required my leadership input? When my family needed so much from me?

That kind of thinking almost put me over the edge. I let myself get so depleted that I couldn't find my way out. I ended up in a Christian counselor's office, and he pushed me to do the things that replenish me—and do them regularly. He challenged me to find some form of recreation that gave life to my soul. And that's how I got into boating. Being on the water pours huge streams of replenishment into my bucket.

At first, it was hard. I told my counselor I felt horrible being a pastor who would go boating in a world where people are still poor and where a lot of people are not headed to heaven. What right did I have to be out on the water?

This counselor helped me understand the heart of God in a new way. He helped me understand that recreation means to *re-create* energy and vitality in your inner person. He kept saying, "Bill, God wants for you to re-create energy and vitality so you'll have much to offer others."

> God wants for you to re-create energy and vitality so you'll have much to offer others.

So I race sailboats and hang around sailors, and savor the spray of the water and the sound of the waves and the feel of the wind in my face. Recently, my grandson Henry and I took our eight-foot wooden rowboat out on a little adventure in South Haven, Michigan. We explored the shoreline of the Black River and spotted at least a dozen turtles. We made memories I won't soon forget. When I get back from little excursions like this, I am filled up to overflowing.

What is it for you? What fills you up? Is it reading, cooking, golfing, gardening, camping, stamp collecting? Whatever it is, you need to find something that re-creates your energy and vitality, and you must install it as a regular stream of replenishment in your life. You need the replenishment of recreation to keep you filled up.

For me, it's boating. And just for the record, I think it's biblical:

> When Jesus heard what had happened, he
> withdrew by boat privately to a solitary place.[7]

So you see, Jesus was a boater! I'm in good company. Feel free to golf or rock climb or garden, or do whatever fills you up, but I'm sticking with the thing Jesus did!

Exercise

The final replenishment activity that fills my energy bucket is exercise. For many years, I have made exercise a significant and regular part of my life. I come from a genetic line that has not been kind to Hybels males. My father died of a heart attack at age fifty-four, when I was just twenty-seven. Losing him when I was in my twenties devastated me, and I will do anything I can to keep my kids from having to experience what my siblings and I went through.

Years ago, I made a commitment to good health. Running, lifting weights, getting adequate sleep, and eating healthy foods are the norm for me. And though I made that commitment for the purpose of physical health, I have discovered that these activities also boost my mental health and energy reserves in a way that far exceeds the amount of time and investment they cost me.

Read any study on the topic of what adds energy and vitality to your life, and you'll find that most experts agree: Exercise and proper rest patterns give about a 20 percent energy increase in an average day, average week, average month.[8] *A 20 percent increase in energy.* If you're not motivated to exercise for the purpose of physical health, do so as a simple, effective way to increase your energy—and with it, your overall quality of life.

Diet also maximizes my energy levels. Because of my dad's heart history, I have always been cautious about cholesterol intake, staying away from too much red meat, too much cheese, etc. But in recent years, largely due to the influence of Shauna, Aaron, and Lynne, I have cranked up the healthy-eating habit a notch or two. I've been doing a Hybels version of the Paleo diet—for the most part, eating just fruits, nuts, vegetables, small portions of meat, and the like. The difference in my energy levels has been striking. If you struggle with sluggish energy, especially in the afternoon, I highly recommend increasing the health of your diet.

Maximizing your energy requires more than eating the right foods; it also requires eating at the right intervals. Jack Groppel is an expert and pioneer in the science of human performance and an authority in fitness and nutrition. He wrote a book called *The Corporate Athlete*, which talks about energy being the fundamental currency of organizations.[9] We brought Jack in to train our staff on the subject of energy management a few years back, and it changed the way we all look at our energy investment. Simple changes, such as eating nutrition-packed foods at work when energy gets low, have helped our team keep our energy buckets full.

Adequate sleep isn't very exciting to talk about, but it is fundamental to increasing your energy reserves. When I travel internationally, jet lag is a killer. The cost is worth it—I love the work I do with global pastors and leaders—but it takes its toll on my energy levels during and after each trip. When I get home, I'm reminded firsthand why experts insist that sleep patterns matter. As far as I'm able, I make it a priority to engage in regular sleep patterns at home.

My greatest bursts of energy come in the morning, so for me, getting to bed at a decent hour is a nonnegotiable if I want to maximize the most productive hours of my day. If you are a night person and find that your best thinking and productivity come late at night, adjust your schedule so you can sleep longer in the morning. Identify your best hours of the day and modify your daily routine accordingly.

BEGIN WITH A FULL BUCKET

In the coming chapters, as you assess key practices to simplify your life, it is essential that you first make course corrections to move from exhausted to energized. That's the starting point. Depletion has got to stop, friend. When you're at the bottom of your fullness bucket, you're dangerous. Living this way has consequences for your marriage, your children, your team, and your colleagues at work. They know it, and you know it. You can feel it too. You're in a rut, and it's hard to get out of it. If you have spent too long at the bottom of your bucket, you're not living the way God designed for you to live. He designed a better future for you.

> Learn how to fill up your bucket and keep it filled. God created you to live your life with your energy reserves filled to the top.

Learn how to fill up your bucket and keep it filled. God created you to live your life with your energy reserves filled to the top. That's how He created all of us to live. My prayer for you is that you will put a stake in the ground that says, *I'm done living on empty. I'm done staying in a depleted condition.* May you have the kind of humility and conviction it takes to mark today as the day that living on empty *ends* for you.

Get creative. Get motivated to find the activities that will start pouring life into your empty bucket. No one can do this for you. It's your life. It's your future. You're on the right path, and I admire you.

Feel free to engage the Action Steps below with a friend or two, or even a small group, as you self-assess your movement from exhausted to energized. Often our friends can reflect back to us valuable insights, showing us things we cannot see in ourselves. Those who know you best are the ones most likely to help you spot patterns and trends that keep your bucket drained. Likewise, in the company of friends, it can be fun to brainstorm life-giving activities that will bring you refreshment.

You will be your best self when you live at the top of your energy bucket. You'll do God's bidding more eagerly. You'll love more effectively. And you'll leave a legacy for your family when you live your life out of a full bucket.

· · ·

ACTION STEP: TAKE AN HONEST ASSESSMENT

The first step in learning to fill your bucket is to take a sober assessment of where you are now.

In your journal or on a piece of paper, draw a bucket and put a line to mark where you feel your energy level is right now. Be realistic. Are you filled up? Are you half full? A quarter full? Are you depleted? Don't lie to yourself. Be honest. (If your instinctive reaction to this assignment is, "Take a flying leap, Hybels. I'm not going to do it," then I know where your line is—you're depleted!)

Once you've marked your energy level on your bucket, ask yourself, "Why do I let myself get this depleted? What drives me, *really*?" Ask God to give you insight into what's underneath your propensity for running on empty. When you are living this way, what inner hunger are you feeding that should be fed in healthier ways? Is there someone you're trying to please? If this type of reflective digging has you stumped, ask a trusted friend or a Christian counselor to help you gain insight.

■ ■ ■

ACTION STEP: CRAFT A CUSTOM REPLENISHMENT PLAN

The second step in filling your bucket—and this is fun, but it's not simple—is to design a custom replenishment plan that fits you.

A bucket-filling plan will look different for every person. We're all filled up by different replenishment streams. Don't worry about what works for other people. Just craft a plan that fits you.

What are the replenishing people, dynamics, activities, and engagements that predictably fill you up when you've gotten a little low in the tank? What things work uniquely for you?

Don't worry yet about how to fit these into your current, overbooked schedule. We'll deal with that in the next chapter. For now, envision a blue-sky day in which your assignment is to do nothing but what suits you—the things that bring you the most joy, the deepest sense of God's pleasure with your life. They may be ventures you've never done before but want to try. They may be activities you used to enjoy but have let slide. What are those things?

To stimulate your thinking, glance back at my top five replenishers: connecting with God, time with family, satisfying work, recreation, and exercise. Do any or all of those ring true for you? Feel free to add your own replenishers, completely different from what works for me.

Next, scan your list and choose one or two replenishers you can do starting tomorrow; one you will do by week's end; and one you will try by the end of the month. The point isn't to fill yourself up quickly, but rather, to train yourself to begin the habit of prioritizing the replenishing streams that breathe life into your soul and leave your bucket filled. There are no shortcuts. Change begins with small, daily steps. Start now.

chapter two

from overscheduled to organized

Harnessing Your Calendar's Power

WHEN YOU COMPLETED your Action Steps for chapter 1, you identified the activities that pour emotional, spiritual, and physical energy into your life.

But as you look at your current schedule, you may be thinking, *Thanks a lot, Bill. Sounds good in theory, but how do I squeeze these "replenishing streams" into my already packed schedule?*

Great question! And you're not alone. No matter where I am in the world, I hear a common complaint:

"I'm overscheduled."

"I don't have time."

"I'm too busy."

I hear it from the guy next to me on the airplane and from the people I talk to at church. I hear it from friends, neighbors, and coworkers. Sometimes I hear it from my own lips. We say these words so often that we become immune to how repetitive we sound. Our schedules are packed so tight, we couldn't slip a razor blade between appointments. We have no wiggle room, no margin, not a moment to spare—let alone an hour, a day, or a week.

We almost brag about it, don't we? It makes us feel a little important: *I am much too busy to do such and such. No time. More pressing commitments.* It feeds something unhealthy in us—and the cost is severe.

A runaway calendar will keep you from simplifying your life. It holds you hostage to tangible things—meetings, appointments, and projects—without giving proper priority to the intangibles: who you are becoming, your relationships with family and friends, your connectedness to God. Without conscious intervention, this pattern of chronically overscheduling ensures that the priorities you care about most will take a backseat to the urgent priorities of others every time.

GRABBING THE REINS

Often when people describe their too-busy lives, they make it sound as if the overscheduling *happened* to them unwittingly, like they had no choice in the matter. "It's not *my* fault. It's my boss's fault. It's my family's fault. It's my teammate's fault." They truly believe they are mere victims of the very responsibilities and commitments they said yes to.

News flash: *You* are the boss of your schedule. It's your responsibility to keep command of your calendar—and you must, in order to simplify your life.

Many people I know are doing the best they can to control the mayhem. Yet despite their valiant efforts, their lives show little change. No doubt you, too, have tried to simplify your overscheduled life. You bought a new planner. You installed a new calendar app on your phone. You attended a time-management class or listened to an audiobook about being more organized. You even managed to sync your work calendar with your home calendar, trying to corral everything into one system, hoping this would solve the problem. But reshuffling the same deck of cards will faithfully deal you the same too-busy hand.

What if you could grab the reins of your runaway calendar? What if you could turn your schedule into a powerful tool to help you live out your endgame priorities?

A simplified life begins with well-invested hours each day. You can harness the true power of your calendar by filling in each square *holistically*, creating room for both the outward activities and inner priorities in your life. Your calendar is more than merely an organizer for what needs to get done; it's the primary tool for helping you become who you want to become.

IF GOD WERE IN CHARGE

A couple of years after I became a Christian at seventeen, an older guy from my church began spending purposeful time with me as a mentor. I admired him as a husband, a father, and a businessman, and I was very grateful for his time and attention. One day, he took me out to lunch and broached the subject of time management.

"Christ followers should think totally differently about time," he told me. He explained Paul's teaching in the book of Ephesians, which says, "Be very careful, then, how you live—not as unwise but as wise, making the most of every opportunity."[1]

I must admit that, from my youthful vantage point at the time, life looked plenty long and the future seemed far away. Why was it so important to *make the most of every opportunity*?

Perhaps my friend sensed I wasn't catching his point. Near the end of our lunch, he looked me in the eye and said, "Here's the question I want to leave with you: How would you spend your time if God were in charge of it?" With that, he put a twenty-dollar bill on the table, said his good-byes, and left.

I sat alone in that diner booth with his question echoing in my head. Up to that point in my life, I had been the undisputed boss of my time. I went to school, went to work, hung out with friends, took girls on dates—I did whatever I wanted to do whenever I wanted to do it. But the longer I pondered my mentor's question, the more it got under my skin.

I asked the waitress for a pencil and paper, and I wrote down this question: *What would my schedule look like if God were in charge of it?*

This idea was a brand-new concept for me. I'd never thought about it before. But that lunchtime meeting inspired a lifelong discipline for me. Ever since that day, I've been asking myself the question, *How would God have me spend my time today?*

Schedules—my own and others'—fascinate me. In fact, a few years ago, that fascination prompted me to study how Jesus invested His time. I searched through the Gospels to see what I could learn about His daily schedule, His weekly schedule, His monthly schedule—even His yearly schedule—in keeping with the traditions of His Jewish faith. I found it all very interesting.

> A lot of people who led fascinating lives kept very strange schedules.

I've also studied the schedules of great leaders throughout world history. A lot of people who led fascinating lives kept very strange schedules. Did you know that Winston Churchill worked a considerable amount of time from bed? He often stayed up until 2:00 or 3:00 a.m. and then went to bed, awakening around 7:00 a.m. and working from bed until 11:00 a.m. or noon. Given Churchill's role in history, few can question the effectiveness of this eccentric schedule for an eccentric world leader.

Leonardo da Vinci was reputed to take two-hour naps whenever he got tired, regardless of the time of day, so he wouldn't "waste" eight solid hours sleeping every night. His daily schedule was punctuated by these bursts of naps. Leonardo's polyphasic sleep pattern has come to be known as "the sleep of genius."

Thomas Edison, too, was a power napper. He strategically placed sleeping cots throughout his house and laboratory to accommodate his twenty-minute naps throughout the day.

These leaders and others—including Benjamin Franklin, Nikola Tesla, Thomas Jefferson, and Napoleon Bonaparte—utilized a polyphasic schedule to maximize their waking hours.

What I appreciate about these examples—and what I hope you will apply to your own life—is that these people experimented with their schedules until they found a formula that really worked for them. They didn't try to shoehorn themselves into a "normal" schedule that looked like anyone else's. They understood, *My rhythm doesn't have to work for anybody but me.*

My most productive hours are in the morning, when I am well rested and my mind is fresh. Several years back, I made a shift in my schedule to capitalize on those first hours of each day—and I only wish I had made this change decades earlier!

Once I step onto the campus of our church and head to my office, it's off to the races. Meetings, phone calls, e-mails, and appointments can devour every moment of my day.

I have learned this about myself: In order to stay spiritually centered, to be in tune with God's whispers, to be able to listen for *His* guidance for my day, rather than my own or someone else's, I must protect those quiet, peaceful, uninterrupted morning hours and surrender them to God.

> In order to stay spiritually centered . . . I must protect those quiet, peaceful, uninterrupted morning hours and surrender them to God.

Every morning around 5:30, I climb out of bed and get directly on my knees for prayer. If I don't do this, I'm too apt to become distracted with "doing" and never return to prayer. After I pray, I spend time in a favorite chair, or in the unhurried setting of my home office, where I open God's Word and invite its wisdom into my soul. I write in my journal, asking myself hard questions about my actions, my words, my relationships, my character. What sin pattern is God illuminating in me that warrants confession and a change? What relationships need repair? Where is God inviting me to grow? What opportunities does He want me to say yes to? Where is He telling me to take a pass? Where is He praising me for a job well done?

These early morning hours are my most fruitful of the day. The uninterrupted solitude clears my mental space for sermon preparation, active learning, and big-picture dreaming. Once I have filled my soul by spending time with God, I put my hands to the plow and start the day's work.

I don't head into the office until 11:00 a.m. By then, I have already invested several hours in the inner priorities that might otherwise be swept aside by the busyness of the day. And I have made a good dent in the day's workload before setting foot in the office. This schedule works for me. It's not a traditional 9:00 to 5:00 routine, but it works.

Is your current schedule working for you?

Is it *really*?

If it's not, it's up to you to find a schedule that does work for you. You may not have the luxury of flexible work hours, which means you'll need to get creative with your nonwork time so your personal priorities don't take a hit. I'm of the opinion that the thoughtful arrangement of your daily and weekly calendars is one of the holiest endeavors you can undertake. Drafting a new, proactive, holistic schedule is tantamount to writing a whole new script for the next season of your life. Your calendar plays a critical role in determining who you will become as a person, as a Christ follower, as a family member, and as a friend. It has the power to change the trajectory of your present and your future. I believe to my core that when you sit down to rewrite your schedule, you will be making choices with far greater implications than you might imagine.

At this stage of my life, with nearly four decades of church work behind me, I am still learning that my schedule is far less about what I want to get done and far more about *who I want to become*. Let me repeat: My schedule is far less about what I want to get done and far more about who I want to become.

How do most people plan their schedules? They grab their calendars and start plugging in all their appointments—where they need to be, and when, to avoid losing their jobs or forgetting to pick up the kids at the soccer field after practice. After they've accounted for everything they'd get in trouble for forgetting to do or neglecting to accomplish, they squeeze in the next most urgent to-do items. With any luck, there's still room to fit in some sleep and a shower and maybe even a meal or two with the family.

At the end of a good day, if they've made all their appointments and crossed everything off their to-do lists, they fall into bed and pray, "God, help me pull this off again tomorrow."

> The thoughtful arrangement of your daily and weekly calendar is one of the holiest endeavors you can undertake.

Confession: This is how I put together my schedule all the way through high school, college, during my years in the family business, and even into the early days of Willow Creek.

There is a better way.

A NEW WAY OF FILLING THE SQUARES

If it weren't for a little girl named Shauna, who stole my heart the day she was born, I might still be putting together my schedule based on urgencies and other people's expectations. But one night in the early days of our church, when Shauna was just three years old, she followed me to the door as I was heading out for yet another meeting. As I bent down to kiss her good-bye, she looked up at me with her bright-blue eyes and asked me a question—not out of anger, but out of sheer curiosity: "Daddy, are you going to be gone again tonight?"

"Gone . . . again . . . tonight?"

With those few, simple words, my approach to scheduling came crashing down. I felt a tension growing inside me as I drove to the church, and I began asking myself, *Why exactly am I gone again tonight?*

Well, the answer was simple: Tonight's meeting was on my schedule, just like last night's meeting and tomorrow night's meeting. They must be important meetings or they wouldn't have made it onto my calendar, right?

And then, if you can believe it, for the first time in my life, it hit me: *What if my weekly schedule also included my nonwork responsibilities?* For me, this idea was groundbreaking. How holistic could (or should) my schedule be? Must it only contain work stuff and logistical stuff, or should it be more comprehensive?

As I pulled into the parking lot at Willow, I asked myself, *Am I looking at this from the right perspective, or not?*

And then came the clincher: *How much do I involve God and prayer and the wisdom of the Holy Spirit when I put together my schedule? Am I just trying to crank out more work and cram more activity into the same number of hours each day?* I thought back to that lunch I'd had with my mentor several years earlier, and I remembered the question I'd written on a piece of paper that day: *What would my schedule look like if God were in charge of it?*

> What would your schedule look like if God were in charge of it?

The next morning, I went to a coffee shop with a sharp pencil and a fresh piece of paper in hand—and Shauna's innocent question seared onto my heart. I wrote a new question: *What investment of time will it take for me to be a great dad to that precious little girl?*

For me, this particular question was steeped in personal pain. I grew up with a largely absent father. I knew firsthand what it felt like to have my dad gone night after night. I knew he loved my siblings and me. But, to be honest, his business priorities drove his schedule. Shauna deserved better. My son, Todd, who was just a baby at the time, deserved better.

So I asked: What investment of my time will it take to be not an average dad, just getting by, but a fantastic father during Shauna's and Todd's fleeting, growing-up days and years?

I asked for God's wisdom as I sat pondering this question, and the Holy Spirit seemed to whisper, *Four nights. Four nights a week at home. Start there. You can adjust it as the kids get older. But for this season, it's four nights.*

I blinked. Four nights seemed like a lot, given my pace and responsibilities at the time. Some guys pride themselves on making every Friday or Sunday evening "family night." One night a week. But *four* nights?

And then came what I would describe almost as an out-of-body experience. In my gut, I felt courage welling up, and I decided then and there, *I don't care what other dads do. I don't give a rip if some guy says he can be a great dad with only one night, or two, at home. God gave me Shauna and Todd as treasures to enjoy and to bring up. And I know I need to be home four nights a week if I want to be as great a dad as I can be—the kind of dad they deserve.*

For the first time ever, I wrote on my calendar four simple letters that changed everything:

H-O-M-E.

Right there on my work calendar, I filled in four evenings' worth of squares and elevated *home* to the same stature as any other important meeting—any business or ministry appointment, elders meeting, board meeting, ministry meeting, or property acquisition meeting.

As I looked down at my new week, the impact and power of a

God-in-charge schedule gripped me for the very first time. By writing one simple word four times on a piece of paper and then following through on my new commitment, I could forever change the destiny of a three-year-old, blonde-headed girl and her curly-haired brother.

Today, more than thirty years later, I can see how that one crucial decision had *generational* implications for our family. Our family time is still one of God's greatest gifts in my life. Both of our children are leading full lives with God at the center, and our grandsons are following their example, even at their young ages. I'm deeply grateful that God led me to begin that pattern all those years ago.

> Redrafting your personal schedule holds implications for your future that you probably can't yet imagine.

As I began to recognize the power of a commitment on a calendar page, I had a head-popping moment in that coffee shop. By including my nonwork priorities in my work schedule, I was making sure that the things most important to me would no longer take a backseat to the inexhaustible stream of hour-eaters that came my way most days. I was taking proactive measures against overscheduling my life. It was such a simple concept, but the impact was immense.

I don't know if you've ever had a similar moment of awareness over something as mundane as a calendar, but I promise you that redrafting your personal schedule holds implications for your future that you probably can't yet imagine.

WHO DO YOU WANT TO BECOME?

Simplicity cannot be achieved without clarity about the big-picture target of your life. To create a schedule that reflects your most important life goals, you must begin with the right question. The question isn't, "What do I want to get done in the next thirty days?" but, "Who do I want to become in this next season of my life?" Once we answer that key question, calendars and schedules are terrific tools for helping us accomplish our life goals, both interpersonal and practical.

Many years ago, I decided I wanted to become a pilot. My father had been a private pilot, and our family company owned airplanes when I was growing up. I had a strong sense that flying would be one of those life-giving streams of replenishment for me, so I decided I would learn how to fly and earn my pilot's license.

Here's the secret to how I became a private pilot: *I wrote it on my calendar.*

There was more involved, of course—such as booking the lessons, paying for them, showing up, and doing the work. But in the simplest of terms, writing "Flying Lessons" on my calendar was step one in my commitment of setting aside a couple of hours each week for six months to take lessons.

The process is really not that hard. You just have to put it on your calendar, show up, pay your dues, do the training, and take the test. That's how you become a private pilot.

And that's how you can accomplish any number of life changes. Anyone can change direction in life, add or subtract priorities and activities, or reshuffle the matrix to put priorities in a better order. That's the transformative power of a schedule.

A friend of mine was in a dead-end job. He couldn't bear the thought of grinding out decade after decade in his mind-numbing, low-paying company. One night, he was thumbing through a community college brochure that had come in the mail, and he spotted a night

> Anyone can change direction in life. . . . That's the transformative power of a schedule.

class in the exact field he had dreamed of going into someday. He signed up for the course and wrote it on his calendar. He went to the first class and loved it. Before long, he had decided to take a class in that field every Tuesday night for the next two years. He put it on his calendar.

One hundred and four Tuesday nights later, he received his professional degree in the field of his dreams. Soon he changed jobs and embarked on a fulfilling, financially rewarding career. Today, he's comfortably retired. His whole life changed when he wrote "Night Class" on the Tuesday-night squares of his calendar—and then followed through for those two years.

American novelist John Grisham was an attorney who hated his job. He wanted to become an author, but he didn't know where to begin. Finally, he decided to start by writing a one-word message to himself on the early-morning squares of his monthly calendar: "Write." Grisham said to himself, "I'm going to get to work sixty minutes early each day, and I'm going to write just one page per day."

And that's what he did.

He started getting up an hour earlier during the week and showing up at his desk an hour before the normal start time at his firm. He began writing . . . and he kept writing. Today, he is one of the most prolific and appreciated novelists of our day. That's the power of even a single word written on a schedule and lived out. For me, it was *Home*. For John Grisham, it was *Write*. What's your word?

One weekend, following a message I gave at Willow, I had an interesting conversation that demonstrates the power of our schedules. I spoke to a guy who said he was rather confused about the Bible, and he wasn't sure Christianity was true. He asked a lot of really good questions, and he seemed open-minded. After listening to him for a few minutes, I asked him something that surprised him: "You got a calendar on you?"

He looked a little skeptical, but he humored me and pulled out his smartphone.

"Can you punch the word *Alpha* into your calendar?" I asked. I gave him the date and time of an amazing class we hold at the church, which teaches the essence of Christianity over a ten-week period.[2]

So the guy entered "Alpha" into his calendar for the next ten Sunday nights. "And promise me you'll go," I said.

"Ten weeks—that's a big commitment," he said.

"So is Christianity," I replied. "So is eternity. So is your life. But you're standing here talking to a pastor, and I think you ought to go to Alpha for ten weeks. There's great information about the big questions in life, and you'll learn a ton about Christianity."

I explained that he'd be sitting around a table and discussing this stuff with other people who were also exploring and who were open-minded like he was. "It's cool," I promised. Because it is.

"All right," he said. "I'll check it out." And off he went.

I didn't see him again until our June baptism, almost a year later. I was standing in the lake, and the next person waiting to be baptized was a man who looked familiar and who was grinning from ear to ear.

"Do you remember me?" he asked. "I'm the guy you told to punch 'Alpha' into his smartphone."

"And you did, didn't you?"

"Yep!" he said. "Here's how it happened. I went to the first four sessions, and it was tough—sort of confusing at first. A lot of new information. I almost bailed. But I had already entered 'Alpha' into my calendar. I had already set aside the time, and I only had six sessions left, so I just decided I'd finish out what I had on my schedule."

> "I had already set aside the time, . . . so I just decided I'd finish out what I had on my schedule."

Out there in the water, standing next to me, he got a little emotional.

"The very next Sunday night," he said, "I asked some more questions, and some of the puzzle pieces that had eluded me finally started to fall into place. After that night, it got really exciting, and by the end of those ten weeks, I knew deep down that Christianity was absolutely true and that I needed to commit my life to Jesus Christ. Which I did."

Then he looked at me and said, "Thanks for challenging me about Alpha. Now, would you please baptize me?"

Which I did—with great joy.

Just one word in a smartphone—*tap*. Ten Sunday nights—*tap*. Eternity changed. Family changed. Every day of this man's life changed. How important is a commitment on a calendar? It changed his life. It could change yours.

(If you're exploring Christianity, take a moment and look into Alpha. You can check it out online at http://guest.alphausa.org or www.alpha.org. There are thousands of Alpha courses all over the world—and likely one near you. Add it to your calendar—*tap!* Ten sessions over dinner—*tap!* What could be simpler? You won't regret it.)

I don't know your story. I don't know which parts of your life are in need of a do-over or a makeover, but I bet you do. And by utilizing your schedule as a holistic tool for all areas of your life, you can ensure that each square on your calendar is centered on things that matter to you, rather than being consumed month in, month out by the same time-suckers that leave you feeling overscheduled and exhausted.

Let's use the framework from chapter 1 as a means of examining the places in your life that could benefit from a new, holistic schedule. The areas that fill my energy bucket reflect vital values for me. My guess is they will serve a similar function for you.

CONNECTING WITH GOD
Church Attendance

As a pastor, I am struck by how often I hear the comment, "I almost didn't come to church today." It's usually after I've given a message that, by God's grace, spoke to some people in a powerful way, and they are telling me how timely the sermon was. "And to think I almost didn't come," they'll say.

One Sunday recently, a guy I was talking to used that phrase several times. Finally, I took the bait. "Really?" I teased him. "You almost didn't come today? 'Church' isn't on your regular calendar? So, on Sunday mornings, you and your family start flipping coins to decide whether or not you're going to show up?"

During the next service, several more people made the exact same comment, and I became even more emphatic about the importance of regular church attendance—and how it greatly enhances the likelihood we will stay connected with God.

By the final service that day, my intensity on this topic was pretty high. I might have upped the volume just a bit as I challenged our congregation: "Really? You don't have church on your calendar?"

From the upper deck of our auditorium, a little kid yelled out, "Nope!" He outed his family—and in church! I thought, *That kid's gonna be sitting in a time-out chair until he's about fifteen!*

> If you want to hear more from God, be where His Word is taught. Regularly. Weekly.

People laughed, as did I, but the truth is, it breaks my heart when parents don't commit themselves—and their kids—to weekly church attendance. "Nope, it's not really on our calendar" is a far-too-common refrain. "We're still flipping a coin every week. Some weeks we come; some weeks we don't."

If you want to hear more from God, be where His Word is taught. Regularly. Weekly.

Church attendance was part of Jesus' weekly rhythm: "On the Sabbath day he went into the synagogue, as was his custom."[3]

Who do you want to become? If you have even the vaguest interest in becoming a more dialed-in Christ follower, someone who knows a little more about your faith, who is becoming a little more like the one you claim to follow, then there are a few words you need to write on your calendar—and *church* is one of them.

If you want more of God's direction and purpose in your life, you need to adopt the same weekly rhythm that Jesus practiced. Church was on His calendar. It's on my calendar too. Add it to yours—and make it a nonnegotiable part of your schedule.

Chair Time

When people tell me they just wish they felt closer to God, or they describe how they never really hear much from Him like other people seem to, I wonder about their personal connection with Him. If they don't understand some of the basic truths of the Christian faith—or they're having a hard time living out those truths in their everyday lives—I ask them one question: "How's your daily time with God?"

I can predict their answer: "What daily time with God?"

The second key practice for staying connected to God is allocating purposeful time with Him every day. As I suggested in chapter 1, find a spot you like—a chair in your home where you can sit uninterrupted, or a booth in a coffee shop, or a bench on your patio. Wherever it is, meet God there every day. Open God's Word, read it for fifteen minutes or so, consider how it might apply to your life, and then pray. You can tell God something simple like this: "Thank You for Your careful watch over my life. If You have anything You want to whisper to me, I'll listen and obey."

> If you want to become more connected to God, be consistent with those fifteen-minute blocks of time with Him.

Your chair time doesn't have to be an in-depth Bible study or an hour-long meditation exercise. But it should be purposeful and slow and protected from distraction, at a time of day that works best for you. Most important, it should be daily.

If this is new for you, begin with just five minutes a day. Get yourself into a daily rhythm. You'll be surprised by how powerfully this small increment of time can affect your life when you surrender it to God.

If you want to become more connected to God, be consistent with those fifteen-minute blocks of time with Him. Write them on your calendar at the time that corresponds best with how you're wired, and then follow through.

MARRIAGE AND FAMILY

A married couple in another state called me a few months back to tell me they were giving up on their fifteen-year marriage. Just like that, it was over. I reminded them in the conversation that they have two precious kids, but they were unmoved. Too much pain. "We're done," they said.

I listened as they shared their situation, and I was praying the whole time, *God, give me something to say. What can I tell these people?* Finally I thought, *Well, here comes a Hail Mary pass.*

"Hey, listen," I said, "I know a Christian counselor who lives in your city. I've met him through my travels, and he's a wise, well-trained guy. I would be happy to arrange for you to get in touch with him before you throw in the towel on your marriage. You've been married for fifteen years. Would you be willing to do just fifteen sessions with a trusted Christian counselor? One session per year of marriage. That's all I'm asking. And can I remind you that there are kids involved?"

Begrudgingly, they agreed. But after meeting with the counselor only three times, they stopped going. They just quit. And then they got divorced. That's how this unfortunate story ended.

Maybe they would have gotten divorced anyway. But I wish they had played it out for all fifteen weeks—just fifteen one-hour blocks on their calendar—because marriages are worth fighting for. Families are worth fighting for. Kids are worth fighting for.

If your marriage is teetering, put it on your calendar. See a Christian counselor. Set aside the time needed for hard-but-healing conversations. Marital fractures don't heal themselves without wise guidance and the strategic investment of time. Use your calendar to protect the time and space necessary for your marriage and your family.

When I meet deliriously happy married couples, I often quiz them: "How can you still be so in love with each other?" Among a number of deeper reasons they may give for why their marriage is so great, I hear one particular common denominator more often than not: "We have a date night." Depending on their stage of life, it might not be every week. Sometimes it's every other week. Sometimes they describe where they go or what they do on their dates. These conversations are delightful.

> Use your calendar to protect the time and space necessary for your marriage and your family.

Typically, their plan is quite simple: They put their date night on the calendar, and then they protect it. It's not hit-or-miss. They don't flip a coin. It's an investment in their relationship and their future together. It's who they want to become.

Lynne and I share a quirky, adapted version of date night at this season of our lives, now that our kids are grown and gone. Because both of us are very involved in global issues—Lynne in the Middle East and the Congo, and I in other places around the globe—we both travel a fair amount. We've decided that whenever we're both home, we'll meet in our family room every evening to watch *NBC Nightly News with Brian Williams.*

I know this may not sound like a romantic date night for many people, but for us it's very life-giving. We watch the news together for half an hour, then click off the television and catch up with each other: "How are you doing?" "How did work go today?" "How was your latest trip?" "What did you write today?" The news provides a shared experience from which to launch into rich conversation. Sometimes, if I'm traveling and the evening news comes on, I'll shoot Lynne an e-mail: "Wish we were home, watching the news together."

And there's an added bonus: Whenever guys brag to me, "Hey, I have a date night every week," I can counter with, "I have a date night every night—and it's free!"

SATISFYING WORK

Let's talk about your work schedule.

When you signed on the dotted line and said yes to the employment you're engaged in right now, you made a commitment. Every workplace has requirements about starting time, length of breaks and lunch, and quitting time. When you signed the employment contract, you gave your employer your word that you would abide by that code of conduct and meet those agreed-upon expectations.

Jesus challenged His followers, "Let your 'Yes' be 'Yes,' and your 'No,' 'No.'"[4] In other words, "Keep your word." If the start time is 8:00 a.m., don't roll in at five after. If your lunch break is an hour, don't take an hour and a half. Keep your word.

At Willow Creek, if you serve on the paid staff, you learn quickly that promptness is just about next to godliness. We start our meetings on time. And we have a rule: If anyone comes late to a meeting, they apologize to the whole team. No need to explain why they're late—because of the traffic or the snow or the train that took too long. They simply say, "Hey, gang, sorry I'm late." No one has to grovel, and no one gets scolded. That's not the point.

> Jesus challenged His followers, "Let your 'Yes' be 'Yes,' and your 'No,' 'No.'" In other words, "Keep your word."

But about the third time we hear, "Sorry I'm late," we start to suspect they're really not very sorry. We recognize that their "yes" to a ten o'clock meeting isn't truly a yes and that the teachings of Jesus really aren't all that important to them in this regard. If the problem persists, we will speak with that staff member and say, "You know, we used to think that your lack of promptness was a matter of carelessness; but now we think it's about character. We think it's about giving your word but not keeping your word. And around here, character matters. So we encourage you to reconsider this pattern. We want your yes to be yes. We want you to show up on time out of respect for your teammates." If the person can't make the correction, in due time we have a different sort of conversation. It's that important.

Let your *yes* be yes and your *no* be no in every area of your life. Be realistic and schedule enough time for travel around the events on your calendar so you can show up when expected and fulfill the commitments you've made. When it comes to honoring Christ in your role at work, does your schedule include enough travel time so you can clock in when expected? Do you focus and give your best efforts to your employer during your allotted work hours? And do you keep healthy boundaries by not allowing work to leak into your home hours? If not, use your calendar to make those adjustments.

> Schedule enough time for travel around the events on your calendar so you can show up when expected and fulfill the commitments you've made.

RECREATION

My calendar is absolutely the most efficient tool I possess when it comes to guaranteeing that I schedule regular, adequate, and thorough times of recreation into my life. Every January, Lynne and I and the kids plot a year's worth of family vacations and protect them on our calendars. This is especially important now that our kids are grown and on their own, as we must coordinate three groups of schedules to find dates that will work for everyone. And by planning ahead, we get the best reservations and the best airline ticket prices—a high value that honors my Dutch heritage.

But the main reason we plan ahead is this: Family vacations are high priorities for us. They get protected far in advance on our calendars. Our vacations don't get nibbled away by new opportunities or commitments. We gear up for them by planning ahead and saying no to work obligations during the days we've blocked out. That way, we aren't tempted to turn a family trip into a working vacation with our laptops and smartphones. And we maximize our anticipation as the countdown begins for each trip.

How important is your family? Do you want to become someone who fosters rich, lasting memories with your loved ones? My guess is you do. If so, write "Family Vacation" on your calendar—in ink.

EXERCISE

I have a friend who's been out of shape—and I mean seriously out of shape—for about twenty years. When we'd go out together, he used to complain about it: "Look at me—I'm just a slug," he would say, "but, man, you should have seen me in high school!"

Then, some time ago, he decided he was going to exercise three days a week. Just an hour-long workout—no personal trainer, no private chef.

"I put it on my calendar," he told me.

To be completely honest, I wasn't optimistic, given the bellyaching he'd been doing about his weight for as long as I had known him.

But he put it on his calendar—and then he lived it out. Today, he's forty-five pounds lighter than he was back then. He feels better than he has for twenty years. All from three squares a week that he protected on his calendar with the words "Work Out."

The power of words added to a calendar and then lived out changes who we become.

The power of words added to a calendar and then lived out changes who we become.

■　■　■

I want to end this chapter by telling you the story of a businessman in my community who started attending Willow some years back. At first, he came only when his wife put enough pressure on him. But every once in a while, he'd attend and stay after the service, and occasionally he and I would talk.

Eventually, he began attending more frequently. Before long, I noticed a shift in this guy's demeanor. Something seemed to click, and he got all fired up about God. He had a ton of questions and asked for books to read. He came to our midweek service and sometimes attended two of our weekend services. Finally, he jumped in with both feet and committed his life to Christ. I had the honor of baptizing him. Soon he was in full flight spiritually. He knew who he wanted to become.

He wanted to become a new man in Christ.

One day we were having lunch together, and he said, "I memorized my first Bible verse."

"Well let's hear it," I said.

He recited Matthew 6:33: "Seek ye first the kingdom of God, and his righteousness; and all these things shall be added unto you."[5]

"Awesome!" I said. "So that's really the first verse you ever memorized?" It was. Then I had a little fun with him. I asked, "Do you plan to go around quoting this verse and showing off about it—or do you have any intentions of actually living it out?"

This was a new concept for a man who was young in his faith. "How would you live out *that* verse?" he wanted to know.

So we engaged in an animated conversation about what it looks like to seek God's Kingdom first. I told him, "One way you can start seeking God's Kingdom first is by redrafting your schedule and filling it up the way God would fill it if He were in charge of your time, your schedule, your calendar."

"But I run a business," he said. "I have to do what I have to do."

"We all have stuff we have to do," I said. "But if you put the God stuff in first—if you start by plugging in the time slots on your calendar that determine who you want to become—and then fill in the other stuff around it, you'll gradually become the kind of person you want to be."

"I want to become a God-first person," he said. "I really do."

I believed him.

He began drafting different attempts at a God-first schedule, and he would occasionally run them by me. When he landed on the final draft—the version with all the "God stuff" slotted in first—we prayed over it, and this guy decided to live it out, courageously and with conviction.

By his own admission, he had some marriage repair to do, so he put it on his calendar and slowly, purposefully repaired his relationship with his wife. His kids had never been a priority in his life, but now that his spiritual values had shifted, family was much higher on the priority list. In fact, he started planning family nights and family vacations. He had always been too busy for family vacations, but not anymore. It wasn't too late to start.

He scheduled time to participate in a men's Bible study, and that Bible study rocked his life. Then he arranged some time to volunteer in some of the ministries at church he felt passionate about.

> One calendar square at a time, this guy became a totally different man, all because he redrafted his schedule and then lived it out.

Over the next couple of years, one calendar square at a time, this guy became a totally different man, all because he redrafted his schedule and then lived it out.

Little did he know that this new schedule would indeed be his final draft, because cancer came his way. As it ravaged his body,

"regrets" department. Four simple letters can make all the difference: *H-O-M-E*.

If you're in a dead-end vocation, do something about it! Sign up for a night class. Attend the development training your company offers. Plan regular times on your calendar to update your résumé and look for a new job. Do something that will eventually get your life on a better track.

chapter three

from overwhelmed to in control

Mastering Your Finances

FEW THINGS HAVE THE POWER to throw our lives into chaos like financial stress. An out-of-control financial picture leaves us vulnerable to unspeakable pain. We dread answering the phone or opening the mail for fear of facing another late bill—or worse, a foreclosure notice. We're always waiting for the other shoe to drop. No matter how full our energy buckets are or how intentionally we've designed our schedules, a dysfunctional relationship with money will result in an ever-present feeling of being beset and besieged.

I hear it all the time: "I'm just overwhelmed."

I hear it from people who are underwater financially: "I'm overwhelmed with bills. I'm overwhelmed with debt. I'm overwhelmed with what to do to keep our heads above water, let alone set aside funds for our kids' education."

I hear it from people who have adequate incomes and cash flow: "I've worked so hard to get where I am, and now I dread making a mistake and losing it all."

There is no way to simplify your life if your relationship with money is out of control.

WHY TALK ABOUT MONEY?

First, a disclaimer: As a pastor, I frequently fight the stereotype that what pastors really care about is getting people to give more money. We've all seen or heard of money-grubbing preachers whose sole focus seems to be lining their own pockets.

I cannot speak to what motivates these people, but I can speak for myself and for countless other Christ-following pastors who are compelled to address the issue of money because we cannot ignore the crystal-clear message of Scripture. Judging by the sheer number of verses related to money, it's obvious that a right relationship with our finances is of great importance to God. Directly and in parables, Jesus spoke frequently about both money and stewardship. As a Christian leader, I take my responsibility seriously to educate fellow Christ followers about what the Bible teaches in this regard.

> It gives me genuine joy to equip people to move from feeling *over-whelmed* to *in control* regarding their finances.

It gives me genuine joy to equip people to move from feeling *over-whelmed* to *in control* regarding their finances. I am unapologetic when it comes to talking about money, because I've witnessed up close the freedom that good stewardship can bring. Time and again, I've seen the life-changing peace that permeates people's hearts when they surrender their finances to God's guidance. I've experienced this peace in my own life, and I want it for you as well.

THE BREAKING POINT

Let's begin by examining the life of a guy in Scripture who had a fractured relationship with money. In my opinion, his terrible financial mind-set left him increasingly filled with guilt and shame. But then he encountered Jesus:

> Jesus entered Jericho and was passing through. A man was there by the name of Zacchaeus; he was a chief tax collector and was wealthy. He wanted to see who Jesus was, but because he was short he could not see over the crowd. So he ran ahead and climbed a sycamore-fig tree to see him, since Jesus was coming that way.
>
> When Jesus reached the spot, he looked up and said to him, "Zacchaeus, come down immediately. I must stay at your house today." So he came down at once and welcomed him gladly.
>
> All the people saw this and began to mutter, "He has gone to be the guest of a sinner."
>
> But Zacchaeus stood up and said to the Lord, "Look, Lord! Here and now I give half of my possessions to the poor, and if I have cheated anybody out of anything, I will pay back four times the amount."
>
> Jesus said to him, "Today salvation has come to this house, because this man, too, is a son of Abraham. For the Son of Man came to seek and to save the lost."[1]

If you grew up in the church, this story is not new to you. It's likely you heard about Zacchaeus many times in Sunday school. Perhaps you can still sing the song about this "wee little man." He is a well-known biblical character from a well-known passage of Scripture.

Yet in my more recent studies of this episode in Luke's Gospel, something entirely new fascinates me about this tax collector's story. I sense a raw, human element just below the surface of

Zacchaeus's carefully constructed, rich-man facade. The emotional undercurrent of his messed-up life bubbles up through the cracks as he encounters Jesus.

Luke tells us that because Zacchaeus was short of stature, he needed to climb a tree in order to catch a glimpse of Jesus. He couldn't see over the heads of the crowd. Seems straightforward enough, right?

But doesn't it make you wonder what would drive a wealthy man to go to this extreme, sacrificing his dignity by hiking up his tunic and climbing a tree in broad daylight on a crowded street? Why was he so determined to see Jesus?

Almost everyone in Palestine had heard of Jesus, the teacher and miracle worker. For the past couple of years, He had been healing people, feeding them with miraculous multiplications of bread and fish, and turning barrels of water into a fine pinot grigio or chardonnay. The word had spread. Perhaps Zacchaeus was simply a Jesus fan, like those who crowd around movie stars or rock stars today, seeking autographs. No doubt plenty of people in Jericho were crowding Jesus in a similar way. Zacchaeus could have been a mere curiosity seeker.

> Jesus' teachings of grace and forgiveness had given hope to a man steeped in guilt for his dishonest ways.

But Zacchaeus took it a step further. He risked ridicule by climbing a tree—the unsettling act of a desperate man.

My hypothesis is this: Zacchaeus wanted to do more than simply catch a glimpse of the famous rabbi known for hanging out with sinners and tax collectors. He wanted help.

Perhaps Jesus' teachings of grace and forgiveness had given hope to a man steeped in guilt for his dishonest ways. Years—maybe decades—of extorting money from his own people on behalf of their Roman oppressors had finally caught up with him. Zacchaeus had become wealthy, to be sure, but he found his riches did not satisfy. Just the opposite, in fact.

Perhaps this desperate man clung to more than a sycamore tree that day. Maybe he clung to the hope that this miracle worker could work a miracle in his life and free him from the bondage of his crippling relationship with money.

Not only had Zacchaeus obtained his money unethically, but it seems evident from Scripture that he kept his ill-gotten gains for himself. Instead of using a portion of his wealth to serve the poor, he ignored their plight. He essentially said of the needy around him, "Let them eat cake." He hoarded his riches, no doubt making him even more of a pariah in that Jewish community. His money-obsessed lifestyle had caught up with him and corroded his soul, leaving him tortured and guilt ridden.

On this particular day, it was more than Zacchaeus could stand. He seems to have reached the same point an addict reaches when he or she finally admits, "I'm powerless to change my behavior." Overwhelmed with the weight of self-reproach, perhaps Zacchaeus realized it would take something major in his life to free him from his bondage to money. It would take a power greater than his human strength.

■　■　■

Over the course of my thirty-eight years of ministry, I have had countless conversations with people wrecked by their relationships with money. Grown men and women have buckled over and burst out crying as they told me their stories, because of the self-hatred and shame associated with mishandling their finances. I've too often seen the long-term effects in people's lives when they live as slaves to money. Guilt and shame leave an indelible mark.

> I've too often seen the long-term effects in people's lives when they live as slaves to money.

I have spoken with many professionals over the years—doctors, dentists, lawyers, accountants—many of whom made hundreds of thousands of dollars a year, but who were now asking how they could possibly explain to their spouses and kids that they were going bankrupt. The "for sale" sign is going up on the front lawn, the cars are being repossessed, and all remaining assets, including watches and jewelry—and even wedding rings—are now frozen. They ask, "Bill, can you help me break this news to my family?" The level of shame in these conversations is so deep and humiliating that I cannot adequately describe it.

People in these kinds of financial situations tremble with self-reproach. Can you relate? If your true financial condition were put up on a billboard for all your friends and family to see, would you feel satisfaction and peace? Or would you feel deep embarrassment?

·   ·   ·

Back to our tree climber, Zacchaeus. I believe he was at a point where the accumulated years of shame were killing him inside. When he heard about a miracle worker passing through town, a man of compassion with some sort of supernatural power, he felt a glimmer of hope and had to see for himself.

Imagine how the scene unfolded: Jesus spotted Zacchaeus in the tree and invited Himself over for dinner. It was the kind of thing Zacchaeus normally would live for—an important rabbi coming to visit, a boost for his ego, an acknowledgment of his standing in the community. And just imagine the kind of house Zacchaeus had. With wealth like his, it wouldn't be a one-room hut. It would be a status symbol—gated, spacious, beautiful.

Perhaps when they turned onto Zacchaeus's street, he had to walk Jesus past beggars and hungry women and children who frequently gathered outside the gates of his house—people who knew Zacchaeus had money to spare, though he never gave them a penny. You can feel the tension building.

No doubt it got more uncomfortable once they stepped inside. Was Zacchaeus's house filled with lavish furniture and expensive artwork—all purchased with money extorted from fellow Jews? In days past, giving people a tour of his home might have been an ego boost for Zacchaeus, but now he saw his luxuries through the eyes of Jesus, who knew that blood money had purchased every painting and each fine piece of furniture. Zacchaeus's perspective on his wealth was being transformed. What had once made him proud, now left him ashamed.

Scripture doesn't tell us how the dinner conversation evolved that night, but we know something happened in Zacchaeus's heart that rocked him to the core. His life was turned upside down. And at long last, he surrendered the idol of his life—his wealth. He paid back fourfold the money he'd cheated, and he showered the poor with half his wealth. The shackles that had kept him a prisoner to his money now fell to the ground. He was free.

> Something happened in Zacchaeus's heart that rocked him to the core. His life was turned upside down.

Jesus said to the crowd of onlookers, "Salvation has come to this house." Someone who was lost had just been found. Someone who was feeling deep guilt and shame had been cleansed. Someone who felt powerless over his problem had found a higher power. Someone far from God—in many ways *at war* with God—had been reconciled with Him.

Zacchaeus is one of the only people profiled in Scripture who experienced not just one reconciliation with Jesus, but two. The first was, of course, the spiritual reconciliation: Salvation came to Zacchaeus's house. He was forgiven of his sin, and he came into a spiritually reconciled relationship with God.

But at that same dinner, Zacchaeus experienced a second reconciliation—a financial one. With friends, foes, and the poor he'd victimized as his witnesses, he expressed complete repentance for his past financial sins. He confessed the vile track he'd been on—the path that had led to terrible regret and self-reproach.

The text in Luke points to a complete change of heart in this man and his relationship with money. He rectified the damage he had done in his lifetime of greed and hoarding. He reconciled himself financially to a holy God. He chose to go a new way—God's way—from that day forward. By the end of dinner, Zacchaeus was spiritually and financially reconciled before God.

A SECOND RECONCILIATION

In my opinion, far more Christ followers have spiritual reconciliation experiences with Jesus than financial reconciliations with Him. I don't know how else to explain why so many sincere, serious-minded, card-carrying Christ followers have such ongoing, tormented, dysfunctional relationships with money. When Christ redeemed you, He forgave your moral indebtedness and your wrongdoing. You were spiritually reconciled to God. This is the single most important inner shift in the life of any Christian.

But if you haven't yet experienced a second reconciliation—a financial reconciliation in which the power of God breaks the power of money in your life, His love cleanses your shame and guilt about your financial state, and the Holy Spirit fills you with the power to move ahead with all-new financial practices—well, friend, in my opinion, you're still one reconciliation short. You cannot be fully free from shame and guilt until you experience that second redemption.

> Imagine if money no longer had the power to tie you in knots and leave you overwhelmed.

Imagine what it would be like if money behaved properly in your life instead of making you do all the insane things it has made you do. Imagine if money no longer had the power to tie you in knots and leave you overwhelmed. Sound tempting? Read on.

How does a financial reconciliation with God happen? Fair question. Let's take a look at an example of a spiritual reconciliation in Scripture and then explore any parallels between the two.

Luke records a spiritual reconciliation in Acts 16. One night, a military leader approached the apostle Paul and his ministry partner Silas. This was easy for the leader to do because Paul and Silas were sitting in a jail cell and the guy was their jailer. You might say he had a "captive audience."

When the jailer asked how he could be reconciled to God spiritually, Paul and Silas boiled down the entire doctrine of spiritual redemption into a brief sentence: "Believe in the Lord Jesus, and you will be saved."[2] That's it. Just believe.

The key word here is *believe*.

Believe that Jesus is God's Son.

Believe in the power of His atoning death on the cross.

Believe that His resurrection defeated sin and death on your behalf.

Believe that God will guide you into your future.

Believe that He will make your eternity secure.

Paul and Silas told the jailer, "If you fully embrace Jesus Christ and believe in Him in the fullest sense of the word, you can be reconciled to God and saved—this instant."

Within a few hours, the man and his family, who also believed, were saved and then baptized. These life-transforming stories of total spiritual reconciliation never get old for me. That's the power of God's Spirit at work in the world.

Financial reconciliation is similar to spiritual reconciliation, in my opinion. There are some strong parallels. In my study of Scripture over the years, I've found that five central tenets form the foundation for full financial reconciliation with God. To experience this in your life, I believe you must fully embrace these key financial beliefs.

FIVE BELIEFS OF FINANCIAL RECONCILIATION
BELIEF #1: All I Have Comes from God.

None of us got where we are in life today 100 percent on our own power. We haven't bootstrapped ourselves into our current positions without help—from teachers, parents, bosses, and others who influenced us or gave us a break. These were gifts directed our way from God. As Scripture boldly states, "Every good and perfect gift is from above, coming down from the Father."[3]

God gave you life. He gave you talents and aptitudes. He gave you learning capabilities. He has opened educational and vocational doors for you throughout your life. A humble person with any degree of sound judgment will readily admit, "I didn't get here on my own. Everything I have came my way from the loving hand of God."

> You are a daughter or son of a loving Father who has given you everything you have.

Do you believe this? Do you have a right understanding of the depth to which, contrary to our culture's mind-set, you are not a self-made woman or self-made man? You are a daughter or son of a loving Father who has given you everything you have, and who invites you to steward your talents, gifts, education, opportunities, and possessions for His purposes in the world.

BELIEF #2: I Live Joyfully *Within* God's Current Provision for My Life.

It is human nature to look for greener pastures, to wish for better circumstances, more affluence, an easier life. We think, *If only I had a better job, a nicer house, a newer car, I would be happy.* Seems logical, right?

According to this logic, people in the United States should be among the happiest people on earth. We enjoy greater wealth per capita than most countries. We have more opportunity for education, medical care, home ownership, car ownership, food availability, freedoms, and so on.

But a 2012 Gallup Poll ranked the United States *thirty-third* in the world on a happiness scale. Having more doesn't increase our happiness. In fact, seven of the top ten countries were in Latin America, which generally ranks low on the typical economic indicators we might associate with happiness.[4] Civil war–torn Guatemala, which ranks just above Iraq on the United Nations' Human Development Index, is seventh highest in the world in terms of positive emotions. Despite escalating gang violence that produces one of world's highest homicide rates and cripples the economy, Guatemalans are happy. A similar story is reflected in Panama.

> These data may surprise analysts and leaders who solely focus on traditional economic indicators. Residents of Panama, which ranks 90th in the world with respect to GDP per capita, are among the most likely to report positive emotions. Residents of Singapore, which ranks fifth in the world in terms of GDP per capita, are the least likely to report positive emotions.[5]

Translation: More money doesn't equal greater happiness.

Paul would concur. Few of us have experienced circumstances like he faced in his lifetime. In 2 Corinthians 11, Paul cites an alarming list of his personal hardships and provision shortages, including being imprisoned, flogged, stoned, shipwrecked, cold, naked, homeless, hungry, and thirsty. Did this dictate Paul's happiness? Examine what he says in his letter to the Philippians:

> I have learned to be content whatever the circumstances. I know what it is to be in need, and I know what it is to have plenty. I have

> learned the secret of being content in any and every situation, whether well fed or hungry, whether living in plenty or in want. I can do all this through him [Christ] who gives me strength.[6]

These are beautiful words. Someone fully reconciled to God financially can joyfully accept God's current level of provision for his or her life. That provision might go up or down throughout the course of a lifetime—from plenty to want—but we can be content in both. It is our responsibility to make adjustments so we can live within God's provision and be joyfully content whether He provides a little or a lot in any given season.

This belief comes with some implications. For starters, when God increases someone else's provision, do you covet it? Do you become envious? Do you get angry and ask, "Why him and not me? Why her and not me?" Do you get jealous and want what others have? Or are you able to say—and mean it—"Hey, you got a raise. I'm happy for you. You got a better-paying job. You got a new car. God increased your level of provision, and I'm glad. I'm living contentedly within His current provision for my life, and I can rejoice when good things come your way." Can you do that?

> It is our responsibility to make adjustments so we can live within God's provision.

A second implication centers on the issue of debt. By definition, debt comes from wanting more than God's current provision for your life and arranging other ways to get it. Let that sink in. *Debt comes from wanting more than God's current provision for your life and arranging other ways to get it.*

God's provision may include some ups and downs over the course of your lifetime. Job changes, the economic climate, decisions you make and decisions made by others, and sometimes just good or bad timing will all affect your provision levels.

You will only know true financial peace when you learn to live joyfully *beneath* God's provision in *every* season of your life. The apostle Paul unpacks the key to contentment in Philippians 4. To paraphrase, he says, "I make adjustments as needed and live beneath God's provision level—whatever it may be. I build some margin between my spending and God's provision, and that margin leads to contentment, which leads to peace."

Week after week, month after month, year after year, I meet with sincere Christ followers who love God but spend more than what God has chosen to provide. They incur large amounts of debt and experience the shame and pressure that accompanies it. And they wind up feeling overwhelmed.

When you overspend to maintain an inflated, artificial lifestyle, it's like telling God, "Hey, You blew it. You messed up my provision level. You got it wrong. I need more money. So I'm going to use debt to arrange a level of provision beyond what You are providing through my income." Through excessive spending, maxed-out credit cards, outrageous car loans, staggering mortgages or home equity loans, and the like, debt dupes you into enjoying—temporarily— a false level of provision. It might feel good for a moment, but debt puts you in bondage to the lender. And eventually, when it all comes crashing down, and you are suffocating under the weight of bills you cannot pay, you find yourself overwhelmed and with a deep sense of shame.

> When you overspend and rely on debt to maintain an artificial lifestyle, it's like telling God, "Hey, You blew it."

Friend, God wants something better for you. Simplifying your life means diligently living within God's provision for you and diligently working to free yourself from whatever debt you carry.

Are you living within God's provision for you? If not, can you drive a stake in the ground and say, "Beginning today, I commit to living joyfully within God's current provision for my life"? As you make adjustments in your spending along the way, the margin it creates in your life will breed contentment, which leads to peace. Whether you're in a season of plenty or in a season of less, you can live with contentment and peace.

When it comes to your finances, the implications of simplified living are enormous, especially for your children and grandchildren. When you set up future generations to live within God's provision, with their finances under control, it's a beautiful thing.

If the very thought of living *beneath* God's provision petrifies you, just imagine what it would feel like if you were granted freedom from your debt for even one day. Just one day to live debt-free—what would that day be like for you?

Imagine a whole day of owing nothing, of carrying no debt, of savoring and enjoying the things you can afford—a home that doesn't keep you house poor, a car whose title reads "Paid in Full," a meal with people you love that fills your soul without breaking your budget. The sun shines brighter when you're debt-free; the air you breathe feels fresher when you're debt-free; your conscience feels cleaner when you're debt-free.

How would you feel near the end of those twenty-four hours of debt-free living? My guess is you would say, "I want to feel like this for the rest of my life. I don't care what possessions I need to sell, trade, or walk away from in order to get out of debt. I'm going to attack my debt with a chain saw. And I'm going to keep at it until I am totally debt-free. Never again will I submit myself to the shackles of living beyond my means. I commit myself to living joyfully within God's provision for the rest of my life." When you make that decision, it's Financial Emancipation Day.

Sound too good to be true? Are you hearing a little voice saying,

"You're in too deep. You can't get out"? That voice is not from God. It's a lie from the evil one, and it's not true. You *can* get out. If you commit to these principles, you can become debt-free in less time than you imagine.

During a weekend service at Willow recently, a young couple named Ryan and Chelsea shared their story of financial reconciliation. Their struggle with debt began during the planning stages of their wedding when they said yes to expenses that were beyond their provision—and paid for them, as many of us have, with little plastic cards that sat in their wallets.

> If you commit to these principles, you can become debt-free in less time than you imagine.

"Within the first weeks of our marriage," Chelsea said, "those bills came due, and we soon found ourselves buried in debt. The total amount was ginormous. We were ashamed at how foolish we had been to rack up such a debt, and we were overwhelmed."

The financial strain of those bills put their brand-new marriage on the rocks. They fought regularly over how to manage the debt they were under. The honeymoon was over.

But this is a bright young couple. Rather than wait until their marriage crumbled or the bankruptcy court was their only option, they sought help. They signed up for a finance class that our church offers.

"We started developing some great tools for having productive financial conversations," Chelsea said.

"And we decided we would cut up each credit card as it was paid off," Ryan said. "We cut up six credit cards during the ten-week class."

They set a goal to be free of their crazy credit-card debt by the end of that year. It was a steep goal, to be sure. But by sticking to their plan, they accomplished their goal with a week to spare and were able to wrap up the year with a huge sense of joy and freedom. No more shame, no more weight of debt, no more feeling overwhelmed.

The story doesn't end there. Just two weeks after paying off their credit-card debt, they received an e-mail making them aware of a financial need within a ministry close to both of their hearts. Because they were now living beneath God's provision for them, they had margin in their budget to respond to that ministry's need.

"God placed a really large number on my heart," Chelsea said.

"When Chelsea presented her number to me, it was about ten times more than my number!" Ryan said. "But I sensed God asking us to meet this need too. I met Chelsea right there."

"For the first time in our lives, we were able give over and above our regular tithe, and writing that check was a freeing and joy-filled experience," Chelsea said.

"I think my wife has the gift of giving, because she receives so much joy through this," Ryan said. "Looking back through this experience of getting out of debt, a year ago I couldn't have imagined us being in this position. But God, within His provision, made it possible."

> God truly can be trusted to provide. He simply asks you to trust Him by living beneath His provision.

What a courageous couple. And God truly can be trusted to provide. He simply asks you to trust Him by living beneath His provision. Perhaps for you the next step is to find a class that can help you, or a financial counselor who can guide you. Fill in the squares of your calendar with financial next steps and then follow through. It will simplify your life like you can't begin to imagine, and it will move you from overwhelmed to in control. You'll experience joy and freedom and peace. You won't regret it, I promise.

BELIEF #3: I Honor God by Giving the First Tenth of All My Earnings to His Purposes in the World.

The disclaimer I made earlier about the stereotype of pastors talking about money comes into play with this third belief. But I am unapologetic about communicating what Scripture teaches about tithing and giving. I have no dog in this hunt. It won't benefit me or my church a single penny if you get your finances in order in the area of tithes and offerings. I talk about it solely for your benefit, because the promises of God are not difficult to discern in this area:

> Honor the LORD with your wealth, with the firstfruits of all your crops; then your barns will be filled to overflowing, and your vats will brim over with new wine.[7]

> "Bring the whole tithe [a full 10 percent] into the storehouse, that there may be food in my house. Test me in this," says the LORD Almighty, "and see if I will not throw open the floodgates of heaven and pour out so much blessing that there will not be room enough to store it."[8]

Whenever I teach on this subject, the room gets really quiet because so many people feel guilty about their finances. So, before you continue, allow me to declare these next few pages a guilt-free zone. *Guilt-free.*

When the Bible asks us to take the first tenth of our earnings and give it to God's purposes in the world, this obviously requires faith. It requires faith because it means we are setting aside 10 percent of God's provision—and we're committed to living beneath His provision, right? So we have 10 percent less to work with, in order to keep that healthy margin between God's provision and our spending.

Imagine two friends—let's call them Mike and Jim—who are Christ followers. They have been Christians for exactly the same amount of time, but Mike has a little more faith in the area of God's provision. Jim, not so much. Jim says, "Hey, listen, Mike. I've got to get from A to B financially, and it's going to require 100 percent of my earnings to do so. It's simple math; these calculations work. For me to get from A to B, I need 100 percent of what I earn."

Mike, on the other hand, listens to what God's Word says about this and decides, "I need to get from A to B too. But I believe God can take me from A to B on just 90 percent of my earnings. I'm going to give 10 percent, as I've been instructed in Scripture, as a tithe to support the purposes of God. I believe that, as a reward for my faith and obedience, God will take me not only from A to B, but from B to C, as well. In His Word, He promises to pour out blessings until they're overflowing, and I want to take Him up on it."

This new place, C, isn't even on Jim's radar. He's doing the simple math. His road map ends at B. But Mike finds in Scripture that C is described as a place of blessing, a place of favor. Mike doesn't know exactly what C will look like, but he has a hunch it will be far more exciting and rewarding than ending his journey at B.

Friend, *every single Christ follower I've ever known* who applied this faith-filled practice in their lives has some "C stories" they can tell you—stories of answered prayer, favor, protection, new friendships, new opportunities, and unexpected blessings coming their way. There is nothing quite like living in obedience from A to B and knowing that God has a "C story" in mind for you. The anticipation alone brings energy, joy, and delight.

> "In God's Word, He promises to pour out blessings until they're overflowing, and I want to take Him up on it."

But here's what utterly fascinates me: *Both Mike and Jim think the other guy is an idiot.*

Jim looks at Mike's 90 percent plan and says, "Are you kidding me? Really? You think you're going to get from A to B on just 90 percent? Can't be done. It's simple math. Don't be an idiot."

Mike looks at Jim and says—a little more kindly, perhaps—"No offense, man, but *you're* the idiot, because the most you can ever hope to accomplish is to move yourself from A to B. Big deal! *Boring!* That's what every average person is signed up for. On your 100 percent plan, you'll get from A to B just like I will, but you'll never get to experience the joy of the journey from B to C. You will never know the feeling of God's supernatural activity in your financial life. You will never experience the sense of being favored and blessed. You will never get the privilege of seeing what God might do in your life beyond point B. The real living happens between B and C, my friend. And pardon the pun, but *that's* where the money is! Sign me up for the B-to-C life, anytime."

I ask you right here and right now: Which idiot do *you* want to be?

I want to be the faith-filled idiot, like Mike. I've been that kind of idiot ever since I started earning wages, and I could regale you for a long time with the B-to-C stories God has invited me to take part in throughout my life. In fact, *my entire life* is a B-to-C story. I would never go back to living anything less.

I actually feel sorry for Christ followers who settle for the A-to-B life. They sing songs in church like, "All to Jesus, I surrender . . . ," but when it comes right down to it, they don't surrender all; they won't even surrender 10 percent. It's more like this: "God, I'm totally surrendered to You, but steer clear of my money."

These people talk a good game, but until they surrender all to God—*including* their finances—they're robbing themselves of one of the coolest parts of Christianity, which is the supernatural part.

I ask you: At what point in your life history will you finally put a stake in the ground and say, "Sign me up for the B-to-C life, starting today. The first tenth goes to God, by faith."

Here's a free tip that will make being faithful with your tithe a little simpler: Set up your giving electronically, if at all possible. If your church or ministry of choice doesn't have the ability to receive funds electronically, use your own bank's website to schedule your checking account to set aside your tithe amount each pay period. Utilizing technology in this way helps you get in the rhythm of regular giving. You can prayerfully make a decision that reflects a surrendered heart in the area of giving, and then put that decision to rest by scheduling it to happen whether or not you're "in the mood." This minimizes any temptation to tell yourself, *I'll just pay these bills first and give my tithe later.* Once you've made a prayerful decision to give, setting up an automatic-withdrawal payment system frees you from those hit-or-miss impulses and helps you remain faithful. It's that simple.

> Set up your giving electronically, if at all possible. . . . Utilizing technology in this way helps you get in the rhythm of regular giving.

Give God the full 10 percent of your tithe and trust Him to take you not just from A to B, but also from B to C. It's a key step toward simplifying your life. No guilt, no shame—just a purposeful decision that lines up with being fully reconciled to God. Over the course of your life, you will be glad you moved to this point.

BELIEF #4: I Set Aside a Portion of All My Earnings into a Savings Account for Emergencies, Giving Opportunities, and My Later Years.

In just two short verses in the book of Proverbs, King Solomon paints a word picture that communicates volumes on the topic of savings.

> Take a lesson from the ants, you lazybones. Learn from their ways and become wise! Though they have no prince or governor or ruler to make them work, they labor hard all summer, gathering food for the winter.[9]

Ever go through a "winter season" with your finances? Most of us have been in wintertime financially for the last several years because of the recent economic downturn. Perhaps you know what it's like to lose a job and go through the wintertime of unemployment. You got laid off, or you got moved to part-time, or for whatever reason, the regular income you counted on is just not there anymore.

Have you ever experienced the wintertime of unforeseen expenses? Stuff breaks down—the furnace conks out, the car acts up, the washing machine finally dies. It's as if a pack of gremlins broke into your house and took over. Everything is giving out at once. Then your kid falls and breaks her wrist, and you have a stack of medical bills that weren't budgeted. It's like you're living Murphy's Law: "Anything that can go wrong will."

But if you're the kind of person who has adopted the savings pattern of the ant, you have already set aside a portion of each paycheck into a savings account as an emergency fund for just such a time as this. You can use that emergency money to fix the car and the furnace, buy a new washer, and pay your kid's ER bill. No worries. You planned for winter, so you weren't caught off guard when winter came.

Since the early days of Willow Creek, our board of directors made sure we set aside a portion of every offering and put it in a capital replacement fund for emergencies, equipment failures, unexpected repairs, and so on. Last summer a huge air-conditioning unit for one of our buildings—an unusually expensive unit—died an ugly death during the most

> If you're the kind of person who has adopted the savings pattern of the ant, you have already set aside a portion of each paycheck.

severe heat wave of the summer. Not a problem. I didn't need to beg our congregation to give more money for a new AC unit. In fact, they never even knew the old one died. They didn't have to worry about it, because we have equipment replacement funds ready for situations like this. We just called the HVAC contractor, who came over and took the dead unit out and installed a new unit. Simple. We never skipped a beat. And now we're building the emergency fund back up for the next thing that goes wrong.

You can greatly simplify your life by adopting the wisdom of the ant. Set aside money from every paycheck—you choose a percentage, whatever percentage you feel will meet your need—and put that money into a savings account. And no matter what "winter" comes your way—emergencies, medical bills, retirement—you will be prepared. You will even be prepared for giving opportunities when "wintertime" strikes in the lives of others.

Here's another free tip: I have found that following a 10-10-80 principle prepares me well for whatever wintertimes come my way. I set aside the first 10 percent of my earnings for God's purposes; I save the next 10 percent for emergencies, giving opportunities, and my future; and I live on the 80 percent that remains. This brings simplicity to my life. I'm not overwhelmed, even when unforeseen expenses land in my lap.

When you're fully reconciled to God financially, and you live your life accordingly, no "winter blizzard" has the power to overwhelm you. Being prepared takes the stress out. It brings simplicity to your financial world. It brings peace.

BELIEF #5: I Live Each Day with an Open Ear toward Heaven, Eager to Respond to Any Whisper from God regarding My Resources.

When you are spiritually reconciled to God, you're in a dynamic two-way relationship with Him throughout the course of your day. Christianity isn't a static creed or set of rules; it's not just going to church. In its essence, Christianity is a dynamic relationship between you and God. You pray; He listens and responds. He whispers; you listen and respond. You sense His presence. Just like breathing, you inhale and exhale, listen and pray, relating to God throughout the day.

When you are financially reconciled to God, your conversations with Him might go something like this: "God, I'm living joyfully within Your provision level. I'm not shackled by debt. I'm honoring You with my tithes. And I'm setting aside savings for those winter seasons in my life." And then you have the freedom to add, "So, God, if You want to whisper any guidance to me about redirecting any of the resources You have entrusted to me, I'm listening. If there is a person or a cause that needs resources and You want to use me to provide some of those resources, it's cool; I'll do it. No problem. It would be joyful for me." That's B-to-C living, friend.

> Just like breathing, you inhale and exhale, listen and pray, relating to God throughout the day.

About a month ago, I was sitting in a booth at a crowded diner, working on a sermon. The waitress was one who had waited on me before at this particular restaurant, and she was struggling to keep up with a whole bunch of tables. She was under quite a bit of stress.

At one point, in between orders, she went off to the side, picked up her phone, and read a text message she had received. I saw her face cloud over and her eyes grow moist, and I couldn't help but notice she got emotional. But in the next moment, people were summoning her for more coffee, or to place their orders, so she put away her phone and hurried to the next table.

Just then, the Spirit of God whispered something unmistakable to me: *Bill, you're writing a sermon right now, but your sermon can wait. Here is a woman under a lot of pressure, so just stop what you're doing and change direction. Write her an encouraging note on a piece of your sermon paper.*

God's whisper seemed pretty clear, so I set aside my sermon and started writing a note of encouragement. And then the prompting came to me just like this: *Oh, and Bill? Leave her a breathtaking tip.*

Now I was distracted—and a little worried—because I didn't know what a "breathtaking tip" meant. *Well, first,* I thought, *let's just finish the note.*

After finishing the note, I swallowed hard and prayed, *Uh, God, what exactly did You mean by 'breathtaking tip'? Is it, like, 30 percent of . . . my coffee and sandwich?* (That's double a standard tip, right? I was just giving God a little coaching, helping Him define "breathtaking.")

Then God said clearly, *Leave her one hundred dollars, Bill.*

Yeah, a hundred bucks. That was breathtaking, all right.

So I folded the note, tucked a hundred dollars into it, put my coffee cup on top, and left the restaurant.

Just last week, I went back to the same coffee shop to work on another sermon. The same waitress waited on me. She just took my order and didn't say anything, which was fine, because I was working. When I was done, I paid her and began to gather my things. As I was leaving, the waitress slipped a card into my hand and said, "Read this sometime later." Here's what the card said:

> You will never know what your note and gift last month meant to me. That morning, my husband served me with divorce papers. He controls all of our money, and he took all of our money and our only car. That day was one of the worst days of my life. Then I found your note and your financial gift. It just reminded me that God is faithful and He will take care of me.

When you're spiritually and financially reconciled to God, you get a front-row seat to watch God use your resources like this. You get to have B-to-C experiences and touch the lives of others in some small way. You're on the joyful side, the peaceful side, the open-ear-toward-heaven side of this whole crazy money equation. And God wants that for you. He didn't set you free from your sin so that you could live in bondage to debt for the rest of your life. He wants you to be free. And He wants you to experience the privilege of watching your resources help other people—there's nothing else like it.

DECISION TIME

I would be guilty of leadership malpractice if I challenged you with these five beliefs and then didn't invite you to make a decision about each one of them. It's decision time.

When I sense God inviting me to make a significant decision in my life, I often begin with a self-assessment, and I surrender to Him that part of myself that needs His transforming power. To borrow a line from a famous hymn, my prayer goes something like this:

> Just as I am, God, without one plea—a moral screwup, a financial failure.
>
> Just as I am, without one plea. I have no excuses, God. I made all those crazy decisions. I'm that idiot who doesn't trust You. I'm that guy. I overspent. I've done this to myself. Here I am, God, without one plea.
>
> And here You are, God, with love and forgiveness, ready to cleanse me from all that past insanity. Extend Your hand of grace to me so I can start fresh. Help me simplify my life by mastering my finances and experiencing a full spiritual and financial reconciliation with You.[10]

If these five beliefs intrigue you but leave you feeling conflicted, frightened, or unsure of what to do next, I exhort you: Choose faith. Go God's way. You will never be able to simplify your life until you master your out-of-control finances. You serve a God of fresh starts, of second chances, of new days. When you give

> You serve a God of fresh starts, of second chances, of new days.

Him control of your financial world, you are making a decision of great importance that could change destinies. It could change your family's values for generations to come. Stop the financial insanity today. Ask God to help you get this financial thing right.

You will never regret being fully reconciled to Him—spiritually and financially.

* * *

ACTION STEP: COMMIT TO THE FIVE BELIEFS OF FINANCIAL RECONCILIATION

Consider the five beliefs we have talked about. Do you believe them, or don't you? Can you mark today as the day you go on record as saying, "I want to be financially reconciled to God"? As you read each statement below, prayerfully invite God to shine a light on areas in your life that need to be surrendered to Him. Then commit yourself to each belief.

Whenever I'm wrestling with an area of surrender, I find it helpful to *write* my prayer to God, rather than praying aloud or silently. Use your journal or a piece of paper to process each of these beliefs as you commit every area of your finances to God.

BELIEF #1: ALL I HAVE COMES FROM GOD.

Can you say to God—and mean it—"All I have has come my way by Your loving hand"? When you are tempted to pat yourself on the back for your gifts, talents, opportunities, and possessions, can you humbly remind yourself that these things have been entrusted to you by God, who is counting on you to steward them well?

BELIEF #2: I LIVE JOYFULLY WITHIN GOD'S CURRENT PROVISION FOR MY LIFE.

Financial patterns are frequently passed down from one generation to the next. Perhaps you inherited yours. But you don't need to pass them along. Somebody has to stop the financial insanity. Let that somebody be you, and let it begin today. For the sake of your family throughout the ages, get it right. Take a stand and say, "No more living beyond God's provision in this family."

You have a chance right now to commit yourself to living joyfully within God's provision for your life. Take a stand and declare, "I'm not going to live as if God messed up and His provision level for me is not right. I'm not going to raise my provision level through debt. I'm going to pay off the debt I'm carrying, and I'm never going to return to it. From today forward, I'm going to create margin between God's provision and my spending—and live with contentment and peace for the rest of my life."

BELIEF #3: I HONOR GOD BY GIVING THE FIRST TENTH OF ALL MY EARNINGS TO HIS PURPOSES IN THE WORLD.

Ask yourself: Which kind of idiot do you want to be—the idiot with small faith who does the simple math and gets himself from A to B with 100 percent of his earnings, or the idiot with just a little more faith who actually believes God will get him from A to B and then from B to C? Be the faith-full kind of idiot who decides, "I'm going to step out in faith and commit the first tenth of my earnings to God."

BELIEF #4: I SET ASIDE A PORTION OF ALL MY EARNINGS INTO A SAVINGS ACCOUNT FOR EMERGENCIES, GIVING OPPORTUNITIES, AND MY LATER YEARS.

Few things can make you feel more out-of-control than unforeseen expenses you cannot afford. Don't be caught off guard by winter. Simplify your life by being prepared for the unexpected. From this day forward, will you commit to taking a portion of your earnings and putting it in a savings account for emergencies, giving opportunities, and your later years?

BELIEF #5: I LIVE EACH DAY WITH AN OPEN EAR TOWARD HEAVEN, EAGER TO RESPOND TO ANY WHISPER FROM GOD REGARDING MY RESOURCES.

By committing to the first four beliefs of financial reconciliation, you create financial margin that helps you respond to God's guidance when it comes to allocating your resources. You are one decision away from living every day with an open ear toward heaven, responding to God's whispers regarding your resources. Will you partner with Him to extend compassion and usher in maximum Kingdom impact through the resources He has entrusted to you? This is B-to-C living at its best!

chapter four

from restless to fulfilled

Refining Your Working World

HERE'S A WAKE-UP CALL: You will spend roughly one-third of your life at work. And because your work will consume eight to ten hours per day, every weekday of your life, your experience on the job will either add significant levels of joy and fulfillment to your life, or it will create a misery index that will be tough to overcome with the remaining hours of the day. Being stuck in a miserable job complicates your life like nobody's business. Examining your work life, therefore, is a significant step in simplifying your life.

It should come as no surprise that the writer of Ecclesiastes weighs in on the subject of work:

> This is what I have observed to be good: that it
> is appropriate for a person to eat, to drink and
> to find satisfaction in their toilsome labor under
> the sun during the few days of life God has given

> them—for this is their lot. Moreover, when God
> gives someone wealth and possessions, and the
> ability to enjoy them, to accept their lot and be
> happy in their toil—this is a gift of God.[1]

Put more simply, one of the greatest blessings in life is to love your work, to be satisfied in your daily labors.

Do you know people whose jobs make them miserable? Let me guess *how* you know this detail about their lives: They make *your* life miserable by telling you every time they see you how unhappy they are at work—right? Misery does love company.

By contrast, I met with a young man recently who loves his job and is quick to rattle off all the classic "love my job" lines: "Time just flies when I'm at work." "I work with the best people ever!" "My coworkers are like family." "There's always a new challenge at work—tons of variety every day. Never a dull moment." And here's the capper: "I'd work there for *free* (but don't tell my boss)."

"The other day," he told me, "I was driving home from a fantastic day at work, and the thought occurred to me, *They* pay *me to do what I love to do! This shouldn't be legal.*"

We both had a good laugh. This guy tells everyone he knows how much he loves his job. He views it as one of the greatest blessings in his young life.

HOW A SATISFYING JOB SIMPLIFIES YOUR LIFE

How satisfied are you with your job? On a scale of one to ten, how high would you rate your job satisfaction? Finding fulfillment at work has the power to simplify your life in a number of key ways.

Energy

When you invest the best hours of your day in a rewarding job, your energy level not only stays high throughout the day; it gets refilled by being at work. A miserable job, on the other hand, sucks the energy right out of you, and then it sucks even more energy to keep your attitude in check, doing things you don't really enjoy doing, with people you don't really like. You finish your workday drained, knowing you must return for another energy-draining day tomorrow and the day after that. When you arrive home, you have little energy left for life-giving activities that might otherwise refill your bucket. It's a downward spiral.

> Finding fulfillment at work has the power to simplify your life in a number of key ways.

At the end of a workday in a job you love, you have expended appropriate energy throughout the day doing tasks you enjoy in a culture that is life-giving. The energy you spent on work was naturally refilled throughout the day by the rewarding environment and the pleasing role you play. When it's time to clock out, your tank is still nearly full, leaving you ample energy to engage in family, hobbies, friendships, and other fulfilling endeavors in your after-work hours—meaning you begin your workday tomorrow fully refreshed.

Peace

Conflict, frustration, poor decisions, chaos, inefficiency, and the emotionally toxic environment of a miserable job create an inner turmoil that robs you of peace. You cannot check the turmoil at the door when you leave work at the end of the day; it lingers in your gut and leaks out through your words and attitude in your after-hours world. Your spouse hears about it, your friends hear about it, and your mental energy is spent rehashing it rather than engaging with those you love or doing things that give you life after work. When chaos reigns in your job, your life is anything but simplified.

By contrast, a job with a healthy culture, in which roles are well defined, directions are clear, and responsibility levels are commensurate with the authority needed to carry them out—this type of environment brings a deep sense of peace. Energy is spent doing the actual work, not trying to fight the system to get the work done. People are free to excel at what they do best, with teammates and supervisors who are rooting for them. When you engage in a job like this, you breathe easier inside. Not only is your workday simplified by such a rewarding environment, but your off-work hours and your weekends are simplified as well. You are able to leave the job at the office, where it belongs. When you check out at the end of the day, no cloud of turmoil follows you home. When peace prevails at work, you feel it, your coworkers feel it, and you carry it with you into your simplified, post-work hours.

> When peace prevails at work, you feel it, your coworkers feel it, and you carry it with you into your simplified, post-work hours.

Self-Confidence

A miserable job eats away at your self-confidence through ingratitude, petty jealousy, disregard, lack of respect, lack of development, and an invisible ceiling, above which you can never rise.

A job you love, on the other hand, boosts your self-esteem in healthy ways. You get to do things God uniquely wired you to do well. You see tangible results for your efforts. You experience intangible rewards by witnessing the positive effects of your labor. You know you are making a difference, and you are compensated accordingly— not just financially, but with increased responsibilities.

There is a simple joy that comes from being in a job where you know your contribution matters—to your boss, to your clients, and to yourself. At the end of a workday in this kind of job, you're a better version of yourself. You become more fully the person God made you to be. And you carry that better version of yourself into your after-work world.

A satisfying, fulfilling, rewarding job that you love simplifies your life. When the main hours of your day are spent in a healthy work environment, doing worthwhile tasks that fit your gifts, talents, and skills, your energy level stays high, your emotional reserves stay filled, and you are a little more confident and joyful about what you contribute to the world than you were before you invested those eight or ten hours.

BRINGING YOUR JOB INTO ALIGNMENT

So what do you look for? How do you find a job you will love so much that it actually simplifies your life? When assessing your current job—or any job you might consider in the future—I find it helpful to filter the role or position through four foundational alignments: *passion, culture, challenge,* and *compensation.*

ALIGNMENT #1: Passion

King David reminds us we are "fearfully and wonderfully made."[2] Somewhere in everybody's hardwiring is a passion for something. Though passions vary from one person to the next, when it comes to finding a job that satisfies us, getting the *passion alignment* right plays a vital role.

> How do you find a job you will love so much that it actually simplifies your life?

Even if I live to be a hundred, I will never get over the mystery of the sheer diversity of passions that God places in people: a passion to paint, to fly planes, to sing, to cook, to write, to build, to lead, to administer, to orchestrate, to garden. A passion for law, medicine, construction, accounting, aviation, filmmaking, child rearing, farming. A passion for landscaping, architecture, welding.

I sat next to a mortician on a flight one time. "I love my job," he told me, "because I get to help families during the most difficult times in their lives." Wow. His perspective was right on. Then he added, "I also love my job because it's so quiet!"

Yeah, I thought. *Dead quiet!*

Contrast that with a friend of mine who flies fighter jets and lands them on aircraft carrier decks in the black of night in the middle of the ocean. "I love my job," he says, "because it's life-or-death stakes every time I fire up the engines!" He has a passion for jets, risk, adventure, and adrenaline.

A young man I know is passionate about providing a pastoral influence in the lives of kids who live in poverty. He was a youth ministry major in college, but rather than going the youth-pastor route, he earned his certification in math and became a public school teacher instead. As a middle-school algebra teacher in an under-resourced school district in Southern California that is about 80 percent Spanish-speaking, he uses his bilingual fluency to connect with his students and their parents. He likes math, but his real satisfaction comes from being a source of encouragement and guidance to his students.

The technical director at our church has a very specific passion: utilizing technology to maximize the impact of God's message through the musicians, artists, and teachers in our church's weekend and midweek programs. He views those with technical skills as artists in their own right, and he gets great job satisfaction from equipping them to use sound, lighting, video, and graphics to help God's message reach our audience.

> By identifying our God-given passions and finding jobs that align with them as closely as possible, we can put ourselves in position for great satisfaction.

Willow's copy editor is passionate about providing professional polish to our church-wide communications. She enjoys grammar, punctuation, and words, but her real satisfaction comes from knowing that her contributions help minimize the distraction of typos and mistakes. "I get to help people focus on the message God might have for them, rather than being sidetracked by a mistake," she says.

By clearly identifying our God-given passions and finding jobs that align with them as closely as possible, we can put ourselves in position for great job—and life—satisfaction. The best book ever written on the subject, in my opinion, is *Let Your Life Speak* by Parker J. Palmer. If you are curious about identifying your vocational passion, Palmer's book could help you.[3]

ALIGNMENT #2: Culture

Aligning our jobs with our passions isn't the only alignment that matters. The culture of your work environment also plays a vital role in creating true satisfaction and fulfillment. If the culture alignment is off-kilter, your job can quickly become a drain. For example, you might have a passion for technology—a worthy field of endeavor—but if you work in a dysfunctional, divided, autocratically ruled IT department, chances are you are not going to love your job. Your passion is in proper alignment, but the culture is not. Right vocation, wrong company (or wrong supervisor).

1. Ask the right question. I was talking with a dad recently whose daughter just finished grad school. She is being courted by a dozen high-profile companies, many of which seem appealing—at least on paper. "But how can you predict which of these companies will have the right culture in which my daughter can thrive?" he asked me.

He's asking the right question. He knows how important a healthy culture is to job satisfaction. He knows that the job description might fit his daughter to a tee, but if the culture fosters poor leadership, gender bias, unhealthy competition, and the like, even a perfect job won't matter a lick. She will be miserable.

When you're looking for a new job, look beyond the daily tasks and responsibilities. Investigate the company's *climate* and *culture*. You might learn more by taking an employee to lunch than you'll ever learn in an interview with HR or the manager. How does the culture intersect with your passion, personality, priorities, and relationship style? Is this a place where you could thrive?

2. The truth is your friend. When you've worked at the same job for a number of years, you get a strong sense of your company's culture. I don't think I can brag enough about the staff at Willow Creek today. We have fantastic people who create a fantastic culture! But this hasn't always been the case. If you are curious about how a work culture can turn itself around, allow me to tell you about our journey over the past several years.

> How does your passion intersect with your personality, priorities, and relationship style?

Six years ago, when I stepped back into my operational leadership role at Willow Creek after a number of years focusing more on my Willow Creek Association role, I had a strong sense that our culture was really in the ditch. Our leadership team concurred, and Colby Burke, our human resources director, tried to talk me into hiring an outside firm to survey our staff for the purpose of assessing the health of our work culture.

At first, I balked. We had just watched three senior leaders leave. There was confusion in the air. There were muffled conversations in the hallways. There were tears by the watercooler and peel-out marks in the parking lot. I knew all of this tension would show up if we let our staff fill out an *anonymous* survey.

This survey was going to hurt—like a root canal with no pain-killers. "The truth is our friend," Colby kept reminding me—every day for a year. I knew it was the right thing to do. He finally wore me down, and we hired the consulting firm, surveyed the staff anonymously, and then braced ourselves for the results.

The results came back every bit as ugly and painful as I had imagined. This was pain on a stick! And it was one of the best moves we ever made.

The survey tool we used (and still use) is called the Best Christian Workplaces engagement survey. It invites every staff member to rank a series of fifty-eight statements on a scale of one to five—from "strongly disagree" to "strongly agree." The results are then tallied and the answers are averaged within each department. Here is how the Best Christian Workplaces Institute describes staff culture:

- **Toxic** (*scores of 3.74 and below*): Teams scoring in this range exhibit low trust, hurt feelings, fear, high friction, unresolved conflict, and the like. People who work in this kind of staff culture are saying to themselves, *It's résumé time!* Alarm bells should be sounding.

- **Critical Moment** (*scores of 3.75 to 3.99*) is the space between "Toxic" and "Healthy." It's a "critical moment" because teams are moving in one direction or the other. There is *movement*, but the outlook is uncertain and unclear.

- **Healthy** (*scores of 4.00 to 4.24*): For teams scoring in the "Healthy" range, things look good, but not great. Trust levels are building. People are comfortable, but not enthusiastic. There is nothing worthy of panic, but nothing to brag about either.

- **Flourishing** (*scores of 4.25 and above*): This is where the magic happens. This is where the power lies. Teams scoring in this range are running on all cylinders, the flywheel is spinning, and everything is moving up and to the right.[4]

Our staff completed their anonymous surveys that first year, the results were tallied, and the big reveal came. We scored 3.82—*just .08 above toxic!* And that was after I filled out twenty-seven surveys myself, just to get us that high! (I'm kidding.)

I was devastated. I stayed up late every night for a week reading hundreds of individual comments from the staff. Some were positive and hopeful, but far too many were filled with hurt and disappointment.

> With God's help, we committed ourselves to do whatever it took to move our staff culture to a much higher level of health.

Our executive team processed the results and began putting together an action plan to remedy the situation. With God's help, we committed ourselves to do whatever it took to move our staff culture to a much higher level of health. We held hundreds of meetings, listened to people's stories, and made a lot of apologies. I needed to make a lot of apologies myself. And some people made apologies to me. We began building a new foundation of trust. We all rolled up our sleeves and got to work.

Twelve months later, when we took the same survey again, we showed marginal signs of improvement. We scored a 3.95—which was still below the "Healthy" category and a long way from "Flourishing." But even though it wasn't huge progress, we were nonetheless encouraged because we had made a lot of amends; we knew that it takes time to rebuild genuine trust. Over the next two years, we kept working, kept meeting, kept praying, and kept talking. We established better lines of communication between our leaders and the teams they led.

By the third year, we were well into the "Healthy" range—scoring a 4.07—and in the hallways and by the watercoolers, you could begin to feel the progress we were making. The old bounce-in-the-step was coming back among our staff members.

We learned some important things along the way, such as, "People join organizations, but they leave managers." Perhaps you can relate.

Maybe you feel great about your company, but your manager makes your job unbearable. This was true at Willow as well. In exit interviews, we heard time and again, "I love Willow's mission and vision, and I wanted to stay and pursue that vision, but my supervisor is *crazy!*" By "crazy" they meant controlling, inattentive, uninspiring, uncaring—or, worse yet, mean-spirited. We installed a series of manager training courses and made huge progress there. We also had to let go a number of our managers who had become blocked learners. They had stopped trying to grow as people managers, so they lost the opportunity to lead people on our staff.

We also modified our staff performance evaluations to make it crystal clear to our leaders that we are every bit as dedicated to building our staff culture as we are to building the church. These days, the staff at Willow is measured every six months—not only by *what* was achieved but also by *how* it was achieved. In other words, it's great if we accomplished a lot of tasks, but did we display Christlike attitudes? Did we inspire teammates? Did we resolve conflict quickly and biblically? Did we communicate our concerns in a timely and uplifting fashion?

In year four, we made it to the "Flourishing" level, scoring a 4.25. Our staff engagement consultant told us we had entered the rarefied air of "elite organizations" with thriving, life-giving cultures, which evidently are few and far between.

> We are every bit as dedicated to building our staff culture as we are to building the church.

And more than just seeing it in the stats, you could really feel it in the hallways. The staff's enthusiasm and joy were palpable. People were happy, and their work showed it. And their senior pastor was happier as well!

Today, we're not resting on our laurels. We remember too well the pain of working in a near-toxic environment. We don't ever want to go back there again. We continue tinkering, making course corrections, and doing whatever we can to keep people thriving in their roles under leaders who care about culture as much as they care about finish lines. And just a few months ago, in our fifth year, we scored a 4.33! Our staff engagement consultant told us he'd never seen anything like it—in any organization. He said it's very rare to see a score above 4.30, mainly because a staff culture depends so heavily on "imperfect human beings." Certainly this is true at Willow, because I'm part of that culture!

As a senior leader, I can honestly say I'm as proud of the staff culture improvements we've made over the past five years as I am of almost any ministry achievement our church has played a role in to date. Why? Because when a culture is working right, we are able to give God our very best offerings. Our energies are now being spent on the right things, rather than being wasted on trying to survive in a toxic environment. We have become better stewards of everything God has entrusted to us. I thank our staff—and especially our HR team—for fighting for these gains, for tinkering and challenging and pushing us to build a more Christlike culture.

A flourishing staff culture not only contributes significantly to everyone's job satisfaction; it also contributes greatly to performance improvement. A 2013 study by the Gallup organization, titled "State of the American Workplace," revealed that only 30 percent of workers are "excited" about their jobs, 52 percent are "disengaged," and a full 18 percent are so ticked off about what's going on at work that they are actively trying to do harm to their organizations![5] Leadership consultant Mark C. Crowley describes it this way: "Imagine a crew team out on the Potomac River where three people are rowing their hearts out, five are taking in the scenery, and two are trying to sink the boat."[6]

Contrast this with ten people in the boat, all rowing intensely and enthusiastically. Who is going to win that race every time?

3. Culture builder or culture buster? No matter what level of the company you're on, you have a choice about what you will contribute to the culture. You're not a victim. You have at least some degree of control. But are you maximizing the control you have?

We continually remind our staff that every interaction they have throughout the course of a day either builds up our culture or breaks it down. It either blesses other people or burdens them by adding unnecessary drag. Builder or buster? Blessing or burden?

> No matter what level of the company you're on, you have a choice about what you will contribute to the culture.

We regularly challenge our staff members to be culture builders. We ask them to spend at least fifteen minutes of "chair time" with God before they drive onto our campus. We ask them to be filled with the Holy Spirit and eager to display the fruit of the Spirit, so their interactions throughout the day will be a blessing to their teammates.

I make the same challenge to you. No matter how healthy or dysfunctional your work culture is today, you can choose, by the power of Christ, to become a *culture builder*. You can be someone who blesses every person who crosses your path, from senior executives to entry-level workers.

I've learned that when I show up for work committed to being a culture builder, my job becomes even more fulfilling than it already is. In some way, my culture-building efforts lift other people's spirits, which in turn lifts my spirits. Even my smallest attempt to add value to the life of a fellow staff member seems to make a difference, and I pray that it helps that other person move closer to Christ.

What would happen tomorrow morning if you walked into your workplace fired up to build a healthier culture and create a more joyful, Christ-honoring work environment? I think all of heaven would rally behind your efforts.

I know it's not easy. In no way am I minimizing the monumental task of transforming a toxic work culture. It's hard to stay on your game in such an environment. In fact, in some situations, when the culture is so toxic that you are asked to make moral compromises, you need to get out. Pray for God to guide your steps to a new job that has a better climate and culture.

But in most cases, even a toxic environment can be improved—and you always have a choice. You always have a role to play. You are not a victim, and no one can ruin your attitude without your permission. Reframe your situation and look for small steps you can take to keep your attitude in check, to be buoyant in the face of adversity, to bless even those who curse you. Solicit a trusted coworker to partner with you in this, and see if your combined culture-building efforts can become a team-wide endeavor. Your work life will be greatly simplified when you focus on becoming a culture builder and a blessing to those around you.

> Be strong and courageous; assess your team's culture. Then take the steps necessary to improve. You won't regret it.

Side note to leaders: Truth is your friend. You will not regret taking the bold step of measuring the culture of your staff or those you lead. The insights you gain can be leveraged to bring about change that will simplify the lives of everyone you lead, from the top down. Speaking from our experience, the payoffs are huge. I urge you to summon your courage, pray the prayer of Joshua to "be strong and courageous,"[7] and assess your team's culture. Then take the steps necessary to improve. You won't regret it.

ALIGNMENT #3: Challenge

Whenever I mentor leaders, I often ask this question: At what challenge level do you do your best work? Is it when you're under-challenged, appropriately challenged, or dangerously over-challenged? I ask this question because operating at the optimal challenge level brings the deepest satisfaction. It can mean the difference between a job that leaves you feeling fulfilled at the end of each day and a job that leaves you either frazzled or bored.

When you think of your role at work, do you feel over-challenged, under-challenged, or somewhere in between? And at which of these levels do you do your best work? At which challenge level do you *thrive?*

It's a trick question. The obvious answer would seem to be "appropriately challenged," right? *Wrong.*

Before I give away the answer, let's look at each challenge level.

1. Under-challenged. At this level of challenge, most people eventually quit. As a human being, you are wired to work against some level of resistance. When you're not adequately challenged, your mind begins to wander, you lose your sense of accomplishment, and you start to think, *What's the point?*

You don't do your best work when you're under-challenged. If you're currently feeling over-challenged, you might think I'm crazy to say such a thing. "If only I had a season of *boredom* at work," you might be saying, "I could finally let my creative side come out to play. I could accomplish all the things I don't have time to do now."

That's a fallacy. When people are under-challenged, their skills atrophy and their motivation coasts to a standstill. Instead of becoming more productive, they actually become lackadaisical and are prone to depression. Stay under-challenged at work for any length of time and you'll soon be looking over the fence for a new job. Leaders, under-challenge your employees and you will lose them.

2. Appropriately Challenged. This must be the sweet spot, right? Nope. When you are appropriately challenged, you do not do your best work. You accomplish your work on your own power. No need to rely on teammates. No need to hit your knees and ask for God's wisdom, strength, or intervention. There's no punch in "appropriately challenged." It's the vanilla of 31 Flavors. You might accomplish your to-do list each day, but there's no sense of adventure. Your job feels muted and a little unimportant. You're not thriving. You're just getting the required amount of work done.

3. Dangerously Over-challenged. Not only do you not do your best work in the "dangerously over-challenged" range, but if you stay in this range for very long, something in your life will break. I don't care how resilient you are, how much energy you naturally possess, or how much mental toughness you think you have; something will break. You will not be exempt from this law. Your health, marriage, connection with your kids, relationship with God, emotional well-being—something is going to crack.

> There's no punch in "appropriately challenged." You might accomplish your to-do list each day, but there's no sense of adventure.

I've raced a lot of stuff with engines in my life—boats, cars, motorcycles. Most things with engines have a tachometer, which is a little meter that tells you just how high your engine is revving. The higher the revs, the faster you go, and the higher your tachometer needle climbs. Every tachometer includes a danger zone, usually indicated by a red line. In a close race, you can rev your motor up past the red line for short bursts of time—maybe six or seven seconds. But if you keep your RPMs in the danger zone for too long, something will blow up. And that's both expensive and dangerous.

It's the same way at work. You can't run past the red line for very long there either. Something will blow. In the end, the gains you thought you made by pushing it too hard for too long will come crashing down, either personally or at your job—or both.

So if we don't do our best work in any of these three zones, at what challenge level do we bring our A game to the field?

4. Appropriately Challenged–Plus. Believe it or not, you do your best work just above the "appropriately challenged" level, as you inch toward the low end of "dangerously over-challenged," but before you dip into the danger zone. Let's call this zone "AC+." Here, you feel an excitement, a need for God, a need to work as a team. You're in just enough over your head that you must swim hard and fast—but you're not drowning.

Working at the AC+ level has a feeling similar to when you're working out a muscle and you get that little burn—not the destructive pain of a torn muscle or a sprain, but that "hurts so good" burn where you know your muscle is becoming stronger because of the workout. You want to keep the momentum going.

The sweet spot at work is just above "appropriately challenged." When you can find that level of challenge in your job, your work satisfaction really begins to climb. You know you're bringing your A game nearly every day, and it feels fantastic.

Whose job is it to get you to the right challenge level at work? Whose job is it to make the adjustments, up or down? It's *your* job.

In every job, there are seasons when we need to rev it up above the red line for short periods of time. If you're in church work, you know that Christmas is one of those seasons. As I write this, our team is preparing for twelve Christmas services. Confession: At the end of twelve Christmas services in four days, I will be spent. But I can do it once a year, for a short season. It's okay to bump up into the dangerously over-challenged level for short periods of time—just don't stay there. If your work culture is such that you find yourself continually over-challenged, you must decide, *I'm not going to stay here forever*, and take steps to bring it down to a sane level.

The same is true when you find yourself under-challenged at work. A woman I know took a new job as an orthodontic assistant in a small office. It was her first job in this field, and she had a lot to learn. At first, she felt over-challenged. But her boss was a great teacher, and she soon picked up the skills she needed.

Before long, she found herself "appropriately challenged"—or perhaps dipping just a bit below that. Rather than expecting others to fix her "challenge alignment," she began looking around for ways she could improve the general operation of the office. With her boss's blessing, she reorganized the supply cabinets and brought order to the drawers at each station. She created forms to help record what was accomplished during each patient's visit.

These things had nothing to do with being an orthodontic assistant. They weren't in her job description, which meant she had to find space for them without negatively affecting her main job of patient care. But it gave her deep satisfaction to help her little team function more efficiently, and these projects kept her functioning at just above "appropriately challenged," where she did her best work.

If you find yourself needing more challenge at work, don't wait for those challenges to land in your lap. Be proactive. Talk to your manager and get permission to do more. Show that you can handle more. Ask for greater levels of responsibility. You'll discover that when you function at the AC+ level, you can accomplish far more than you thought you could—and with greater satisfaction. Finding the appropriate level of challenge at work is a key part of simplifying your life. It's like tuning your engine to operate at peak efficiency.

ALIGNMENT #4: Compensation

There's an exchange that occurs in every employment situation: You put in the labor, and the company pays you wages. Jesus said it this way: "The worker deserves his wages."[8]

Pretty straightforward, isn't it? But there's a breathtaking range of compensation in the marketplace—between teachers and professional athletes; waiters and actors; bank tellers and investment bankers. The income disparity is often dramatic. But there's more to "compensation" than cash wages. There's also the degree to which a job satisfies our passions and challenges our abilities.

1. Pay versus Passion. Every college student faces a dilemma when choosing a major: "Do I follow my passion, or do I pursue something that will pay a larger salary?" Parents face a challenge when their excited sophomore calls home and announces, "I'm going to Broadway!" or, "I'm going to be a poet!" Inevitably, the wet-blanket question comes next: "Yes, but how will you pay the bills?"

And so, in the age-old debate, *pay* sits on one side of the teeter-totter and *passion* sits on the other. If you have to choose, should you follow your passion and perhaps earn less money, or should you go for the paycheck—and the financial stability that goes with it—and downplay or disregard your passion?

> Should you follow your passion and perhaps earn less money, or should you go for the paycheck and downplay or disregard your passion?

It's a beautiful thing when passion and pay align, allowing you to do something you love *and* be well paid. If this is your situation, thank God on your knees every day, because you are living the dream. Very few people ever experience the perfect balance between passion and pay. It is one of life's rare and precious blessings.

Most of us have tough decisions to make along life's path, trading off between passion and pay. It can be agonizing, and I rarely give a simplistic answer when asked to weigh in on the question.

On the one hand, I've seen otherwise sane, able-bodied Christ followers bankrupt their families, tank their credit, and go into foreclosure, all because they refused to take a job they weren't 100 percent passionate about. This seems hard to justify in light of the apostle Paul's clear directive: "Anyone who does not provide for their relatives, and especially for their own household, has denied the faith and is worse than an unbeliever."[9]

Strong words. Paul seems to be saying, "Put passion aside if you must (at least for a season), and put food on the table. If you're called to provide, you must provide, even if you cannot do so in your area of passion. That's your first priority."

On the other hand, I've seen women and men make career decisions based solely on a big salary and then lose touch with their God-given passions. These men and women become shells of the people they would have been if they had simply trusted God and done everything in their power to find jobs that stoked their passions. They live in large, well-decorated houses and drive the latest cars. But when you look at these people, there's nothing alive in them. They're not fired up about going into work, they're not stretched, and they're not growing the way God would want to see them grow. But they have fat paychecks, beautiful homes, and someone to mow their beautiful lawns.

> Some people choose to stay in a lower-paying job that aligns with their passion and then figure out how to supplement their income.

When I talk to people who are either stuck in jobs that don't align with their passions or have jobs they love but can't pay the bills, I tell them to pray fervently, because they need God's wisdom to solve this complex conundrum. The people I know who are trying to balance the pay-versus-passion dilemma generally choose one of two paths. They either find a way to pursue their passions and supplement their income, or they take the higher-paying jobs and find ways to supplement their passions.

2. Low Pay + High Passion = Supplement Your Income. Some people choose to stay in lower-paying jobs that align with their passions and then figure out creative ways to supplement their income. They find part-time work or do odd jobs to put food on the table so they can continue to work in the jobs they are passionate about.

When Lynne and I started Willow, we both took on multiple part-time jobs because Willow was our passion but the church couldn't pay us for the first three years. We didn't abandon our passion; we just said, "Let's find other sources of income." So we did. It was tough—and time-consuming. But we had to pay the bills, and we refused to give up our passion.

3. High Pay + Low Passion = Supplement Your Passion. People who work in higher-paying but less-enjoyable jobs can find ways to supplement their satisfaction levels by doing volunteer work that fills them with joy. I know scores of people who are not all that thrilled by their daytime jobs, but this work provides enough resources to keep food on the table and still allows them to pursue God's purpose for them at their church, in the community, or around the world. They fill their tanks by investing in something outside of work, doing whatever brings them joy. Their volunteer roles balance the passion equation for them. They work hard at their marketplace jobs, but they don't expect those jobs to satisfy their passions.

Bob Goff, author of the *New York Times* bestseller *Love Does*, lives out the "supplement your passion" principle masterfully. He is an attorney by trade, and his marketplace job provides a good income. But his passion lies elsewhere. Bob founded Restore International, a nonprofit human-rights organization that pursues justice for those who cannot afford legal representation in Uganda and India. He views his work as a lawyer as "fund-raising" for his personal ministry, which includes his involvement in Restore International and his role in inspiring others to follow their own God-given passions.

Why not look for a job that will align your passion, culture, challenge, and compensation needs?

Both of these paths can work for people who want to balance the pay-versus-passion equation. They find ways to make ends meet without sacrificing their passions. Which of these paths works best for you? There's no limit to the number of creative ways you can balance this equation in your life, and it's vitally important that you do this if you want to simplify your life.

You're going to spend at least a third of your life at work, so why not look for a job that will align your passion, culture, challenge, and compensation needs? Pray your best prayers, step out on limbs of faith, and put your best efforts into it, because if you get all four of these critical alignments working together, you will experience one of the greatest gifts afforded in life: the feeling of loving your job.

"YOU STILL LOVE THIS, DON'T YOU?"

Decades into the one job I've held since 1975, I still love my work as a pastor. I feel more energy and passion for what I get to do every day than I did in my twenties. Most days at work, I deliberately avoid looking at the wall clock in my office, because I know it will show that it's later in the day than I want it to be and that quitting time is close at hand. I am blessed to have all four alignments in order in my job. I love what I get to do. I can't imagine anything that beats it.

Lynne and I spent a recent Friday night at a home on the North Shore of Chicago, near one of Willow Creek's regional congregations. Willow North Shore currently meets in a rented school facility, but they dream of owning their own building and grounds so they can establish a lasting presence in their community.

The home that night was crammed full of people eager to make sacrificial financial gifts for a capital campaign that will build Willow North Shore—the first new evangelical church on the North Shore in twenty-five years. Their new building will stand on fourteen beautiful acres of prime real estate, and it will welcome people from that community to explore faith and to consider letting God fill the void in the center of their lives. It was a night of high energy and contagious excitement as this congregation launched their building campaign.

On the drive home, Lynne looked over at me and said, "You still love all of this, don't you?"

"A little," I said. She grinned. Evidently, passion shows.

That night capped off an amazing week for me that included a series of inspiring meetings with our staff and 416 adult baptisms. Then the next morning at work, I found an anonymous note on my desk. It read, "God bless you. Willow saved my life." Once again I was reminded how high the stakes are when we give ourselves to the work that God sets before us.

AND YOU?

I cannot leave the topic of work without asking you one final question: Have you ever been tapped on the shoulder by God, or has the Holy Spirit ever whispered to you and asked you to cancel out of your current gig and become a pastor? Or to pursue a similar career that helps bring God's Kingdom to earth? If so, did you brush it off? Or laugh it off?

I did. For almost two years, I ignored God's tap on my shoulder. At the time, I was well established in the business world, and I brushed off God's prompting to pursue vocational ministry. But eventually I couldn't ignore Him any longer. I figured, *What the heck?*

In the highly unlikely event that God actually knows what He's doing, I'll humor Him by following His guidance, changing vocations, and becoming a pastor. Undoubtedly it would end in disaster, and then I could shake my finger at God for the rest of my life and tell Him with great confidence that He had His wires crossed.

Forty years later, look who's gotten the last laugh. Almost every night, I drift off to sleep, thinking, *You knew better, God. Your ways are always higher than my ways. Thank You, thank You, thank You for pushing me to become a pastor.*

My life as a pastor has not been without complications. It has demanded more of me than I thought I had in me to give. But pursuing my passion and using my spiritual gifts in my sweet spot is tremendously simplifying. I have clarity. There's no confusion, no "what if" questions that haunt me. I *know* I am working where God wants me, and that knowledge simplifies my life. Had He not kept pushing, had I continued to ignore Him, I would have missed the adventure of a lifetime.

> Life is short. Don't waste another minute ignoring God's tap on your shoulder.

What adventure is God calling you to? Find a way to pursue your passion, either by making a vocational change or by continuing your current vocation and pursuing your passion in the off-hours. When you know you are following God's path, you will experience a tremendous, simplifying freedom. I can promise you the work will be high challenge. It will demand your best. God's work always does. But the work will be clear, focused, and rewarding; and you won't have to fight off the "what ifs." You can simply put your hand to the plow and give God the best hours of your day. Trust Him. He won't lead you astray.

Life is short. Don't waste another minute ignoring God's tap on your shoulder. I dream of the day when, as you drift off to sleep, you can say, "Thanks, God! You knew best. I followed Your prompting. I listened to Your whisper. I changed or adjusted my vocation to follow Your lead and pursue my passion. And You were right. Your ways are higher than my ways. Because I followed You and found my passion, my work is one of the greatest blessings of my life."

■　■　■

ACTION STEP: ASSESS YOUR ALIGNMENTS

How well aligned are you with the job you currently hold? Write your thoughts about each of the four alignments below, and include an action step that will help you improve your alignment in each area:

1. **Passion Alignment:** Does your job fit your area of passion? What can you do to bring this into alignment?

2. **Culture Alignment:** Is the culture of your workplace life-giving to you? What can you do to be a culture builder rather than a culture buster?

3. **Challenge Alignment:** Are you above or below the AC+ challenge level in your current job? What changes do you need to make, or what conversations do you need to have, to right-size your challenge level to the optimal AC+ alignment?

4. **Compensation Alignment:** If *pay* and *passion* are not aligned in your current job, which solution below will lead to the most satisfying alignment for you? What steps can you take to help equalize the pay and passion in your life?

Low Pay/High Passion = Supplement Your Pay

High Pay/Low Passion = Supplement Your Passion

chapter five

from wounded to whole

Making Room for Forgiveness

You can't live in this world for very long without being wronged. On any given weekend at church, if I were to ask for a show of hands of how many people have ever been wronged, certainly every hand in the house would be raised. My hand would shoot up, and I'm guessing yours would too.

We've all been wronged. In my role as a pastor over the past several decades, I've had countless people pour out their hearts to me, telling me how they have been mistreated, victimized, and offended. I've heard tales of betrayal and heartache I will never forget. I've heard stories that wrecked me for days. I've also heard stories that left me shaking my head at the graciousness of the person doing the sharing. And I've listened to everything in between.

Sometimes we grossly underestimate the true cost of living with a relational rift. We think we can go about our lives unaffected by conflicts and fractures with people we care about; but this, of course, is far from true. Relational breakdowns extract energy from us. They take up head space and heart space. They hang over us like a dark, gray cloud.

I know a guy who, for whatever reason, has a pattern of broken relationships in his life. When a misunderstanding happens or someone is wounded, he makes little or no attempt to set things right. "It takes too much time and energy," he says. "I just move on." And he leaves a path of desolation in his wake.

> Relational breakdowns extract energy from us. . . . They hang over us like a dark, gray cloud.

If this guy were to tally the number of hours it has cost him over the years to *avoid* dealing with the relational wounds that have come his way (not to mention those he has dished out), he would find the opposite is true. It is much more time-efficient—and brings much greater peace of mind and satisfaction with life—to heal a relational rift rather than let it linger or avoid it altogether. We cannot live simplified lives without attending to broken relationships.

WHAT'S INSIDE SHOWS

No one understood the cost of broken relationships better than Jesus. In fact, in one of His final prayers, as He hung dying on the cross, Jesus offered words of reconciliation to the very people who had unjustly accused and convicted Him—the people who were killing Him: "Father, forgive them; for they know not what they do."[1]

Jesus' prayer is one of the most extraordinary prayers ever uttered. It's not a lengthy prayer; it's only ten words long. Yet these ten words have rocked the lives and hearts of readers throughout history.

Right in the midst of being wronged, Jesus forgave those who wronged Him.

The executioners were no choirboys. They were not model citizens who just happened to draw the short straw on crucifixion day. These men were Roman soldiers so filled with violence and rage that the only roles fit for them in the Roman army were those of coldhearted executioners. They were professional killers, legalized hit men who excelled at their craft. They had already beaten Jesus beyond recognition. And now they sledgehammered crude spikes into His hands and feet. Their next bit of amusement would be to play poker for the robe they had stripped from His back. As these profane, bloodthirsty thugs stood jeering and gawking, Jesus hung on the crossbeam, fighting for breath, bloodied and broken.

And in the midst of it all, naked, wounded, and exposed, Jesus forgave.

What kind of impact did Jesus' short prayer have on those in attendance at His crucifixion? As Mark's Gospel records, "When the centurion, who stood there in front of Jesus, saw how he died, he said, 'Surely this man was the Son of God!'"[2] Years later, the apostle Paul would write in his letter to the church in Rome, "While we were still sinners, Christ died for us."[3] *Still sinners.* The prayer that Jesus prayed while He hung on the cross—for the men who put Him there—left its mark on the foundations of the Christian faith. While we were still sinners, in the midst of our wrongdoing, Jesus forgave us.

You can tell a lot about someone's heart by how that person prays when he or she has been wronged. Your prayers provide a unique window into the true condition of your soul. In life and in death, Jesus valued people—even those torturing and killing Him. Before He breathed His last breath, He forgave the soldiers who killed Him.

> You can tell a lot about someone's heart by how that person prays when he or she has been wronged.

We live in a world filled with wrongdoers. They're everywhere. I'm one of them. In fact, I am a serial wrongdoer. So are you. It's human nature to put ourselves before others—and when we do, we cause harm.

RESPONDING TO WRONGS

Over the years, I've developed three categories in my mind that help me determine how to respond to those who have been wronged.

People often stop me after a service, or in the parking lot, or at an airport. They figure a pastor should care about this kind of stuff, so they approach me and start explaining how they've been wronged: Who did it. Where it happened. Time of day. How it felt.

As they describe the insult or injury, I start praying, *God, give me discernment about how to assess their situation and how to be wise in my response.* Next, I look at the expressions on their faces. I read their body language. I search for nonverbal cues because I want to put the offense in the proper category in my mind before I open my mouth, so I can offer good counsel.

CATEGORY 1: Minor Offenses

Sometimes, within a minute or two, I've heard enough, seen enough, and prayed enough to know that this is a Category 1 transgression.

In a Category 1 offense, the "wrongdoing" is nothing more than a slight—if that—but the offended party has lost track of reality and the ability to see the other person's perspective on the issue, and he or she has stepped into "poor me" mode.

> When I recognize a Category 1 situation, I believe the most helpful thing I can do is to offer the person a friendly reality check.

When I recognize a Category 1 situation, I believe the most helpful thing I can do as a pastor is to offer the person a friendly reality check, looking at the situation from an outsider's point of view, with both sides taken into account.

At first, I just let the person share, hoping that hearing himself recall the details of the tiny little slight will be enough of a wake-up call. Sometimes this works, and the person will say, "I guess it's not that big a deal, but thanks for listening."

If that doesn't work, I have a single word I rely on for Category 1 offenses when the affronted person insists on playing the victim card. As the aggrieved party rattles on, plumbing the depths of the other person's transgression, I wait for the perfect moment to interject my magic word—delivered with a grin and all the sarcasm I can muster:

"*Really?!* You feel wronged by that? *Really?!*"

This gentle ribbing often helps the person take a step back from the perceived offense and see it with more objectivity. It helps to *right-size* the impact of the Category 1 minor offense.

I started using this technique as a youth pastor when high school students would describe to me the unthinkable persecution inflicted on them by their heartless parents—and how they'd never get over the trauma of it. They would regale me with how cruel and unreasonable their parents were, and I'd respond, "*Really?!* Really?! You got caught doing sixty in a twenty-five-mile-an-hour zone, and it was an hour past curfew. Your folks grounded you, and now you're upset with them? You've been wronged? *Really?!* With all the evil in the world, this is your big cry of injustice. *Really?!*"

That's Category 1.

One time, a young wife—fighting huge tears—told me how deeply she'd been wronged by her husband. "We decided we were going to have friends over to watch the Bears game on TV, and my husband said he was going to invite a few guys from work."

"And . . ."

"He thought three guys would come, but six showed up! And we ran out of chips by the third quarter!" She was mad and embarrassed. "I've never felt so humiliated."

She was turning her husband into a wrongdoer, when, by her own description, he had invited only three guys. This wasn't his fault. He couldn't have seen it coming—and the "harm" done to her was very slight indeed: They ran out of Doritos.

Out came my Category 1 response: "*Really?!* You're going to put him on the couch for that? Really?! Come on. Really?!"

My playful invitation for a reality check did its work, and she right-sized her perspective. The jolt gave her just the motivation she needed to reevaluate whether she'd actually been wronged—or if perhaps she was overreacting. "I guess those guys didn't need the extra Doritos anyway," she said.

I tend to lose a little patience when I hear Christ followers say with great emotion, "So-and-so said such and such or did this to me, and I feel mortally wounded. I feel so wronged."

I try to be a good pastor. I do. I try to listen. But sometimes I reach my Popeye moment: *That's all I can stands. I can't stands no more.*

"Really?! With all the garbage going on in the world, you're concerned about *that*? That's child's play. Keep it in perspective, friend." Category 1.

Here's what I'm driving at: First Corinthians 13:5 exhorts everyone who claims to be a Christ follower, saying we ought to be people who are "not easily angered." Other translations say "not provoked." The idea here is that, as Christ followers living under the ever-flowing fountain of God's love, our hearts should be so filled with His daily kindness, graciousness, and love, that we should have the resilience not to be angered or provoked when the minor irritations of life come our way—the everyday injustices, the normal little frictions that happen in families and friendships. We should have enough grace to easily overlook the little speed bumps, to forgive the minor injustices, to quickly forget about them and get on with life. Keeping Category 1 offenses in proper perspective simplifies our interpersonal world. It keeps our relational slates clean.

> We should have the resilience not to be angered or provoked when the minor irritations of life come our way.

When an everyday speed bump comes your way, don't make an issue of it. It's child's play. Let it go. It's Category 1.

I was traveling recently with a Christian colleague. After a long day, we were looking forward to getting to the hotel. As we pulled up to the entrance, he began ribbing me.

"You know, I got an upgraded room."

"Well, I didn't even try," I said. "Cheapest room is fine with me."

"If you're lucky," he teased, "I might invite you up and let you walk around in my suite."

We got to the front desk, and I signed for my room. Then my colleague stepped up and asked for his upgraded room.

"I'm sorry," said the person behind the desk, "but that suite was given to someone else; it's not available."

Imagining my friend's response after all his big talk, I thought, *This ought to be good.*

But without batting an eye, he smiled at the clerk and said, "No worries! First-world problem. I'll take whatever room you have left. Thanks for trying."

I was impressed. You can't fake that kind of response. His natural reaction was to care for the feelings of the stranger across the desk, a dedicated customer-service employee who might feel uncomfortable about disappointing him. My colleague understood what mattered most. He prioritized others over himself. And at the end of the evening, when his head hit the non-upgraded pillow, I bet he drifted to sleep without regret over how he'd handled this minor disappointment. He had no low-level sense of shame for having played the victim or for treating the desk clerk poorly.

His response was so automatic that I'm sure he never gave the incident another thought.

That's simplified living.

In moments when things don't go your way or something isn't said just the way you wish it had been said, the con-

> If you have enough of God's grace filling your heart, you can see the situation in its proper perspective.

dition of your heart is revealed for all to see. How do you react? If you have enough of God's grace filling your heart, you can see the situation in its proper perspective.

Speed bump.

Child's play.

First-world problem.

No worries. You can easily overlook it. You can easily forgive.

Or you can do the opposite. You can play the victim. You can stand on your "rights" and let everyone know you've been slighted. You can let anger and annoyance bubble to the surface.

Really?!

Category 1 offenses do a great job of revealing the state of your heart.

From time to time, when my heart is not in the right condition and I get easily offended or provoked—or a little wrong comes my way and I say something I regret, or I lash out at someone as if his or her little transgression were a major offense—the Holy Spirit will grab hold of me and whisper, *Category 1, Bill. This is child's play. Let it go.*

When I slip up and act like a jerk, I take a deep breath and say a modified version of Jesus' ten-word prayer from the cross: "Father, forgive me, for I know not what I do. I've lost perspective. I've lost the narrative of Your grace and Your love. I've lost sight of the fact that I'm a treasured child of the Most High God and I've been redeemed. I have the Holy Spirit in my life. I've been blessed beyond measure. I have spiritual gifts. I have a wonderful church. I have an incredible family. I have good health. I have a future. Heaven is awaiting me. And I'm getting tripped up and mad about speed bumps? *Really?!* Father, forgive me, for I know not what I do."

Being too easily offended or provoked is common to human nature. When I respond too strongly to a Category 1 offense, it makes me curious. Why did such a minor slight trigger such a disproportionate response from me? What's going on inside me that needs exploring? Sometimes the source of my irritation is understandable, but the trajectory of my response is way too high. What's that about?

When I start poking around inside, asking for the Holy Spirit's enlightening truth, sometimes I find there's a legitimate issue that needs some attention—but I have let it come out sideways, rather than addressing it in an appropriate, mature way. Why?

Or I'll discover I took offense for reasons I'm embarrassed to admit: My ego was dinged, or my shortcomings were exposed, or I had unrealistic expectations, or an overinflated perception of my right to a trouble-free life. When this is the case, I'll turn my focus from the offender to myself. I'll investigate the area in my life that God is revealing, which clearly needs some work.

> Sometimes the source of my irritation is understandable, but the trajectory of my response is way too high.

In both these situations, the minor offense serves as a helpful directional arrow, pointing me toward an area in my life where I need to grow.

Other times when I am offended too easily, it's a clear indicator that I am spiritually and emotionally depleted. My bucket is low, and I need to fill it up with streams of replenishment that allow God's grace to flood my heart.

If you've been too easily irritated recently, take time for a quick confession, and join me in this inverted version of Jesus' prayer: "Father, forgive me, for I know not what I do. I've lost the narrative of Your grace and Your love. My perspective is out of whack. Help me remember that I'm a treasured child of the Most High God. Help me live that way when I experience everyday Category 1 offenses."

Richard Carlson, one of the world's foremost experts in happiness and stress reduction, wrote a book in 1997 that struck a chord with people all over the world. *Don't Sweat the Small Stuff* spent one hundred weeks on the *New York Times* bestseller list. Carlson highlights the importance of not overcomplicating your life by getting worked up about things that aren't worth your energy.[4] "Don't sweat the small stuff" became a mantra that still works today. If you are prone to sweating the small stuff—blowing things out of proportion and being easily offended or provoked—figure out why. If you're not sure why these Category 1 offenses set you off, make a commitment to do some exploring to figure out what triggers your out-of-proportion reactions.

> When you keep your bucket filled, the minor irritations and little injustices of life lose their power to rob you of emotional time and energy.

Simplify your life by letting go of Category 1 offenses. When you understand your reactions to everyday annoyances, and also keep your bucket filled, the minor irritations and little injustices of life lose their power to rob you of emotional time and energy. Your relational world will run more smoothly, and you'll find it easier to overlook offenses and forgive those who commit them.

CATEGORY 2: Legitimate Wounds

Category 2 wrongdoings are more complex. They're not just minor offenses; they lead to legitimate wounds that require resolution and healing. These kinds of infractions happen to all of us sooner or later. They are a consequence of living in a world where wrongdoing is ever present.

I've listened to thousands of Category 2 stories over the years. Here's an example of one I heard recently:

"Bill, I've been wrestling with something in a private area of my life that I'm not proud of. I've struggled with it for years, and I finally gathered the courage to take it out of hiding and share it with a brother I trust. We went out to dinner, and I talked to him about it. He listened. He understood. At the end, I pleaded for him to keep it totally confidential. He promised he would. He agreed to walk alongside me as I struggled to gain victory in this area of my life. But within twenty-four hours, our entire small group knew about it, as well as half my colleagues at work. The guy talked! I'm angry. I feel embarrassed. I feel deeply wronged."

As this man recounted his situation, I prayed for discernment, and I knew which category matched his situation: Category 2, legitimate wounds. This is more than a speed bump. It's a betrayal. It's more than just a "minor irritation." An otherwise-trusted friend didn't keep his promise of confidentiality—and his big mouth had big consequences.

When someone tells me of a situation that fits in Category 2, my response is gentle.

"Oh, I am so sorry, friend," I say with genuine sincerity. "I am so sorry. That brother should not have broken his promise. That betrayal should never have happened to you. I am so sorry."

I offer comfort as best I can, and then we pray about it. Invariably, though, the person asks, "So, what should I do? He wronged me. I'm the innocent party. There ought to be justice of some sort, right?"

That's a legitimate question. And it fits with the common thinking of our world. It's the Old Testament concept of "an eye for an eye, a tooth for a tooth."[5] Wrongdoers deserve punishment, right?

The trouble with that sort of thinking is that it doesn't give the depth of satisfaction the aggrieved person thinks or hopes it will. And focusing our energies on revenge-seeking doesn't lead to a simplified life. As understandable as it is to want the people who hurt us to pay in some manner, justice-seeking alone never leads to relational peace. There is certainly a time and place for justice, especially if the wrongdoing has legal implications. But at the end of the day, we each must come to terms with what has happened to us, and we must forgive.

Forgiveness is not a simple process. Believe me, I know. It means we fully acknowledge the wrong that was done to us, grieve over what has been lost, and yet eventually let the other person off the hook.

We release them. We let them go. Not for *their* sake, but for our own and for Christ's.

When I talk to someone who has been legitimately wounded, I try not to minimize that person's pain. I don't offer a quick fix. I don't say, "If you really loved God, you would just forgive." Sadly, countless people who have experienced legitimate Category 2 wounds have been victimized again by well-meaning Christ followers who offer simplistic advice that adds guilt and shame onto already-broken hearts.

> Forgiveness means we fully acknowledge the wrong that was done to us . . . and yet eventually let the other person off the hook.

But the truth is, forgiveness in God's time is the only door to healing.

I say this boldly from my own experience. No matter the depth of my wounds, no matter how justifiable my desire to see the wrongdoers get what's coming to them, justice will not bring the peace and healing I desire. In the end, clinging to my desire for justice doesn't cost the other person anything; it only enslaves *me*.

When I sense that people are truly open to hearing the hard truth about their painful situations, I tenderly address the work they need to do on the forgiveness side of the equation.

I tell them, with all sincerity and compassion, "Wow, your situation is tough. I don't envy you. But in my honest opinion, at some point you need to do what Jesus did when He was mistreated. Jesus was horribly wronged at the cross, and yet His response to the wrongdoers was, 'Father, forgive them; for they know not what they do.' He surrendered His right to revenge. He gave it up, right there on the spot."

Some people respond, "Well, that's just ridiculous. He was Jesus, and I'm not. End of story." They get stuck on the justice-seeking road, which makes sense to them.

But other times, someone will respond, "Do you think I could actually forgive? What would that look like? How would I go about trying to forgive this person?" These people are hungry and curious.

Whenever people are willing to attempt forgiveness, I walk them through three Scripture texts to help them understand what forgiveness looks like in practical terms. These texts can be summed up with five "go" instructions:

> At some point you need to do what Jesus did when He was mistreated.

1. Go. In Matthew 18:15, Jesus outlines what to do in situations when you've been wronged. "If your brother or sister sins, go and point out their fault." If there's a relational rift, no matter who caused it—*you go.* You take the first step. It doesn't matter whether it's the other person's problem or your problem or something in between; *you* initiate a reconciliation attempt. Don't sit by the phone, waiting for the wrongdoer to call you. If there is friction in your relationship, or any kind of breakdown, Jesus says, *Go. You take the first step.*

2. Go alone. Furthermore, Jesus adds, "Go in private."[6] Don't hold a pre-meeting. Don't call all your friends together and say, "You know what Joe did? I'm going to go talk to him in a couple of days, but first I want to tell you the terrible thing he did. He breached confidentiality. He did this. He said that." Too often, people who are betrayed through a breach of confidence or through gossip then go and tell others about how they were betrayed—committing the same offense that was committed against them. They don't see the irony.

Go alone. Don't tell anybody else the details of your conflict. Take it to the offender directly.

If someone comes to me and says, "Hey, Bill, I need to talk with you about a little problem I'm having with you—and for the record, I haven't talked to anybody else about this; you're the first to hear it," that is really impressive to me. When someone says, "I came straight to you," I know he takes seriously the guidance Jesus offers in Matthew 18. He came to me directly, and he came to me in private. My admiration level instantly rises, and my heart is all the more open to hear what he has to say.

3. Go to reconcile the relationship. When Jesus instructs us to go in private to someone who has offended us, He has a goal in mind: to reconcile the relationship. "If they listen to you, you have won them over," He says.[7] When you go to someone who has wounded you, do so in a spirit of reconciliation.

Ever have someone come to you to discuss an issue, and you can tell that all that person wants is a pound of flesh? He says he wants to talk about a wrong you have committed, but you're not sensing any desire on his end for reconciliation. He's mad. Accusations are flying. He's making you feel worse, with no hope of the two of you making things right.

That's not the way it's supposed to go down. I've been on the receiving end of this approach, and it actually makes it harder for me to see the error of my ways. It's harder for me to offer the appropriate apology or work toward restoring the relationship when I'm busy defending myself from a barrage of attacks.

It's human nature to go on the defensive when attacked, so this approach is not effective. But in Matthew 18:15, Jesus says, "Go. Go in private. And go to set things right, to restore the relationship."[8]

When you go seeking reconciliation, try an approach like this: "Hey, Joe, we've been friends for a long time, and I'd like us to be friends for a long time to come. But something has come off the rails, and we need to talk about it. I feel wounded by it, but I know it's likely I haven't fully taken into account your perspective. I'm coming to you believing that if we talk about this, we can understand one another better. We can forgive each other, and I believe our friendship will be even closer and more trust filled on the backside of this. Can we talk about it now, Joe?"

You go. You go alone. You go to restore the relationship. My rough guess is that about 90 percent of relational breakdowns can be healed by applying this one verse.

If you attempt a restorative conversation and the other person doesn't respond well, Jesus offers counsel for a follow-up. If you can't get the issue worked out during the first meeting, you might need to take a trusted, mutual friend with you and try again. You might need to involve a church elder at some point. But most of the time, if you go right away, in private, with a spirit of reconciliation, you can work things out.

> If you attempt a restorative conversation and the other person doesn't respond well, Jesus offers counsel for a follow-up.

4. Go now. Imagine that your friend "Joe" has breached confidentiality or wounded you in some other way. You know from Matthew 18:15 that you need to go to him; you're not going to tell anybody else; and you're going to go with a spirit of reconciliation. How long should you wait before you try to set things right? One day? Ten days? Thirty days? Is there a sense of urgency to reconcile a broken relationship?

Jesus addresses the "when" question in Matthew 5. Say you're in a worship service, and it's packed. People are singing and worshiping, and during the middle of the service, the Holy Spirit taps you on the shoulder and reminds you that you and Joe are not okay. It's partially Joe's fault; partially yours. It doesn't matter. You and he aren't doing well.

Get up and leave the worship gathering, Jesus says. Crawl out over the ten people in your row. Miss the rest of the service. People might stare. But it's more important for you to resolve your broken relationship with Joe than it is for you to keep singing worship songs to God.[9]

The first time I taught these principles, I was speaking to a group of about 250 high school students. I was teaching with a lot of passion, going through Jesus' instructions—and while I was talking, about a third of the students got up and left! At first I thought I had offended them. But then I realized they were listening to me and simply practicing what Jesus had told them to do. They were going to make amends. I was really proud of them because they took God's Word for what it says. They got up and they left to start making amends, offering apologies, having the tough conversations that can lead to restoration and reconciliation.

This happened again when I was teaching on this passage recently: People got up and left when I got to this point in the lesson. They were convicted by Jesus' words and needed to make a phone call or drive to someone's house. When others in the gathering realized why people were leaving, they started applauding for those who were putting into action their desire to reconcile their relationships. It was quite a moment.

> Take that first step. Reconciling your relationships is a vital step toward simplifying your life.

Perhaps as you're reading right now, the Holy Spirit is bringing to mind a relational fracture in your life, and you know you need to take that first step. The Spirit is whispering to you to go, go alone, go to restore the relationship—and go now.

Close the book and go. This chapter will be waiting for you when you get back. Take that first step. Reconciling your relationships is a vital step toward simplifying your life.

5. Let it go. Sometimes you can do everything right—you go, go alone, go to restore the relationship, and go now—but the other person won't reconcile. Instead, he or she says, "The heck with you. I want to hang on to my anger. I want to hold on to this grudge, and you're messing it up by coming to me to reconcile. I don't want to fix this."

What do you do now? Are you forever saddled with a broken relationship?

No.

The apostle Paul tucks a beautiful verse into Romans 12 that addresses this very issue: "If it is possible, as far as it depends on you, live at peace with everyone."[10]

You can't control other people's responses. They might choose to play it badly for the rest of their lives. If you've done your best and the other person won't reconcile, you're clean before God. You're released.

If you're not confident that your attempts at reconciliation have matched Jesus' guidelines, give it one more try:

Go.

Go alone.

Go to restore the relationship.

Go now.

Before you begin, pray, "God, give me the courage to seek to work this out." I am confident He will give you the strength you need to attempt restoration in good faith.

If the relationship is restored, give God the glory. If the relationship cannot be restored, despite your best efforts, get on with your life.

Let it go.

CATEGORY 3: Life-Shattering Injustices

I define a Category 3 wrongdoing as a life-shattering injustice that comes your way, often out of nowhere; an unthinkable tragedy that forever changes the landscape of your life. By God's grace, not everyone will experience a Category 3 offense in their lifetime.

My wife, Lynne, has become friends with two remarkable people who have experienced Category 3 wrongdoings. She met Robi

Damelin and Bassam Aramin during her travels in the Middle East. Their stories demonstrate, like few I've ever heard, what it looks like to navigate a Category 3 injustice with a heart toward relational restoration. I had the privilege of hearing their stories recently.

Robi is an Israeli woman whose twenty-eight-year-old son, David, was a former officer in the Israeli Defense Force. He later became a teacher at a university and a peace activist who opposed his government's occupation of Palestinian territory. He was called upon to serve another term in the IDF—this time within the occupied territories, the very thing he opposed. Nevertheless, he went, knowing that he would treat with respect every Palestinian he met, and that his soldiers would follow his example and do the same. But shortly after being deployed, David was killed by a Palestinian sniper.

"It is impossible to describe what it is to lose a child," said Robi. "Your whole life is totally changed forever. It's not that I'm not the same person I was. I'm the same person *with a lot of pain*. Wherever I go, I carry this with me."[11] Yet the first words out of Robi's mouth when she was told of David's murder were words of peace: "Do not take revenge in the name of my son."

They have chosen to steward the injustices that have shattered their lives—not toward revenge, but toward relational reconciliation.

Bassam's experience is similar. He is a Palestinian Muslim whose ten-year-old daughter, Abir, was shot in the head and killed by an Israeli soldier while standing outside her school with some friends. She had just taken a math test, and in her pocket was some candy she had purchased but never had a chance to eat.

"Abir's murder could have led me down the easy path of hatred and vengeance," Bassam said.[12] But this is a path neither he nor Robi has chosen.

Both Robi and Bassam are parents whose hearts were broken through life-shattering injustice: children killed in the Israeli-

Palestinian conflict. These are Category 3 levels of wrongdoing that none of us should have to go through, but some of us do. Today, Robi, Bassam, and many others who have lost loved ones in this conflict work together toward peace through the Parents Circle Families Forum. They have chosen to steward the injustices that have shattered their lives—not toward revenge, but toward relational reconciliation.

Nothing can bring back the precious children these parents lost. They will forever have a Category 3 ache in their hearts that few of us can begin to understand. But by working toward reconciling the broken relationships that led to the deaths of David and Abir, Robi and Bassam minimize the seeds of bitterness that could flourish in their hearts. They simplify their inner worlds by putting their energies toward reconciliation and peace.

A New York woman named Victoria Ruvolo was minding her own business one snowy night, driving her car down a New York motorway. She didn't realize she was minutes away from a Category 3 wrongdoing.

A group of teenagers out joyriding that night approached Victoria in the opposite lane of the same motorway. One of the teenagers, eighteen-year-old Ryan Cushing, reached into a grocery bag, pulled out a twenty-pound frozen turkey they'd purchased with a stolen credit card, and just for grins, lobbed it out the back window and into the lane of oncoming traffic.

That large frozen turkey smashed through Victoria Ruvolo's windshield and crushed nearly every bone in her face. She almost died at the scene of this horrific accident—and she was in a coma for weeks. Ryan was soon arrested for the crime.

Victoria is no stranger to personal loss. The youngest of seven children, she had already lost two older brothers, a nephew, and a beloved brother-in-law in unrelated accidents and a murder. Then, when she was thirty-eight, her full-term baby died. Now this. If anyone had a reason to feel like a victim, Victoria fit the bill.

After several surgeries, months of recuperation, indescribable levels of pain, and permanent scarring, Victoria decided to attend the sentencing of the young man who had done this horrible thing to her. The judge gave Victoria permission to speak in the packed courtroom.

With a steady voice, she said, "There is no room for vengeance in my life, and I do not believe a long, hard prison term would do you, me, or society any good.[13] . . . I truly hope that by demonstrating compassion and leniency, I have encouraged you to seek an honorable life. If my generosity will help you mature into a responsible, compassionate, honest man, whose graciousness is a source of pride to your loved ones and your community, then I will be truly gratified, and my suffering will not have been in vain."[14]

In a public courtroom, she forgave him. She said, in effect, "Father, forgive him. Forgive Ryan; he had no idea what he was doing that night."

Upon hearing Victoria's words of forgiveness, Ryan broke down in the courtroom and wept. The judge was so moved that she sentenced Ryan to six months in prison and five years of probation instead of the maximum penalty of twenty-five years.

As Ryan was being led from the courtroom to begin serving his greatly reduced sentence, he stopped in front of Victoria, speechless, with tears streaming down his cheeks. She wrapped him in her arms and hugged him. "I was the last person to hug him before he went to prison," she later recounted. Victoria did the hard work of forgiveness, and it changed the trajectory of Ryan's life—and her own.

> By God's grace, genuine forgiveness for Category 3 offenses is indeed possible.

But notice that Victoria didn't extend mercy to Ryan flippantly or immediately. It was a hard-earned, multidimensional process.

One of the privileges of being a pastor is having a front-row seat to profound acts of forgiveness. I have seen grown victims of sexual abuse do the hard work of forgiving their perpetrators—not releasing criminals from the legal consequences of their actions, but releasing themselves from the desire for revenge. I have seen marriages reconciled in spite of adultery on the part of one or both spouses. I have seen addicts enter recovery and make amends with the forgiving families they devastated, bankrupted, and betrayed. By God's grace, genuine forgiveness for Category 3 offenses is indeed possible. It's hard work, and it doesn't happen overnight. For many, it requires a lifelong journey of working out their forgiveness.

Adam Hamilton, senior pastor of The United Methodist Church of the Resurrection in Leawood, Kansas, has written an excellent book on this topic, called *Forgiveness: Finding Peace Through Letting Go*.[15] On his blog, Hamilton describes the two dimensions of forgiveness:

> There is your internal release of bitterness, anger, or desire for revenge, and there is the extension of mercy toward the one who has wronged you.
>
> Regarding your release of anger, bitterness, and desire for revenge, you must forgive. The more serious the wound, the longer the process may take. But failure to forgive in this sense gives power to the one who wronged you. It is you, not they, who are hurt by your unwillingness to forgive.
>
> But in the second dimension of forgiveness— extending mercy to those who have wronged us— *we may actually harm wrongdoers if we extend mercy too quickly*. Wrestling with the hurt they have caused is a part of their redemptive process, and for Christians, redemption should always be the goal.[16]

As Christ followers, the first dimension of forgiveness begins right away. Depending on the depth of the offense, the process of forgiveness may take moments, days, months, or years. But the second dimension—the act of extending mercy, especially for serious offenses—requires wisdom and discernment, with redemption of the other person as the ultimate goal. Removing the natural consequences of someone's offenses can actually be harmful to the redemptive process. A flippant "I forgive you!" in the face of a significant act of harm prevents wrongdoers from feeling the full weight of what they have done, making it harder for them to experience the redemption that comes from wholehearted repentance.

A DIFFERENT KIND OF HEART

Radical forgiveness is a powerful thing. It takes people's breath away. It causes them to ask, "How could you do this? The normal human heart seeks revenge. How did you find it in your heart to forgive?"

It takes a different kind of heart to choose forgiveness rather than revenge. Jesus modeled this kind of heart when He forgave His murderers even as they were killing Him.

> When we have an accurate understanding of our own shortcomings before a holy God, it empowers us to choose radical forgiveness.

What changes a normal human heart into a new, different kind of heart—a heart that can express radical forgiveness even in the face of Category 3 tragedies?

It starts when we experience the forgiveness of our own sins through the Cross of Christ and the transforming grace of God. When we have an accurate understanding of our own shortcomings before a holy God, it empowers us to choose radical forgiveness too.

Jesus said of a prostitute who had anointed His feet with expensive perfume, "I tell you, her sins—and they are many—have been forgiven, so she has shown me much love. But a person who is forgiven little shows only little love."[17] When we fully comprehend the radical forgiveness God extended to us while we were yet sinners, that's a heart changer too. It is much easier to extend forgiveness to others when we are fully aware of how much God has forgiven us.

When your heart is filled every day by the kindness of the Father, you have enough of His grace overflowing that you can extend His grace to others. When your heart is seared with the practical truths from God's Word about what to do when wronged, you will have some insight as to how to navigate Category 2 and Category 3 situations. You will understand the alternatives to hostility, bitterness, and revenge-seeking. If your heart has been taught that revenge-seeking slowly destroys the souls of people who attempt it, the only viable option—even if you have been horribly wronged—is to return to Jesus' prayer: "Father, forgive them; for they know not what they do."[18]

Not long ago, a woman stopped me after a service. As soon as she started describing the wrong that had come her way, I knew this was a Category 3 life-shattering injustice: Her only daughter had been hit by a drunk driver and killed. I simply hugged her and said, "There are no words. I am so sorry." We prayed, and then we talked some more.

You can bet I didn't fill her ears with any quick-fix platitudes. She is still so steeped in grief that she cannot yet begin putting her energies toward forgiveness. I introduced her to someone from our pastoral care team, so our church can walk alongside her, provide her with some grief counseling, and do whatever else we can to help her navigate this tragedy.

But one day, down the road, she and I will have to sit down and talk again—because, at some point, she's going to have to decide what to do with that drunk driver. The only thing more heartbreaking than a woman losing her only daughter might be for that heartbroken woman to spend the rest of her life enslaved to bitterness.

And if she asks me, I have only one thing to tell her in this situation. As tenderly as I can, I will direct her attention to a ten-word prayer prayed by Someone who was wronged in the worst conceivable way. The injustice cost Him His life, but Jesus freed Himself from the temptation of bitterness through these profoundly simple words: "Father, forgive them; for they know not what they do."

Over the years, I've seen tragically wounded people set free from the tyranny of bitterness and vengeance-seeking. I've seen people greatly abused and mistreated who were liberated from decades of hostility and wishing the worst for someone; I've seen people released from the soul-scorching acid of the need for revenge. It's not easy for them. Forgiveness is a lifelong process. And every once in a while, they have to circle back and get their hearts right again. Many find it helpful to stay close to Jesus' ten-word prayer. Some pray it every day, just to stay clean before God and to remain free of bitterness.

> I've seen tragically wounded people set free from the tyranny of bitterness and vengeance-seeking.

The tragedies that these heroes have experienced do not go away just because they have forgiven those who have wronged them. But neither do those offenses multiply and breed. These people's lives are simplified by their commitment to follow Jesus' example.

Don't let unforgiveness hold you captive. Don't let it rob you of time and energy that would be better invested in meaningful pursuits. The sooner you can pray a prayer of forgiveness and release those who hurt you, the sooner you can live in a new kind of liberation. When you move from wounded to whole, you move to a more simplified life.

■ ■ ■

ACTION STEP: RELEASE MINOR OFFENSES
CATEGORY 1: MINOR OFFENSES

Do you often feel violated by little things? Do others tell you that you're too sensitive or that you blow things out of proportion? If so, friend, you're too easily offended. You're too easily provoked. It's speed-bump stuff. Let it go.

When you feel you've been wronged by a minor offense, ask yourself (with a little sarcastic edge in your voice, if possible), "*Really?!* Am I *really* going to let this little wrongdoing suck up my valuable thoughts, time, and energy?"

Perhaps it's time for you to reboot your perspective. Pray, "Father, forgive me. Forgive me for being a too-easily provoked, too-easily offended Christ follower. That's got to stop." Here are three practical steps you can take to help you release minor offenses:

1. **Do some exploring inside.**

   What's causing you to blow a gasket so easily? What's at the root of it? Write out your best guesses at the underlying cause of your quick trigger. Once you have a clearer picture of what's driving your overreactions to the everyday speed bumps of life, invite God to help you grow in those areas. Ask Him to help you catch yourself when you're going into victim mode.

2. **Fill up your heart.**

   Be purposeful about getting your heart filled with God's love, so life's little annoyances can be easily forgiven, forgotten, and dealt with graciously.

3. **Ask for God's help.**

   When you feel yourself getting offended, ask God for His perspective. Learn to ask yourself, "Is it worth my energy to get upset over this? Or is this something I can let go?" If you've had a long-term pattern of taking offense quickly—or if a specific minor offense comes to mind—you might have some relational repair work to do. Reach out to those who have been victims of your easily provoked nature and tell them, "Hey, I know it hasn't taken much to irritate me. But I see now that it's Category 1 stuff. Speed bumps. Child's play. And I'm sorry. Will you forgive me?"

· · ·

ACTION STEP: RESOLVE LEGITIMATE WOUNDS

Do you have an unresolved Category 2 offense in your life? Perhaps somebody disappointed you, abused you, betrayed a confidence, or broke a promise, and you've got a legitimate reason for being wounded. But you've been holding on to that wound for too long now. It's got to go.

Examine the five "Go" principles for reconciling relationships. Where has your reconciliation with this person broken down? Note the "go" level that has you stuck:

1. Go.

2. Go alone.

3. Go to restore the relationship.

4. Go now.

5. Let it go.

Wherever your reconciliation has stalled, pick it back up and see it through to the end. By God's grace, it can end well. If it doesn't—if the person is hell-bent on clinging to a grudge—you have the release of Romans 12:18 on your side: "If it is possible, as far as it depends on you, live at peace with everyone."

If the person who has wronged you ever has a change of heart toward you, be open to it. But until then, let it go. Get on with your life.

. . .

ACTION STEP: FORGIVE LIFE-SHATTERING INJUSTICES

If you have experienced a Category 3 wrongdoing—a life-shattering disaster—first of all, you have my deepest sympathies and my respect. I would not want to walk in your shoes. I admire your courage.

Second, I invite you to continually move toward forgiveness. Perhaps you think there is no way you will ever be able to forgive the person who did that horrible thing to you or to someone you love. May I humbly suggest that the Holy Spirit will give you the power to forgive, in time, if you offer Him your desire to do so.

Forgiveness is a journey, and you can choose the difficult but better way of dealing with wrongdoing. Like Robi Damelin and Bassam Aramin, you can become known for peacemaking, reconciliation, and restored relationships. You can become that kind of person.

Forgiveness at the Category 3 level is complex. There is no quick solution that can speed you along. But perhaps the following "mile markers" will help you take some steps in the forgiveness journey.

MILE MARKER 1: NAME WHAT HAPPENED.

Many who have experienced life-altering trauma at the hand of another find it helpful to set aside some time to relive the details of the ordeal—not for the purpose of rehashing painful events or remaining stuck in the past, but in order to fully appreciate the depth of what happened. Some find comfort in reading the police report or accident report, attending the trial, or speaking with those who witnessed the incident. Sometimes the details they gain can provide answers to questions that have nagged them, thus allowing them to fully validate the extent of their loss.

Find healthy ways to name what happened to you: If you have unanswered questions, get them answered, if possible. Then write out the details of how you were hurt, or share your story with a trusted friend or Christian counselor, someone who has experience in helping people navigate trauma. In doing so, you will take a significant first step toward forgiveness.

MILE MARKER 2: IDENTIFY WHAT YOU LOST.

When you experience a significant wrongdoing, it can feel more comfortable to stay at Mile Marker 1 on your grief journey—to stay focused on what someone else *did*, where emotions like anger, bitterness, and even hatred make sense. But eventually these emotions lead to a dead end. You have further work to do.

At some point, you need to move from what someone *did* to you, to what you *lost as a result*. At Mile Marker 2, you make that shift and say yes to a more vulnerable emotion: *sadness*. Here are some examples of how this Mile Marker shift looks in action:

Mile Marker 1: "He drove drunk and killed my only daughter."
Mile Marker 2: "I will never walk my daughter down the aisle." "I will never hold a grandchild in my arms."

Mile Marker 1: "He gambled away our life savings!"
Mile Marker 2: "I must now keep working at my job well beyond retirement age." "I can no longer trust him with our finances."

Mile Marker 1: "She cheated on me!"
Mile Marker 2: "The purity of our marriage has been violated." "I can't trust her." "I feel betrayed."

Can you see the shift? Write out a few similar sentences about your Category 3 experience, and let yourself begin to feel the sadness your loss has caused. Take it in small doses, as you are able. By making the shift from identifying *what happened* to describing *what you lost*, you will take a significant step in your grief journey.

MILE MARKER 3: BE OPEN TO FORGIVENESS.

Once you have given yourself sufficient time to grieve the sadness of your loss, you will eventually be ready to say yes to the possibility of forgiveness. You will be able to envision the day when you can fully surrender (or re-surrender) to God the gaping wound of your tragedy.

You may not be ready today to embrace your victimizer the way Victoria Ruvolo hugged Ryan Cushing. But you can take a baby step. In Mark 9:24, the father of a demon-possessed boy tells Jesus, "I do believe; help me overcome my unbelief!" Perhaps you can make a similar statement to Jesus: "I do forgive; help me with my unforgiveness."

By saying yes to *someday* forgiving those who have wronged you in a Category 3 way, you begin to clear the path to being able to pray, "Father, forgive them; and help me to forgive them too. I release my right to exact revenge. I release my desire for control. Forgive them; for they know not what they do." And that, friend, is a prayer that will greatly simplify your life.

chapter six

from anxious to peaceful

Conquering Your Fears

WHEN SOME FRIENDS of mine moved into a rental house recently, the landlord asked them to make note of any preexisting damage. A handful of things were evident to the naked eye—a few obvious dings in the walls, a missing doorknob on one of the closet doors—and my friends jotted a list to give to the landlord.

The morning after they moved in, something else caught their eye. A few tiles in the upstairs shower were not plumb. Upon closer inspection, they noticed some of the grout was cracked and showed signs of mold.

"I pushed gently against the tiles and immediately felt them give way," my friend told me. Moisture damage beneath the surface had weakened the wall.

The next day, the landlord stopped by with a handyman to fix the visible scuffs and dings. When my friend showed them the tiles in the shower, the handyman did some exploring and discovered that many of the tiles were completely detached and the Sheetrock behind the entire wall of the shower was soaked, crumbling, and caked with black mold. If this problem had continued undetected and my friend had leaned unknowingly against the tiles, the whole wall would have caved in. The landlord asked his handyman to tear out the entire shower and redo the upstairs bathroom.

At first glance, the damage to the shower wall hadn't looked too bad; yet with a small push, the damp, moldy Sheetrock disintegrated. The weakened undergirding couldn't provide the strength needed to withstand even the slightest pressure. What looked fairly good on the outside was in fact not good at all. The wall needed to be rebuilt.

> Simplifying our lives means eradicating pockets of fear wherever they lurk.

The same can be said of us when it comes to the topic of fear. We may have succeeded in simplifying significant areas of our lives, and we may look pretty good on the outside. But if fear runs rampant below the surface, we're in danger of collapsing like soggy Sheetrock when the least bit of pressure is applied to our lives. Simplifying our lives means eradicating pockets of fear wherever they lurk.

LIVING IN *SHALOM*

God's preferred state for humankind is that we live free from fear, experiencing *shalom*, or peace. From Genesis to Revelation, Scripture is packed with references that emphasize God's desire for a fear-free, peace-filled world.

In the book of Numbers, God instructs Moses to give this blessing to the Israelites:

> "The LORD bless you and keep you; the LORD make his face shine on you and be gracious to you; the LORD turn his face toward you and *give you peace*."[1]

Peace is also one of the last gifts that Jesus imparted to His followers before He ascended into heaven:

> *Peace I leave with you*; my peace I give you.
> I do not give to you as the world gives. Do not
> let your hearts be troubled and *do not be afraid*.
> . . . I have told you these things, so that *in me*
> *you may have peace*. In this world you will have
> trouble. But take heart! I have overcome the
> world.[2]

In addition, both Paul and John refer to *shalom* in their letters to the early church:

> *Do not be anxious* about anything, but in
> every situation, by prayer and petition, with
> thanksgiving, present your requests to God.
> And the *peace of God*, which transcends all
> understanding, will guard your hearts and your
> minds in Christ Jesus.[3]

> There is *no fear in love*. But perfect love drives
> out fear.[4]

These are but a few of the numerous passages about *shalom* found in Scripture. God's preferred state for the world—and for each individual in it—is that His peace would prevail. Fear cannot rule in the hearts of people who allow God to reign fully.

WHERE'S THE PEACE?

If you're completely honest with yourself, you no doubt can identify at least a few pockets of fear nestled in the recesses of your inner world. So can I. I know very few people who live consistently with "peace which transcends all understanding" reigning in their hearts. But why do so few people experience peace?

Fear is the fundamental barrier to peace, and it's a deal-breaker when it comes to leading a simplified life. Fear is debilitating. No matter how much we've simplified our calendars, relationships, finances, and the like, when fear strikes, the whole deal blows up. No matter how good we look on the outside, we will crumble if fear has seeped beneath the veneer of our lives.

> Fear is the fundamental barrier to peace, and it's a deal-breaker when it comes to leading a simplified life.

When I was in college, I had a roommate whose life looked dialed-in. He got decent grades, had good friends, and held a part-time job. But just beneath the surface, he was harboring some deep scars that made true inner peace impossible.

Sometimes, in the middle of the night, he would bolt straight out of bed and shriek in horror at the top of his lungs. He had recently completed a tour of duty in Vietnam during the war. Though you would never guess it by looking at him, he had been horribly wounded there. His scars were on the inside.

Though my roommate was safe in a quiet dorm at a college in the middle of an Iowa cornfield, half a world away from southeast Asia, the fear and horror he had experienced on the battlefield still lurked behind the tiles of his inner world.

PEACE BUSTERS

It's easy to understand why, for years, my roommate couldn't find peace. He suffered from post-traumatic stress disorder—for which he eventually sought help. But even if we don't have PTSD, we all encounter peace busters that rob us of the *shalom* God desires for His people.

Peace busters are forces or circumstances that shatter our internal tranquillity. They smash into our lives uninvited. They incite fear. They cause anxiety. And left unattended, they seep behind our walls and put us at risk of collapsing under life's pressures when our fears are triggered.

Perhaps you've experienced one of these common peace busters: financial pressure, relational breakdown, unexpected bad news, moral failure, impending mortality. Or maybe you're smack in the middle of one right now. We've already spent some time on the first two—financial and relational issues—so let's take a brief look at the other three.

> Peace busters are forces or circumstances that shatter our internal tranquillity. They smash into our lives uninvited.

Unexpected Bad News

A telephone call. A certified letter. An e-mail marked "urgent." A knock at the door. A pink slip in your mailbox at work. In an instant, bad news thrusts itself in your face, and the placid waters of your life turn into a tsunami. You have stepped across the threshold from your old, relatively peaceful life into a new, uninvited life where tragedy and chaos want to reign. You wish you could turn back the clock and undo what has happened, but it's beyond your control. *Shalom* has left the building.

Moral Failure

When you cross a serious moral boundary, the wave of fear, remorse, guilt, and shame that floods your soul washes away any sense of peace that once resided there.

Here's how it goes: The last time you caved in to a certain temptation, you felt so guilty before God, so filled with anxiety and shame, that you confessed your sin to Him and said, "This is never going to happen again. I'm going to live by Your power and walk in Your ways. I will never do that again."

But when the temptation comes your way the next time, you do a swan dive back into the same old pit. You're mad at yourself, and you feel dirty and ashamed. The very notion of peace with God—*shalom*—seems distant and forever lost. Swirling in your mind are words like *judgment, shame, hiding, secrecy,* and *fear.* How can peace reign in your heart when you have broken the moral boundaries God has set—the boundaries He knows protect us from shame and remorse? Few things shatter our peace like moral failure.

Impending Mortality

Someday—and no one knows when that day will come—we will all reach a moment when we come face-to-face with our own mortality, when we recognize that life is winding down.

Perhaps you already live with physical challenges. Maybe there's a bad medical report lying on a desk at home somewhere. Maybe you've hit middle age and you realize there are more years behind you than still ahead. Or maybe you're just getting older and you've reached the age where it's likely you won't see another ten years, or five, or one. How do you let the peace of God reign when you know you will be moving into the next life in the not-too-distant future? That's the tension. Our impending mortality can be a major peace buster.

> How do you let the peace of God reign in your life when you know you will be moving into the next life in the not-too-distant future?

I'll never forget the day one of my friends called me from his car while he was driving home from work. He didn't sound right, and he told me he'd already been lost five times since leaving the office, which was only a three-mile drive from his house. His route home wasn't complex; it required only about three turns. Something was very wrong. I hopped in my car, drove to where he was, and helped him get to a hospital. There, the doctors discovered he had inoperable brain cancer.

From that day until his last, he woke up every single morning and asked himself, *Am I going to live in God's peace today? Or will I allow my circumstances to rob me of* shalom? And despite his circumstances, most mornings he was able to usher a deep sense of God's peace into his day. He didn't allow his impending mortality to be a peace buster in his life.

Peace busters like bad news, financial woes, relational break-downs, moral failures, and our impending mortality have the potential to keep the peace of God from reigning in our lives. They can shatter our *shalom*.

When a peace buster comes crashing into your life, what do you do? Do you simply bail on the idea of peace? Do you rationalize to yourself, *Well, I'm just a natural worrier. I've always been a little fear-prone. That's just how I'm wired*? Do you resign yourself to living with a low-grade level of fear and an ever-present sense of anxiety?

You can do better than that. You can live in *shalom* regardless of the peace busters that try to undermine your life. When fear threatens to overturn your applecart, you can stand up and fight. You simply need to learn some new fear-fighting skills.

CONSTRUCTIVE FEAR

Before we go any further, it would be good to note that, sometimes, fear is a good thing. Some fears should not be fought; they should be heeded. I call these *constructive fears*.

When you get a little anxious while driving on icy roads, that fear might keep your foot light on the pedal and your car out of the ditch. When you fret over a huge presentation at work, or an exam at school, a certain amount of that fear motivates you to prepare and do your best. In some situations, a little fear helps you value an opportunity, so that you don't squander the privilege of your job or education. That is constructive fear.

> Some fears should not be fought; they should be heeded. I call these *constructive fears*.

When you successfully avoid a temptation because you're afraid of the harm it would cause—or even if you're just afraid of getting caught—that fear keeps you alert and realistic about the consequences of your actions.

When you decide to say no to a dangerous dare because you're "chicken," we call that kind of constructive fear *good judgment.*

Constructive fear is a good thing. It motivates us to fasten our seat belts, show up for work every day, and pay our taxes.

Over the years, I have failed to heed the wisdom of constructive fear at times, especially when I was younger and drawn toward thrill-seeking activities. One of the most terrifying experiences of my life happened many years ago when we were in a construction phase at Willow. We were adding a balcony to our auditorium, which involved laying steel I-beams from one side of the room to the other, about twenty feet above the auditorium floor.

As I walked through the building one morning, monitoring the balcony's progress, I noticed those freshly set beams. I went upstairs to check the construction—as if I knew anything about what a properly set I-beam should look like!

While I was up there, I was gripped by a strange desire to walk from one side of the auditorium to the other on top of those ten-inch I-beams, as I had seen the construction guys do the previous day.

Constructive fear screamed in my ear, telling me to say no to this crazy urge. But I ignored it. *How hard could it be, right?* I'm not afraid of heights. I have a pilot's license, and I have tackled skydiving, bungee jumping, and other head-rush activities before, with no problem. So, no big deal.

Like Karl Wallenda on the high-wire, I started walking, one foot at a time, as I had seen the steel erectors do with such ease the day before. *This isn't so hard. . . .*

When I was about halfway across the beam, a staff member walked into the auditorium and spotted me. I think it was the look of sheer horror on his face that did it, but something hit me. I don't know the medical definition of a panic attack, but standing on a ten-inch-wide strip of steel, twenty feet above the concrete floor of the auditorium, I experienced shortness of breath, a racing pulse, light-headedness, paralysis, emotional overload—the whole nine yards. I felt an overwhelming desire to shout a four-letter word—*Mama!*

> Twenty feet above the concrete floor of the auditorium, I experienced shortness of breath, a racing pulse, light-headedness, paralysis.

What had I been thinking?! It was a moment of pure terror. After forcing myself to get a grip on my emotions, I eventually completed my first and last high-wire act.

There's a verse in the Old Testament that describes someone who is having a panic attack. I came across this verse shortly after my Wallenda episode: "His face turned pale and he was so frightened that his legs became weak and his knees were knocking."[5]

I believe the phrase in the original Hebrew means, "He was scared out of his mind!"

Constructive fear not only warns us about physical dangers, but it also tries to warn us of deeper, spiritual dangers as well. Jesus, who often told His listeners to "fear not," also had this to say: "Do not be afraid of those who kill the body but cannot kill the soul. Rather, be afraid of the One who can destroy both soul and body in hell."[6]

Some fears are legitimate and important. We ought to live with one eye on eternity. There is a heaven and there is a hell, and real people choose one place or the other for eternity. Jesus warns us to fear things that could imperil our eternal destiny. That's constructive fear.

Getting the eternity question wrong carries the deepest of consequences. I saw a bumper sticker the other day that said, "True success is winding up in heaven." No mincing of words there. Failing to navigate your final destiny invites a real fear that will last for eternity.

Constructive fear keeps us alert and helps us deal with the realities of life and eternity, but we must defeat another kind of fear if we hope to lead simplified lives.

DESTRUCTIVE FEAR

Unlike the constructive fear that benefits our lives, there's a *destructive* fear that is baseless, useless, and crippling. It doesn't protect us from reasonable dangers or call us to ponder eternity with a serious mind. It simply nips away at our emotional well-being, cluttering and complicating our lives by erecting false barriers in our work, our relationships, and even our recreational pursuits.

Destructive fear diminishes the quality of our lives. It tricks us into believing, beyond what is reasonable, that the world is an ominous and dangerous place. It mutes our joy and robs us of satisfaction. It causes us to anticipate the future with dread rather than exhilaration.

Destructive fear must be stopped in its tracks or it will undermine the life God invites us to live. History is filled with men and women who said *no* to destructive fear and changed the world. But imagine if they had given in to the paralyzing effects of fear on their lives.

> Destructive fear must be stopped in its tracks or it will undermine the life God invites us to live.

Imagine the apostle Paul, fearing resistance or rejection, choosing to stay home rather than embarking on the missionary journeys that took the message of Christ throughout the known world.

Imagine Reverend Martin Luther King Jr. giving speeches filled with gentle hints about the evils of segregation, because he feared pushing too hard. Instead, King championed the civil rights movement against racial segregation in the United States. Though we still have a long way to go as a country when it comes to ending racism, King's legacy is extraordinarily important.

Imagine Rosa Parks, during that same era in American history, meekly submitting to the bus driver's command to give up her seat to a white person. Instead, she resisted, and her powerful protest against racial segregation became a lightning rod that culminated in the Montgomery Bus Boycott and helped catalyze the civil rights movement during the 1960s.

Imagine Nelson Mandela looking the other way when he witnessed and experienced apartheid in South Africa, because he didn't want to make a fuss. Instead, he spent twenty-seven years imprisoned—eighteen of those years in a tiny cell on Robben Island—and brought apartheid onto the world's radar, helping end the centuries-old regime of oppression.

Imagine Malala Yousafzai passively quitting school, because she was too frightened by the death threats she received from Taliban extremists, who abhor education for girls. Instead, she became even more vocal about the educational rights of children and women, survived a 2012 assassination attempt, and was a Nobel Peace Prize nominee in 2013 and 2014. Her in-your-face response to fear has brought the oppressive plight of women in the Swat Valley of Pakistan—and in gender-oppressed cultures around the world—to the international spotlight.

Imagine yourself, fully aware of the mission and vision God has placed in your heart to advance His Kingdom in this world, yet held hostage to phobias, irrational worries, and destructive fears of failure, harm, or rejection. If you don't fulfill the mission God assigned to you, who will?

The apostle Paul, in a letter to his protégé Timothy, writes, "God has not given us a spirit of fear and timidity, but of power, love, and self-discipline."[7]

God does not want you to live with a spirit of timidity, under a blanket of destructive fears. He wants you to live with a spirit of power, love, and a sound mind—a disciplined thought pattern.[8]

He wants to help you conquer the debilitating, paralyzing, and joy-wrecking worries that hold you back.

A healthy understanding of what the Bible says about conquering our fears is vital to experiencing *shalom*. Some people who teach Christian truths create a bit of a false impression when it comes to conquering fear. They overstate the biblical case, promising that God will take away all your fear if you just ask Him. Some add a dollop of spiritual shame to the equation by saying, "You wouldn't even have fears if you only had enough faith."

> God wants to help you conquer the debilitating, paralyzing, and joy-wrecking worries that hold you back.

This overstatement sets people up to fail and gives an incomplete picture of the process for overcoming our destructive fears. In my estimation, the Bible presents the journey toward overcoming fear as a joint venture, in which we partner together with God. God will play His role. He'll come through. And you must play your role as well. It's a partnership.

CONQUERING YOUR FEAR

If you're serious about simplifying your life by overcoming destructive fears, be prepared for some pretty tough work. But there is much hope. When you do your part and God does His part, you can fully expect to reap the rewards of a life no longer in bondage to fear.

When I'm struggling with a destructive fear—as we all do, from time to time—I find there are a handful of steps that help me enter into the fear-busting venture with God and do my part to bring about my own freedom from fear.

STEP 1: Understand Fear's Origin

Before you can conquer a fear, you must understand where it originates.

A child-and-family counselor I know relayed a heartbreaking story—names and details omitted—from a client she had recently seen. The client was a school-aged boy, brought to the clinic because of outbursts, tantrums, and extreme phobias he could not control. He was afraid of the dark, afraid of new places, afraid of crowds, and afraid of people. His fears were so crippling, they affected his ability to function at home, at school, and in public. Each morning, he resisted leaving the house to go to school, and once at school, he would resist going outside for recess or leaving the classroom to walk to the cafeteria or the gym.

Upon exploration, the psychologist learned that when the boy was younger, he'd had a propensity for running outside unattended. In an attempt to protect him, his mother had repeatedly warned him of dangerous and scary stuff that could happen if he went outside alone in their neighborhood. He could be mugged. He could be kidnapped or shot.

This boy had an active imagination that quickly filled in the blanks. Having already experienced more trauma in his young life than any child deserves, he now imagined unspeakable horrors, based on his mother's warnings, that led to fears of the outside world and the evil people waiting to do him harm. No wonder he was petrified to go to school. No wonder he was terrified of the dark and afraid of crowds and people. In trying to protect her son from the real dangers of running outside alone, his well-meaning mother had fueled a host of imaginary fears that were now crippling his life.

Many people live their entire lives tormented by a particular fear that resulted from a single traumatic event.*

Only by understanding the origin of this little boy's fears could the counselor and her team begin to help him overcome them.

Dr. Joseph Wolpe, a twentieth-century South African psychiatrist who dedicated his career to understanding the origins of people's phobias, discovered that many people live their entire lives tormented by a particular fear rooted in a single traumatic event in their childhood.

For example, a grown man refuses to go near the water because when he was eight or nine years old, a neighbor kid dunked him in the public pool and held him under, and he felt certain he was going to drown. From that one, frightening episode evolved an extreme phobia of water—not just a reluctance to take swimming lessons, but a lifelong fear of water, boats, beaches, the whole thing. His life-altering phobia originated from one bad experience early in life.

Public speaking tops the list of the most common phobias. Dr. Wolpe discovered that almost everyone who experiences high degrees of fear about speaking in front of an audience can recall a time when they gave an oral book report in elementary school, or a three-minute talk in a seventh-grade speech class—or a similar time when all eyes in the room were focused their way—and somebody laughed, the talk didn't go well, or the teacher embarrassed them in some way. From that moment on, the mere thought of speaking in public has caused fear and trembling.

I know a Christian leader who writes books and does live radio and television shows. He speaks with utter confidence in front of thousands of people, but he will only travel to those speaking engagements by car or train, because he is afraid to fly. Earlier in his life, he was in an electrical storm one night while on a small commuter plane, and that single frightening experience has kept him on the ground for the past thirty-five years.

I know people who won't drive because they put a car in a ditch thirty years ago. I know people who won't go out on boats because they got seasick once when they were fourteen. I know people who will not pursue deep relationships because they're afraid they will be hurt like they were twenty years ago. So many people stay far away from God and all things religious because they once had a negative experience at church.

It's heartbreaking to see how some people go through their entire lives held captive by debilitating fears. When you peel back all the layers of self-protection that cover up these destructive fears, you'll often find one or two significant events at the core. These events may not even seem all that terrifying to the casual observer, but they were just scary enough to start tripping the dominoes, causing the person to erect walls of avoidance.

STEP 2: Expose Fear's Lies

Once you have a firm understanding of the origins of your destructive fears, the next step is to expose fear's lies. In John 8:44, Jesus refers to the evil one as a liar and the father of lies, thereby revealing evil's primary strategy for bringing about our defeat and destruction: *deception.*

Here's how it works.

Imagine you're in a serious dating relationship and your significant other says, "I'll call you tonight." When he or she hasn't called by 11:00 p.m., fear makes its move. Destructive fear starts spinning nightmares into your imagination, and they often take one of two predictable tracks: *tragedy* or *betrayal.* It's either, *He's lying dead by the side of the road,* or, *She finally dumped me.* Thoughts like these are good for soap operas and country music songwriters, but they're not good for your emotional health.

> Once you have a firm understanding of the origins of your destructive fears, the next step is to expose fear's lies.

The technical term for manufacturing worst-case scenarios is *catastrophizing.* The evil one loves to help you spin your worst-case scenarios, because they consume, distract, and derail you. When fear has you in a stranglehold, it's easy to take your eyes off of God's power and provision.

Let's say you have serious concerns about the corrupt environment at work. You feel it's a violation of your relationship with God to continue working for that company, and you sense God encouraging you to look for another job. But then destructive fear starts talking and the lies start spinning. You think, *If they find out I'm looking for another job, they'll fire me. No one will ever hire me again. I'll be out on the street, and my house will be foreclosed, and, and, and—and my family will starve to death before my very eyes!*

You can become so paralyzed by destructive fear that you don't even bother looking for the job God wanted to guide you toward. All because you listened to destructive fear and became too afraid to move.

Or imagine you need to confront your spouse on a serious issue. Perhaps there's an unhealthy pattern to how you've been relating lately that warrants a heart-to-heart talk. But then fear takes over: *If I bring this up with my spouse, it won't go well. We'll just end up fighting again, and maybe he [or she] will walk out the door and never come back. I'll be a single parent. Our children will be scarred for life, and my parents will disown me.*

In reality, the heart-to-heart discussion might be risky—but so is saying nothing. This is how catastrophizing works. If you listen to the catastrophic lies spinning in your head and decide to keep silent, you invite a whole new host of troubles your way. Your hostility toward your spouse will likely increase, your warmth and affection will decrease, and you will walk around with an energy-sucking, joy-draining knot in the pit of your stomach. And the opportunity to improve your marriage will be missed. Score one for Team Fear.

> Fear thrives on deceit. . . . Exposing the lies that fuel your fears is often half the battle.

Fear thrives on deceit. Listen for the lies it tells—those frenzied worst-case scenarios fanned by the evil one. Exposing the lies that fuel your fears is often half the battle.

STEP 3: Face Fear Head-On

Studies show that avoiding our fears only causes them to escalate. Experts in the field of fear management agree that the power of fear begins to diminish when a person takes the time to understand its origins, expose its lies, and face it head-on.

The Spirit of God will do His part in helping you discern the origin of your fears and revealing the lies of the evil one. But there's also work to be done on your side of the equation. You must acknowledge your fears, naming them for what they are (and are not) and taking steps to free yourself from the bondage of destructive fear.

The only way you will conquer your fear is to reach out for the steadying hand of God and face the thing you're afraid of. You have to lean into it and walk through it. There's just no other way.

"One ought never to turn one's back on a threatened danger and try to run away from it," said Winston Churchill, the prime minister who defeated Hitler and led Great Britain to victory in World War II. "If you do that, you will double the danger. But if you meet it promptly and without flinching, you will reduce the danger by half."[9]

First lady Eleanor Roosevelt, a contemporary of Churchill's, expressed a similar view about facing fears: "You gain strength, courage, and confidence by every experience in which you really stop to look fear in the face. . . . You must do the thing you think you cannot do."[10]

You must face your fears. Understanding the origin of your fears is the first step: Talk to friends, replay your memories of the past, journal, write, go to a Christian counselor if needed, and get to the root of what it is that makes those dominoes of fear start falling. All of that is good. But then you must actually "do the thing you think you cannot do." You must face the fear head-on.

A side note to parents: Don't affirm your kids' childhood fears. Too often I hear stories of well-meaning parents who react to their son's or daughter's irrational childhood fears by giving in to whatever comfort or reassurance the child is demanding—without stopping to think about what giving in silently conveys.

> The parent has two options: Give in to the child's fear . . . or help the boy work through his fears.

Imagine this scenario: A dad has a fourth-grade son who wakes up terrified one January night, frightened by a disturbing nightmare. The boy dreamed that he and his dad fell through the ice at their local skating pond. The dad provides appropriate comfort to his boy and helps him fall back asleep.

The next morning, a Saturday on which father and son had planned to play some hockey on the long-frozen pond, the boy begs, "Please, Dad, no! Please! Don't make me go on the ice! I'm afraid we'll fall in!"

The boy's fear is age appropriate and understandable in light of his unsettling nightmare. The parent has two options: Give in to the child's fear and avoid the pond, or help the boy work through his fears despite his protests. Many moms and dads in similar situations believe that the good parenting move is to accommodate their frightened child and stay home. *Maybe next Saturday he'll feel better . . .*

But think this through: If the dad gives in to his boy's demands and avoids the frozen-solid pond, the boy will feel relief—*temporarily*. But the lingering message the son takes away is this: *My dad thinks my fear is legitimate. In fact, he thinks we should avoid the pond.* And this: *I guess nightmares should be believed.* Unwittingly, the father has affirmed the boy's fears rather than assuaging them.

But what if the father took the opposite approach? What if, rather than allowing his fear-filled son to take the lead, he instead helped his son *face* the fear, first by showing him how solidly frozen the pond really is, and then by taking whatever steps are necessary to help the boy once again enjoy skating safely on the frozen pond. In the second scenario, the son not only gains victory over an irrational and destructive fear; he also grows in his confidence that his dad is a trustworthy resource when fears arise.

When your child faces an irrational fear, provide comfort, to be sure. But do whatever you can to keep from affirming that the fear is reasonable.

If you struggle with phobias of your own, do everything you can to keep from passing your fears on to your child. If you're afraid of dogs, for instance, help your child be comfortable around them. Avoid making statements or using body language that give your children a reason to be afraid. Let your desire to be a good parent motivate you to overcome whatever phobias you struggle with, so that they end with you and are not passed on to the next generation.

Destructive fear is a mental battle. Scores of passages in Scripture challenge us to be sober-minded, circumspect, and reflective so we do not become tyrannized by destructive, fear-based thought patterns. In 2 Corinthians 10:5, the classic New Testament passage on this topic, Paul challenges Christ followers to refuse to be tyrannized by fear-inducing ideas: "We take captive every thought to make it obedient to Christ."

> You can bring order and discipline to your thinking by surrendering your fears to the power of Jesus Christ.

Even when your mind is reeling from destructive fears, you can bring order and discipline to your thinking by surrendering your fears to the power of Jesus Christ and taking every thought captive.

STEP 4: Speak Words of Truth

The truth wins, every time. If you want to gain victory over the lies that fear speaks into your life, then it's critical to speak truthfully when fear starts grabbing the wheel of your mind. Here are three types of truthful words you can speak to counter your fears and bring God's *shalom* back into the driver's seat.

1. Self-Talk. Remember my Wallenda-like fiasco? When I was halfway across that I beam, twenty feet in the air, you can bet I did some catastrophizing. Here is what the worst-case scenario voices were saying:

Bill, you are going to fall. There is no way you are going to keep your balance for the rest of this little trek. You've never done this before. You were stupid for trying. You're going to splat on the concrete below. Your life is over. It ends here. You are going to die.

These were the frenzied self-talk messages spinning in my mind as I tried to get myself out of that predicament. At a certain point, when the seriousness of my situation fully hit me, I decided to fight back with truthful words. My self-talk sounded like this:

I'm standing on a sturdy I-beam, not a flimsy tightrope. This is not a quarter-inch cable stretched across Niagara Falls. It's a ten-inch—maybe even a twelve-inch—steel beam. If I were on a sidewalk and someone painted a foot-wide path in front of me, I could easily walk that path for miles.

Then I reminded myself, *I'm a decent athlete. I've had a good sense of balance all my life. I don't make a habit of falling over for no reason at all.*

Finally, I spoke a little more firmly to myself. I remember saying something like, *Bill, just stop. Stop this ridiculous panic stuff. It is not helping! Get a grip. Settle down. Take a breath. Regain your equilibrium. Regroup. Stop.*

As these truth-filled words soaked into my mind, I felt my pulse rate slowly return to normal. The tingling in my hands and legs faded. My vision refocused, and the panic began to subside. I envisioned myself grasping God's steady hand, and I took a step. And then I walked slowly, one step at a time, across that beam to the other side.

I think the coworker on the floor of the auditorium was even more relieved than I was.

Remember the Mennen aftershave commercials from the 1970s, in which a guy would slap himself in the face and say, "Thanks, I needed that"? That's sort of what I did to myself up on that I-beam. I gave myself a mental slap in the face. It worked. Perhaps it will work for you, too.

When you get in a situation where you are overwhelmed by fear, get a grip. Tell yourself to *stop!* Fear-management experts say it may be helpful to say the words out loud: *"Stop it!"* Stop manufacturing worst-case scenarios. Stop exaggerating and catastrophizing. Stop believing that you can't push back panicky feelings with the power of Christ and the power of truthful words, because you can! Speak bold, truthful words about your situation, your own abilities, and God's willingness to help you out in situations like this. It will help you regain your equilibrium, both physically and emotionally.

> Stop believing that you can't push back panicky feelings with the power of Christ and the power of truthful words, because you can!

2. Scripture. Christ followers who overcome fear successfully have learned that when they face their fears, God does His part. He shows up, and His presence is tangible. He is a more than adequate partner for the journey. And He has filled Scripture with words of truth that can keep your fears at bay.

The psalmist David experienced debilitating fears at times, and he found God to be a faithful Deliverer: "I sought the LORD, and he answered me; he delivered me from all my fears."[11]

Joshua, who had the unenviable task of following in Moses' footsteps and leading the Israelites into the Promised Land, received this message from God: "As I was with Moses, so I will be with you; I will never leave you nor forsake you. . . . Have I not commanded you? Be strong and courageous. Do not be afraid; do not be discouraged, for the LORD your God will be with you wherever you go."[12]

God can be counted on to show up and do His part. He will be with you when you face your fear. Speaking words of truth from His promises is key to conquering what you are afraid of. The art of speaking truthfully with words of Scripture is a skill that can be strengthened with practice. Over time it will become second nature, and it will be a powerful weapon in your arsenal against fear.

3. Prayer. The early church was traumatized by genuine, life-threatening fears on a regular basis. Arrests, beatings, and imprisonment by their Roman oppressors and the Jewish religious leaders were common occurrences. When Peter was arrested for refusing to stop speaking the truth about Jesus Christ, what did the church do? Did they scatter? Did they bail? Did they shrink in fear? No. They prayed.

"Peter was kept in prison, but the church was earnestly praying to God for him."[13] The church gathered in a nearby home, and Peter's friends earnestly prayed for him.

> I can relate to praying bold prayers and then being shocked when God actually answers them.

Allow me to push the pause button in the story and pose a question: What specifically do you think they were asking God to do for Peter? The text doesn't say. I like to think they were boldly praying, "God, get Peter out of prison!" When, through a dramatic miracle, Peter was in fact released from prison and showed up at his friends' house, where everyone was praying, they were so surprised, they didn't believe it was him! I love the authenticity of the early church. I can relate to praying bold prayers and then being shocked when God actually answers them.

I've been in plenty of prayer meetings where it seemed to me that certain specific prayers should have been prayed, but the other Christ followers in the meeting didn't feel the freedom to pray that way. Here's an example:

In the early days of Willow, I went to the hospital to be with the family of a man who was about to have open-heart surgery. I showed up just before he was wheeled into the operating room. The wife was understandably distraught. The kids were afraid they might lose their dad in this rather serious procedure, and the dad looked petrified— about how you might expect a guy to look who's about to have his chest cut open.

I huddled the family around their dad's gurney so we could pray. The wife prayed first, and she spoke words to this effect: "Oh, God, I have no idea what to ask You for. I have no clue what Your divine will is in this situation. I have no sense of what would please You in heaven in the situation we're facing as a family here today."

On and on she went, espousing the most vague, benign ideas I'd heard in a long time. I was very tempted to interrupt and say, "Lady, do you want your husband to live or die? I mean, do you like this guy? Is he a keeper? Why are you praying this way?" (This is why they don't let me make hospital visits very often, by the way. These are the thoughts that sometimes go through my head. Not helpful!)

This wife was so concerned about not forcing God's hand that she was overcomplicating things. I worry sometimes we do the same thing. We pray guarded, nonspecific, if-it-be-Thy-will types of prayers, rather than simply telling God exactly what we want Him to do.

Here's how the apostle Paul says we should approach situations when something big is looming and our fears are heightened: "Do not be anxious about anything, but in every situation, by prayer and petition, with thanksgiving, present your requests to God. And the peace of God, which transcends all understanding, will guard your hearts and your minds in Christ Jesus."[14]

Present your requests. When you're facing your fears head-on, pray! Tell God exactly what it is you want Him to do. Keep it simple and bold: "Lord, heal my husband!"

If you feel filled with doubt, begin by repeating back to God all the ways He has answered your prayers in the past. This will help you remember how faithful and reliable He really is. And pray as often as you need to until your fear subsides. Regardless of the outcome of your circumstance, God is with you, and you can expect His peace to follow.

> Regardless of the outcome of your circumstance, God is with you, and you can expect His peace to follow.

PUT TO THE TEST

A few years back, I experienced a frightening situation that gave me the opportunity to put my "speak words of truth" skills to the test when it comes to self-talk, Scripture, and prayer.

I was booked on an international flight out of Bangkok, Thailand. The plane was scheduled to take off at midnight, but the weather outside was horrific. Those of us waiting at the gate eyed the violent electrical storm outside—thunder, lightning, heavy rain. I was doubtful the flight would actually happen.

Nonetheless, the crew let us board, the doors to the plane were shut, and we taxied into position. As the storm raged around us, you could cut the tension in the cabin with a knife. No one was chatting or reading *SkyMall*, and you can bet we were all very compliant with our seat belts!

As the storm raged on, we started down the runway and became airborne.

A few moments after takeoff, while we were still in a steep incline, an alarm buzzer began sounding and a loud, automated voice came over the intercom: "This is an emergency! Put your pillow in your lap. Put your face on the pillow. This is not a test. This is an emergency."

No one argued. People began scrambling for pillows, yelling, screaming. Most everyone around me lost their cool. Near hysteria ensued. It was not a pretty sight.

The voice repeated its terse emergency instructions several more times, in two or three other languages. I didn't have a pillow, but I stayed buckled with my head on my folded arms, as near to my lap as I could reach. All the while, our altitude continued to escalate and the buzzer kept sounding.

Then, suddenly, everything went silent. The buzzer stopped, the voice recording shut off midsentence, and a flight attendant came on the speaker.

"Oops! Sorry about that," she said in a chipper voice. "We accidentally pushed the wrong button. Our bad! Hope we didn't 'alarm' anybody!"

The entire cabin pulsed with anger. We did not share her cavalier attitude. When the pilot realized what had happened in the cabin, he ordered free drinks for everyone for the remainder of the flight. Soon it was a happy plane, but no one would forget that error anytime soon.

> When everyone around me was panicking, my habit of speaking truth to myself kicked in, and I remained calm amid the chaos.

The reason I tell this story is because, in those moments when everyone around me was panicking, my habit of speaking truth to myself kicked in, and I remained calm amid the chaos. The woman sitting next to me commented on it after the panic was over. My inner monologue during those tense moments sounded something like this: *Bill, you've flown on thousands of flights in your lifetime and landed safely every time. You've piloted tiny planes through weather like this, and you've landed just fine. Statistically, the odds are in your favor that this time, too, your plane will land safely on the ground.* This truthful self-talk kept me centered on reality.

And then I thought about how, even if the worst-case scenario happened, I was in right standing with God. I reviewed the promises of Scripture in my mind: *God says, "Believe in the Lord Jesus, and you will be saved."*[15] *And Romans 10:9: "If you declare with your mouth, 'Jesus is Lord,' and believe in your heart that God raised him from the dead, you will be saved." Bill, you believe these truths. You've centered your life on them. If you were to die on this plane, you know where you would go. Your eternity is secure.*

These Scripture verses, which I committed to memory many, many years ago, spoke words of spiritual truth into my soul at that moment. They steadied my pulse and kept my fear at bay.

If you don't already have a bank of powerful, fear-fighting Scripture verses committed to memory, consider this one of your Action Steps. Nothing brings peace of mind quicker than letting the truth of God's Word wash over your soul.

Then I prayed something like this: *God, help us land safely. But if we don't, I know You will be faithful to take care of my family, just as You took care of me when my own dad died at a young age. You have been that Father to me, and I've treasured this one and only life You entrusted to me. Thank You. And heck, if things don't work out at twenty thousand feet with this plane, I'm already halfway to heaven!*

> It's time to face your fear. You have suffered under the tyranny of anxiety and fear long enough.

Self-talk, Scripture, and prayer paid dividends by quelling my anxiety during that flight—and in countless other moments of fear since then. I am confident they will do the same for you. When we're freed from fear's bondage, we're liberated to experience the powerful, simplified life that God dreams for us.

IT'S TIME

Nothing complicates our lives faster than being paralyzed by destructive fear. It robs us of *shalom*, the soul-satisfying peace God desires for humankind. No one is exempt from fear, but that's not the end of the story. We can equip ourselves to fight those destructive fears instead of remaining in bondage to them.

It's time. It's time to face your fear. You have suffered under the tyranny of anxiety and fear long enough. You have paid your dues. You don't owe that cruel taskmaster Fear another minute. He's robbed you of enough joy and fulfillment and peace. You're done.

It's time for you to reach out for God's hand and face the fear you've always wanted to face, if you only had the courage. It's time to accept God's divine assistance and start living your life unencumbered by destructive fear. It's time to face the little phobias that silently plague your life and keep you from enjoying the life "to the full" Jesus invites you to live. [16]

It's time to start doing the activities you've longed to do—but felt you couldn't because of the shackles of fear that held you captive. It's time to visit the places you've always wanted to see, but haven't because fear said no.

It's time to embark on the mission God has given you—but you've never had the courage to attempt because fear held you back. It's time to launch out on new dreams and new visions that your timidity has kept you from starting.

It's time to let go of your fear of committing your life in its entirety to Jesus Christ. It's time to throw open the doors of your heart to Him and say, "No more holding back; no more fear. I'm not standing on the sidelines anymore. Jesus Christ, come into my life. Forgive the ways I've messed things up. Guide me. I choose to be a member of Your family, beginning right now, beginning today."

Make this day a defining moment in your life.

Friend, it's time to take a stand against fear. Make this day a defining moment in your life—the day you decided to begin facing your fear and take a step toward freedom.

■ ■ ■

ACTION STEP: NAME YOUR FEAR

We all have pockets of fear eroding our lives. What are those fears for you? Think through each of the peace busters below. On a sheet of paper or in your journal, name every fear that affects you. Don't be overwhelmed if the list is lengthy; you don't need to conquer each fear today. But an honest "state of the union" is a powerful starting point.

1. Unexpected bad news
2. Relational breakdowns
3. Financial problems
4. Moral failures
5. Impending mortality
6. Other

Now read through your list. Which of these fears causes the most destruction in your life? Which exacts the greatest toll on those you love? Which would be easiest to tackle first, as you develop your "fear-conquering muscles"? Circle the fears you want to eradicate first.

For certain deep-seated fears and phobias, it will be necessary to enlist outside help. Certainly if you suspect that a trauma has left you suffering from PTSD like my Vietnam vet roommate, consult a Christian counselor who specializes in your unique situation. For other fears, be bold about bringing family, friends, a mentor, or your small group into the loop. Choose people who are "safe" emotionally and whose godly wisdom you trust. Let them know you're working on this fear—and invite them to help you along the journey.

． ． ．

ACTION STEP: CRAFT A STRATEGY FOR OVERCOMING YOUR FEAR

When it comes to unseating fears that have held you captive for months, years, or decades, change doesn't happen without deliberate intent. Choose one of the fears you identified above and consider the prompts in the four steps below. By writing out your answers, you will craft a strategy to begin the process of breaking free from the grip of fear.

1. **Understand Fear's Origin:** Describe the first time you can recall experiencing your fear. Can you identify the source? Record any incidents that followed that might have solidified your phobia.

2. **Expose Fear's Lies:** What are the lies that fuel this fear? (Remember, they may not feel like lies. They may seem rational.) Why do these lies seem believable?

3. **Face Fear Head-On:** What is one baby step you will take to face this fear?

4. **Speak Words of Truth**
   - **Self-Talk:** What strengths do I possess that will help me say no to this fear? What is the logical truth that most people believe about this fear? (Examples: "The elevator is safe"; "Most dogs are friendly.")
   - **Scripture:** What are two key verses you can commit to memory that will help quell your fear? If none come to mind, look up a key word, such as *fear*, to find verses that speak to you. Then memorize them so you can remind yourself of God's truth when you face your fear.

- **Prayer:** What specific request do you want God to answer regarding your fear? Write your request in one short sentence. Pray this prayer as often as you need, whenever fear strikes.

chapter seven

from isolated to connected

Deepening Your Relational Circles

IF YOU WERE TO DIE TONIGHT, how many friends would come to your funeral? Not how many *family members*—they're bound by blood. But beyond your family, how many *friends* would show up at your funeral?

If you're like most people, your guess is high—way high. I don't mean to burst your bubble, but one of the realities I've witnessed again and again in my role as a pastor is that people have fewer true friends than they think. Here's an example:

A guy dies in his late fifties from heart trouble. I meet with his wife and their two adult children. They're grieving; they're shocked. We pray together, reminisce, and eventually, in order to plan the memorial service, I have to ask the family how many people will come to the funeral. We want to find the right-size room to hold the service. It's a practical question that must be asked.

And then the widow and the kids begin: "My husband was an

extrovert," or, "Dad had tons of friends, going all the way back to high school and college. All of them will come. All of his golf buddies will come, and everyone from work. And the whole neighborhood will be there, plus all the guys from the park district football teams he used to play on." In short, they guess between five hundred and a thousand people will be there for the funeral.

In the early days of my pastoring, I would go with whatever number the family said. If they said they expected between five hundred and a thousand guests, we'd hold the service in our Lakeside Auditorium, which can easily accommodate such a crowd.

And then the funeral day comes. People file in, and (at most) a hundred people show up—in a 4,300-seat auditorium. And seventy-five of them are family.

After the graveside ceremony, the widow and kids make a beeline to me and ask, "Where in God's name was everyone? He had all these friends. And only a hundred people came?"

I've now been through this so many times that I go into protection mode on the family's behalf right up front. Now, before I ask how many people they expect at the funeral, I offer some disclaimers, such as, "I'm sure this loved one had lots of friends, but in today's economy, not everyone can get off work, and travel costs are high if people are coming from out of town. That will probably cut down significantly on the number of people who will be able to make it." I try to protect the hearts of families already stricken with grief—because nine times out of ten, they will overestimate the number of friends who will show up.

> The number of people we *know* does not equal the number of true friends we have.

The number of people we *know* does not equal the number of true friends we have. Solomon puts it this way: "One who has unreliable friends soon comes to ruin, but there is a friend who sticks closer than a brother."[1]

It's sad enough when you overestimate a loved one's friendships for a funeral service, but when you wrongly assess the friendship levels in your own relationships, the cost can be much higher. An unevaluated, underdeveloped relational world can wreak havoc on your life. If your relationships are in disarray, simplified living will be a distant dream, rather than a present reality. By evaluating, pruning, expanding, bordering, and deepening your relationships, you can maximize the energy and joy they bring to your newly simplified life.

DEFINING FRIENDSHIP

If I were to wrestle friendship in all its complexities down to just a few short words, I would define it like this: *to know and be known.*

In a true friendship, you move beyond pretending to be someone you're not. You take off your mask, and you say to the other person, "Here's who I really am." And it's reciprocal. A true friend accepts you as you are and says in return, "Here's who I really am too— without my mask." You are accepted, and you accept that person.

True friends love one another, even though we're all a little quirky. We accept each other's faults and unique wiring. There is tremendous acceptance and deep safety in a true friendship.

True friends serve one another. You do what is best for your friends above what is best for yourself. You put their interests ahead of your own, and they reciprocate. There's a give-and-take that satisfies both parties in the friendship.

True friends celebrate with one another. You show up at each other's important life events. You cheer one another's victories. You mark life's milestones together.

Knowing and being known; accepting and being accepted; loving and being loved; serving and being served; celebrating and being celebrated. These are the hallmark ingredients of a true friendship. Who wouldn't want to experience a friendship like that? Our lives would be all the richer.

Too often, though, we settle for "friendships" that fall far beneath this standard.

Relationships, like every other area of life, require regular evaluation, pruning, and strengthening.

EVALUATING YOUR RELATIONSHIPS
Stupid Rubs Off

When I was a boy, one of my good friends moved to the South, and I occasionally visited him for three or four days at a time. I always brought my mitt because we would play baseball at a park near his house every chance we got.

> Relationships, like every other area of life, require regular evaluation, pruning, and strengthening.

Every time we left the house to go play ball, my friend's dad would say in his deep Southern drawl, "Watch out who you hang with after the game, boys, because stupid rubs off."

Stupid rubs off. That was an expression I'd never heard up north, but I knew what he meant. He was warning us not to be influenced by other boys' stupid decisions, things we knew better than to do.

Stupid rubs off in our grown-up world too. Perhaps you work in an environment where profanity flows like a polluted river all day, every day. Can profanity rub off?

Maybe you work in the financial services industry, where the whole game is making more money, no matter what it takes to get it. Can greed rub off?

At parties where the main event is alcohol consumption, can over-drinking rub off?

I went to a Blackhawks hockey game a few years back, and there were about a half-dozen fistfights during the game. Late in the third period, a bench-clearing brawl broke out. When the game ended, the crowd was all hyped-up. As everyone tried to exit, the normal jostling that happens when thousands of people exit a stadium soon turned into elbow throwing, shoving, and pushing. I wondered, *Can anger and violence rub off?*

Solomon, the wisest man who ever lived, was so aware of this unalterable reality that he admonished us to choose our friends wisely: "Walk with the wise and become wise, for a companion of fools suffers harm."[2]

I've heard different versions of the same story about a thousand times: Someone approaches me after a church service, or out in the community, or in

> "Walk with the wise and become wise, for a companion of fools suffers harm."
>
> PROVERBS 13:20

a social setting, and says, "Hey, Bill, do you remember me? A long time ago, you baptized me," or, "You helped me find a place to serve around Willow," or, "You got me connected to a small group."

Then the story comes out: "I was doing great, but then I started hanging out with a group from work that went out together on Friday nights. And then we started hanging out on Saturday nights too. And some of the Saturday nights got a little crazy, and I couldn't make it to church on Sundays. Then I had to drop my volunteer work because of the time I was spending with those friends. Everything sort of went south from there. I guess I moved God out of the equation." Then they tell me about some stupid decisions they made, and now their life is a rip-roaring mess—which is why they are speaking with me at this moment. "Will you pray for me?"

And I do. I pray for them. But between you and me, I am so sick of this story. There are a hundred variations of it, but it's the same stuff-rubbed-off story: "I was good with God; then I started hanging around with some folks, and I started going their way instead of God's way—and then my life hit a new low. Now everything is a mess. Pastor, will you pray for me?"

Parents start warning their kids about this in junior high: "Don't hang out with the wrong kids at school." Stuff rubs off.

Fathers walk their sons around the block before they drive off to college: "Hey, son, find a good set of friends when you get to campus." Stuff rubs off.

I counsel people at church whose jobs transfer them to other cities around the country or around the world: "Find a great church, a church that teaches God's Word, where there's high-integrity leadership; a church that encourages you to be the hands and feet of Christ in the world. Then take some time to build quality friendships with godly, mature people in the church and lean into those relationships. If you do, you'll do fine in that new city." I encourage them in this way because stuff (good and bad) rubs off.

What Solomon says is absolutely true: *"Walk with the wise and become wise, for a companion of fools suffers harm."* When we surround ourselves with foolish people, we become like them. And when we surround ourselves with wise, mature, good people, their high character rubs off on us too.

Seven Warning Lights

Taking an assessment of your friendship circle is vital to simplifying your relational world. As uncomfortable as it may make you feel, you must be willing to make necessary course corrections in your friendships. This isn't being judgmental or condemning anyone; it's simply being a good steward of your life and having a realistic understanding of others' natural influence on you.

Plenty of foolish people are perfectly likable, especially when you first meet them, and it takes careful evaluation to peer into the inner core of a person's character. Solomon lists seven character traits that are so offensive to God, they should act as red warning lights, flashing "Danger!" when we spot them in a friend or acquaintance. His list is helpful when assessing the character of those in your friendship circle:

> There are six things the LORD hates, seven that are detestable to him: haughty eyes, a lying tongue, hands that shed innocent blood, a heart that devises wicked schemes, feet that are quick to rush into evil, a false witness who pours out lies and a person who stirs up conflict in the community.[3]

Solomon says if you see any of these traits in people who are in your circle of acquaintance, put up your guard. You can be kind to them, pray for them, or help meet a need in their lives. Invite them to church with you. Try to point them to faith in Christ. But don't even think about inviting them into your inner circle of friendship. Why? Because stuff rubs off. No matter how strong you are, people who are prideful, dishonest, mean-spirited, and divisive will negatively influence your character, inhibit your development as a person, and impede your spiritual growth.

> As uncomfortable as it may make you feel, you must be willing to make necessary course corrections in your friendships.

The apostle Paul puts it this way: "Bad company corrupts good morals."[4]

A look at each trait in Solomon's list will help you understand why it's important to filter your close friendships by this standard.

1. Pride ("haughty eyes"). People who have haughty eyes look down on others. We might call it *arrogance*. Perhaps you've met someone like this: "I matter; you don't. I'm sophisticated; you're plain. I'm educated; you're ignorant. I'm beautiful; you're average. I'm slender; you're chunky. I'm married; you're single. I'm spiritual; you're secular. I'm young; you're old. I'm a career woman; you're a stay-at-home mom. I'm a businessperson; you're a laborer. I'm a Chicagoan; you're a Burb." (I didn't even know what a "Burb" was until recently when a guy from Chicago told me I was one because I live in the suburbs instead of in the city.)

What does the Bible say about pride?

"God opposes the proud but shows favor to the humble."[5]

"Pride goes before destruction, a haughty spirit before a fall."[6]

"Do not think of yourself more highly than you ought, but rather think of yourself with sober judgment, in accordance with the faith God has distributed to each of you."[7]

Pride is corrosive, and it rubs off. You're going to have a tough time developing Christlike humility and thinking of yourself with sober judgment if your close friends are arrogant, full of pride, and looking down their noses at everyone else.

2. Dishonesty ("a lying tongue"). Most of us know to steer clear of people who blatantly lie. But it's equally important to keep our distance from people who fudge the truth or exaggerate; people who think little white lies don't matter. Be kind to these people, pray for them, invite them to church; but someday they will hurt you if they're in your inner circle. It's easy to slip into the same habits they exhibit—exaggerating to make your story more colorful, or dancing around the truth because it's easier than speaking honestly. It's tough to become a truth teller if your close friends have "a lying tongue." Stuff rubs off.

> It's tough to become a truth teller if your close friends have "a lying tongue." Stuff rubs off.

Incidentally, omissions are lies. When we allow our silence to imply agreement, it's no different from overtly telling a lie. If your friends intentionally deceive others by keeping secrets, they are liars. And that stuff rubs off too. Steer clear, friend.

3. Mean-Spiritedness ("hands that shed innocent blood"). This is a no-brainer, right? Don't invite an ax murderer into your small group. Actually, the meaning of this phrase is a little broader than that. Solomon is warning us to be wary of people who use their power to exploit others. Beware of those who oppress the weak. Beware of individuals who throw their weight around and like to "stick it" to people. Beware of folks who are mean-spirited. It's a danger signal.

A scene recently returned to my memory that I hadn't thought about for fifty years. I hesitate to share it, because it still makes me sick, and even though I was only a boy, I wonder if I should have done more at the time.

When I was ten years old and attending a two-week summer camp, I was assigned to a cabin with eight guys I'd never met. The first day of camp, we were all sizing each other up. Even at the young age of ten, we already had a sense of trying to figure out who the leader would be, who the cool guy would be, and so on.

One kid in our cabin was a little older than the rest of us, and he had an infectious kind of charisma, so we all wanted to be his friend. One day, this kid trapped a gopher outside the cabin, using a trash can—which, if you know anything about gophers, requires Olympic-level talent. The rest of us were in awe when he brought his prize into the cabin.

We gathered around, watching the scared little brown creature scurry around in the bottom of the bucket. Then the kid who had caught him pulled out a pocketknife and said, "Let's torture him!" And he started jabbing at the gopher with the knife.

Most of us had mixed feelings about this plan, but we all wanted to be this guy's friend. One by one, the other kids got out their knives and joined in.

I was only ten years old, but I knew this was wrong. I knew in my spirit that this was not cool, that this gopher was created by God, and that hurting it for fun was wrong. I knew it was so wrong that

I was willing to risk being "the loser kid" for the next two weeks of camp, if it came to that. So I told the kid holding the bloody knife, "Let the gopher go."

"It's just a gopher," he said. "They're hard to catch. And I'm going to torture it to death. Are you in or out, Hybels?"

"I'm out," I said. While the other kids opened their pocketknives and eventually stabbed the poor gopher to death, I went outside the cabin and puked my guts out because I could hear what was going on inside.

I hadn't thought about that episode in fifty years, but when I read the phrase about being wary of someone who sheds innocent blood, it stirred my memory. Proverbs 12:10 speaks specifically to this scene: "The righteous care for the needs of their animals."

> When I read the phrase about being wary of someone who sheds innocent blood, it stirred my memory.

I *hate* violence. I hate it in any form. I hated knowing those kids were carving up that gopher and making it suffer. I hated fistfights in high school. When kids would start pounding each other in the hallway, I went the other way. It made me sick. I refuse to watch cage matches and other violence-for-sport entertainment on TV. I've walked out of more than one movie over the years when the senseless fighting got out of control. I hate violence.

In my late teenage years, right after the Vietnam War, I walked through Walter Reed Medical Center, the military hospital outside of Washington, DC, which has since closed. But at the time, Walter Reed had fifty-five hundred rooms, comprising twenty-eight acres of floor space.

The day I walked those halls changed me. Every room was filled with soldiers coming back from Vietnam. I saw hundreds of young men and women—just a few years older than I was—with mangled bodies, missing limbs, faces burned beyond recognition, vacant stares, little hope for a bright future; and it made me hate war. *Hate it.* It made me distrust warmongering leaders and politicians, not just in the United States but all over the world.

Violence seems so contrary to the heart of God. It seems so out of sync with God's basic nature and character. When Jesus was arrested in the garden of Gethsemane, His friend Peter resorted to violence to protect Him. Peter grabbed a sword and cut off the ear of an assistant to the high priest, one of the men who had schemed to frame Jesus.

"But Jesus answered, *'No more of this!'* And he touched the man's ear and healed him."[8]

In the face of raw violence, Jesus healed. He reached down, picked up the guy's ear, and gently restored it. He healed a man who was there to arrest Him and carry Him off to be crucified.

Jesus hated violence. He taught against it. He modeled a degree of gentleness (power under control) that the world had never seen. Even as soldiers were beating Him mercilessly, ripping His beard from His face, and leaving Him naked and exposed, Jesus forgave them.

We live in a violent culture. In fact, our culture sees violence as entertainment, and I wonder if we've lost our way. Violence in sports, violence on TV and in the movies, violence in children's video games—it's become so normative we don't even blink. But stuff rubs off. Have we become so inoculated with it that we don't even notice violence? Have we drifted into an acceptance of violence that the Holy Spirit would have us resist and repel? Does God's Spirit wish we would puke our guts out a little more reflexively at the sight of senseless violence, the shedding of innocent blood?

It's hard to cultivate a heart of gentleness in today's violence-saturated world—and it's even harder when you surround yourself with chest-thumping, violence-loving, bar-brawling buddies. If you hang around with a bunch of people who are enamored of violence and have lost their sense of horror at the shedding of innocent blood, that stuff rubs off.

I have a hard enough time pursuing gentleness. I don't need any bravado junk rubbing off on me. I need more of the Holy Spirit instead.

4 & 5. Looking for Trouble ("a heart that devises wicked schemes, feet that . . . rush into evil"). We all have read about people who indulge in get-rich-quick schemes or business ventures that prey on the vulnerable. We hear about scams of one kind or another on the news. Solomon warns about such people who have no qualms about making a quick buck off someone else's vulnerability or gullibility.

> I have a hard enough time pursuing gentleness. I don't need any bravado junk rubbing off on me. I need more of the Holy Spirit instead.

I met a guy one time who felt called by God to leave a very lucrative career to launch an effort to end the production and distribution of child pornography in the United States. Gripped by the evil of an industry that preys on the most vulnerable, he threw himself wholeheartedly into this venture, and I respect him for doing so. I met with him one day, to hear about and support his efforts.

He told me about all the things he was doing to try to end the production and distribution of child pornography, which is a very complex problem. As I tried to get my head around it, I finally asked, "How does anybody in that industry sleep at night, knowing they're profiteering from the rape and abuse of little boys and little girls?"

He smiled at me, as if to say, *You really don't get it, do you?* Then he explained, "In the porn business, the on-camera people call it 'acting,' the directors call it 'art,' the distributors call it 'free enterprise,' and the video stores call it 'entertainment.' Everybody justifies their part—therefore, nobody is guilty, see?"

I sat at the table shaking my head, thinking, *Are you kidding me? Really?*

You can tell when people are devising a scheme or promoting a scam, because they go out of their way to justify it. When you ask one of these people what they do for a living, they don't say, "I profit from the rape of little girls and little boys." With a straight face, they justify their evil schemes that line their pockets at the expense of the innocent and vulnerable.

You can pray for these people. You can warn them. If they're violating the law, you can call the police to stop them. If they're hurting a child, you'd better stop them! But don't hang around with these people. The devising of evil schemes and the justifying habit that minimizes wrongdoing rubs off.

There are a lot of wicked schemes that don't sink to the level of child pornography. But don't fall into the trap of contrasting such filth with your "little shortcuts here and there" and acquitting yourself by comparison. Sure, you're not selling porn. But in God's eyes, your "corner cutting" and "little integrity lapses" are a big deal. If you're building a business, you know it's hard to run a squeaky-clean, high-integrity company in an ethically gray world. If you wanted to, you could make a few extra bucks by skirting the edge. But don't do it. And don't surround yourself with people who do. Compromise is a slippery slope you don't want to be on.

> In God's eyes, your "corner cutting" and "little integrity lapses" are a big deal.

6. Spreading Gossip and Slander ("a false witness who pours out lies"). People who are eager to spread false information for the sheer delight of tearing down someone else—these are folks to avoid. Solomon warns: "A gossip betrays a confidence, but a trustworthy person keeps a secret."[9]

If someone always gives you the lowdown on other people, you can be certain he or she is giving other people the lowdown on you. Don't set yourself up for slander. Keep away from people who tell you the juicy stuff—whether it's true or not. Gossip and slander are the last things you need to rub off on you. We need to be truth tellers and confidence keepers.

7. **Divisive** ("a person who stirs up conflict"). Beware of anyone who *spreads dissension*. Proverbs 16:28 says, "A perverse person stirs up conflict." It doesn't take long to figure out whether someone is fundamentally a polarizer or a unifier; a bridge builder or a bomb thrower.

I was in a social setting recently, enjoying a pleasant conversation in a circle of people I didn't know very well. A guy with a cocktail in one hand and a plate of hors d'oeuvres in the other came up and began opinionating about politics and the presidential candidates. He started lambasting one of the candidates, saying what "idiotic ideas" this person had, and so on. Within thirty seconds, everyone in that previously congenial group had squared off, sharing pieces of their minds they couldn't afford to lose.

I stood watching all this, shaking my head in amazement at how quickly one person had polarized everyone in the circle, causing dissension and strife. I extricated myself from the unpleasantness of that conversation and stepped outside for some fresh air. A verse of Scripture came to mind: "If it is possible, as far as it depends on you, live at peace with everyone."[10]

> I have no shortage of strong opinions, but I have tried all my life to be a bridge builder.

Jesus said, "Blessed are the peacemakers."[11] I have no shortage of strong opinions, but I have tried all my life to be a bridge builder. Any progress I've made toward that end has been greatly assisted by choosing close friends who are as committed to bridge building as

I am. Today, it just wears me out to be around polarizers and bomb throwers, people who gladly divide groups and people.

One of the greatest blessings of being married to Lynne is that she's an extremely effective bridge builder. She spends many weeks a year in some of the most strife-ridden places on the planet—the Democratic Republic of the Congo, which has been called the rape capital of the world;[12] and Israel and Palestine, where generational conflict and violence rip apart families, villages, and cities. Lynne invests tremendous physical, emotional, and spiritual energy building bridges between people groups, taking part in reconciliation forums, trying to get bitter enemies to talk to one another instead of spilling the blood of their sons and daughters for yet another generation. When you live with a reconciler, a peacemaker, a bridge builder, it rubs off. I am very grateful for all the ways that Lynne's peacemaking has rubbed off on me.

If you're trying to become more of a bridge builder and less of a bomb thrower, keep on the lookout for bridge-building friends to add to your circle. And put a little distance between yourself and the bomb throwers and polarizers. Again, you can pray for them and invite them to church, where they'll be able to hear about the teaching and the life of Jesus Christ, the greatest bridge builder and reconciler in human history. But don't hang with these kinds of people, because stuff rubs off.

Solomon's seven warning lights give us a head start on evaluating those in our friendship circles, so we can make adjustments accordingly. Don't be duped into thinking it's no big deal to hang with people whose character is marked by these signs. They will affect you. Their traits will become yours. Take a step back—and look for people whose strong character will rub off on you instead.

Nine Welcome Signs

Let's turn this "stuff rubs off" idea on its head: You're at a worship concert for two solid hours. The people around you are singing their lungs out, hands raised high. You don't know them; you may have never even met them. But it doesn't matter. You share a common bond. Does the spirit of worship rub off? Of course it does.

At work, your department is led by a cheerful woman who stays on her game eight hours a day; she lifts the spirits of everyone in the department. Does a positive attitude rub off? Yes, it does.

> Does the spirit of worship rub off? Of course it does. . . . Does a positive attitude rub off? Yes, it does.

You work out at a local health club three days a week. During the forty-five minutes you're there, the same people show up regularly. They're fit; they're disciplined; they're fired up. They do their sets. They drink their protein shakes. They push themselves physically. Do healthy work-out habits rub off? Absolutely!

You're at a twelve-step meeting, listening to the other women and men do their work.[13] They're admitting mistakes. They're encouraging each other. They're committing themselves to pursue a different path in life. Does life-altering courage rub off? Beyond a doubt.

In life, through our relationships, stuff rubs off. Good and bad, it rubs off.

The apostle Paul offers a corollary to Solomon's seven warning lights. If you're looking for people whose character will rub off on you in a positive way, Paul's list is a great place to start:

> The fruit of the Spirit is love, joy, peace, patience, kindness, goodness, faithfulness, gentleness, self-control; against such things there is no law.[14]

This list of character traits is not for the faint of heart. In a world that is more drawn to selfishness, violence, and entitlement, it takes grit to live out these traits. It requires daily, relentless fortitude to be loving, joyful, peaceful, patient, kind, good, faithful, gentle, and self-controlled regardless of the ebb and flow of circumstances. When searching for friends to draw deeper into your inner circle, look for people who exhibit these foundational fruits of the Holy Spirit. They will influence your life in positive ways. Their character will rub off on you.

Three Levels of Friendship

Once you have a benchmark of warning lights and welcome signs to help you assess the inner character of your friends and acquaintances, the next step is to determine the depth of friendship you have with each person. Taking an honest assessment of your friendship levels helps you be intentional about making adjustments, moving friends of high character deeper into your inner circle and perhaps creating safe distance from those whose weak character will rub off. Again, this is not for the purpose of casting judgment.

No matter a person's character, he or she is of infinite value to God and as such should be of infinite value to you. But having a clear understanding of where each person fits in your life helps you clarify your expectations. And holding reasonable expectations of what you can expect from each friendship will help you

> Having a clear understanding of where each person fits in your life helps you clarify your expectations.

simplify your relational world, minimize disappointments, and maximize the energy and effort you give toward your inner-circle friends.

1. Circumstantial Friends. The people we say hi to at work, the fellow jogger at the gym, the checkout person at the grocery store, the dry-cleaning guy—these are all very nice people. They're friendly to us, and we're friendly to them. But are they true friends? Or are they friends only because of the circumstances in our lives?

They're circumstantial friends. They're not coming to your funeral. They're not coming to mine. They are friends by circumstance, and when circumstances change, the friendship ends. It's that simple.

Occasionally, someone who is a friend by circumstance becomes a true friend. But most of the time, if your usual checkout lady at the grocery store transfers to a new location, you don't track her down and change grocery stores so you can continue your "friendship." If the guy who has worked out near you at the gym for the past four years is suddenly AWOL, you don't do an online search to find him. If your dentist retires, you look for another one, but you don't start making lunch dates with your old dentist every six months to keep up. You just accept the fact that life moves on. These kinds of relationships come and go.

Circumstantial friends are not *fake* friends. You're not being insincere when you converse with them. But what brought you together was a job, a business connection, or a service they provided. And when these circumstances change, there's a strong likelihood you'll never see these people again. So be friendly, but be careful about adding circumstantial friends to your projected list of funeral attendees.

A few months ago, I was chatting with some people in a small group I've been a part of for about fifteen years. One of the professional women in the group, who has thrown her heart and soul into her team at work for two decades, shared that she felt God was whispering to her to pursue a different vocation in the next season of her life. She was pretty sure God wanted her to move into this new vocation, but she was reluctant to make the announcement at work because she felt bad about letting her team and boss down.

"I can't work up the courage to go in and resign, because we're just like family," she said. "They will be devastated."

Then she stopped and waited for a response from the group.

Silence. As sensitively as I could, I said, "Hey, my friend, if God is telling you to move into a different career, you've got to move on. I know you don't want to disappoint anybody at work, but the fact is, the day after you tell them you're quitting, they'll have a plan in place for how they're going to replace you. It's not that they won't miss you, but they'll move on without you."

She burst out crying. Not the reserved, sentimental type of crying, but the slobbery, messy, uncontrollable kind. At first, I was worried she might leap across the table and strangle me. But she settled down and said, "Bill, you're absolutely right. They *will* move on without me. They will be fine. I let myself believe that we're family, that we're true-to-the-end friends, when really we've just been brought together by work circumstances. We care about each other because of the years we've worked together, but we're not *actually* family." She was right. She and her coworkers were wonderful, warm, circumstantial friends, but they were not true friends or family.

Circumstantial friends matter. You can and should have lots of them. You should be radically loving and kind in every exchange you have with your circumstantial friends. You ought to pray for them and invite them to church with you. But if you consider these people true friends, you will be disappointed. Again, they're not coming to your funeral.

Don't spread yourself too thin with circumstantial friendships. You have only so many relational dollars to spend, and you must steward them wisely. "The righteous choose their friends carefully, but the way of the wicked leads them astray," Solomon cautions in Proverbs 12:26. Make sure you choose your true friends carefully—and leave yourself enough energy to invest in those true friendships.

> You should be radically loving and kind in every exchange you have with your circumstantial friends.

2. True Friends—for a Season. In the early days of our church, I built a friendship with a guy of high character. Our friendship grew stronger and evolved to the "true friend" level. I thought it was going to be a lifelong friendship. We had twenty years invested in it.

The two of us hung out with a small group of guys in those days. One day, my friend came to our small group meeting at a local restaurant. As he sat down at the table, he announced, "Hey, I sold my company over the weekend, and I'm going to move to a sunshine state next month. Thanks for all the great memories. I'm still going to root for the Bears, though. You know me—I'm a Bears fan through and through."

I sat at the table, stunned. It had never occurred to me that this guy's friendship would be torn out of my life. Really, I was just floored. This is how a twenty-year friendship ends? With, "I'm moving to a sunshine state; thanks for the memories—I'll be a loyal Bears fan"? *Joke's on me.* I thought my friendship with this guy was going to make it for the long haul. Sure, we could still call and e-mail. We could still visit once in a while. But the closeness we shared by living our lives side by side, day in and day out, was shattered. I was disillusioned about friendship for quite a while after that.

> I wish someone had taught me when I was a much younger man that even the true friendships I develop will actually be *seasonal friendships.*

I wish someone had taught me when I was a much younger man that even the true friendships I develop—like the relationship I had with this guy, and maybe even the majority of true friendships—will actually be *seasonal,* rather than lifelong. Our lives ebb and flow in seasons, and our friendships follow this pattern.

Around the same time my Bears-loving friend announced his impending move, another friend, by God's design, sent me a CD out of the blue. He is a leadership-oriented lecturer, and in that CD lecture, he reflected on how some of his most meaningful friendships had lasted for only five, ten, or even twenty years; and then, for all good reasons, they changed. Someone moved. Someone started spending winters in Florida. Some friends went through a divorce, and things got all funky. Whatever the reason, there was an event that redefined the friendship dynamic.

My friend's point was that many of us will invest in and fully enjoy some very meaningful, true friendships; but we shouldn't be surprised if, for one reason or another, life reshuffles the deck every so often. Through no one's fault, things change. As wise King Solomon says in Ecclesiastes 3, everything in life has its season—including friendships.

The more I reflected on the seasonal nature of even the best friendships, the worse I felt about my original vision-casting when we started Willow Creek. I was twenty-two years old and naive about friendships and how life works. When I stood before the staff and the tiny little core of Christ followers who met in a rented movie theater in Palatine, Illinois, I would say things like this: "Hey, gang, let's build this really cool church and invite people to come into a relationship with God. Let's work hard together and play hard together, and be like family to one another. Let's do this for forty years or so, and then we'll all retire together in the same retirement community, where we'll sit in rocking chairs all day, sipping lemonade and drooling and talking about the good old days. Let's put our hands in the center of this circle and let's do our whole lives together. Are you in?"

And because that vision was so powerful and attractive, a lot of people put their hands in the center of the ring and said, "We're in. We're in for life!"

But every few years, stuff would happen. A core family would get transferred because of work. Another family would move across the country to take care of aging parents. In some cases, families simply decided there was another church that fit them better. And the pain of those departures went extra deep because it felt like the death of the dream I'd had. I really thought we would do our whole lives together.

> The high bar of expectation I had set was not realistic for how long our friendships could last in the real world.

I now see that my vision was naive and perhaps caused unnecessary pain for those who moved out of the circle. The high bar of expectation I had set was not realistic for how long our friendships could last in the real world.

3. Lifelong Friends. Sometimes circumstances and chemistry align in such a way that friendships really do last a lifetime. By God's goodness, the four original couples who started our church—Joel and Cathy Jager, Scott and Laurie Pederson, Tim and Erin VandenBos, and Lynne and me—are all still here, forty years and counting, serving together and doing life together. Many others who threw their hands in back at the beginning still attend our church and are actively involved—many of them on staff. It has been one of God's most generous gifts in my life.

For obvious reasons, we cannot force or manufacture lifelong friendships. They are forged in the trenches of everyday life—and, by definition, they take a lifetime to develop. I believe if we invest ourselves fully and freely, even as we hold these relationships with open hands, God in His grace will allow us a certain number of friendships that *stick* for the long haul of life. These friendships are a treasured blessing.

These days, when I talk to our staff and key volunteers at Willow, I describe our relationship a little differently. I say, "Hey, gang, listen. God has knit our hearts together during this exciting era of our church. No one knows how long this season will last, so let's soak it up and enjoy it to the fullest. Let's receive it as a gift from God and squeeze every drop of potential from the love we share together. If someday, for whatever reason, this season draws to a close and God deploys you to another assignment in His Kingdom, let's thank Him on our knees that we got to live this season of friendship and ministry together."

When I cast the vision in this way, it feels truer to the Scriptures, and I know I'm setting a more realistic bar of expectation about how life and friendships really work. And it frees people to follow God's leading with an open heart through the seasons of their lives.

We need this reality check once in a while. Viewing each true friendship as a season heightens our gratitude for each day and week and month that we get to enjoy those people. I'm not minimizing how deep and how loving seasonal friendships can be. They can be transforming. They can be life-giving and fun. But you might not make it all the way to the retirement porch where the rocking, lemonade sipping, and drooling are going on. You might actually retire with a whole different set of friends than the ones you have right now. It's possible. And they might prefer shuffleboard over rocking chairs; you never know.

> Viewing each true friendship as a season heightens our gratitude for each day and week and month that we get to enjoy those people.

PRUNING YOUR RELATIONAL CIRCLES

A friend told me a story that illustrates the process of making adjustments to our friendship circles. Many years back, her parents bought a home that was twenty years old. The house was in good repair, but the yard needed some work. Two apple trees on the property had clearly never been pruned. Hundreds of tiny limbs shot out in every direction, crisscrossing one another, blocking the sunlight and keeping air from circulating through a tangled morass of leaves. As a result, even though the trees were quite large, only a few small apples hung from the branches.

One afternoon, the husband got out his chain saw and began hacking away at those trees, leaving nothing but the trunks and central branches. Huge piles of leafy twigs were all that remained of the foliage. His wife was appalled. "But the trees were so beautiful!" she complained.

"These trees are meant for apples, not just beauty," he told her. "Trust me, this is what was needed."

Once the wife got over the horror of her husband's assault on the trees, his brutal pruning job became a bit of a joke. Every time she looked at those apple trees, she laughed at how sparse they looked. But the following spring, her husband got the last laugh when the trees grew new, healthy branches that allowed plenty of light and air throughout. By May, the new branches were covered in white blossoms, and in September, the couple harvested buckets of juicy, red apples. The wife was now a believer: Pruning works!

> Harsh as it may sound, you probably have some relationships that belong on the brush pile.

We have arrived at the most difficult part of this chapter: *pruning your friendships*. Harsh as it may sound, you probably have some relationships that belong on the brush pile. You may have some friends whose "stuff" is rubbing off on you, and you need to cut back the time you spend with them. And you can probably think of a handful of people you wish you could spend more time with. By purposefully pruning your relationships, you will make room for new, healthier friendships—relationships that will bear fruit.

Perhaps your list of friends and acquaintances doesn't require the level of butchery that the apple trees required. You can put down your chain saw. But take seriously the challenge to make some adjustments that might be long overdue—cuts that will make room for new growth and new fruit in your life.

EXPANDING YOUR FRIENDSHIP CIRCLE

Once you've completed some much-needed pruning in your relation-ship circles, you'll find you have room for healthy, new growth in the area of friendships. You'll have margin for making investments in friendships that will bring energy and joy to your now-simplified relational world.

Chances are, you need some new friends anyway—people whose high character will rub off on you. You need wise friends whose faith is important to them and who want to move forward on this God-guided adventure. How do you find these people? Where do they hang out? Probably not at Hooters or the local pub. Probably not at a cage-fighting event.

If you're looking to meet like-minded Christ followers who are serious about growing in their faith, start hanging out where people of faith gather. Join a Bible study at work. Attend a church function. Sign up to serve at a faith-based charity event. Start socializing with your Christian friends and meet *their* Christian friends.

But let me be crystal clear about one thing: It's not your church's job to pro-vide you with a new set of really wise, cool friends who live near you, enjoy all the same interests, and have kids the same age as yours. The church may provide an environment where you can find these friends, but it's *your* job to take the initiative. It's *your* job, as the Holy Spirit prompts you, to take those risks. As you step out in faith, God will guide and provide.

> If you're looking to meet like-minded Christ followers who are serious about growing in their faith, start hanging out where people of faith gather.

BORDERING YOUR FRIENDSHIPS

Reordering your friendships can be tricky, but I can tell you what I've learned from the times I've seen it done well.

Bring Them Along

Perhaps you're in a season where you're growing in your relationship with God faster and more sincerely than ever before. But the same cannot be said of your close friends. This is a little awkward.

Try your best to bring your close friends along on your spiritual adventure. This thought never even occurs to some sincere Christ followers, but it is actually quite normal in most other areas of friendship. Example: A couple of friends decide to take a cooking class, and they say to the rest of their friends, "Let's take the class together!"

Or a couple decides to sign up for ballroom dancing lessons. They say to their friends, "Let's all give it a go. What have we got to lose?"

Or perhaps a guy who plays on a park district basketball team invites the rest of his team to volunteer with him at a soup kitchen over Thanksgiving. He says, "I know this is out of our comfort zones, but why not stretch ourselves? We'll all be better for the experience."

If only one or two of your close friends are interested in doing some spiritual exploring with you, that's okay. Bring them along!

If your spiritual life is igniting in new ways these days, why not try to fire up your friends as well? Invite them to a church service or special event. Invite them to your small group. Invite them to a class designed for people exploring faith. It's what friends do. They try new stuff together.

If all goes well, perhaps you and your entire circle of friends will walk into your spiritual futures together. I've seen this happen. I've seen groups of people come to Christ together and grow in faith together because someone in their group said, "Let's try this adventure together." I've seen groups of friends get baptized together, and then learn how to serve together and grow together. They forge friendships that can last for eternity.

If only one or two of your close friends are interested in doing some spiritual exploring with you, that's okay. Bring them along!

Let Them Go

It's possible that some of your friends will not be interested in pursuing the spiritual journey with you. What then?

The best solution is to get on your knees and ask for wisdom from God. You don't want to blow up relationships unnecessarily. I've heard too many horror stories of friends who essentially fired their non-Christian friends with a spirit of judgment. Those friends are left shaking their heads, asking, "What did we do? We're the same people as before. We were good enough for you *before* you got all spiritual on us. What happened?"

It's much better to proceed slowly, sensitively, and with great discernment, because friendships matter, and they shouldn't ever be uprooted or pruned in a cavalier fashion. I advise you to talk warmly, openly, and humbly with your circle of friends about this topic. It's perfectly appropriate to say, "Hey, gang, I love you guys. I love each one of you. Lately, my faith has begun to mean more and more to me. It's causing me to rethink some things. And because of how much our friendship means to me, I want you to be a part of this journey I'm on. Would you join me?"

If you talk openly to your circle of friends, who knows where that conversation might lead? Some of your friends might freak out or bolt. That happens sometimes. You can't stop people from opting out. If this happens, you need to let them go.

Obviously, stay in touch with them, even from a distance. Who knows? Someday they might become more open to pursuing faith, and you might be the only person of faith they know. If you keep in touch, they can reach out to you when they're ready.

Say Good-Bye

Sometimes you need to create space in a relationship, or even end a friendship altogether. "Walk with the wise and become wise," Solomon says, "for a companion of fools suffers harm."[15]

To put it bluntly, certain friendships are harmful to you. They can hold you back. The very people you call "friends" can beat you down. If the wrong kind of stuff is rubbing off on you; if your friends aren't cheering you on or looking out for your best interests; if they want you to stay in the same rut they're in, the one you used to enjoy together but you know isn't good for you—it's time to move on.

> There's no easy way to say good-bye to a friendship, but some ways are better than others.

Sometimes the friend who is stuck in the rut is your spouse. This gets tricky. Because you've made a covenant before God and promised "for better or worse," you cannot be flippant about cutting off this relationship. While God hates divorce, Scripture does allow room for an abused or abandoned spouse to find protection through the ending of that marriage. If you are married and your spouse is harming you, *do not wait around, thinking things will magically get better.* They won't. Take action. Seek wise counsel on how to best proceed, especially when children are involved.

There's no easy way to say good-bye to a friendship, but some ways are better than others:

Don't choose avoidance. Don't start hiding from your friends. Don't ignore their texts or voice messages. Don't no-show to commitments you've made. In short, *don't do things that would make you less than a friend.* Just because your life is switching onto a new track, that doesn't invalidate the friendships you've had. You can bow out gracefully without "disappearing." Treat your old friends the way you would want to be treated.

Don't be judgmental. Don't make value statements about how poor their life choices are compared to your now-better choices. Remember, those were *your* life choices too, until recently! Let your example speak for itself. Make changes in your life that will be evident to your friends over time.

Choose honesty and grace. If you need to part ways with a certain friend, sit down with the person and say, "I'm moving on with my life. I'm changing direction. What worked for me for many years is no longer working for me. I think I'm figuring some stuff out, and I wish you would come along with me. If you're dead set against it, I understand. But I have to move on!"

These are excruciatingly difficult conversations. But they need to happen.

Continue to pray for your old friends and occasionally circle back to touch base with them, hoping you'll see some movement. But don't let an old friendship keep you from taking the journey God has called you to take. Nothing and no one should hold you back. Sometimes you just need to move on!

JESUS' RELATIONAL CIRCLES: 72-12-3-3

Jesus set a precedent for us and showed us how to border friendships and maintain healthy friendship circles. He had a large circle of friends—at least seventy-two who were close enough to be called *disciples* (according to Luke 10:1). These were the people He sent ahead to the villages and towns He planned to visit. They did ministry together, and Jesus coached them.

He also hand-selected twelve disciples to be His "small group." For the entire three years of His ministry on earth, these twelve men lived their day-to-day lives with Jesus. Jesus also had two inner circles of friends—the men and women who knew Him best.

His first inner circle included Peter, James, and John, His

three closest friends. These were the three He asked to join Him to pray on a high mountain, where they witnessed Jesus' transfiguration. These same three men accompanied Him deeper into the garden of Gethsemane while the rest of the disciples stayed back, just before Jesus was arrested.

> Jesus set a precedent for us and showed us how to border friendships and maintain healthy friendship circles.

Do you think it was awkward when Jesus singled out these three friends as His inner circle? I do. But Jesus understood that it was more important for Him to invest in these three close friends than to worry too much about others feeling jealous or left out. He needed the intimacy of an inner circle, and He recognized that bordering His inner circle included making some cuts. He was still close to the other nine, but He *chose* the three. And He held to that decision.

His second inner circle was with three siblings—Mary, Martha, and Lazarus—as we discussed in chapter 1. These three were not part of the twelve, but they were likely part of the seventy-two. Jesus felt at home with this family. They were His "kitchen table" friends. He could relax with them. He could bank on good food, a comfortable bed, and warm conversation whenever He stopped by. He found friendship and safety at the home of Mary, Martha, and Lazarus.

If the Son of God required two distinct inner circles of friends, what does that suggest for us as His followers?

Perhaps God has been nudging you long before now about pruning your friendships. Maybe He's prompting you to get your relational world in better order. Might it be time for you to redefine some of your current relationships and forge new friendships along the way?

DEEPENING YOUR INNER CIRCLE
Take Small Steps
Few things are more awkward than beginning a friendship with someone who makes a great first impression, diving headfirst into that new relationship, and then quickly discovering that this person is not someone you want to get closer to.

Another person, who's a little bit harder to get to know, might be worth the extra effort because he or she has the depth and wisdom you seek. Be patient. Take small steps—and avoid having to take awkward steps back because you jumped in too soon.

Invest Time
Deepening friendships takes time. Your simplified, holistic calendar, which contains your commitments to work, home, church, and friendships, is a great tool to use when it comes to carving out time for deepening your relationships. If you're prone to letting the urgent (appointments, work commitments) take priority over the important (relationships), discipline yourself to schedule time for these new friendships.

> Be patient. Take small steps—and avoid having to take awkward steps back because you jumped in too soon.

Create Shared Experiences
Getting together for coffee or lunch provides an opportunity for conversation, which is the foundation of getting to know people better. But shared experiences beyond a casual get-together can augment and cement a developing friendship. A friend of mine knows he is prone to not prioritize friendships as much as he should, so he invited a new friend to join him in a shared hobby—photography. They walk trails together with their cameras, taking photos and engaging in conversation during these shared experiences.

My wife, Lynne, is good at creating shared experiences with friends. She often invites a girlfriend along when she travels to speak or participate in conferences or events. They inevitably get into some adventures together and create memories through these shared travel experiences. My preference is to invite friends onto sailboats or powerboats. We join together doing the work of sailing or motoring, and we enjoy good food and conversation on the open water. Memories are made there that cannot be made over a sedate cup of coffee or a restaurant meal.

Volunteering is another effective shared experience when it comes to building friendships. Find a common cause and engage in it together.

Wait for the Volley

If you find you're doing all the initiating in a new friendship, it might be wise to wait for your new friend to return the volley. Make sure that he or she is interested in deepening the friendship with you—and that he or she has the time and desire to invest in your relationship. If you are unsure where you stand, *ask*. Make sure the interest in a deeper friendship is mutual before putting all your eggs in that basket.

Take Off Your Mask (First)

When you have taken some baby steps into your new friendship and you feel confident that the desire for a deepening friendship is mutual, begin to take off your mask.

Don't freak out the other person by unpacking all your dirty laundry over coffee at Starbucks. Rather, start with a small truth about yourself that you don't share with just anyone, and see how the person handles the responsibility of that truth in the coming weeks. If your confidence is kept and your friend is willing to reciprocate by sharing at equal depths, you are well on your way to a rewarding friendship.

Free tip: Beware of people who want you to do all the sharing and never reveal anything of significance from their own lives. An inability, or unwillingness, to be vulnerable to another, or a resistance to seeing one's own flaws—these are major red flags.

There is a place for people who do all the sharing. It's called a counselor's office. But in a true friendship, the sharing needs to be reciprocated by both parties.

In a Crisis, Show Up

You cannot orchestrate this last tip. You cannot (or at least you should not!) plan a crisis in your life or your new friend's life. But in a deepening friendship, when a crisis arises, *show up*. Deep friendships are forged in the fire of pain. If your friend experiences a personal loss of any kind, extend yourself. Don't wait to be asked; depending upon the depth of the pain, your friend may not have the emotional energy to ask for help. Show up with food, time, assistance, or whatever the situation calls for. Most of all, be present.

> Beware of people who want you to do all the sharing and never reveal anything of significance from their own lives.

If you're the one who encounters a season of pain, let your friends walk alongside you. Don't isolate yourself. Let them in. Time and again, relationships have moved from mere acquaintanceship to inner-circle friendship during a season of crisis.

A SIMPLIFIED LIFE WORTH LIVING

You will greatly simplify your life when you fine-tune your relational world. Prune wisely and with determination. Create space for new growth that will bear fruit in your life—spiritual, emotional, and relational fruit. Life is too rich with opportunity to walk it alone. Invest yourself in people whose high character will rub off on you.

The effort you put forth to prune your relational world, expand your friendship circles, and deepen your inner circle of friends will pay huge dividends. When you simplify your friendships, you are well on your way to leading a richer, fuller, more joy-filled life. You are on the path toward a simplified life worth living.

■ ■ ■

ACTION STEP: IDENTIFY YOUR CURRENT RELATIONSHIP CIRCLES

In your journal or on a computer spreadsheet, create five columns and label them as follows: Seventy-two, Twelve, Three, Distant, and Potential.

SEVENTY-TWO

In the first column, list your current acquaintance-level friendships. This list includes people from all areas of your life: coworkers, neighbors, church friends, committee members, family, etc. Maybe you can think of only twenty-five people for this column; or maybe there's a hundred. The names on this list are people you don't know well. Most likely you have never socialized with them one-on-one or as couples, and you've never shared a significant conversation.

> When you simplify your friendships, you are well on your way to leading a richer, fuller, more joy-filled life.

TWELVE

In the second column, list your current friends, your "twelve." There might be six people on this list or there might be twenty, depending on your personality and season of life. This list represents people you know a little better, socialize with occasionally, and would consider a friend—family included. These are the people you do life with throughout the week.

THREE

In the third column, list your current inner circle. This might include a spouse, adult children, or best friends. Again, it doesn't have to be exactly three. But it should be a smaller handful.

DISTANT

In the fourth column, list your significant relationships with people who live out-of-town. These are people who might be in your "Twelve" or "Three" columns if they lived nearby.

Note: While these are valuable friendships, it's not realistic to expect the same kind of "doing life together" relationships from these people that you can experience with those who live near you. If you want to keep them in your inner circle, develop a strategy for connecting at least weekly.

POTENTIAL

In the last column, list a handful of people you wish you knew better, who might be potential friends. These should be people you have a realistic chance of becoming friends with. Don't put Oprah on your list unless you live next door to her. Don't add Chris Tomlin unless you play backup in his band and have regular contact with him. Be realistic. Who do you know and admire for their Christlike character? Who do you think might be worth making an initial volley of friendship toward? Put them on your list.

Once you've completed your five lists, save them. Then begin making adjustments to the columns, creating a blue-sky picture of where you'd like to see your relational world a year from now. Move people from one column to another, and highlight names you know need to go.

ACTION STEP: PRUNE YOUR CURRENT
RELATIONSHIP CIRCLES

Review the highlighted names of current friends who you know aren't healthy for you—and plan to create a safer distance between you and them. Over the next couple of weeks, begin praying for God's wisdom in making the necessary adjustments in those friendships.

Put a date on your calendar two weeks out. This is the date when you will begin the process of engaging these people in the kind-but-honest conversations we discussed. Don't avoid. Don't delay. Honor these friends by being proactive, compassionate, and straightforward.

ACTION STEP: EXPAND AND DEEPEN YOUR
NEW FRIENDSHIP CIRCLES

EXPAND

List three risks you can take in the next month to expand your exposure to potential new friends. Make your list and add each item to your calendar.

DEEPEN

Review your "Three" column and your "Potential" column. Write the names of three people you wish you had a closer friendship with, and write a small step you can take with each potential friendship. Perhaps set up a coffee date. Invite them to a movie and then grab dessert. Ask if they want to volunteer with you at your church's next event. Pick something easy and nonthreatening, but something that will help the two of you explore your friendship a little more closely.

Making adjustments to our relational circles takes prayer, discernment, and a fair amount of fortitude. But it's one of the most effective energy investments we can make when it comes to simplifying our lives.

chapter eight

from drifting to focused

Claiming God's Call on Your Life

MY FATHER AND I had a number of hair-raising adventures over the course of my younger years. He was not a man of caution, to say the least. One such adventure marked me deeply, and I remember it as clearly as if it were yesterday.

I was eight years old, and my dad had taken me out sailing on Lake Michigan. If you've ever been on Lake Michigan, you understand how utterly inadequate the word *lake* is to describe this massive body of water. Plunging to a depth of 925 feet, it holds a volume of 1,180 *cubic miles* of water, with a surface area of 22,300 square miles—roughly the size of West Virginia.[1] The weather on Lake Michigan is volatile, and the bottom is littered with the hulls of ships, large and small, that never made it back to port. My dad loved to regale me with stories of past shipwrecks, which heightened my respect for Lake Michigan's dangers.

On this particular day, around midmorning, we set out from South Haven, Michigan, heading for Chicago, where my dad had some business to conduct for the produce company our family owned. The fresh breeze that filled our sails in the harbor developed into a stiff wind once we were out on the lake. By noon, it was a full-blown gale, and visibility was poor.

We fought the storm for more than ten hours, making sluggish progress, before darkness fell as the sun dipped below the western horizon. Even as a boy, I knew how easy it would be to miss the entrance to the harbor in the dark. We both knew we must be very close, but the weather conditions made it nearly impossible for either of us to see anything. My mind raced, but I kept quiet, not wanting to interrupt my dad's concentration.

"There," my dad said at last, pointing into the dark just off the starboard bow. I turned my gaze in the direction he was pointing, and in the distance, a vivid pinpoint of red light could be seen above the crashing waves—the Chicago Breakwater Lighthouse.

Built more than 120 years ago, this lighthouse has welcomed innumerable vessels of all sizes to safety. Twenty long, drenching minutes later, we passed beneath the lighthouse's beam and entered the gentle waters of the Chicago Harbor, safe and sound.

The image of the lighthouse in the midst of the huge storm was indelibly seared into my mind—so much so that, later that week in art class, I painted a picture of our experience. That little painting hangs in our kitchen today. Although it boasts all the artistic talent of an average eight-year-old schoolboy, that picture always takes me back to that experience of feeling utterly lost in the darkness, spotting the lighthouse shining above the waves, and watching my dad steer our sailboat to safety and dry land.

In life, as on the open water, we need a light that directs us back to safe harbor. Scripture is that light:

> Your word is a lamp for my feet, a light on my
> path.[2]

Just as the Chicago lighthouse guided my dad and me toward the entrance of the harbor, we all need a vivid point of light from Scripture—a particular verse that resonates with us personally, to guide our paths and give us a reference point, no matter the size of the waves. When circumstances batter us about and we are most prone to go off-course, a single, well-chosen verse can guide us back toward the things that matter most. A "life verse" is a powerful, clarifying tool when it comes to simplifying our lives.

> A "life verse" is a powerful, clarifying tool when it comes to simplifying our lives.

WHAT IS A LIFE VERSE?

A life verse is a short passage of Scripture that serves as a rallying cry to guide and focus the current season in your life, or your life as a whole. Carefully chosen after prayerful consideration, a life verse resonates with you in a personal way and serves as a lighthouse that continually guides you back to God's mission and vision for your life.

Let me begin by saying there is no explicit biblical mandate for the practice of having a life verse. You won't find "life verse" in your Bible's concordance. However, the life-centering principle of relying on Scripture is so evident in the words of Jesus and the writings of the apostles, and of David, that I can comfortably build a case for choosing a life verse without fear of steering you wrong.

I have found my life verse to be remarkably helpful when it comes to keeping my life simplified. I have adopted an overall life verse—1 Corinthians 15:58—and at various times I have leaned into several other verses that have helped me navigate specific seasons.

My life verse keeps me anchored to the truth and continually calls me back to the things that matter most, helping me not lose sight of why God put me on this earth. My life verse is a lighthouse that beckons me back to the harbor when I stray too far offshore.

It functions as a powerful tool for helping me filter decisions and opportunities that come my way.

THE POWER OF ADOPTING A LIFE VERSE

Over the years, I have encouraged Christ followers to adopt a life verse as a tool to help them stay centered on God's call in their lives; and by many reports, having such a verse has borne much fruit.

Allow me to describe the role that my life verse has played, tell a few stories I've heard about other people's life verses, and discuss the characteristics to look for in choosing a life verse of your own.

MY LIFE VERSE

Over the years, I could point to times when adverse circumstances left me so deeply dejected and forlorn that I couldn't find words to express to God how I felt. At those times, I simply wrote my life verse over and over again on the pages of my prayer journal to refocus my mind on God's truth. I would read the verse aloud, just to hear its words echo in my ears. I would let it soak deep into my soul. And those words of Scripture had a healing effect, leaving me centered, anchored, and renewed once again. I could get back to work and engage with God and the people around me. So, what is this awesome, life-altering verse?

> I have encouraged many Christ followers to adopt a life verse as a tool to help them stay centered on God's call in their lives.

Here is my life verse, 1 Corinthians 15:58:

> Therefore, be steadfast, immovable, always abounding in the work of the Lord, knowing that your work is never in vain if it is in the Lord.[3]

The apostle Paul penned these words to the church in Corinth, and there are three key reasons why I've chosen it as my life verse.

REASON #1: It Clarifies What Matters Most

I love this verse, first of all, because it brings clarity to what matters most in the world. It clearly establishes that there is a "work of the Lord" for each of us to do. There are many *good* things you could choose to do with your one and only life, but those good things can easily distract you from the *best* thing God has called you to do. What is that best thing—that "work of the Lord"—for you?

If you are a Christ follower who has invited God to lead your life, He has given you an assignment in this world for which He has uniquely gifted you. Your assignment is different from mine; it is unique to you. Your life verse will reflect God's particular guidance in your life.

When God tapped me on the shoulder decades ago, I knew one of His key assignments for me was to use my spiritual gift of evangelism to help people spend their earthly lives and their eternities with Him. Another assignment was to use my gifts of leadership and teaching to help equip and encourage pastors to maximize the Kingdom impact of their local churches. My life verse directs my attention to God's unique calling and assignments in my life. It clarifies for me how my best efforts should be spent: "abounding in the work of the Lord." (This verse also fits my personality, which my wife and staff will attest can be rather steadfast and immovable at times.)

> My life verse directs my attention to God's unique calling and assignments. It clarifies for me how my best efforts should be spent.

Because my life verse begins with the word *therefore*, I need to understand what the *therefore* is there for. Earlier in 1 Corinthians 15, Paul seeks to convince his audience that because Jesus was resurrected from the dead, all human beings, too, will be resurrected in spirit the moment they die. In 1 Corinthians 15:52, he says, "In a flash, in the twinkling of an eye," people who die will awaken into a new reality. In 1 Corinthians 15:53, he adds, "This perishable must put on the imperishable, and this mortal must put on immortality."[4] Everyone will be resurrected to stand before God and to give an account of their lives: what they lived for; who they lived for; how they spent their one and only lives.

In this day and age, what do most people think will happen to them when they die? Throughout history, the majority of people have not believed in immortality. Most people on this planet, with its varying faiths and worldviews, believe that when they die—*poof!*— their candle simply goes out and they suddenly cease to exist. They believe there's no resurrection on the other side, no eternal life, no standing before a holy God, no giving an account of their lives here on earth. No rewards, no consequences, just a sea of nothingness. Eternal, unconscious nothingness. Statistically, this is still what most people believe today.

This was the prevailing belief in Paul's day as well. Most of his listeners still believed in the "candle goes out" theory of death. Paul implores the Christians in Corinth to understand that this theory is simply not correct. If you follow the candle theory through to its logical conclusion, life on earth loses all meaning. How we live our lives would make no difference whatsoever.

Paul writes, "If there is no resurrection of the dead, . . . our preaching is useless and so is your faith."[5] Why does anything in this life matter at all? He borrows from the secular thinking of his day: If all we do after death is pass into eternal nothingness, "if the dead are not raised, 'Let us eat and drink, for tomorrow we die.'"[6] What difference does it make?

If there is no resurrection, then the eternity of the modern-day sex trafficker is the same as that of Mother Teresa, who spent seventy years serving the poor and trying to save little girls and their families from such horrific experiences. With the eternal-nothingness theory, neither of their lives really mattered. The serial rapist, abuser, or murderer would enjoy the same quiet nothingness after death as Martin Luther King Jr., Nelson Mandela, and Billy Graham.

Paul says, "Not on your life." Every human being is going to be resurrected and stand before a holy, living God and a resurrected Jesus to give an account of the life he or she lived on this earth—behavior, words, deeds, actions, attitudes, and beliefs. Paul writes, "Christ has indeed been raised from the dead, the firstfruits of those who have fallen asleep" (a euphemism for dying).[7] Paul explains that everyone who dies will be resurrected into the new reality the moment they exit this world—consciously, immediately, bodily.

"Therefore," Paul says in 1 Corinthians 15:58, "be steadfast, immovable . . ." Be *steadfast* in these core Christian beliefs and how you live them out. Be *immovable* when it comes to your convictions about who Christ is, what He taught, why He died, and how God raised Him from the dead. Be immovable about the fact that you and every other human being who has ever lived is going to be resurrected. Be immovable when everybody else tries to sell the "candle goes out" theory. When the culture around you says, "Eat, drink, and be merry, for tomorrow we die," don't buy it. Think it through. Stay focused on living out your core Christian beliefs. "*You*," Paul says, "be steadfast. *You* be the immovable one." When we are steadfast and immovable in our commitment to core Christian beliefs, it clarifies how we live our lives. It has a simplifying effect.

> When we are steadfast and immovable in our commitment to core Christian beliefs, it has a simplifying effect.

Time for a little truth telling that I'm not particularly proud of: Part of the reason I chose 1 Corinthians 15:58 as my life verse many decades ago is because of how tempting it is for me to fall into the "eat, drink, and be merry" mind-set. It was tempting when I was young, and I am still tempted by it today. I catch myself secretly wishing I could just live for myself a little bit more often. Indulge my own desires, blow off my commitments, stop focusing my energies on the condition of the world, and spend money like a drunken sailor—which I am fully capable of doing. Oh, to set aside being Dutch for just a week—or a month!

In my darker moments—and I'm not proud of this either—I sometimes wish that it all ended with the candle going out and that no one would have to give an account of their life, myself included. I spend a lot of energy worrying and praying about the lives and afterlives of people I care about. And sometimes, in my darker moments, it would just be so convenient to believe that nothing exists beyond the grave, and it's all just eternal peace and quiet. It would make my life so much easier. Selfish as it sounds, these are the inner stirrings I sometimes wrestle with.

But whenever I find myself ruminating about these ideas, my life verse smacks me right in the jaw. It reminds me, "You've got one life, Bill. Don't buy that 'nothingness' belief. It doesn't add up. Someday, every man, woman, and child—including you—is going to stand before God, and they will all have to explain how they invested their lives."

I read, write, or recite my life verse *every day*, and it always re-centers me on my purpose. "Be steadfast. Be immovable. Never lose sight of reality." It motivates me to live every day with resurrection realities in the forefront of my mind. It drives my attitude, behavior, and actions. Can you see why I love and need this verse?

Do you live with a high sense of urgency about the lives and the afterlives of people you love? Do you pray with fervency for people at work, for people in your neighborhood, for your friends and relatives? Friend, there is an eternal clock ticking, and if you've gotten sucked into the idea that it's all going to come out in the wash and there's nothing really at stake, you need a wake-up call, just like I do.

My life verse keeps me praying for the people I love when I feel like giving up. It reminds me of what's truly at stake with my friends. It keeps me taking risks to extend Christ to them; it keeps me giving away another Bible, book, or CD that might resonate with someone at an eternal level.

I love this verse because I need it. It knocks me upside the head every day. It calls me back to the simple truth. Maybe you would do well to choose a life verse that does the same for you.

REASON #2: It Calls Out the Best in Me

My life verse calls out the absolute best in me. It minces no words; its marching orders for my life are blindingly clear: "Always abound in the work of the Lord." Another translation says, "Always give yourselves fully to the work of the Lord."[8]

There's no wiggle room in this verse. No halfway. Giving myself fully leaves no room for "if it's convenient," or throwing God a bone, or dabbling periodically in His work. "Always abounding" means I'm *all in, all the time.*

Paul sets the bar about as high as it can be set. He chooses two words—

> My life verse calls out the absolute best in me. It minces no words; its marching orders for my life are blindingly clear.

always and *abound*—that are full-bucket words. Every day, rain or shine, come what may, even if your biorhythms are low or the planets aren't aligned to perfection in your world, "*always abound* in the work of the Lord." Every day, move His purposes forward intentionally, strategically, passionately.

In case you think Paul is a little overzealous in his challenge to Christ followers, take a look at these words from Jesus:

> As long as it is day, we must do the works of him
> who sent me. Night is coming, when no one can
> work.[9]

> The harvest is plentiful, but the workers are few.
> Ask the Lord of the harvest, therefore, to send out
> workers into his harvest field. Go! I am sending
> you out like lambs among wolves. Do not take a
> purse or bag or sandals; and do not greet anyone
> on the road.[10]

Jesus makes Paul look like a lightweight. This world matters, Jesus is saying. Go! Do God's work while it is still daylight, because a season is coming when darkness will fall and you'll no longer be able to work for God. But today you can advance His purposes.

> This is to my Father's glory, that you *bear much
> fruit*, showing yourselves to be my disciples.[11]

Not just a smattering of fruit, Jesus says. Not just a little seed here and there. We're to bear *much* fruit with our one and only lives.

Life passes quickly, so *abound in the work of the Lord*, and *bear much fruit*, for the night is coming.

A few years back, I had the privilege of interviewing Dallas Willard, one of the great spiritual thinkers and writers of our day. His passing in 2013 was a deep loss for the Christian community, though heaven's gain. Everyone who knew Dallas can attest to his joy-filled, optimistic, loving, outgoing personality, and it was a pleasure to speak with him.

After the formal interview was over, I asked Dallas if anything ever got him down.

"I'll tell you what gets me down," he said without missing a beat. "It bothers me that Christ followers require so much prompting and cajoling to do God's work in the world. I know many pastors who must beg people to show up for events. They must beg people to use their God-given spiritual gifts to further His Kingdom. They must beg people to read their Bibles and pray and tithe. Churches spend thousands of dollars producing emotional videos to move people to care for the poor, because if they didn't show those videos, their congregations wouldn't really care for the poor."[12]

I was taken aback by his bluntness, but I can affirm his description of what most pastors go through. Dallas shook his head and said, "It just shouldn't have to be this way. A Christ follower's motivation should come from within."[13]

People who live by 1 Corinthians 15:58 don't require pep talks from pastors or pleadings from exhausted ministry leaders to step up and get involved with the work of God. The life verse that echoes in their minds all day long keeps them fired up. They're the kind of people who say, "Today will be an abounding day. Just show me a need—I'm going to abound. This is what my life is all about. It's what God wants. These are my marching orders."

In the moments right after you die, when you're resurrected "in the twinkling of an eye" and you stand before the sovereign God of the universe, you will fully grasp that this whole world was His, and His purposes were the most important things ever going on in it. And you'll be so unbelievably grateful that you abounded in the work of the Lord with your one and only life. You'll be so glad that you lived full-on for Him.

> My life verse motivates me every day to "abound in the work of the Lord." Your life verse should motivate you similarly.

By contrast, imagine how horrible it would be to stand before this loving, awesome God and admit that, during your one shot at this life, your main focus was to eat, drink, and be merry. Your main purpose was chasing money, power, pleasure, or self-indulgence.

My life verse motivates me every day to "abound in the work of the Lord." Your life verse should motivate you similarly.

REASON #3: It Brings Comfort

The final phrase in 1 Corinthians 15:58 gives me enormous comfort: "knowing that your work is never in vain if it is in the Lord."

I detest doing stuff in vain. If I accidentally take the long way when driving somewhere, rather than a more expedient route, or I forget to save something on my computer and have to redo it, it makes me a little crazy. I don't like wasting time. I like my time and energy to be well invested.

Many years ago, an excavator friend of mine spent three days digging out a guy's backyard to install an inground swimming pool. The project went well, and my friend felt the deep satisfaction of a job well done. The hole was squared nicely, set at the perfect depth, and all the specs were just as they should be, ready for the pool company to come and install the pool.

Then the homeowner returned from vacation. He saw the hole and said to the excavator, "I didn't order a swimming pool. What address do you have for where you were supposed to dig this hole?"

My friend had missed the correct address by one house. He had to fill back in the perfectly dug hole and resod the entire yard. He had dug that huge hole for nothing.

Because I hate doing things in vain, I love that my life verse reminds me that every effort I expend to advance the purposes of God in this world—no matter how big or small, how visible or hidden—is never in vain. God Himself notices and appreciates it.

Sometimes, when I put my all into an endeavor I hope will make a difference in people's lives, or their church, and it goes unnoticed, my life verse reminds me it was not a waste. God noticed. I do what I do, ultimately, for an audience of one. Every prayer prayed, every gift given, every kind deed or act of service, every sermon well preached, every flight across another time zone to encourage some fellow pastors—it's all recorded on the ledger sheets of heaven. And someday, God will reward it accordingly. None of it is in vain.

Doing things that would be rewarded in eternity motivated the apostle Paul as well. In fact, in 1 Corinthians 9, Paul records this vivid comparison of two kinds of races:

> Do you not know that in a race all the runners run, but only one gets the prize? Run in such a way as to get the prize. Everyone who competes in the games goes into strict training. They do it to get a crown that will not last, but we do it to get a crown that will last forever. Therefore I do not run like someone running aimlessly; I do not fight like a boxer beating the air. No, I strike a blow to my body and make it my slave so that after I have preached to others, I myself will not be disqualified for the prize.[14]

Think about how much time, effort, and training go into every Olympian's attempt to win a single race. Years of their lives and plenty of blood, sweat, and tears all go toward winning a race that might last only a few short minutes. And all the winners get for their efforts is a medal—some bling on a ribbon to wear for the rest of the day. Then it goes in a drawer or on a wall somewhere.

In Paul's day, instead of giving gold medals for winning first place in an Olympic event, a crown of olive or laurel leaves was placed on the winner's head. By the time the athlete went home that night, the wreath would already be wilting and falling apart. Think of that. All that energy expended for a wreath that didn't last beyond the day.

Paul contrasts this with putting our efforts into running a race of another kind—a race that advances the purposes of God in the world. If you enter into that race and you run hard, God will give you an imperishable wreath, an eternal crown, a reward that isn't wilted by sundown, but that lasts forever.

Are you in the right race? Or have you accidentally drifted into a race that is mostly in vain? Are your best efforts going toward a race that results in fleeting applause? Or do you strive for material gain, which rusts, rots, and depreciates? Or for passing pleasures that don't amount to a hill of beans in the eternal scheme of things?

> Are you in the right race? Or have you accidentally drifted into a race that is mostly in vain?

Paul admonishes us, "Don't get to the end of your one and only life and find out that it was all in vain, and that you dug a swimming pool in the wrong backyard."

Instead, "be steadfast, immovable, always abounding in the work of the Lord, knowing that your work is never in vain if it is in the Lord."

YOU'RE NOT CRAZY

Some years back, I received a phone call from a man I know who has the spiritual gift of giving. He could have retired five times over and spent the rest of his life on the golf course; but, instead, he chose to keep working very hard and living rather modestly in proportion to his substantial income so he could underwrite Kingdom ventures as generously as possible. This guy took his gift of giving very seriously. He was running the right race for the right kind of crown.

On the phone, he asked to meet with me, so we made a lunch date. I feared something horrible had happened to him, but across the lunch table, he said, "Bill, you know I have the spiritual gift of giving. It's the only thing I can do really well."

"I'm well aware," I said. I knew of several substantial Kingdom plays that had been possible solely because this man had been faithful with his gift of giving. "You could have hung it up a long time ago," I told him, "yet you keep working, so you can keep giving."

"Exactly," he said. "But my wife thinks I'm crazy. My business partner thinks I'm crazy. My accountant thinks I'm crazy. And my lawyer thinks I'm crazy. And it would really help me if you could tell me I'm not crazy!"

I burst out laughing. "Not only are you not crazy," I said, "you're actually the smart one who's laying up treasures on the other side. My life verse says, 'Be steadfast, immovable, always abounding in the work of the Lord, knowing that your work is never in vain.' Investing in an imperishable wreath is *not* crazy. People who are running a different race, they'll call you crazy; but you're the smartest guy I know, laying it up on the other side."

> You're not crazy for going all out for God with your one and only life. Your efforts are not in vain.

If you, like this man, are being a good steward of the spiritual gifts God has given you—if you're being steadfast and immovable, abounding in the work of the Lord—you're not crazy. Let me repeat: *You're not crazy!* You're not crazy for going all out for God with your one and only life. Your efforts are not in vain. You will be richly rewarded on the other side.

HATS OR HARDWARE

Sailboat racing is a recreational rush for me. I love being on the water, and I love the precision of teamwork necessary to be successful in the sport. Allow me to share a sailboat-racing word picture that came about as a result of a regatta I sailed in several summers back.

A regatta is a sailboat-racing event. Most regattas consist of anywhere from seven to ten races. Points are awarded by order of finish in each race, and whoever achieves the lowest overall score wins the regatta. They win the crown, if you will. It's actually a trophy, but sailors are way too cool to call it a trophy. They refer to the champion's trophy as simply "the hardware."

When a crew wants to psych themselves up at the dock, while getting their boat ready to go out on the course, they might say, "Hey, are we going for some hardware today?" "Yeah, we're going for some serious hardware." Not a trophy. *Hardware.*

During the individual races, if your boat comes in first, everyone on the crew receives a smaller prize—often a sailing cap with a corporate logo, like Quantum Sails, Mount Gay Rum, or Harken. The hats are nice, but no one cares much about the hats. It's the hardware that counts. That's what we're racing for—the hardware.

One particular summer, the team I raced with went to a major regatta. Some experienced America's Cup racers were sprinkled among the crews. All the big dogs were there. Needless to say, it was extremely competitive.

As the regatta progressed through the first several races, our boat was doing very well. In fact, we had finished first in a few individual races and already had some hats. One other boat had taken a few firsts as well, but everyone else was pretty deep in the pack. Coming into the final race, it was between our boat and the other one. Who would win the overall prize and take home the hardware?

Before the race began, our crew had a little talk at the starting line. We all agreed on a winning game plan: We didn't need to come in first in this final race; we just needed to finish ahead of that one other boat. If we simply kept that boat behind us, no matter where we finished in the race, we would get the hardware. We reminded each other, "Focus, focus, focus!"

We fired off the starting line with a perfect start. We were in third place out of thirty or so boats. The boat we had to beat was just off our hip, as they say. All we had to do was stay in front of them to take home the hardware.

Our tactician, an America's Cup sailor, kept his eye squarely on the boat we had to beat. Some of us who were in other positions on the crew started looking at the boats ahead of us. Wouldn't it be great to win this final race? We were gaining on the second-place boat, and pretty soon the chatter started:

"Hey, if we just go a little left, we could pick off that number two boat."

"And if we went just a little farther left, we might pick off the leader as well!"

In the heat of the moment, we turned our focus away from the one boat we had to beat, to the boats ahead of us—boats that didn't matter a bit in the race for the hardware.

Our veteran tactician listened to our chatter for a while, until he'd finally heard all he could stand. With brilliant brevity, he called us all back to our central purpose: "Boys, it's hats or hardware."

In other words, "If you want to win another hat, we can go pick off those guys ahead of us—and risk letting the one boat we have to beat get around us. Or we can stay focused and bring home the hardware. Are you going to put a cheap hat on the mantle at home? No. It's hats or hardware. You make the call."

We immediately realized that we had lost our focus.

"Hardware, John. Hardware," we all said, duly embarrassed. We refocused and stayed in front of the one boat we had to beat. And at the end of the day, we took home the hardware.

> My life verse helps me keep my life simplified and focused on "hardware."

My life verse helps me keep my life simplified and focused on "hardware." When I get tempted to chase after other boats that don't matter, I am reminded to be steadfast and immovable, always abounding in the work of the Lord, racing for hardware that lasts for eternity.

EXAMPLES OF OTHER LIFE VERSES

Now you've read a thorough explanation of why I feel my life verse should be everyone's life verse. But in the spirit of fair play, I want to give you some examples of life verses that others have chosen—and why.

Billy Graham, at one point in his life, chose Psalm 16:11 as his life verse: "You make known to me the path of life; you will fill me with joy in your presence, with eternal pleasures at your right hand."

I've had the privilege of sharing a conversation or two with Billy, and you can sense the very joy and presence of God in his life. The verse clearly had a formative influence on him.

Reverend Martin Luther King Jr. claimed Amos 5:24 as his verse, which fit his God-ordained passion for righting the wrongs of pre–civil rights America: "Let justice roll on like a river, righteousness like a never-failing stream!"

A friend of mine describes her life verse, Philippians 1:21, as a centering force in her life: "For to me, to live is Christ and to die is gain." She was fresh out of college, asking herself the question, *What is going to be the driving force in my life?* When she learned that the apostle Paul had written those words while in chains in prison, it rocked her world. Today, her all-in commitment to live her life fully for God—as echoed in Paul's words—has driven her to devote herself to issues of compassion and justice in our broken world. God is doing remarkable things through this woman.

An obscure minor prophet in the Old Testament penned the life verse of another friend of mine. Habakkuk 3:2 reads, "Lord, I have heard of your fame; I stand in awe of your deeds, Lord. Repeat them in our day, in our time make them known." This friend lives to see God do the same kinds of amazing deeds in our day as He did in

Habakkuk's day. He and his wife have launched a network of churches in a major city, fully inviting God to do amazing things there. They are well on their way to seeing God fulfill this man's life verse.

Another friend leans into John 15:5: "I am the vine; you are the branches. If you remain in me and I in you, you will bear much fruit; apart from me you can do nothing." This friend puts it plainly: "I don't love my life verse; I just really need to hear it." He describes himself as too easily tempted to do things in his own strength rather than relying on God. His life verse reminds him that he can do nothing apart from Jesus doing it through him. His reliance on this life verse is indeed bearing fruit. Today he keeps his focus on *who God wants him to be*, not what God wants him to do. God is using him and his wife to lead a thriving church of more than five thousand people.

Yet another friend counts on his life verse daily: "Let your gentleness be evident to all. The Lord is near" (Philippians 4:5). This friend, whose Kingdom role includes pastoring in an incredibly difficult environment, admits, "I'm not naturally wired for gentleness, but my life verse reminds me to be gentle in dealing with people, no matter what they may have done. And that 'the Lord is near' part of this verse reassures me that the end result in their lives is not up to me; it's in God's hands. He is near."

A friend whose life has included some deep losses roots her soul in words spoken by Jesus in John 10:10: "The thief comes only to steal and kill and destroy; I have come that they may have life, and have it to the full."

"This verse continually reminds me that my circumstances do not dictate the quality of my life," she says. "The evil one may have intended these painful circumstances in my life for evil, but God brings good even from the deepest of losses, when we invite Him into the mess. Today, I can honestly say I am experiencing 'life to the full,' in spite of what I have lost."

Having a life verse is one of the most powerful tools I know for simplifying your life. Like a lighthouse in the darkness, it keeps you on course. It helps you make wise decisions about where to invest your time, energy, and gifts. It motivates you to ruthlessly trim the waste from your life. It drives you to live each day with fervency and passion.

It's hats or hardware, friend. Choose a life verse that gets you focused on the "hardware," and keep it ever-present in your mind. Let it empower you to run the race that matters, free of distraction. Someday, when you stand before God, your life verse will have helped you receive a crown worth keeping.

■ ■ ■

ACTION STEP: FIND A LIFE VERSE

This action step is a no-brainer: Find a life verse. And use it.

IF YOU HAVE A LIFE VERSE

If you already have a life verse, commit it to memory. Post it in the places you see regularly throughout the day: at your desk, on the bathroom mirror, in the kitchen, in your car. Be strategic about incorporating it into your chair time each day. What is God inviting you to do today as a result of your life verse? What elements in your life is He inviting you to change?

IF YOU NEED A LIFE VERSE

If you do not yet have a life verse, use the resources in Appendix A, "How to Choose Your Life Verse," for suggestions on what to look for in a good life verse, and where to look. Appendix B contains a robust list of potential verses, sorted by topic.

Once you've compiled a list of several verses that resonate with you, pray over them. Don't rush the process—take time to discern which verse would best act as a lighthouse for you, calling you back to God's desires for your life. Which verse keeps you running the right race, giving your all for eternal hardware?

chapter nine

from stuck to moving on

Welcoming New Seasons in Your Life

THE SONG "Turn! Turn! Turn!" was an anthem of changing times during the tumultuous 1960s. Originally penned by Pete Seeger, the song was popularized by The Byrds, who released it in 1965.

I was in my early teens the first time I heard the song on the radio. I thought the lyrics sounded a little familiar, so I did some poking around. Imagine my shock and delight when I discovered that all the verses in the song come from the book of Ecclesiastes in the Old Testament.

I watched with even greater delight as the song rose in the charts, becoming one of the top one hundred songs in the country, then one of the top fifty, then one of the top ten. Finally, on December 4, 1965, it became the number one song in America. With words straight out of the Bible.

Around this time in my life, I spent a chunk of every summer at a very conservative Christian camp. The camp had lots of restrictive rules, including a ban on transistor radios—which was intended to keep us from listening to "secular music" while we were at camp. The camp leaders believed that secular music would corrupt our souls.

"Rock music is from the devil."

"Rock musicians are demon-possessed!"

You get the picture.

Each evening at camp, we gathered for a campfire sing-along. A college kid with a twelve-string guitar—which was as radical as we could get—led us in the singing of church hymns. The uptight camp directors stood guard at the back, making sure that no one made eye contact with anyone of the opposite sex and that no one was chewing gum. We were there to sing songs to God, not to have fun!

One night, a bunch of us junior high kids made a pact. Because we were adolescents and inherently rebellious, we agreed that when sing-along time began, none of us would sing. We would boycott those stuffy old songs.

When we all gathered around the campfire and the college kid began strumming and singing, no one joined in—except the crickets. It was perfect! This infuriated the camp leaders, which, of course, was exactly what we wanted.

Finally, the song leader stopped singing and gave us all the eye, as if to say, *Watch this!* And then he segued into the distinctive opening chords of "Turn! Turn! Turn! "—the number one song in the country! We looked at each other in amazement. *Can this really be happening?*

He started singing the first verse, and we all joined in at the top of our lungs.

> *To everything—turn, turn, turn*
> *There is a season—turn, turn, turn*
> *And a time to every purpose under heaven . . .*

We knew every word (evidently I wasn't the only heathen junior-high student who listened to *secular* music), and everyone sang with great excitement and emotion, our arms in the air.

Of course, the old geezer camp leaders, who had never listened to secular music in their lives, didn't recognize the song as the rock-and-roll hit that was sweeping the nation. They just recognized that the lyrics were from Scripture—and by the sound of our singing, they thought a revival had broken out! We sang that "secular song from the pit of hell" with all our might, and our leaders stood in the back, wiping their eyes, thanking Jesus that these rebellious young people had finally seen the light.

I don't think the camp leaders ever realized that the spiritual revival they witnessed that night was delivered compliments of those "rock musician demons," The Byrds.

With a memory like that, you can imagine I feel a great fondness for Ecclesiastes 3, from which Pete Seeger drew the lyrics for "Turn! Turn! Turn!" In these verses, King Solomon—the wisest man in the world in his day—speaks about the turning of seasons in our lives. And though these words drew my attention in junior high because of their popularity on the radio, today they draw my attention for a more substantive reason: They call for change. They invite us to consider the seasons of our lives through the landscape of eternity—and this is key to simplifying our lives.

> King Solomon invites us to consider the seasons of our lives through the landscape of eternity— and this is key to simplifying our lives.

I hope by now you have made significant changes toward simplifying your life. You've identified areas where adjustments are in order, and you've crafted a game plan to bring about those changes. At this point, I want to invite you to frame your simplifying process in a new way—by thinking of your life in terms of *seasons*.

A STRING OF SEASONS

When we view our lives as a string of random days connected only by the calendar, it's easy to overlook the active movement of God.

Our ability to identify the seasons of our lives increases our ability to cooperate with God, recognize His guiding hand, follow His lead, and accept the end of one season as the beginning of the next.

Solomon was king of Israel in the tenth century BC, and he wrote the book of Ecclesiastes later in his life. He attempted to capture all he had learned about the meaning of life and the things that really mattered. He opens chapter 3 with these words: "There is a time for everything, and a season for every activity under the heavens."

In Solomon's view, life is not a one-dimensional, steady-state trudge from the cradle to the grave; it's an ebb and flow of seasons.

The span of years that forms your life isn't merely a linear path. Nor is your life predictable or controllable. The days don't just pelt you like raindrops, one after the other. Rather, you enter into seasons—weeks, months, or years in length—that have a beginning and an end. You spend some time in that season, and then you move to the next one.

We all have a baseline awareness of what Solomon is talking about. In fact, when people my age talk about our families, we rarely talk about the specific ages of our kids. Instead, we talk about *seasons*.

If Lynne and I are at a party and we see someone we don't know well, we might say, "Don't you have kids about the same age as ours?"

"Yes, we have a daughter with a toddler, like Shauna."

No need to mention their daughter's age. She and Shauna are in the same season, and Lynne and I know exactly what stage of life that is.

Had their answer been, "We have a daughter with three teen-agers," we probably would have said, "Give us her name; we will pray for her every single day!" That's a definite, distinct season: three teenagers in the home.

Had they replied, "Two kids away at college, so it's just us at home now," we could relate to the empty-nest season—and also to the budget-pinching season of college tuition payments for two kids at once!

A couple of weeks ago, I was talking to a woman who casually mentioned she had four preschoolers. *Four preschoolers.* I almost gave her a hug right then and there. She's in the no-sleep, macaroni-and-cheese-for-every-meal, diaper-bag-instead-of-a-purse, minivan season. *Yikes!*

No matter how old you are, you have already lived through several distinct seasons, with more to come. People talk about their high school and college years as a season. For many, that was quite a season! Married folks talk about being honeymooners—a too-short season. Businesspeople talk about the seasons of past jobs, past bosses, and past career directions.

> No matter how old you are, you have already lived through several distinct seasons, with more to come.

Sometimes, adverse circumstances define our seasons. If someone says, "My dad is in hospice," you understand that family is in a difficult season, with an even more difficult one to come. If someone tells you he just lost his job, you understand the pressures and parameters of his new season. If a woman tells you her husband just walked out on her and filed for divorce, you know she is moving from one difficult season (a crumbling marriage) into another (dividing up their lives), and will soon enter a third difficult season (adjusting to being single again, and possibly living on a very limited income with little or no help with the kids).

Sometimes, difficult seasons come in succession, which can be extraordinarily challenging.

Solomon's words suggest that the most accurate way to gauge your life is to discern what season you're in, because the season acts as a subplot to the narrative of your overall life story. But *it isn't your whole life.* This is vital to remember. It's only a season. Good or bad, easy or difficult, every season on this earth is temporary.

For the sake of further exploration, let's look at a few of the seasons Solomon mentions in Ecclesiastes 3:

a time to be born and a time to die,
a time to plant and a time to uproot,
a time to kill and a time to heal,
a time to tear down and a time to build,
a time to weep and a time to laugh,
a time to mourn and a time to dance,
a time to scatter stones and a time to gather them,
a time to embrace and a time to refrain from embracing,
a time to search and a time to give up,
a time to keep and a time to throw away,
a time to tear and a time to mend,
a time to be silent and a time to speak,
a time to love and a time to hate,
a time for war and a time for peace.[1]

Mourn or Dance

Solomon says there's "a time to mourn and a time to dance." Do you know someone in a season of mourning? Are you in such a season yourself? A friend of mine in South Haven just lost his mom. He is in a season of mourning. My own mom died a couple of years ago, and I remember that season of mourning very well. Every week in the news we hear about another random shooting that leaves a trail of mourning in its wake. The shocking news comes, and then loved ones are thrust into a season of mourning they couldn't have seen coming and never would have chosen. But here it is, nonetheless.

Losing a loved one in death is not the only circumstance that can thrust us into a season of mourning. Loss of any kind begets a need for grief. If you have recently experienced the loss of a job, marriage, or home, or another significant disappointment—and if you are honest about its impact—you will give yourself permission to enter an appropriate season of mourning.

A number of factors determine the duration and characteristics of seasons of mourning. The depth of loss plays a factor, to be sure. Our own natural wiring for handling loss also plays a role. Some people are more naturally buoyant than others in the face of loss.

A third factor is the intensity and pace with which a person chooses to grieve. Some people who have experienced significant loss dive headfirst into their season of mourning. They grieve forthrightly and in large doses, figuring the quickest way to get to the other side of this painful season is to plow through it—to cry the tears that need to be cried and feel what needs to be felt. For others, the season of mourning is best experienced in small doses over a longer period of time.

Losing a loved one in death is not the only circumstance that can thrust us into a season of mourning. Loss of any kind begets a need for grief.

There's no "right way" to mourn. The slower, small-doses style doesn't mean the person has experienced less of a loss; nor does the headfirst style mean the person is feeling more pain. The key is finding a style that feels authentic to you, while accepting that others may grieve differently.

Don't confuse different ways of grieving with non-grieving. Non-grieving is not a style. If you're in a season of mourning but are not actually grieving, you're stuck. Be intentional about allowing yourself to feel the loss so that, in God's timing, you can exit this season of mourning.

If you are drowning in your grief—feeling overwhelmed or incapacitated—consider seeking professional help. And remember, though your *loss* may be permanent (as in the death of a loved one), your season of mourning is not. In time, it will dissipate. And life will again hold joy and peace for you.

Be attuned to those in your world who are in a season of mourning. Speak to them. Offer your condolences. Don't pretend nothing happened. Don't excuse yourself by saying, "I don't want to remind them of their loss and ruin their day." I promise you, they have not forgotten their loss. Saying something is not going to "remind" them that their loved ones have died. Rather, your acknowledging their loss is like a cool sip of water on a hot day. If possible, attend the funeral. Reach out. Provide practical help: watch the kids, bring a meal or some groceries, mow the lawn, or tuck a restaurant gift card into your sympathy card. All these acts of kindness will help those who are grieving regain their equilibrium after the shattering disruption of their loss.

If you're reading these words today and you're in a season of mourning, be intentional about attending your church and your small group. Put yourself in the places where people can come alongside you in your grief. They might not get it right. They will likely need some coaching; but if you just stay home, you will deny yourself the possibility that someone can shoulder your grief with you. Remaining isolated only augments your feelings of loss. By coming into a gathering of friends, you give God room to inject a little hope into your equation. Or He may give you some encouragement or perspective through your pastor's message or a song that is sung.

Maybe you'll deepen some relationships during this season or make new friends. Many people who have experienced a season of deep loss reflect that it was during the difficult season that they met people who are now their closest friends. It is a common phenomenon. Perhaps this will be your story too. And in due time, you will move out of your season of acute mourning. New seasons lie ahead.

Solomon says there is also a season for dancing. The long-awaited baby is finally conceived. The adoption goes through. The first house is purchased. The door to employment swings open. The grad school acceptance letter arrives in the mail. The Cubs win the World Series. (For us Chicagoans, that will truly be a season of dancing! If only I have enough faith . . .)

A decade ago, my daughter, Shauna, was preparing to enter a season of dancing. A long-haired musician named Aaron asked for her hand in marriage. She said yes. The wedding date was set, all the plans were made, and I soon realized my *literal* season of dancing was approaching: Shauna wanted me to join her for a father-daughter dance at the wedding reception.

I come from reserved Dutch stock. We are not a demonstrative people. Hugging is a stretch for me. So let's just say dancing isn't my favorite pastime. But you know what? I would do *anything* for Shauna, even if "anything" meant dancing. In public.

A few of the women in our small group forced me to learn a dance step or two, and on that wedding day, I took my little girl into my arms, and we danced as only a father and daughter can dance. It was a moment I will always treasure. This was truly a season of dancing for both of us—in more ways than one.

Scripture is ripe with descriptions of seasons of dancing. The Old Testament is packed with detailed instructions for festivities and celebrations that God not only permitted but *mandated.* God is by nature joyful and celebratory, and He gives us full permission for wholehearted, joy-filled seasons of dancing.

In the course of your lifetime, you will pass through countless seasons of dancing. Don't let them slip by unnoticed. If you're in such a season, dance! Mark the events of your life with celebration. Eat good food, drink good drinks, and take photos to mark the moments. Give words of blessing to those you are celebrating.

Above all else, give words of gratitude to God, whose fundamental demeanor toward you is goodness. From Him come all seasons of dancing.

> In the course of your lifetime, you will pass through countless seasons of dancing. Don't let them slip by unnoticed.

Embrace or Refrain from Embracing

As I mentioned, I am not by nature a hugger, and I'm happy to point out that I have Scripture on my side when it comes to the topic of hugging: There is "a time to refrain from embracing." Wise man, that Solomon.

If we have trustworthy people in our lives, we can wholeheartedly embrace them, not just with physical hugs but with a deepening, trust-filled relationship. If we have people in our lives who have not proved trustworthy, Solomon gives us permission to refrain from letting them get any closer. There is a time when the wise thing is to avoid the embrace.

Keep or Throw Away

In Ecclesiastes 3:6, Solomon says there is "a time to keep and a time to throw away."

Some of us are savers, and some of us are tossers. By nature, my wife, Lynne, is a saver. And by God's good humor, I am a tosser. Every few years, I'll wake up on a Saturday morning, look around the house, and say, in the words of my favorite philosopher, Popeye, "That's all I can stands; I can't stands no more." I'll order a Dumpster to be delivered to the driveway, and I'll buy some industrial-size trash bags, with the intent of pitching everything in our house that's not nailed down. I want to get rid of it all. I want to simplify my surroundings by tossing every trace of clutter.

Usually my throwaway season coincides precisely with the onset of a season of *keeping* for Lynne. I want to throw out that old painting we bought in our twenties, and she wants to keep it. I want to toss that blanket my mom made for us, and she wants to save it. She gets nostalgic and wants to keep this *memorabilia* (her word) or *junk* (my word) to pass on to our kids and grandkids. Right about then, my Dumpster arrives. If I don't handle the collision of these two seasons thoughtfully, I may be rewarded by a season on the couch!

Because you are reading a book about simplifying your life, I'm going to go out on a limb and guess that you are in a season of *throwing away* clutter. You are throwing away commitments on your calendar that don't fit your values. You're throwing away the financial habit of living beyond your means. You're tossing some shallow or harmful relationships in favor of deeper, more life-giving friendships in Christian community. Through the hard work of self-evaluation, you are in a season of clearing out and clarifying. You are simplifying your life. This is your season.

Or perhaps you're in a season of *keeping*—keeping new commitments to make time for your family; keeping your daily chair time and prayer time with God holy and set apart; keeping your alignments at work—passion, culture, challenge, and compensation. There's a time for one and a time for the other. Everything in its proper season.

Be Silent or Speak

In Ecclesiastes 3:7, Solomon says there is "a time to be silent and a time to speak."

With the frenetic pace of our culture, the decibel level in our heads makes it very hard to hear God's quiet whispers of encouragement, guidance, or correction. There is a time for silence.

> With the frenetic pace of our culture, the decibel level in our heads makes it very hard to hear God's quiet whispers.

A serious-minded friend of mine just completed a thirty-day fast from all social media. Social media isn't a bad thing in moderation. I use social media. It can be very helpful. It can also be addictive. The 24/7 connection can create an ambient noise level that is toxic. My friend is serious about growing in his faith, so he decided to fast from all social media.

During the first three days of his fast, he says, he didn't know what to do with his hands. "When I had a spare half minute, I used to pull out my phone without even thinking. I would scroll through e-mail, read tweets, or check for text messages. It was so habitual that I didn't even know what to do with thirty seconds of spare time. I had to relearn how to be still."

That season of silence had such an incredible impact on him that he decided to continue his fast during a portion of each day. Moving forward, he continues his social-media ban until a certain hour in the morning. He makes sure he is in his chair for fifteen minutes, reading God's Word, writing out his prayers, listening for God's whispers without the "noise" of social media crowding his thoughts. He gets his direction and encouragement from God, and he interacts in meaningful ways with members of his family *before* turning on his phone, checking his e-mail, or engaging in the social-media world.

At lunchtime, he spends another ten minutes or so with God, free of electronic interruption and noise. He silences his phone and closes his laptop. "I thank God for a great morning," he says. "I just take some moments in silence to dial back in to Him. The quiet allows my mind to be still, free of information overload. It helps me stay centered throughout the day."

At a certain time in the evening, his social-media ban goes into effect again. This time, he turns off his phone and shuts down his laptop. "I have begun reading good literature for the last thirty minutes of my day," he says. "I'm actually reading some of the classics, just like I did in college. I'm reading things that are stretching my mind and my heart, instead of just frittering away time by texting, tweeting, and reading or watching stupid stuff on the Internet."

My son, Todd, is naturally wired for silence, and I have learned some valuable lessons from him in this area. Todd is an introvert and a thinker. He doesn't fill a room with words just because no one else is speaking. When he has something to say, he says it. But he is comfortable with quiet. When we are together, I don't have to talk the whole time. I don't have to perform. I can just *be*.

In 2007, Todd embarked on an eighteen-month circumnavigation of the globe. His sailboat, *Crisis Mode*, carried him thirty-two thousand nautical miles across the Pacific, Indian, and Atlantic Oceans—a remarkable achievement. His friend Jeremiah, who accompanied him on the second half of this trip, is wired similarly to Todd. Both are men of few words.

"Jer and I could go the better part of a day on this forty-two-foot sailboat and scarcely say a word to each other—and we were both okay with that," Todd says. "The silence wasn't awkward; it was welcomed. We filled those days with reading good books, writing, praying, tending to the maintenance and operation of the boat—and great fishing!"

Todd and Jeremiah both exude a certain peacefulness that I admire. They're comfortable in their own skins. They aren't addicted to noise. They don't let overstimulation distract them from their inner or outer worlds.

When is your time of silence? If your pace of life is nonstop, when do you give God your full attention? Do you set aside times during your day when you can think, pray, read, and engage in meaningful conversations?

> There is a time to be silent, Solomon says, and there is also a time to speak.

There is a time to be silent, Solomon says, and there is also a time to speak. Sometimes it's easier to remain silent, but you sense God nudging you: *This is a time I need you to speak up.*

If you have a friend who is about to make a self-destructive choice, that's not the time for silence. Don't just watch your friend run off the rails and wreck his or her life. Don't excuse yourself from responsibility by thinking, *It's not my place to say anything,* or *I don't want my friend to feel judged.* That's cowardly. Even if it's out of your comfort zone, speak up! Tell your friend, "Hey, I love you. It's hard for me to watch you do what you're about to do. I'm not judging you. I'm just observing that if you go down this path, there's a huge price tag at the end of it. And I ask you to reconsider."

A friend of mine has a boss he really admires and respects, but this boss was considering steering their company toward actions that were right on the edge of integrity. My friend prayed about it, but he wasn't planning to speak up. He didn't want to be a troublemaker.

The closer it got to decision time for his boss, the more insistently the Spirit of God kept saying to my friend, *You've got to speak up. Say something. It's time to speak.*

My friend listened. He walked into his boss's office and said, "I'm not trying to make trouble. You know me. You know I respect you and I love our company. But I feel we're coming close to making a decision that falls short of our integrity standards."

The boss responded with humility. "I think you're probably right," he said. The company backed away from the edge and made a morally strong decision. My friend was glad he had spoken up. Had he remained silent and the company crossed the line, he would have faced a new set of dilemmas more challenging than the question of whether or not to speak up. Even if things had not gone well—if his boss had responded in anger when he was confronted—my friend still would have known he did the right thing. He knew it was "a time to speak," and he had been obedient to God's whisper.

There are times you have to speak up, even when it's risky or unpleasant. When you know it's your time, speak.

IDENTIFY YOUR CURRENT SEASON

In Ecclesiastes 3, Solomon lists a total of twenty-eight seasons, including the ones I've described above. These are just snapshots of the types of seasons you are likely to experience over the course of your lifetime. Some seasons are easy to identify; others are less distinct.

Identifying your current season is vital to simplifying your life. It equips you to be more fully present and engaged. It brings a single-minded clarity to your days. You are more likely to notice God's active hand, to learn the lessons He has for you, and to maximize the character development, wisdom, and spiritual growth opportunities that each season holds.

It's also important to identify your current season so that, when the season comes to a close, you'll be less likely to cling to it, and more apt to make a graceful exit and step wholeheartedly into the new season that is dawning.

WHAT DOES GOD WANT TO TEACH YOU?

You aren't in your current season by accident. God's hand is in it, and there's a purpose to His activity. What does God want to teach you during this unique, never-to-be-exactly-repeated season?

In Ecclesiastes, Solomon seeks to define the meaning and purpose of life. He challenges readers to find sustainable satisfaction by investing their lives in things that matter for eternity. Too many people—Christ followers included—are spinning out of control. We act as if we don't have a clue about God's narrative for our lives.

> You aren't in your current season by accident. God's hand is in it, and there's a purpose to His activity.

A guy in his late twenties recently described to me that he is in a season of restlessness. He felt he was living out his parents' script for his life instead of living his own adventure, instead of pursuing God's purpose for his life. He's not alone. I have spoken to hundreds of young women and men who have come to realize they're living their parents' dreams instead of their own.

"How long have you been in this season of restlessness?" I asked him.

"About three months," he said.

"Well, what are you doing to cope?"

"Honestly?" he said. "I'm drinking massive amounts of alcohol."

"You might want to consider a different strategy," I said, "or you could be stuck in this season for a long time. What do you think God is trying to teach you in this season?" We talked a while longer, and he began to get curious about what God might want to teach him during this season of restlessness.

There's a reason for every season in your life—good or bad, easy or challenging, rewarding or draining. When you're in a hard season, it's very tempting to want to "medicate" yourself (which could be through food, alcohol, distractions, busyness, etc.). It's easy to want to put on the blinders, escape the discomfort, and ignore reality. If you're a Christ follower, God is continually working to refine your character and make you more like Jesus. He has good lessons to teach you, *especially* in the uncomfortable, restless, painful seasons of your life. What are those lessons? Don't squander the opportunities for growth that come with the hard seasons. Learn all you can during them. What are the lessons God wants to teach you right now?

A Season of Success

Many years back, Ken Blanchard wrote a management book called *The One Minute Manager*, which sold more than *thirteen million* copies.[2] It stayed on the *New York Times* bestseller list for more than two years, and it continues to sell about ten thousand copies per month even today. Amazing!

When Ken wrote the book, he was far from God. And as the sales kept climbing, month after month, year after year, he found himself in an elongated season of professional and financial success—with royalty checks and thousands of speaking requests rolling in.

One day he woke up and thought, *Wait a minute, I'm not that good a writer. I'm not that good a promoter. I'm not that clever. Why have I experienced such success?* He wanted to learn whatever lesson he could in this season.

Most people who experience a season of success like Ken's would just thank their lucky stars and not question it. But Ken took it a step further. He said to himself, *There's a* reason *behind all this. Somebody's trying to get my attention, and I'm going to figure out who it is—and why this person wants my attention.*

That launched Blanchard into a season of exploration. He examined Christianity, and a few years later he yielded his life to Christ. Today, he's a fully devoted Christ follower, and wherever Ken's name and fame lead him, he carries the name of Christ.

All of this emanated from an unexpected season of blessing. But Blanchard didn't just bask in his success; he let it drive him deeper. He learned the lesson that God had for him in that season, and it was a game changer.

A Season of Loneliness

One of the most challenging seasons any of us will face is a season of loneliness. It can be terrifying to feel disconnected in the world, to sense you are on your own and no one has your back. It can disrupt your equilibrium to feel as if you have no one walking alongside you in this world. If you're in a season of loneliness, perhaps God wants to teach you about the tangible presence, proximity, and friendship of Jesus Christ.

> One of the most challenging seasons any of us will face is a season of loneliness. It can be terrifying to feel disconnected.

I remember very clearly the day this lesson was thrust upon me, shortly after my dad died.

I went to meet with my college professor and mentor, Dr. Gilbert Bilezikian. He was sitting behind his desk as I walked into his office. I sat down in a chair across from him.

He stopped what he was doing, looked up at me, and said, "What do you want to talk about today, Bill?"

I shrugged. "Your call."

He thought for a second or two. Knowing I had been experiencing a season of loneliness after the death of my father, he replied, "I want to talk to you about the immanence—the closeness—of Christ."

I balked. "Dr. B., I grew up in a tradition where God sits on a throne of some magnitude far beyond my reach, where my prayers take a long time to get to Him—and even longer for Him to respond, if He hears me at all. That's how I've always viewed God."

Dr. B. didn't flinch. "Bill, that's why we're going to talk about how near He actually is."

He pointed to an empty chair against the wall, about three feet away. "The Bible teaches that Christ by His Spirit is in that chair," he said. "He's actually here. He is a part of this conversation you and I are having right at this moment."

This was a head-popping concept to me. "Uh, my weird meter's going to peg, Dr. B.," I said.

"Well, it's true," he said unapologetically. "The presence of Christ is right here with us, so for the next thirty minutes we're going to talk to Jesus right in that chair. I'm going to talk to Him, and then you're going to talk to Him. Then we're going to be quiet and see if He will give us any kind of communication back, by His Spirit. We're just going to communicate with a Christ who is not sitting on a throne far beyond reach, but who is present, right here, right now."

This was extremely difficult for me to wrap my head and heart around. But I knew Dr. B. wasn't a nutcase. He had a deep, theologically grounded, yet intimate faith that I admired. I trusted him. So I assented. Though it felt completely foreign to my very traditional concept of God, I prayed to Jesus as if He were sitting in that empty chair. Then Dr. B. prayed. And then we simply sat in silence and listened for any prompting that Christ might direct our way through His Spirit.

As clumsy as it all felt, there was something true and peaceful about it.

"Your assignment as you drive home is to talk to the one who's riding in the car with you," Dr. B. told me. "Jesus is just as much in that empty passenger seat as He is in this chair."

"That's going to be a stretch too," I said.

"The Scripture is filled with references that teach about the proximity, presence, friendship, and companionship of Christ," he said. "During that time in the car, keep your radio turned off and just talk to Him, Bill. He is with you. He's not a million miles away. It doesn't take a satellite beam from heaven for Him to reach you. He's right here."

Because of my preconceived notions of a distant God, it took some practice before it became the norm for me to sense His immanent presence. But over time, I began to experience what Dr. B. had patiently tried to describe to me that day in his office.

Today I can be anywhere in the world and sense Jesus' presence. Sometimes when I am on a plane late at night—alone, thirty-eight thousand feet up, flying over the ocean in some remote part of the world—I will look out the window at the expanse of nothingness and sky, and I'll become acutely aware of how very close Jesus is. He is right there with me. I do not feel alone. Wherever I am, I have a curious sense of the closeness, presence, and companionship of Christ—just like Dr. B. described.

> Because of my preconceived notions of a distant God, it took some practice before it became the norm for me to sense His immanent presence.

God had a lesson for me in that season of loneliness. Had I not learned that lesson, I might be tempted today to let a season of loneliness consume, depress, or cripple me. I am so grateful for that season, as hard as it was at the time, because it opened me up to the tangible companionship and presence of Jesus. I never feel alone anymore. I know He is always with me. I learned that lesson during a difficult season.

If you are in a season of loneliness, what is God trying to teach you? Could it be He is inviting you to learn the lesson I just described? When you learn it, you can move on to your next season.

Perhaps the lesson God wants you to learn is to get up off the sofa and take some relational risks: Meet some people. Find a small group at your church. Stick your neck out, which can't happen as long as you keep sitting on your sofa, watching reruns or scrolling through Facebook. You need earthly, face-to-face friendships. You need wise, safe people to help you see yourself accurately. Do *something*, because your loneliness won't be relieved until you take some relational risks.

Same season, different lessons. In every season, God wants to teach you something specific. Find out what your unique lesson is for that season, learn it, and then move on to the next season.

BE FULLY IN YOUR SEASON

Recognizing the season you're in helps to simplify your life by giving you a tangible target on which to focus your growth, energies, and direction. Once you name and understand the season you're in, be *fully present* there. Dive in.

Several years back, I had the privilege of interviewing one of the greatest sailboat racers in the history of the sport, Dennis Conner. He won the America's Cup—the oldest international sporting trophy— four times for the United States. He has won twenty-eight world championships in yachting, and he has raced with all sorts of sail-boats. Dennis, known as "Mr. America's Cup," is very familiar with amazing seasons of success.

In our interview, which was in front of a crowd of business leaders, I asked him questions about his many sailing victories and the successful seasons in his life. He shared some spine-tingling stories about those winning seasons.

But anyone familiar with the competitive sailing world knows that Dennis lost the America's Cup to Australia in 1983. By losing that one regatta, Dennis became the first skipper in the competition's 132-year history to lose the America's Cup for the United States.

I asked Dennis about that season of his life. In front of all those business leaders, he got very real and vulnerable, almost to the point of tears.

"When I lost the America's Cup for the US," he said, "I became the most disdained person in the sport of sailing."

I remembered the beating he had taken in the press at that time, and I knew he was not exaggerating.

Dennis grew emotional. "After that loss, I reached such a point of despondency that I didn't know if I wanted to continue with my life."

You could have heard a pin drop as he continued. "The humiliation, the meanness of the press, the self-doubt. But I had a choice to make in that season. I could either give in to the despondency and play the victim, or I could learn what I had to learn and then pick myself up and move on." That's what he did. Dennis and his crew took back the America's Cup from Australia in 1987.

"I learned more about myself during that hard season—as painful as it was—than I learned in all those other seasons of sailing victories," he said. "Today I can actually be grateful for that season, rather than only feeling deep regret."

> "I learned more about myself during that hard season—as painful as it was—than I learned in all those other seasons of sailing victories."

Dennis learned a lesson in that season that he couldn't have learned any other way.

Job, the central figure in the oldest book of the Bible, went through a season of horrendous loss. His kids, his fortune, his herds, his land—everything, gone. On the heels of unimaginable loss, he spoke these words about God: "Though he slay me, yet will I hope in him."[3]

Job had lost everything, and he grieved heavily—which was

appropriate. But he said, "I still have God. He's my only hope. Even if He takes me out, I'll go down still hoping in Him."

The apostle Paul, in an especially painful season of affliction, prayed for God to remove the source of his pain. Instead, God whispered these words to him: "My grace is sufficient for you."[4] When you think your current season is more than you can bear, listen for God's whisper: "My grace is sufficient for you, for my power is made perfect in weakness."[5]

You learn a lot about people when you see them in seasons of pain. I've witnessed seasons of indescribable pain in people's lives. Some people crumble, while others find a strength they didn't know they had—by tapping into God's power. When you're in a season of pain or weakness, you can draw upon a strength that is not your own. Rather than trying to dodge your challenging season, *lean into it*—and learn how God's strength can infuse your frailty. Those who tap into God's power find it marks them forever. It's a lesson they carry with them for the rest of their lives.

> You can greatly simplify your life simply by recognizing when the season you're in is coming to a close; when it's time to move on.

What season are you in? What is God trying to teach you in this season? He is with you in every season, and He wants to teach you critical, lifelong lessons that will bring meaning to each season, purpose to your pain, and a sense of satisfaction that He has a plan at work in your life.

RECOGNIZE WHEN A SEASON IS ENDING

Solomon lists the seasons of our lives in pairings—contrasting one season with the other. Mourn and dance; plant and uproot; keep silent and speak; and so on. Inherent in all these contrasts is an important point: Seasons end, and new seasons begin. You can greatly simplify your life just by recognizing when the season you're in is coming to a close; when it's time to move on.

Unhealthy Relationships

Sometimes couples get sucked into the vortex of a tragically dysfunctional dating relationship. They aren't bad people; they just aren't good for each other. They are lesser versions of themselves when they are together, and those around them see it. But they've been together for so long, they've lost objectivity, and neither one has the courage to pull the plug. Everybody who loves them wants to say two words to these people: *Move on!* There is more to life than a futile, dead-end relationship, and a bad dating relationship will not produce a good marriage. Cut it off before making this thing permanent. Move to the next season, where better days await.

Can't Leave the Party

Some people who enjoyed a good party in college never grew beyond that rut. They like being known as the "party guy" or "party girl," and it's frightening for them to let go of that identity. They just keep letting the good times roll, long after everyone around them grows up and finds satisfaction in the next seasons of their lives.

These people partied too much in college, they partied too much in their thirties and forties, and last week they woke up with a new tattoo—and no idea how they got it. The people who love these partiers want them to hear two words: *Move on!* Find a better season than the one that worked (or didn't) in college. Find a better season before this one turns into an addiction that tanks your life.

Addiction

Some people drink too much, with or without the party. Perhaps it didn't start out that way, but over time, the drinks came too frequently and became too important. Or the painkillers that originally served a legitimate purpose now anesthetize a pain that is no longer physical—and are causing greater pain of their own. Friend, this season needs to end. *Move on!*

If you need to stop drinking or stop overusing your pain meds because you're seeing an unhealthy pattern in your life, do it—and *tell* someone. Name this challenging season, and put someone on alert who can help you exit this season for good. If you need to enter a program for substance abuse, do it now. Find a Christian twelve-step program. Find a sponsor. Find a counselor who can help you understand what's underneath your propensity for overusing. Put that season of substance abuse behind you. More harm will come if you linger. *Move on!*

Mad at the Church

There's a guy I've known for thirty years who had a terrible experience in the church of his youth. Too many rules, too many bad Sunday school teachers, too many hypocrites, and so on. He left church and he left God. Over the decades, he's visited our church several times. He says he loves it. He knows many of our members and loves them.

Every so often, I will gently ask him if he's ready to move into a new season of his life—a season where he would think about the possibility of a relationship with God. But whenever I do, he immediately dredges up how horrible his childhood experience was, with all those rules and hypocrites. . . .

The last time I asked him about considering a faith journey, he started to return to the victim place yet again. But this time, I looked him in the eyes and said, "Dude, that was fifty years ago. *Move on!* We've gone to the moon and back since you had a bad Sunday school class. We've created this thing called the Internet since you had that problem with your pastor. Don't you think it's time to move on?"

So far, he doesn't think it's time to move on. He's still stuck. He has surrendered half a century of his life to some people at a church who probably didn't do things the way they should have. He gave away those years, rather than deciding he could move on and explore a relationship with God in spite of what happened back then.

If you have a spiritual wound like this man has, I invite you to move on. Don't use someone else's bad behavior as an excuse to keep you from exploring the faith question for yourself. Don't let others rob you of experiencing the unbounded grace of a loving God. Move on. Step into a new spiritual season.

> Don't let others rob you of experiencing the unbounded grace of a loving God. Move on. Step into a new spiritual season.

Unforgiveness

Few things keep us ensnared in an expired season like unforgiveness. If you're still waiting for justice from someone who wronged you in the past, *move on.* Don't shackle yourself to a season that will only ever hold bitterness. Don't give the wrongdoers in your life that kind of power over you. Step into a new season where forgiveness can unlock those shackles and free you from being bound to the unkindness, thoughtlessness, or cruelty of another. Draw a line in the sand and say, "Today's the day I move on. I'm done being trapped in that dead-end search for justice. It's holding me captive. I've got to leave this season. There's nothing more to be learned here. It's time to move on. It's time to step into forgiveness and the freedom it brings."

Cynicism

Cynics are a dime a dozen. They think being cynical is intellectually cool, but if you look beneath the surface, cynicism is intellectually cowardly. It takes no courage whatsoever to tear down other people or ideas with a skeptical remark. It takes no creativity to poke holes in things rather than offer support, encouragement, or a better idea. Cynicism doesn't engage reality; it sloughs it off with a cheap laugh.

Cynicism is contagious. It has an insidious way of seeping

undetected into our thought and speech patterns. It's easy to pick up a cynical attitude from people around us. Yet a cynical outlook is contrary to having the mind of Christ. The apostle Paul offers an antidote for those prone to a cynical mind-set:

> Finally, brothers and sisters, whatever is true, whatever is noble, whatever is right, whatever is pure, whatever is lovely, whatever is admirable— if anything is excellent or praiseworthy—think about such things.[6]

If you have slipped into a season of cynicism and find yourself thinking the worst of others or making cheap, negative jokes, humble yourself and take steps to move out of that season. Admit you have become a bit of a cynic, and then tell yourself, *I am no longer going to be that man or woman sitting on the bench taking potshots at others who are actually* doing *things in this world. I'm going to move on from this cynical season, even if it means distancing myself from the cynics around me. Even if it makes me feel uncomfortable, I'm leaving cynicism behind.*

It shows intellectual courage to take a stand like this. But until you do, you will be stuck in the cynical spiral indefinitely. It's time to move on.

Abuse

Some seasons have only one possible happy ending: *getting out.* Women, in particular, let me say something very direct to you: If you are in a relationship where someone is hurting you or hitting you, move on. Move on today.

Physical abuse, mental abuse, emotional abuse, and spiritual abuse are seasons that God never designed for us to experience. If you find yourself in a season of abuse of any kind, for any reason, take action. Don't wait for another season to ease its way into your life. It won't happen. Abusers aren't looking for new seasons; they like you right where you are. You will have to take the steps to move on. And move on you must, not just for your own sake but for the sake of those you love, those who love you, and for the sake of the abuser as well. Don't wait for a new day. Today is that day. Move on.

Change is hard. We get comfortable, even if the season we're in is not a good one. But there is no simplifying your life when you're stuck in an expired season. You must move on. And moving on means saying yes to the unknown. Friend, if you have learned the lessons God has for you in this season, or if you're in a season that

If you find yourself in a season of abuse of any kind, for any reason, take action. Don't wait for another season to ease its way into your life.

has long since expired, it's time for a change. There is nothing for you in this current season, so don't linger. Follow the pattern laid out by Solomon, the wisest man in the world. When you're through with a season, for God's sake, *move on*; for your own sake, *move on*; and for the sake of everyone around you, *move on*.

THE FINAL SEASON

I want to close with one more thought from Solomon:

> He has made everything beautiful in its time.
> He has also set eternity in the human heart; yet
> no one can fathom what God has done from
> beginning to end.[7]

Life on earth is not your final season. From God's eternal perspective, life on this planet—your seventy years, or so—is a long, extended season woven from a string of shorter seasons. Someday, this earthly season will come to a close and a new reality will begin.

Deep in your inner person, God has given you a sense of eternity.

Even many atheists describe the sense deep in their psyche that there's something else after this life. There is a new season. God built that sense into humankind. He has "set eternity" in our hearts.

Scripture is very clear that if, in your season of life on earth, you find grace and forgiveness through Jesus Christ, you can move from one earthly season to the next with your hand in His, learning the lessons God has for you and finding meaning, purpose, and satisfaction along the way. When you get to the end of your earthly seasons, you will be invited into the next season with God in heaven forever, where you can fully experience His companionship, His joy, and His goodness.

> If you're unsure where you will spend your eternal season, resolve it now. Move to a season of spiritual peace and hope.

For those who choose to live their earthly seasons apart from God's extended hand, who choose their own paths rather than the path of forgiveness through Jesus, the eternal season they experience will look much different. God honors the choices we make on this earth; He would never force people who rejected Him during their earthly seasons to spend eternity with Him in the next. Their decision toward God will stand.

The next season is a forever season. Have you reached for the hand of the one who offers forgiveness that lasts for eternity? If you're unsure where you will spend your eternal season, resolve it now. Move from a season with an uncertain future to a season of spiritual peace and hope. Move on. And when you step into that final season, you'll discover a level of satisfaction you could never arrange for yourself here on earth—a satisfaction that lasts for eternity.

SIMPLIFY THROUGH SEASONS

Solomon's words in Ecclesiastes view life as structured around seasons. Your days are clearer, less cluttered, and more focused when you view your life this way. You're less likely to spin your wheels in a season that should have ended long ago, less likely to spend your energy avoiding change, fearing the unknown, and postponing the effort required to step from one season to the next.

When your current season begins to draw to a close, don't fight it. Don't drag your feet. Jump into the new season God is opening up to you and move on! Simplify your life by stepping forward, leaving the old season behind, and looking for the lessons God has for you to learn in the next season. You'll find meaning, purpose, and satisfaction for each season—and beyond.

■　■　■

ACTION STEP: IDENTIFY YOUR SEASON

Without a clear understanding of how God works through seasons in our lives, we are ill-equipped to move from one season to the next. We're more apt to complicate our lives, rather than simplify them, by drifting through each season without purpose or direction. You can bring clarity and simplicity to your life by learning to identify your current season and glean from it each lesson God wants you to learn.

Write your responses to the prompts below.

- What season are you in?

- What is God trying to teach you in this season?

- Are you fully engaged in this season? What could you do to embrace this season, good or bad, more wholeheartedly?

■　■　■

ACTION STEP: MOVE ON

When we keep trying to shoehorn our lives into seasons that no longer fit, we work against the goal of leading simplified lives. As you reflect on your tendency (whether slight or strong) to linger in an expired season, consider the questions below and answer them on a piece of paper or in your journal. Work toward becoming a person who can readily shed a season as soon as it has been fully engaged and its lessons learned—and who can move into the next season with anticipation and hope.

1. Are you currently stuck in an expired season? What makes you feel this season is drawing to a close? How are you resisting the need to move on? Why?

2. What lessons did God teach you during this season?

3. What new season is God opening up to you?

4. What steps can you take to move on?

chapter ten

from meaningless to satisfied

The Legacy of a Simplified Life

EVERY WOULD-BE PILOT has to demonstrate navigational proficiency in order to pass the flying test. Early in my training, an instructor helped me plan a two-hundred-mile round-trip flight to a neighboring state. He was confident I was ready to handle my first solo cross-country flight.

I took off in a small Piper Tri-Pacer, flight plan at my side, and all was going according to plan until an upper-level air disturbance blew me off course. Way off-course. It wasn't long before I had to admit to myself I was hopelessly lost. Below me was nothing but mile after mile of unmarked Indiana plains.

As I watched my fuel level slowly deplete, I knew I was running out of time to sort things out. If I couldn't determine my location soon, this flight was going to end badly.

Just then, a small town appeared on the horizon, with exactly what I needed—a huge water tower—right in the middle. If you've ever seen one of these water towers in the middle of a small Midwestern town, you know that the name of the town will be painted proudly right on the side. I simply dropped down and flew close enough to the water tower to read the name of the town. Then I matched up the town on my navigational chart, and within minutes I had regained my bearings. I charted a new course back to my home airport, landed the plane safely, and told my instructor the flight had been uneventful.

Getting a little off course in that small plane only cost me forty-five minutes of time and about fifteen gallons of aviation fuel. But getting off course in the big picture of life exacts a far higher price. No one wants to look in the rearview mirror of life and realize they spent time and energy heading off-course but didn't know it. You can't retrace those lost years. There is no turning the plane around.

Chapter by chapter in this book, you have done some hard work toward simplifying your life. You've tackled subject matter that is not for the faint of heart. You've taken an honest inventory of specific pockets of your life and made some course corrections. And for your efforts, I hope you've found that your energy bucket is more full, your days marked by less chaos, and your nights wrapped in greater peace.

But how can you be certain you're on course in the big-picture things that matter most? You're on the road to a simplified life, but if you were able to see your life's journey from an altitude of thirty thousand feet, would you find that you're on course for a life of deep and sustainable satisfaction?

> How can you be certain you're on course in the big-picture things that matter most?

HOW SATISFIED ARE YOU?

It's no wonder we often find ourselves looking for satisfaction in all the wrong ways. You and I are deluged from every side by advertising designed to foster dissatisfaction with our current lives. From what I've seen on television, my life would be much more satisfying if I were to eat Special K for breakfast, buy my car insurance from GEICO, and wear a Breitling watch. No one is impervious to advertising's influence.

On a scale of one to ten, take a moment to assess your current satisfaction levels:

How satisfied am I with my job?

How satisfied am I with my income?

How satisfied am I with my marriage? Or with my singleness?

How satisfied am I with my home? With my car? With my computer or cell phone or closet full of clothes?

How satisfied am I with the overall circumstances and conditions of my life?

Here are some harder questions: How satisfied *should* I be? How satisfied *could* I be? Are my expectations too high or too low? Am I in denial about my satisfaction level, or am I expecting a 360-degree paradise on this side of heaven? Should I lower the bar on my expectations?

The real root of our dissatisfaction goes deeper than our response to the blitz of media advertising. It resides somewhere deep in our souls and traces its origins all the way back to Eden. The serpent's question to Eve strikes home in all of our hearts: "Did God really say, 'You must not eat from any tree in the garden'?"[1]

Before this, Eve had delighted in God's provision, but now she wants more. She decides the only fruit that will satisfy her hangs from the branches of the one tree God forbade her to eat from. But upon partaking of the fruit, she finds—as we all have—that living outside of God's boundaries and provision leads to fatal dissatisfaction. Once humanity crossed the threshold into a broken relationship with God, we've been dissatisfied ever since.

WHAT MATTERS MOST?

Few people in history have truly been successful at pushing the quest for satisfaction to its ultimate limits. On the short list of those who have tried is Solomon, son of David and king of Israel during the tenth century BC. History touts him as the wisest man in the world at that time, and he was certainly one of the richest.

If anyone could speak to the experience of having everything his heart desired, it was this guy. With limitless wealth at his disposal, Solomon pursued satisfaction with breathless abandon. He recorded his findings in the Old Testament book of Ecclesiastes—twelve chapters of bare-fisted, intellectual street fighting about what matters in this world and what does not.

Solomon's raw, irreverent reflections on the subject of satisfaction and the true meaning of life are shocking and sometimes offensive. But they're honest. He speaks from his heart as one who's truly "been there, done that." He records what will satisfy us and what will leave us feeling as if all we did with our lives was chase the wind.

Solomon wastes no time in expressing his existential observations. Here's the big opener to his book:

> Meaningless! Meaningless! . . . Utterly
> meaningless! Everything is meaningless.[2]

Now that's a happy thought! Remind me not to invite this guy to the party.

In the first two chapters of Ecclesiastes, Solomon builds a fairly convincing case to support his depressing worldview. One by one, he uncovers the temporal value of the meaningless pursuits most of us think will satisfy. In the end, he says, these worldly pursuits are as productive as "chasing after the wind."[3]

SEVEN SUREFIRE PATHS FOR CHASING AFTER THE WIND
Physical Health
Good physical health is a key "quality of life" indicator, to be sure. Few would deny that being healthy adds to one's enjoyment of life.

If you have always been in good health, you may not have given your physical well-being much thought. But talk with people whose health issues have kept them from enjoying their favorite activities, and you'll understand why people logically assume that physical health and longevity are keys to satisfaction in life.

Solomon cuts to the chase regarding our time here on earth.

> Generations come and generations go, but the earth remains forever. . . . No one remembers the former generations, and even those yet to come will not be remembered by those who follow them.[4]

He looks at the ancient mountains, valleys, rocks, and rivers that surround him and summarizes it like this: Why do you think your life is so meaningful and filled with purpose when you live for only seventy years or so? The world has been around a lot longer than you have, and it will continue long after you die. And whether you've enjoyed fantastic health your entire life or have struggled physically for decades, the end is the same. You will die, and the world will go on.

Keep your life in perspective. You'll disappear from the scene within a few decades, but the world will remain. My *lawn* will outlive me. Next time I mow my grass, I'm going to keep in mind that I'm just its temporary servant. Someday, someone else will take my place. Someone else will own my house and my little piece of land, and the grass will still be there. It will keep growing, and someone else will cut it—until he or she is removed from the scene and someone else comes along to push the mower. That's how big a deal we are. We're all going to die, and the world will keep spinning without us. Pinning our hopes on longevity is not the key to a simplified and satisfied life.

Education

Solomon was renowned for his wisdom. No one knew more than he did in the tenth century BC world. This was no accident—Solomon was purposeful about obtaining knowledge. And for many like him, education seems a logical path to finding a life that satisfies. But will it pay off?

> I applied my mind to study and to explore by wisdom all that is done under the heavens. . . . I said to myself, "Look, I have increased in wisdom more than anyone who has ruled over Jerusalem before me; I have experienced much of wisdom and knowledge." Then I applied myself to the understanding of wisdom, and also of madness and folly, but I learned that this, too, is a chasing after the wind.[5]

I tried this logic on my parents when I graduated from high school and didn't feel like going straight to college. I told them, "Hey, the smartest guy in the world said the pursuit of knowledge is like chasing the wind."

You know what they said? "Shut up and go to college, Bill."

Solomon isn't saying knowledge and education are bad. He's simply saying they won't bring the soul satisfaction you think they will.

Have you known students who finished college and didn't know what to do next so they went on to grad school, thinking it would provide some direction? But after earning a master's degree, they still hadn't found what they were looking for, so they tried postgraduate studies, maybe even earned a doctorate, yet still were unsatisfied. Some people, it seems, are on an endless quest—for more knowledge, more degrees, more dissertations, more credentials, more initials after their names.

If this hits close to home for you, Solomon can save you some time—and some tuition money. He went as far down the knowledge acquisition road as a human being could go, and here's what he found out: "With much wisdom comes much sorrow; the more knowledge, the more grief."[6]

Knowledge as an ultimate pursuit doesn't pay. At the end of the road, you won't find what you're looking for. The endless acquisition of knowledge won't fill that void in your life. No matter how many degrees you collect or academic achievements you amass, the emptiness will still be there. Knowledge wasn't designed to fill that void.

Some of the most cynical, miserable people I've ever met were people who thought that one more round of research, one more archaeological dig, one more published article, one more book with their names on the cover, would give them what they were looking for. They never learned what Solomon learned—that education and knowledge are a means to an end, not an end in themselves. And when these sad folks get all the way to the end, still striving for more knowledge, more education—while sacrificing the things that matter most along the way—they'll find their quest doesn't deliver. They'll be left with sorrow and grief for all those wasted years pursuing the wrong sorts of things at the expense of things that mattered. They had their hearts set on a big payoff, and it never came.

> Solomon's doom-and-gloom tone in the first chapter of Ecclesiastes brightens considerably when he changes his quest.

Pleasure

Solomon's doom-and-gloom tone in the first chapter of Ecclesiastes brightens considerably in chapter 2, when he changes his quest. He regales his readers with a multiyear swan dive into a pool of hedonism, thinking a good bottle—or barrel—of wine will lighten him up and bring him happiness. He engages in unbridled pleasure seeking, a never-ending college frat party. Let the good times roll.

> "Laughter," I said, "is madness. And what does pleasure accomplish?" I tried cheering myself with wine, and embracing folly.[7]

How much wine does it take to fill the void in the inner recesses of your heart? Clue: There isn't enough wine on earth for that. Recovery programs are filled with people who gave it the old college try—and are now pursuing healthier, more effective avenues to fill that void. They learned the hard way that wine (or drugs, sex, gambling, food, or anything else people use to anesthetize their pain) doesn't lead to a satisfied life. It all eventually feels like chasing the wind.

Work or Accomplishments

The term *workaholic* is likely familiar to you, either because you know a workaholic or because you are one. People who pursue work like an alcoholic pursues his next drink have the same disease; they've merely chosen a different drug of choice. The goal for the workaholic isn't the next chemical high—it's acquisition; it's accomplishment. It's being the top dog. Solomon sprinted down this path!

> I undertook great projects: I built houses for myself and planted vineyards. I made gardens and parks and planted all kinds of fruit trees in them. I made reservoirs to water groves of flourishing trees.[8]

Solomon didn't just build a nice home for himself—he built *houses*. Plural. Solomon's places were palatial, with vineyards, gardens, orchards, and ponds.

I know people whose obsession with their careers has produced this kind of wealth. Some are able to manage their work/life balance in such a way that their families don't suffer. Most are not.

A woman I know recalls a friend in high school whom she envied greatly—the girl bought all her clothes from Nordstrom, lived in a huge custom home, and began driving a new Camaro Z28 as soon as she turned sixteen. Both her parents were top performers at an international aeronautics company, and they were extraordinarily focused on their careers, putting in long hours at work while leaving the girl to fend for herself after school. They tried to make up for their absence at home by buying a summerhouse on a lake, a condo in Hawaii for Christmas vacations, and a ski condo in the Cascade Mountains of the Pacific Northwest.

"I envied this girl all through school," the woman told me. "She had everything. But one day when we were seniors, we got to talking, and she admitted she'd trade in all the exotic vacations and fancy material possessions in a heartbeat for parents who were around like mine were. 'Your mom fixes dinner every night for your family,' she said. 'Your dad is home in the evenings, and he's around on the weekends. My parents are gone constantly. They make it clear what matters the most to them. They show me every day. What I have is just *stuff*. I can't buy what you have.'"

My guess is her parents spent their lives in the office, thinking their accomplishments at work would provide meaning and satisfaction for their lives. In fact, all it brought was more stuff. There is no retracing the years they lost while their daughter was growing up. Those years are gone.

> Don't chase the wind by spending all your time at the office.

If this story makes you squirm, it's not too late. Even if your children are grown, you can build and deepen those relationships. Don't chase the wind by spending all your time at the office. And if you're a stay-at-home parent, don't spend all your work time keeping the house perfectly clean; or preparing fancy, time-intensive meals for company; or making a career out of volunteering at your kid's school. An obsession with your career—even a career at home—is chasing the wind. Instead, pursue authentic connection with those you love. Invest your time in the relationships that matter most to you. You won't regret it.

Wealth

It's easy to confuse work with wealth because one often leads to the other. But Solomon differentiates between the two. One involves an obsession with achieving and accomplishment; the other involves an obsession with possessions and material gain.

> I bought male and female slaves and had other slaves who were born in my house. I also owned more herds and flocks than anyone in Jerusalem before me. I amassed silver and gold for myself, and the treasure of kings and provinces.[9]

In Solomon's day, the number of slaves you owned was a symbol of status. Solomon staffed all his houses with plenty of personnel; his obsession with obtaining more possessions—his many houses—led to more acquisitions to maintain his possessions. He had captured the dragon; now he had to feed it.

Livestock was another measurable barometer of wealth. If the fields of your estate—or estates, in Solomon's case—were filled with grazing cattle and sheep, your neighbors knew you were rich. Solomon admittedly wanted to show everyone just how wealthy he was, so he amassed immeasurable herds and flocks to fill the hills and pastures of his property. Of course, he then needed to acquire more staff to tend and care for all those animals.

Nothing shows your wealth more readily than plenty of cold, hard cash. In Solomon's day, this meant silver, gold, and "the treasure of kings and provinces." International trade was a big part of Solomon's business, so the wealth he amassed included treasures from foreign countries.

The arts were another wealth indicator then, as they are today. But only the rich could afford such luxuries in ancient days. The arts were not lost on Solomon. In addition to all the tangible wealth he possessed, he also "acquired male and female singers."[10] Most of us save our pennies and dimes so we can go to a great concert once in a while, but Solomon flat out bought the band. He acquired the best musicians and brought them to his palace so he could have a concert anytime he wanted.

Solomon was driven. He was focused. And thinking wealth would fill the void in his life, he pursued it wholeheartedly until he was the wealthiest man around. Yet he was empty inside.

A few years back, I had an opportunity to interview Bill Gates, one of the founders of Microsoft. At that time, his net worth was somewhere between $55 and $60 billion, which is a mind-blowing amount of money. Bill and his wife, Melinda, were in the process of setting up the Gates Foundation, a charitable foundation that translates billions of his profits into medical treatment in developing countries, finding cures for diseases, agricultural development in Asia and sub-Saharan Africa, educational assistance in poor US school districts, low-income housing in US cities, and other charitable ventures.

As I was interviewing Bill, I asked him, "So you're moving from wealth building to wealth distribution? Why are you doing that?"

His answer echoed the thinking of Solomon. He said, "I woke up one day and I asked myself, 'What's the point? I can earn a billion more dollars, or five or ten billion more. What's the point? How many billions are enough?'" He and Melinda decided to switch gears. And that decision is, quite literally, changing the world.

Few people on the planet must make decisions about how to spend their billions, so let's take this same theory out of Bill Gates's strata and put it into a perspective that hits closer to home. I know people who say, "If I can just stack up ten thousand more dollars in my account, that's it; I'll be satisfied." Or, "If I can just get my business to this number, then I'll be satisfied."

Or, "If I can just get into this larger house . . . or buy that nicer car . . ."

To paraphrase Solomon, who came to this conclusion almost three thousand years ago, "At some point, you wake up and it all begins to feel as if you're chasing the wind. It's meaningless. It does not satisfy."

I have known some staggeringly wealthy people over the years, and I find they generally fall into two categories: those still chasing the wind, who think that just a little more money, or a little more power, will bring them satisfaction; and those who view their wealth as a tool for doing good in the world. You can imagine the difference in the satisfaction levels of these two groups.

> The Christian faith is not fundamentally against material blessings. God gives us good things, and He wants us to enjoy them.

Allow me to put some qualifiers on the topic of wealth: The Christian faith is not fundamentally against material blessings. Although we shouldn't put our *hope* in wealth, God gives us good things, and He wants us to enjoy them. The apostle Paul exhorted his protégé Timothy—who was young, and perhaps still sorting out the "satisfaction" question—with these words:

> Command those who are rich in this present world not to be arrogant nor to put their hope in wealth, which is so uncertain, but to put their hope in God, who richly provides us with everything for our enjoyment.[11]

Those who know me know I own some stuff. I own a Harley (and so did Lynne, until she gave it up for a kayak). For many years, we owned a small sailboat as well, which we kept at our place in Michigan—a simple, two-bedroom cottage we enjoy on weekends and during my summer teaching break, and where we connect as a family. These things are not necessities, clearly, but they have brought us pleasure and added some play and rest to our lives. I readily acknowledge that these types of blessings come from God. I don't worship them. I share them liberally. I enjoy them, to be sure, but I can part with them at any time. Stuff comes and goes. It doesn't have its hooks in me, and I don't feel guilty for enjoying what I have.

As I said, Christianity is not against material blessings, nor is it against *pleasure*. The Old Testament is filled with descriptions of the festivals, parties, and celebrations that God mandated for His people. These were the same festivals Jesus enjoyed during His years on earth. In fact, His first miracle was turning water into wine for a wedding reception. Christianity in its truest form embraces God-honoring pleasure, joy, and fun.

If you have come into a relationship with God—if your void is filled and you have a group of friends whose void has been filled—you can party with the best of them. Few things hold more enjoyment for me than a dinner party, birthday party, or celebration with friends. But the pleasure they bring is temporal. I don't look to them for lasting fulfillment; I accept them for what they are. I make no apologies for walking with God and enjoying His bounty.

> The Bible is brutally honest about what brings deep, lasting satisfaction to human hearts and souls—and what does not.

The Bible is, however, brutally honest about what brings deep, lasting satisfaction to human hearts and souls—and what does not.

And the pursuit and enjoyment of wealth will never bring the fulfillment you think it might.

Sex

Sex is one of the most common forms of futile satisfaction-seeking I hear about as a pastor. People who use sex as a means to fill the ache in their souls are not alone; Solomon tried this path as well: "I acquired . . . a harem as well—the delights of a man's heart."[12]

Scripture records that Solomon acquired "seven hundred wives of royal birth and three hundred concubines."[13] Do the math. He was married to one thousand women. I have a hard time, as a husband, making *one* woman happy—I can't imagine making *one thousand* women happy! Just spending one night with each woman would take him almost three years. These were women from all over the world and from every religion. As Scripture notes, "his wives led him astray."[14]

There are people who, like Solomon, try to fill the void in their lives by having sex with lots and lots of people. It corrodes their souls and leaves them empty. As the great theologian Mick Jagger said, "I can't get no satisfaction."[15]

This path of wind chasing isn't exclusive to men; women, too, seek satisfaction either through sex or by chasing after the "right person." They always have to be in a relationship or they think they have no value. They think finding the mythical Mr. Right will finally make them happy.

Life doesn't work that way. No other person can *make* you happy. No amount of sex can leave you truly fulfilled. Seeking satisfaction through another person is like chasing the wind.

Fame

Solomon sums up his quest for satisfaction with this: "I became greater by far than anyone in Jerusalem before me."[16]

Best education; best houses; best parties, women, wine, and music.

By the world's standards, Solomon had it all—and everyone knew it. He was famous. If there had been paparazzi in ancient Jerusalem, they would have had but one target for their cameras.

In our media-saturated culture, it's easy to think that fame or popularity must bring satisfaction. But a quick scan of the news indicates that the opposite is often true. Famous musicians and actors are notorious for burning through multiple marriages. Celebrities who seemingly "have it all" also make the news with disturbing frequency when they kill themselves, either on purpose or by an accidental overdose of drugs or alcohol. The number of well-known people we hear about who are admitted into recovery clinics reflects but a small percentage of those for whom alcohol or drugs remain a hidden problem. More often than not, fame wrecks lives. It certainly does not satisfy.

BEEN THERE, DONE THAT

Solomon sums up his worldly attempts at filling the void in his life:

> I denied myself nothing my eyes desired; I refused my heart no pleasure. My heart took delight in all my labor, and this was the reward for all my toil. Yet when I surveyed all that my hands had done and what I had toiled to achieve, everything was meaningless, a chasing after the wind; nothing was gained under the sun.[17]

Unlimited acquisition. Unlimited pleasure. Total, unvarnished self-indulgence. If that doesn't fill a void, what will?

Western society operates under the assumption that more is better. This "truth" goes unquestioned, especially here in the United

States. When you were growing up, did you ever have a conversation like this with your parents?

"Mom and Dad, why do I have to study so hard?"

"So you can get into a better school."

"Why do I have to get into a better school?"

"So you can get a higher-paying job."

"Why do I need a higher paying job?"

"So you can afford all the good things in life."

"Um, what happens when I finally acquire all the good things in life? Will I be happy then? Do the good things make me happy? Mom . . . ? Dad . . . ?"

Solomon played by the rules. He worked hard and succeeded in achieving all of his dreams. And yet, in the end, his hedonistic experiment was an absolute bust. He spent his whole life doing things he thought would make him happy, only to have the experiment implode in the end. "In my search for true soul-satisfaction, I can cross wanton pleasure-seeking off my list. Been there; done that. I literally had it all. And it just didn't deliver."

LETTING GO OF THE TRAPEZE

In a small way, I can confirm the outcome of Solomon's experiment— at least as it pertains to money.

I was born into a fairly affluent family and learned at a relatively young age the limits of what money can buy. Not only was this a blessing (though not in the way you might assume), it was also a huge time-saver for me. When you're seventeen or eighteen years old and already have at your disposal a lot of the stuff that many people spend their whole lives working toward, you look around and say, "What's the point? Am I really going to dedicate the next forty or fifty years of my life just to get a car that corners a little better, or a boat that carries a few more people? Really?" I was fortunate to discover early on that money, toys, houses, and travel cannot fill the void.

One of the defining moments of my life happened right around this time, when I was working at our family-owned company. I had done well in a sales contest, and one day the sales manager handed me a nice bonus check. When I took out my wallet to stash the bonus check, I found my last two paychecks—uncashed. I remember looking at the stack of checks and cash in my billfold and having a panicky thought come into my mind: *I can keep fattening this wallet all I want, but it ain't going to do it for me. Ultimately, money won't satisfy. What will?*

In the months that followed that eye-opening realization, I entered the darkest, most disenchanted time of my life. I clearly knew what money *couldn't* buy. I knew what *wouldn't* work to fill the void. But I didn't yet know what would. I was disillusioned with the prospect of working for the rest of my life just to own more stuff. I felt as if I were floating out over an open expanse without anything else to grab on to—like letting go of one trapeze without the next one in sight.

The next couple of years were the darkest of my life. I still carry embarrassment and regret about some stupid things I did, decisions I made, and people I hurt.

But as frightening and painful as that era was, it began to clarify for me who God really is, what a relationship with Him might be like, and what purpose He could bring to my life—and I was hungry for it. I had no other plan on the horizon, no second trapeze, but I was too smart to get sucked back into spending my life heading down roads I knew would leave me dissatisfied. They were dead ends. I was looking for an alternative.

God showed up and started filling my void with His love. And He started filling my mind with His purposes. Shortly after that, in His timing, I connected with a group of people who were discovering the same things about life as I was, and we experienced Christian community together. Through this community of friends—and through what God was teaching me in a college Bible class with my mentor,

Dr. Bilezikian—I got a picture in my mind of what a church could be like if it was working right. We began dreaming of a church that would feed the hungry and embrace the lonely. We envisioned a church where people did life together, helping one another get on a better path and putting their energies toward fixing the broken things in the world.

This was a vision for a life that held meaning. My pulse raced every time I thought about it. And almost forty years later, my pulse is still racing, and I still shake my head in awe at the privilege of giving my life to something that holds such meaning.

> I still shake my head in awe at the privilege of giving my life to something that holds such meaning.

FOR WHAT?

Toward the end of his life, Solomon clearly understood that his "chasing after the wind" activities were never going to provide the soul-satisfying fulfillment he was looking for. And he makes an astute philosophical observation through some painfully honest words:

> I hated life, because the work that is done under the sun was grievous to me. All of it is meaningless, a chasing after the wind. I hated all the things I had toiled for under the sun, because I must leave them to the one who comes after me. And who knows whether that person will be wise or foolish? Yet they will have control over all the fruit of my toil into which I have poured my effort and skill under the sun. This too is meaningless. So my heart began to despair over all my toilsome labor under the sun. For a person may labor with wisdom, knowledge and skill, and then they must leave all they own to another who

> has not toiled for it. This too is meaningless and a
> great misfortune. What do people get for all the
> toil and anxious striving with which they labor
> under the sun? All their days their work is grief
> and pain; even at night their minds do not rest.
> This too is meaningless.[18]

He *hated* life? Solomon gets an A for honesty. But how'd you like to have this cheery guy on your staff or team? His attitude would wreck any employee survey.

Yet I understand his disillusionment. He takes a hard, honest look at reality and comes to this conclusion: "So I bust it for forty or fifty years to build something significant, and just when it's worthwhile and successful, I have to hand it over to some bozo when I retire. And he or she might just run the whole thing into the ground. The sum total of my life's work could evaporate and disappear before my eyes. This is insanity. Meaningless. Chasing the wind. Ridiculous."

A PARKING LOT

The temporal nature of our worldly accomplishments strikes the Hybels family pretty close to home. My grandfather, John Hybels, emigrated from the Netherlands in the early 1900s, and he worked tirelessly to start Hybels Produce Company, headquartered in Kalamazoo, Michigan. The company survived World War I and barely outlasted the Depression; but my grandfather worked hard *and* smart, and he got through it. Then Hybels Produce survived World War II, as well. My grandfather essentially worked himself to an early grave, all to establish and sustain his produce company.

My dad and his brothers took over the business from Grandpa in the late 1940s, and they followed in their father's footsteps, working eighty-hour weeks for decades, and ushering themselves into early graves for the sake of the business. My dad died in his early fifties, and several of my uncles died even younger than that.

When the last of the brothers was gone, no one in the family wanted to run the business, so we all agreed to sell it. It wasn't long before the buyers, a new group of investors, renamed the company and moved it out of Kalamazoo. Today, at the original site of Hybels Produce Company, where a thriving family business operated for decades, there's nothing left but a parking lot.

The last time I was in Kalamazoo, I drove by the old spot where I'd worked as a child and a teenager, and I thought, *I am so glad I didn't pin my ultimate fulfillment on that company, because it's nothing but an asphalt parking lot now.* In a small way, I understood the type of frustration Solomon felt as he looked at the empire he had built and realized, "So what? Now someone else will take it over, and it may all turn to dust."

Solomon's kingdom did, in fact, end at his death, when the nation of Israel was split in two—the northern kingdom of Israel and the southern kingdom of Judah. The lavish Temple he built for God—arguably more stunning than any previous structure of man—was utterly destroyed in 586 BC.

> Be careful where you pin your hopes and dreams. All your hard work might disappear altogether.

We have seen seemingly indestructible empires collapse in our day as well. Who would have thought that companies like Oldsmobile, Blockbuster, and Lehman Brothers—multibillion-dollar companies—would just crumble and disappear?

Be careful where you pin your hopes and dreams. It's not simply the risk that those things might not satisfy—that's scary enough. It's the risk that they might actually evaporate. All your hard work might disappear altogether. And then you'll have nothing. Even if you succeed at building something great with your life . . . when you retire or die, then what? It could all turn to dust in a heartbeat. All your time and effort could end up blowing in the wind.

IN THE END

There's no point in simplifying your life if you are steering toward an end point that doesn't matter to begin with. In my opinion, Scripture records Solomon's hedonistic odyssey to help us avoid wasting our lives like he did. We have the option of learning from his mistakes.

Spare yourself the heartache. Spare yourself decades of chasing rabbit trails. Don't get to the end of your days and realize you spent your one and only life on distractions. Don't arrive at the end of your life still saying (in the words of the U2 song), "I still haven't found what I'm looking for."

Do you ever stop and wonder where you are likely to spend your final days on this planet? No one knows when or where we will die, but statistically, there's a good chance it will be in a hospital room. There's a good chance you'll spend your final hours flat on your back in a hospital bed, surrounded by electronic monitors, IV poles, and the like. Because I'm a pastor, I've been in hundreds of such rooms. I pull up a chair and sit next to people who are right up against the finish line, sometimes in their final hours or moments. I've been through this drill many, many times, and I know how it goes. The pattern seldom varies.

First, though, let me tell you what *never* happens. In all the bedside vigils I've attended, I have never once heard a person say, "Hey, can you bring me that award plaque I got for volunteering at the park district? It's hanging on the wall in my rec room. Bring it in here so I can gaze at it and remember how everyone applauded for me."

Nor has anyone ever asked me to go to the bank and withdraw a suitcase full of their hard-earned cash and bring it to them. No one has ever said, "Just lay it right here on my chest. I want to just hold my money near my heart as I expire."

No one has ever asked me to take their fancy, new BMW to the car wash and then park it outside their hospital room window. No one has ever said, "Get it all cleaned up. Give it a nice wax. And then put it outside so I can gaze upon it as I take my final breath."

No one has ever asked me to run to their lawyer's office and bring them a copy of their company's most recent financial statement. No one has ever said to me, "I worked so hard for that business. I just want to read over the financials one last time."

These simply aren't the conversations that happen near the end of a life. When people are nearing death, do you want to know what they talk about? Two things: whether or not they're right with their families, and whether they're ready to meet their Maker. One hundred percent of the time, these are the conversations I have with people in hospital beds.

> No one has ever said to me, "I worked so hard for that business. I just want to read over the financials one last time."

I talked to a business guy some time ago at a restaurant. He was recuperating from a recent battle with a disease that had landed him in the hospital for more than one hundred days. He had almost died several times but had miraculously bounced back and gotten an extension to his life.

He grew very emotional telling me about it. "There was something extremely disturbing about this long illness," he said.

"Besides the fact that you almost died several times?" I asked.

"Yes," he said. "It was more than that. You see, very few people came to visit me. I mean, literally almost no one. In *one hundred days.*" His eyes filled with tears.

I felt sick to my stomach. "What was that about?" I asked.

"In my company, I've made thousands of people rich, extremely rich," he said. (I know his company, and it's a multinational business, very successful. He was not exaggerating.) "But pitifully few of those people from work came to see me when I was on my back for more than three months. I gave my life for that company, but I suppose to them I was just the CEO, the boss."

"What about your family?" I asked. I knew he had a wife and some grown kids. "Didn't they visit?"

"Well, to be honest, I kind of neglected my family while I was building the business and making all these other people rich," he said. "And so, not all my family made it to visit me while I was in the hospital. Some did. But not all."

Now we both had tears. I didn't know what to say, so I was just honest with him. "Yes, my friend, you got that one wrong," I said. "I am so sorry." We talked for a bit about how, with his extended lease on life, he could make some long-overdue repairs to those relationships.

Contrast that guy's story with another friend of mine, a business owner who was a pillar in our church for twenty-some years. This man spent his one and only life well. He kept the clutter at bay and led simplified days of purpose, significance, and satisfaction. Several years ago, he was diagnosed with a terrible, incurable disease, and he realized his days were numbered. He underwent treatment with the best doctors he could find. But the disease was taking his life.

Near the end, once all reasonable efforts had been made to prolong his life, my friend didn't feel the need to scramble for a medical Hail Mary. He was so secure in his relationship with God that he decided, *I don't want to die in a hospital. I want to die at home.*

I went to visit him there often. When we knew the end was near, he called me and asked, "Could you do me a favor? Could you arrange for some of my friends—my buddies from church—to come over? My family is here, and I'd really love it if we could just get together and sing some worship songs to God. Could you arrange that?"

So a group of us—his singer friends, a band of volunteers he had worked with, and I—gathered at his house with his family. We stood around his bed, and for about an hour and a half, we sang the songs we had sung together in church for more than twenty years. He was lying there in such peace, singing with us as best he could, and saying, "Thank you. Thank you. Thank you." Trust me, there was not a dry eye in that bedroom.

We prayed over him before we left, and I was the last one to leave the room. He grabbed my hand and smiled. "Bill, when you introduced me to Christ and you baptized me," he said, "I found what I was looking for. I love my church community. And God reminded me throughout my whole life that family matters. I have the best family I could imagine. Tonight they were all around me—family and friends. And I know where I'm going when I die. It's been a good life."

> My friend didn't simplify his life by just avoiding or removing the things that don't satisfy; he *filled* his life with the things that do.

Within two days, he was gone.

Quite a contrast, isn't it? My friend was anything but a wind-chaser. He invested his one and only life in things that matter. He didn't simplify his life by just avoiding or removing the things that don't satisfy; he *filled* his life with the things that do.

He understood a vital truth that challenges me daily—and I offer it to you here.

FURNISHING THE SACRED SPACE

When we eradicate clutter from our lives, we create a vacuum that aches to be filled. Once you've uncluttered your soul and swept the place clean, you'll quickly discover that plenty of things beg to crowd themselves back into the sacred space you've so carefully carved out. How do you keep your life from becoming re-cluttered? How should you furnish your new, simplified, inner world? In short, how do you live an *ongoing* life of simplicity?

I have never found it easy to say no to the myriad opportunities that knock on my door. To help ensure that I furnish the sacred space in my soul with the right things, I first run every opportunity, commitment, and relational investment through three filters.

FILTER #1: Satisfaction

Key question: Will it bring true satisfaction? Because Solomon has given us a clear outline of the things that amount to nothing more than chasing the wind, I know better than to get suckered into saying yes to such things. Nonetheless, when a wind-chasing idol comes my way and catches my eye, I ask myself the hard question: *What unmet desire in me is being tempted here?* By understanding the greater desire of my soul, I can better determine God's plan for filling that desire with something that brings true satisfaction. When the God-given desires of my heart are met in God-given ways, it becomes easy to say no to the things I know will never satisfy.

FILTER #2: Purpose

Key question: Does it align with God's purpose for my life in this season? Sometimes I'm tempted to fill a space in my life with something good—but it doesn't line up with God's call on my life, at least not in this season. I find it easier to say no to something when I can tell myself, *Not now. Perhaps later, but not in this season.* If in seasons to come, I sense God redirecting my purpose, I can revisit those things to which I said no earlier.

FILTER #3: Significance

Key question: Does it help me lead a life of significance? By keeping my eye on the eternal horizon, I can filter out those things that hold only temporal value. This doesn't mean I say yes only to deep, spiritually significant commitments. On the contrary! If something of godly but temporal value fills my energy bucket and keeps my life well balanced, I recognize that the balance and emotional stamina it provides empower me to lead a life of significance. Some might say, for example, that a turtle-seeking adventure in a wooden rowboat with my grandson doesn't have deep spiritual significance. But I know better. I know it refuels me like few other sources of joy in my life; and I know it infuses in that young boy a sense of his inexpressible value to me—and to God.

Be quick to say yes to things that empower you—directly and indirectly—to lead a life of eternal significance. These are the legacy builders, friend. Don't miss them.

> When you get to the end of your life, you will ask yourself the same two questions: Am I right with my family? Am I right with my Maker?

When you get to the end of your life, you will no doubt ask yourself the same two questions: Am I right with my family? Am I right with my Maker?

It's pretty simple, really. In the end, everything boils down to this. If you know in your soul that you can answer yes to both these questions, then when it's your turn to lie in that final bed, you will experience the kind of joy, peace, and satisfaction I saw on my friend's face as we gathered around his bed and sang. And you will have left a rich legacy for others to follow.

THE LEGACY OF A SIMPLIFIED LIFE

These days at the Hybels house, I often have the privilege of viewing my life through two sets of young eyes—my grandsons, Henry and Mac. Our daughter, Shauna; her husband, Aaron; and their boys live nearby, so I get regular, life-giving doses of Henry-Mac time.

I had long looked forward to becoming a grandfather, but I had no idea how much these two precious gifts would rock my world. Time with them changes my perspective on my own life. It helps me slow down. It helps me simplify.

When I look at the sheer potential of Henry's and Mac's young lives, I am reminded anew to evaluate my own life. How well am I spending it? Am I living a life that would make them proud? Am I using my grandfatherly influence to mold who they will become and to ignite their fire for following Christ with their lives, as I have tried to follow Him with mine? Am I passing on to them any wisdom born of the life experience that God has directed my way? What legacy in their young lives will I leave behind when I am gone?

These are the brutally honest questions I ask myself, and it would be pastoral malpractice if I didn't ask the same questions of you. What legacy are you leaving behind? On your final day on this earth, when you look in the rearview mirror of your life, will you see a legacy that brings a sense of deep satisfaction? Or will you see a string of cluttered days filled with things that didn't really matter in the end?

You have spent the chapters of this book doing the heavy lifting of self-evaluation, discerning what course corrections you need to make in order to simplify your life. I hope the process has been helpful to you. But simplifying is not merely intended to make your life easier—like uncluttering a drawer or closet might. You simplify your life for reasons that matter for eternity: to give clarity, purpose, and power to the things that matter most in this world.

You intentionally say no to things that clutter the soul—like jam-packed calendars, out-of-control finances, deep-seated fears, and broken relationships. You turn away from rabbit trails that would take you off the main road and distract you from what your life is really all about.

And you say yes to things that matter, like family, friends, Christian community, satisfying work, and ministry roles that maximize the gifts God has given you to further His Kingdom.

Solomon ends the book of Ecclesiastes with this cut-to-the-chase conclusion:

> Now all has been heard; here is the conclusion of
> the matter: Fear God and keep his commandments,
> for this is the duty of all mankind.[19]

This is what life is all about, friend. This is what fills the void in your soul. Do whatever it takes to radically simplify your life. It's the only way you'll be able to say on your final day, "I'm satisfied."

We get one shot at this life. Choose a purposeful, God-first life, and you will reap rewards for today and for eternity. Choose a life where the God-shaped void in your soul is filled to overflowing, and you will leave a legacy for those who follow you. Invest your one and only life with all the clarity and focus you can give it. This is simplified living. This is the life that satisfies.

■ ■ ■

ACTION STEP: ASSESS YOUR WIND-CHASING PATTERNS

We all get distracted at times. I am more tempted by some distractions than by others. For me, work is the biggest distraction. What is it for you? Think through the seven paths for wind chasing discussed in this chapter:

SEVEN PATHS TO WIND CHASING

1. Physical health and longevity
2. Education
3. Pleasure
4. Work
5. Wealth
6. Sex
7. Fame

Now, in your journal or on a piece of paper, write the answers to these questions:

Which path is most likely to distract me from living a life that satisfies?

When am I most tempted to get distracted in this area?

What can I do to catch myself before I get distracted in this area?

Am I currently on such a trail? If so, what steps can I take today to turn around and get back on the main road toward a simplified, satisfied life?

■ ■ ■

ACTION STEP: SIMPLIFY TO SATISFY

What are the things that matter above all else in your life? Take a moment to write one clear sentence that describes a life that would leave you satisfied on your final day. If it helps, use this sentence-starter as a prompt: "I am satisfied with my life when . . ."

(By way of example, here is my sentence: *I am satisfied with my life when I use my gifts to build the local church and I maintain strong relationships with Lynne, Shauna, Todd, Aaron, Henry, and Mac.*)

Keep your sentence concise and clear.

With your guiding sentence in mind, review your Action Steps from each chapter of *Simplify*. Do you need to take any further steps or make any further course corrections to ensure that your steps of simplifying will lead to a life that satisfies? If so, write them on a piece of paper or in your journal. And then work them into the holistic calendar discussed in chapter 2, to help you live out the priorities that matter most.

Here is an index of the Action Steps, to help you review:

Appendix A

how to choose your life verse

WHAT TO LOOK FOR IN A LIFE VERSE

Life verses often reflect an individual's story and personality. I hope by now I have convinced you of the value of choosing a life verse—whether for this current season or as a rallying cry for the rest of your life. What characteristics are important in a life verse of your own? Look for a few key traits.

Call to Action

An effective life verse serves as a call to action. By this, I don't mean it necessarily tells you what to do. My life verse happens to be instructional in this way—*be steadfast*—but many good life verses are not. Nonetheless, the message of a good life verse should call *you* to action. In the examples I cited earlier, the person's life verse reminded him or her to do everything through Jesus the Vine, or to look for life "to the full" in spite of tragic circumstances. A good life verse should motivate you to run the right race for an eternal, imperishable prize. Find a verse that doesn't leave you sitting comfortably on your backside, but rather drives you to *act on the things that matter most.*

Personalized

Find a life verse that speaks to an area in your life where you need extra reinforcement. Don't pick a verse that simply augments an area where you're already strong; look for a verse that supports you where you are weak. Someone who is naturally filled with God's peace doesn't need, "Do not let your hearts be troubled and do not be afraid" (John 14:27), but someone who is in bondage to fear might! Find a life verse that fills the gaps in your life and undergirds you where you need it most.

Short and Sweet

In order for your life verse to serve as an effective rallying cry throughout your day, it must be succinct. Don't choose several verses. Don't choose Psalm 119, which has 176 verses! Look for a single verse—or, at most, a short two- or three-verse passage. It should be concise enough to memorize and to be recited in the heat of battle as you go about your day.

Hope-Filled

Choose a life verse that leaves you feeling better than you did before you read it. You don't need harsh words of truth or conviction repeatedly drilled into your mind throughout the day. So, don't choose Romans 3:23, for example: "For all have sinned and fall short of the glory of God." We need the truth of this Scripture, to be sure. But for your life verse, find a verse that emphasizes God's benevolence toward you rather than your shortcomings before Him. Choose a life verse that is encouraging, uplifting, and positive; one that motivates you and infuses you with hope.

WHERE TO LOOK FOR A GOOD LIFE VERSE

I have included a catalog of possible life verses in Appendix B. These verses are sorted by topic to make it easier for you to find a verse that fits you. Other places to look for potential verses include your Bible, an online Bible, a book that lists God's promises by categories, or a Bible promise app on your mobile device.

Your Bible

If you're in the habit of underlining and highlighting Bible verses as I am, flip through your Bible's pages and read the verses you have marked. Perhaps you've already underlined the verse you will choose as your life verse. If you find several, make a list of the top contenders.

If your Bible has a concordance, you can search it for key words that resonate with you, such as *peace, joy, faithfulness,* etc.

Online Bible

Use free online Bible software such as YouVersion (www.bible.com) to search for key words. If you think a verse on joy would serve you well, search for "joy" and then scroll through the verses in the Bible that contain that word.

Bible Promise Books

Several publishing companies have published inexpensive, pocket-size books that contain hundreds of promises from Scripture, categorized into dozens of topics, such as anger, contentment, eternal life, hope, God's love, peace, redemption, salvation, trust, worry, and so on. These books are available as e-books and in different versions of the Bible. Pick up the book that matches the Bible version you prefer to read—and then search according to the topics that most resonate with you.

- New Living Translation: *The NLT Bible Promise Book* (Tyndale House)
- New International Version: *Bible Promises for You* (Zondervan)
- King James Version or New Life Version: *The Bible Promise Book* (Barbour)

Bible Promises App

Same idea as a Bible promise book, but mobile friendly. Go to the app store on your device and search "Bible promises." A number of inexpensive or free apps are available to help you search Scripture by key word or topic.

CHOOSING YOUR LIFE VERSE

Using the resources described above, create a list of verses that resonate with you, and then prayerfully consider each one. Don't make a quick decision; rather, give it time until you feel a sense of clarity about which verse to pick.

Once you have selected a life verse, commit it to memory and post it in places you will see throughout your day to keep it fresh in your mind.

CHANGING YOUR LIFE VERSE

There are no hard-and-fast rules about life verses. You can change verses at any time. Though I have chosen a main life verse (1 Corinthians 15:58), I have also leaned in to other verses for different seasons. Aim for finding a verse that will serve you for the long haul, one that can be a lighthouse for you throughout the journey of your life.

life verse catalog

ASSURANCE

PSALM 3:3-4 You, Lord, are a shield around me, my glory, the One who lifts my head high. I call out to the Lord, and he answers me from his holy mountain.

LAMENTATIONS 3:22-23 Because of the Lord's great love we are not consumed, for his compassions never fail. They are new every morning; great is your faithfulness.

ZEPHANIAH 3:17 The Lord your God is with you, the Mighty Warrior who saves. He will take great delight in you; in his love he will no longer rebuke you, but will rejoice over you with singing.

JOHN 10:27-29 My sheep listen to my voice; I know them, and they follow me. I give them eternal life, and they shall never perish; no one will snatch them out of my hand. My Father, who has given them to me, is greater than all; no one can snatch them out of my Father's hand.

ROMANS 8:38-39 I am convinced that neither death nor life, neither angels nor demons, neither the present nor the future, nor any powers, neither height nor depth, nor anything else in all creation, will be able to separate us from the love of God that is in Christ Jesus our Lord.

ROMANS 10:13 Everyone who calls on the name of the Lord will be saved.

EPHESIANS 1:13 You also were included in Christ when you heard the message of truth, the gospel of your salvation. When you believed, you were marked in him with a seal, the promised Holy Spirit.

AWE

NEHEMIAH 9:6 You alone are the LORD. You made the heavens, even the highest heavens, and all their starry host, the earth and all that is on it, the seas and all that is in them. You give life to everything, and the multitudes of heaven worship you.

PSALM 27:4 One thing I ask from the LORD, this only do I seek: that I may dwell in the house of the LORD all the days of my life, to gaze on the beauty of the LORD and to seek him in his temple.

PSALM 71:5-6 You have been my hope, Sovereign LORD, my confidence since my youth. From birth I have relied on you; you brought me forth from my mother's womb. I will ever praise you.

PSALM 116:1-2 I love the LORD, for he heard my voice; he heard my cry for mercy. Because he turned his ear to me, I will call on him as long as I live.

HABAKKUK 3:2 LORD, I have heard of your fame; I stand in awe of your deeds, LORD. Repeat them in our day, in our time make them known; in wrath remember mercy.

PHILIPPIANS 4:4 Rejoice in the Lord always. I will say it again: Rejoice!

COMPASSION

PSALM 82:3-4 Defend the weak and the fatherless; uphold the cause of the poor and the oppressed. Rescue the weak and the needy; deliver them from the hand of the wicked.

PROVERBS 19:17 Whoever is kind to the poor lends to the LORD, and he will reward them for what they have done.

MATTHEW 25:37-40 Then the righteous will answer him, "Lord, when did we see you hungry and feed you, or thirsty and give you something to drink? When did we see you a stranger and invite you in, or needing clothes and clothe you? When did we see you sick or in prison and go to visit you?" The King will reply, "Truly I tell you, whatever you did for one of the least of these brothers and sisters of mine, you did for me."

JAMES 1:27 Religion that God our Father accepts as pure and faultless is this: to look after orphans and widows in their distress and to keep oneself from being polluted by the world.

1 JOHN 3:17-18 If anyone has material possessions and sees a brother or sister in need but has no pity on them, how can the love of God be in that person? Dear children, let us not love with words or speech but with actions and in truth.

CONTENTMENT

PSALM 119:37 Turn my eyes away from worthless things; preserve my life according to your word.

MATTHEW 6:33 But seek first his kingdom and his righteousness, and all these things will be given to you as well.

MATTHEW 6:34 Do not worry about tomorrow, for tomorrow will worry about itself. Each day has enough trouble of its own.

PHILIPPIANS 4:12 I know what it is to be in need, and I know what it is to have plenty. I have learned the secret of being content in any and every situation, whether well fed or hungry, whether living in plenty or in want.

PHILIPPIANS 4:19 My God will meet all your needs according to the riches of his glory in Christ Jesus.

HEBREWS 13:5 Keep your lives free from the love of money and be content with what you have, because God has said, "Never will I leave you; never will I forsake you."

COURAGE

JOSHUA 1:9 Have I not commanded you? Be strong and courageous. Do not be afraid; do not be discouraged, for the Lord your God will be with you wherever you go.

PSALM 27:1 The Lord is my light and my salvation—whom shall I fear? The Lord is the stronghold of my life—of whom shall I be afraid?

ISAIAH 41:10 So do not fear, for I am with you; do not be dismayed, for I am your God. I will strengthen you and help you; I will uphold you with my righteous right hand.

JOHN 16:33 I have told you these things, so that in me you may have peace. In this world you will have trouble. But take heart! I have overcome the world.

ROMANS 1:16 I am not ashamed of the gospel, because it is the power of God that brings salvation to everyone who believes: first to the Jew, then to the Gentile.

PHILIPPIANS 4:13 I can do all this through him who gives me strength.

1 TIMOTHY 6:12 Fight the good fight of the faith. Take hold of the eternal life to which you were called when you made your good confession in the presence of many witnesses.

2 TIMOTHY 1:7 The Spirit God gave us does not make us timid, but gives us power, love and self-discipline.

1 JOHN 4:4 You, dear children, are from God and have overcome them, because the one who is in you is greater than the one who is in the world.

FAITHFULNESS

DEUTERONOMY 6:6-7 These commandments that I give you today are to be on your hearts. Impress them on your children. Talk about them when you sit at home and when you walk along the road, when you lie down and when you get up.

JOSHUA 24:15 But as for me and my household, we will serve the Lord.

PROVERBS 3:5-6 Trust in the Lord with all your heart and lean not on your own understanding; in all your ways submit to him, and he will make your paths straight.

ISAIAH 40:30-31 Even youths grow tired and weary, and young men stumble and fall; but those who hope in the Lord will renew their strength. They will soar on wings like eagles; they will run and not grow weary, they will walk and not be faint.

JOHN 15:5 I am the vine; you are the branches. If you remain in me and I in you, you will bear much fruit; apart from me you can do nothing.

1 CORINTHIANS 10:31 So whether you eat or drink or whatever you do, do it all for the glory of God.

COLOSSIANS 3:23-24 Whatever you do, work at it with all your heart, as working for the Lord, not for human masters, since you know that you will receive an inheritance from the Lord as a reward. It is the Lord Christ you are serving.

2 TIMOTHY 2:15 Do your best to present yourself to God as one approved, a worker who does not need to be ashamed and who correctly handles the word of truth.

GRATITUDE

PSALM 139:13-14 For you created my inmost being; you knit me together in my mother's womb. I praise you because I am fearfully and wonderfully made; your works are wonderful, I know that full well.

ROMANS 15:13 May the God of hope fill you with all joy and peace as you trust in him, so that you may overflow with hope by the power of the Holy Spirit.

COLOSSIANS 2:6-7 So then, just as you received Christ Jesus as Lord, continue to live your lives in him, rooted and built up in him, strengthened in the faith as you were taught, and overflowing with thankfulness.

1 THESSALONIANS 5:16-18 Rejoice always, pray continually, give thanks in all circumstances; for this is God's will for you in Christ Jesus.

JAMES 1:17 Every good and perfect gift is from above, coming down from the Father of the heavenly lights, who does not change like shifting shadows.

HOPE

PSALM 18:2 The Lord is my rock, my fortress and my deliverer; my God is my rock, in whom I take refuge, my shield and the horn of my salvation, my stronghold.

PSALM 25:4-5 Show me your ways, Lord, teach me your paths. Guide me in your truth and teach me, for you are God my Savior, and my hope is in you all day long.

JEREMIAH 29:11 "For I know the plans I have for you," declares the Lord, "plans to prosper you and not to harm you, plans to give you hope and a future."

MICAH 7:7 As for me, I watch in hope for the Lord, I wait for God my Savior; my God will hear me.

MARK 10:27 Jesus looked at them and said, "With man this is impossible, but not with God; all things are possible with God."

ROMANS 8:28 We know that in all things God works for the good of those who love him, who have been called according to his purpose.

PHILIPPIANS 1:6 Being confident of this, that he who began a good work in you will carry it on to completion until the day of Christ Jesus.

HUMILITY

JEREMIAH 9:23-24 This is what the Lord says: "Let not the wise boast of their wisdom or the strong boast of their strength or the rich boast of their riches, but let the one who boasts boast about this: that they have the understanding to know me, that I am the Lord, who exercises kindness, justice and righteousness on earth, for in these I delight," declares the Lord.

2 CORINTHIANS 12:9-10 But he said to me, "My grace is sufficient for you, for my power is made perfect in weakness." Therefore I will boast all the more gladly about my weaknesses, so that Christ's power may rest on me. That is why, for Christ's sake, I delight in weaknesses, in insults, in hardships, in persecutions, in difficulties. For when I am weak, then I am strong.

EPHESIANS 2:8-9 For it is by grace you have been saved, through faith—and this is not from yourselves, it is the gift of God—not by works, so that no one can boast.

PHILIPPIANS 2:3-4 Do nothing out of selfish ambition or vain conceit. Rather, in humility value others above yourselves, not looking to your own interests but each of you to the interests of the others.

PHILIPPIANS 3:7 Whatever were gains to me I now consider loss for the sake of Christ.

JAMES 4:10 Humble yourselves before the Lord, and he will lift you up.

JUSTICE

PROVERBS 31:8-9 Speak up for those who cannot speak for themselves, for the rights of all who are destitute. Speak up and judge fairly; defend the rights of the poor and needy.

ISAIAH 1:17 Learn to do right; seek justice. Defend the oppressed. Take up the cause of the fatherless; plead the case of the widow.

JEREMIAH 22:3 This is what the LORD says: Do what is just and right. Rescue from the hand of the oppressor the one who has been robbed. Do no wrong or violence to the foreigner, the fatherless or the widow, and do not shed innocent blood in this place.

MICAH 6:8 He has shown you, O mortal, what is good. And what does the LORD require of you? To act justly and to love mercy and to walk humbly with your God.

ZECHARIAH 7:9-10 This is what the LORD Almighty said: "Administer true justice; show mercy and compassion to one another. Do not oppress the widow or the fatherless, the foreigner or the poor. Do not plot evil against each other."

LOVE

JEREMIAH 31:3 The LORD appeared to us in the past, saying: "I have loved you with an everlasting love; I have drawn you with unfailing kindness."

MATTHEW 22:37-39 Jesus replied: "'Love the Lord your God with all your heart and with all your soul and with all your mind.' This is the first and greatest commandment. And the second is like it: 'Love your neighbor as yourself.'"

JOHN 13:34-35 A new command I give you: Love one another. As I have loved you, so you must love one another. By this everyone will know that you are my disciples, if you love one another.

ROMANS 12:9 Love must be sincere. Hate what is evil; cling to what is good.

EPHESIANS 4:1-3 As a prisoner for the Lord, then, I urge you to live a life worthy of the calling you have received. Be completely humble and gentle; be patient, bearing with one another in love. Make every effort to keep the unity of the Spirit through the bond of peace.

COLOSSIANS 3:13 Bear with each other and forgive one another if any of you has a grievance against someone. Forgive as the Lord forgave you.

1 PETER 4:8 Above all, love each other deeply, because love covers over a multitude of sins.

PEACE

EXODUS 33:14 The LORD replied, "My Presence will go with you, and I will give you rest."

PSALM 46:10 Be still, and know that I am God; I will be exalted among the nations, I will be exalted in the earth.

MATTHEW 11:28-30 Come to me, all you who are weary and burdened, and I will give you rest. Take my yoke upon you and learn from me, for I am gentle and humble in heart, and you will find rest for your souls. For my yoke is easy and my burden is light.

ROMANS 8:1 There is now no condemnation for those who are in Christ Jesus.

ROMANS 12:17-18 Do not repay anyone evil for evil. Be careful to do what is right in the eyes of everyone. If it is possible, as far as it depends on you, live at peace with everyone.

PHILIPPIANS 4:6-7 Do not be anxious about anything, but in every situation, by prayer and petition, with thanksgiving, present your requests to God. And the peace of God, which transcends all understanding, will guard your hearts and your minds in Christ Jesus.

1 PETER 5:7 Cast all your anxiety on him because he cares for you.

PERSEVERANCE

ACTS 20:24 I consider my life worth nothing to me; my only aim is to finish the race and complete the task the Lord Jesus has given me—the task of testifying to the good news of God's grace.

1 CORINTHIANS 9:24 Do you not know that in a race all the runners run, but only one gets the prize? Run in such a way as to get the prize.

1 CORINTHIANS 15:58 My dear brothers and sisters, stand firm. Let nothing move you. Always give yourselves fully to the work of the Lord, because you know that your labor in the Lord is not in vain.

2 CORINTHIANS 4:7-9 But we have this treasure in jars of clay to show that this all-surpassing power is from God and not from us. We are hard pressed on every side, but not crushed; perplexed, but not in despair; persecuted, but not abandoned; struck down, but not destroyed.

GALATIANS 6:9 Let us not become weary in doing good, for at the proper time we will reap a harvest if we do not give up.

PHILIPPIANS 2:12-13 My dear friends, as you have always obeyed—not only in my presence, but now much more in my absence—continue to work out your salvation with fear and trembling, for it is God who works in you to will and to act in order to fulfill his good purpose.

PHILIPPIANS 3:14 I press on toward the goal to win the prize for which God has called me heavenward in Christ Jesus.

HEBREWS 12:1 Since we are surrounded by such a great cloud of witnesses, let us throw off everything that hinders and the sin that so easily entangles. And let us run with perseverance the race marked out for us.

JAMES 1:2-3 Consider it pure joy, my brothers and sisters, whenever you face trials of many kinds, because you know that the testing of your faith produces perseverance.

JAMES 1:12 Blessed is the one who perseveres under trial because, having stood the test, that person will receive the crown of life that the Lord has promised to those who love him.

PURITY

PSALM 51:10 Create in me a pure heart, O God, and renew a steadfast spirit within me.

PSALM 139:23-24 Search me, God, and know my heart; test me and know my anxious thoughts. See if there is any offensive way in me, and lead me in the way everlasting.

PROVERBS 4:23 Above all else, guard your heart, for everything you do flows from it.

EZEKIEL 36:26-27 I will give you a new heart and put a new spirit in you; I will remove from you your heart of stone and give you a heart of flesh. And I will put my Spirit in you and move you to follow my decrees and be careful to keep my laws.

ROMANS 12:1-2 I urge you, brothers and sisters, in view of God's mercy, to offer your bodies as a living sacrifice, holy and pleasing to God—this is your true and proper worship. Do not conform to the pattern of this world, but be transformed by the renewing of your mind. Then you will be able to test and approve what God's will is—his good, pleasing and perfect will.

PHILIPPIANS 4:8 Finally, brothers and sisters, whatever is true, whatever is noble, whatever is right, whatever is pure, whatever is lovely, whatever is admirable—if anything is excellent or praiseworthy—think about such things.

SACRIFICE

ISAIAH 6:8 Then I heard the voice of the Lord saying, "Whom shall I send? And who will go for us?" And I said, "Here am I. Send me!"

JOHN 13:14-15 Now that I, your Lord and Teacher, have washed your feet, you also should wash one another's feet. I have set you an example that you should do as I have done for you.

JOHN 15:13 Greater love has no one than this: to lay down one's life for one's friends.

GALATIANS 2:20 I have been crucified with Christ and I no longer live, but Christ lives in me. The life I now live in the body, I live by faith in the Son of God, who loved me and gave himself for me.

EPHESIANS 5:1-2 Follow God's example, therefore, as dearly loved children and walk in the way of love, just as Christ loved us and gave himself up for us as a fragrant offering and sacrifice to God.

PHILIPPIANS 1:21 For to me, to live is Christ and to die is gain.

1 PETER 4:19 Those who suffer according to God's will should commit themselves to their faithful Creator and continue to do good.

notes

CHAPTER ONE: FROM EXHAUSTED TO ENERGIZED
1. Luke 10:38-42
2. Luke 10:25-37
3. Every sports team has its archrival. For fans of the Chicago Bears, near my hometown, it's the Green Bay Packers.
4. Gary Thomas, *Sacred Pathways: Discover Your Soul's Path to God* (Grand Rapids, MI: Zondervan, 1996).
5. Psalm 127:3, TLB
6. Ecclesiastes 5:18, author's paraphrase
7. Matthew 14:13
8. Sam Fahmy, "Low-Intensity Exercise Reduces Fatigue Symptoms by 65 Percent, Study Finds," *UGA Today*, February 28, 2008, http://news.uga.edu/releases/article/low-intensity-exercise-reduces -fatigue-symptoms-by-65-percent-study-finds.
9. Jack Groppel, *The Corporate Athlete* (New York: John Wiley & Sons, Inc., 2000).

CHAPTER TWO: FROM OVERSCHEDULED TO ORGANIZED
1. Ephesians 5:15-16
2. Alpha can be found at churches, coffee shops, bars, and homes all over the world. More than 18 million people have taken the course. For more information about Alpha, visit http://guest.alphausa.org or www.alpha.org.
3. Luke 4:16
4. Matthew 5:37, NKJV
5. Matthew 6:33, KJV

CHAPTER THREE: FROM OVERWHELMED TO IN CONTROL
1. Luke 19:1-10
2. Acts 16:31

3. James 1:17
4. Michael Weissenstein, "Happiest People on Planet Live in Latin America, Gallup Poll Suggests," *Huffington Post*, December 19, 2012, www.huffingtonpost.com/2012/12/20/happiest-people-on-planet -latin-america_n_2336772.html.
5. Jon Clifton, "Latin Americans Most Positive in the World," *Gallup World*, December 19, 2012, www.gallup.com/poll/159254/latin -americans-positive-world.aspx.
6. Philippians 4:11-13
7. Proverbs 3:9-10
8. Malachi 3:10
9. Proverbs 6:6-8, NLT
10. Adapted from Charlotte Elliott's hymn "Just as I Am, Without One Plea."

CHAPTER FOUR: FROM RESTLESS TO FULFILLED
1. Ecclesiastes 5:18-19
2. Psalm 139:14
3. Parker J. Palmer, *Let Your Life Speak* (New York: John Wiley & Sons, 2000).
4. These descriptions of the levels of health in a workplace culture are adapted from unpublished direct research by the Best Christian Workplaces Institute. All rights reserved.
5. "State of the American Workplace," Gallup, 2013, www.gallup.com /strategicconsulting/163007/state-american-workplace.aspx.
6. Mark C. Crowley, "Gallup's Workplace Jedi on How to Fix Our Employee Engagement Problem," *Fast Company*, June 4, 2013, www.fastcompany.com/3011032/creative-conversations/gallups -workplace-jedi-on-how-to-fix-our-employee-engagement-problem.
7. Joshua 1:6
8. Luke 10:7
9. 1 Timothy 5:8

CHAPTER FIVE: FROM WOUNDED TO WHOLE
1. Luke 23:34, KJV
2. Mark 15:39
3. Romans 5:8
4. Richard Carlson, *Don't Sweat the Small Stuff and It's All Small Stuff* (New York: Hyperion, 1997).
5. Exodus 21:24, NLT
6. ". . . just between the two of you" (Matthew 18:15).
7. Matthew 18:15
8. Author's paraphrase

9. See Matthew 5:23-26.

10. Romans 12:18

11. Robi Damelin, "A Chain of Change," The Parents Circle Families Forum, November 18, 2005, www.theparentscircle.org/Story.aspx?ID =201. Italics added.

12. "Bassam Aramin (Palestine)," The Forgiveness Project, April 19, 2010, http://theforgivenessproject.com/stories/bassam-aramin-palestine/.

13. Steven Waldman, "Beliefnet's Most Inspiring Person of 2005— Victoria Ruvolo," http://www.beliefnet.com/Inspiration/Most -Inspiring-Person-Of-The-Year/2005/Beliefnets-Most-Inspiring -Person-Of-2005-Victoria-Ruvolo.aspx?p=2.

14. Victoria Ruvolo, Robert Goldman, and Lisa Pulitzer, *"No Room for Vengeance . . ." In Justice and Healing* (N.P.: No Vengeance Press, 2011), 109.

15. Adam Hamilton, *Forgiveness: Finding Peace Through Letting Go* (Nashville, TN: Abingdon Press, 2012).

16. Adam Hamilton, "The Two Dimensions of Forgiveness," August 1, 2012, www.adamhamilton.org/blog/view/49/the-two-dimensions-of -forgiveness#.Uss9ZP2Ects. Italics in the original.

17. Luke 7:47, NLT

18. Luke 23:34, KJV

CHAPTER SIX: FROM ANXIOUS TO PEACEFUL

1. Numbers 6:24-26, italics added.

2. John 14:27; 16:33, italics added.

3. Philippians 4:6-7, italics added.

4. 1 John 4:18, italics added.

5. Daniel 5:6

6. Matthew 10:28

7. 2 Timothy 1:7, NLT

8. See 2 Timothy 1:7, KJV

9. Winston Churchill, "Miscellaneous Wit & Wisdom," National Churchill Museum, www.nationalchurchillmuseum.org/wit-wisdom -quotes.html.

10. Eleanor Roosevelt, *You Learn by Living* (Louisville, KY: Westminster John Knox Press, 1960), 29–30.

11. Psalm 34:4

12. Joshua 1:5, 9

13. Acts 12:5

14. Philippians 4:6-7

15. Acts 16:31

16. John 10:10

CHAPTER SEVEN: FROM ISOLATED TO CONNECTED

1. Proverbs 18:24
2. Proverbs 13:20
3. Proverbs 6:16-19
4. 1 Corinthians 15:33, HCSB
5. James 4:6
6. Proverbs 16:18
7. Romans 12:3
8. Luke 22:51, italics added.
9. Proverbs 11:13
10. Romans 12:18
11. Matthew 5:9
12. Fiona Lloyd-Davies, "Why Eastern DR Congo Is 'Rape Capital of the World,'" CNN, November 25, 2011, www.cnn.com/2011/11/24/world/africa/democratic-congo-rape/.
13. Twelve-step meetings are for people recovering from various addictions, whose recovery is based on the Twelve Steps of Alcoholics Anonymous.
14. Galatians 5:22-23, NASB
15. Proverbs 13:20

CHAPTER EIGHT: FROM DRIFTING TO FOCUSED

1. "Lake Michigan," United States Environmental Protection Agency, July 22, 2013, www.epa.gov/greatlakes/lakemich/intro.html; "Lake Michigan Facts and Figures," Great Lakes Information Network, February 26, 2014, http://great-lakes.net/lakes/ref/michfact.html.
2. Psalm 119:105
3. Through years of repetition and rehearsal, I have slightly paraphrased 1 Corinthians 15:58 from the original version I found in the New American Standard Bible (NASB).
4. 1 Corinthians 15:53, NASB
5. 1 Corinthians 15:13-14
6. 1 Corinthians 15:32
7. 1 Corinthians 15:20
8. 1 Corinthians 15:58, NIV
9. John 9:4
10. Luke 10:2-4
11. John 15:8, italics added.
12. Dallas Willard, interview with Bill Hybels and Nancy Beach, July 2008.
13. Ibid.
14. 1 Corinthians 9:24-27

CHAPTER NINE: FROM STUCK TO MOVING ON

1. Ecclesiastes 3:2-8
2. Kenneth Blanchard and Spencer Johnson, *The One Minute Manager* (New York: Blanchard Family Partnership and Candle Communications Company, 1981).
3. Job 13:15
4. 2 Corinthians 12:9
5. Ibid.
6. Philippians 4:8
7. Ecclesiastes 3:11

CHAPTER TEN: FROM MEANINGLESS TO SATISFIED

1. Genesis 3:1
2. Ecclesiastes 1:2
3. Ecclesiastes 1:14
4. Ecclesiastes 1:4, 11
5. Ecclesiastes 1:13, 16-17
6. Ecclesiastes 1:18
7. Ecclesiastes 2:2-3
8. Ecclesiastes 2:4-6
9. Ecclesiastes 2:7-8
10. Ecclesiastes 2:8
11. 1 Timothy 6:17
12. Ecclesiastes 2:8
13. 1 Kings 11:3
14. Ibid.
15. The Rolling Stones, "(I Can't Get No) Satisfaction," 1965.
16. Ecclesiastes 2:9
17. Ecclesiastes 2:10-11
18. Ecclesiastes 2:17-23
19. Ecclesiastes 12:13

acknowledgments

THREE HIGH-CAPACITY WOMEN brought this book into being:

Jan Long Harris, from Tyndale Momentum, whose pit bull–like tenacity eventually convinced me to move ahead with this project. Thanks, Jan!

September Vaudrey, a family friend, who was kind enough to set aside her own book project to help me write these pages. Her enthusiasm was a constant inspiration to me. Thanks, my friend!

Shauna Niequist, author of *Bread and Wine* and two other fine books, who felt pity for her dad and helped me with the final edits. Her contribution was invaluable. Thanks, Shauna!

about the author

BILL HYBELS IS the founding and senior pastor of Willow Creek Community Church in South Barrington, Illinois, one of the largest and most influential churches in North America. He is the bestselling author of more than twenty books, including *Just Walk Across the Room, Too Busy Not to Pray, Becoming a Contagious Christian, Axiom, Holy Discontent,* and *The Power of a Whisper.*

Hybels is chair of the board for the Willow Creek Association, a not-for-profit organization that equips and empowers more than 15,000 Christian churches from 90 denominations. Each year, he convenes the Global Leadership Summit (GLS), a two-day, world-class leadership event that trains 190,000 leaders in 105 countries. With almost two million participants to date, the GLS is the largest leadership event in the world.

An exceptional communicator, Hybels speaks around the world on strategic issues related to leadership, personal growth, and building thriving churches. He holds a bachelor's degree in biblical studies and an honorary doctorate of divinity from Trinity College in Deerfield, Illinois. He and his wife, Lynne, have two grown children and two grandsons.

Bring **simplify** *to your church or small group!*

Simplify
DVD Experience

Four video sessions with
Bill Hybels, leading you
on a journey toward
discovering a simpler life

978-1-4143-9124-3

Simplify
Participant's Guide

A companion workbook
to the DVD that will guide
your members through
each week's study

978-1-4143-9125-0

WILLOW CREEK ASSOCIATION

Vision, Inspiration, and Resources for Church Leaders Worldwide

Founded in 1992, the Willow Creek Association (WCA) serves pastors and leaders through world-class experiences and resources. WCA is committed to a singular idea: that inspired, encouraged, and equipped Christian leaders create thriving local churches that impact their communities for Christ.

In addition to the Global Leadership Summit (WCA's two-day, world-class anchor event), we share ideas and build partnerships. Through the Global Leadership Summit, WCA membership, and strategic partners, we deliver vision and inspiration to more than 190,000 leaders in 650+ cities and 105 countries.

Learn more about WCA's leadership resources and experiences at willowcreek.com.

Willow Creek Association
P.O. Box 3188
Barrington, IL 60011-3188
Phone: 800-570-9812
willowcreek.com